CREATING ACADIA NATIONAL PARK

Creating Acadia National Park

~

The Biography of

GEORGE BUCKNAM DORR

· Ronald H. Epp ·

FRIENDS OF ACADIA
BAR HARBOR, MAINE

Friends of Acadia
43 Cottage Street, Bar Harbor, ME 04609
www.friendsofacadia.org

Published in the United States by Friends of Acadia

Library of Congress Control Number: 2015956685

ISBN 978-0-9968614-0-3 (paper)

10 9 8 7 6 5 4 3 2 1
First Edition
Printed in the United States of America on acid-free paper
Book design by Z Studio, Bar Harbor, Maine

Portions of this book originally appeared in the *Friends of Acadia Journal*

Cover: George B. Dorr, detail from 1919 photograph from the collection of the Abbe Museum, Bar Harbor, Maine. Aerial photograph showing Sand Beach with Cadillac and Dorr mountains in background by Aimee Beal Church/Friends of Acadia. **Front Inside Cover:** Unattributed illustration from page 1 of George B. Dorr's Sieur de Monts Publication I (1916); Dorr and Interior Secretary Franklin Lane atop Cadillac Mountain, August 1917. Courtesy of the National Park Service, Acadia National Park. **Back Inside Cover:** Dorr, NPS Director Stephen T. Mather, and party, June 1922. Herbert W. Gleason, photographer. Courtesy of the National Park Service, Acadia National Park.

Dedicated to the memory of my wife

Elizabeth Clewell Epp (1943–2013)

Contents

Foreword

I remember the first time I heard the name "George Bucknam Dorr."

It was the summer season of 2009, and my husband and I were new year-round residents on Mount Desert Island. We were not entirely unfamiliar with the island or Acadia National Park, as we were coming from Gardiner, just a couple of hours inland, and had spent many a weekend hiking and camping here with our family over the previous two decades. I worked that summer as a V.I.P. (Volunteer in the Park) at Acadia. Much of my time was spent assisting the interpretive rangers who staffed the Sieur de Monts Nature Center, located at the base of Dorr Mountain and adjacent to both Mr. Dorr's beloved spring and a monument commemorating his name and achievements. For myself as for many visitors, this was my first introduction to the man who is known as the "Father of Acadia."

I was not unlike the millions who come to Acadia never having heard of George B. Dorr. I had, however, the luxury of time. With a penchant for history and inspired by what little I knew of the man, I began to research and read more—starting with summarized park information and continuing on to Dorr's own memoir, *Acadia National Park: Its Origin and Background*, written sixty-five years prior. Numerous accounts of Mr. Dorr, I found, had been written over the past decades, many more anecdotal than factual. As I discovered each of these "histories," I realized that a comprehensive account of George Dorr's life had yet to be produced. Perhaps more importantly, one based on archival records seemed a necessity.

The following summer season I continued as a volunteer ranger for Acadia's Interpretive Division. I conducted both informal and formal visitor programs, but was honored and most happy to be asked to lead the "Missing Mansion" interpretive walk and talk, which leads visitors through Mr. Dorr's Oldfarm property at Compass Harbor, introducing them to the "Dorr Story." To prepare for the program, I continued my bibliographic search of primary as well as secondary sources and paid many visits to local archives, libraries, and historical societies. It was then that I encountered Dr. Ronald Epp's name for the first time, associated with seemingly every scholarly article I uncovered. The quantity and quality of his research on the subject of George B. Dorr was astounding, and was further evident in the trail of Ronald Epp's lectures, presentations, and journal literature.

The Missing Mansion program saw high participation and positive feedback from visitors. Often the small parking lot filled, creating a challenge to accommodate everyone. But this was good news! The more visitors who could be introduced to Mr. Dorr by interpretive rangers, the better. The program generated much interest and inspired further questions: "What was George Dorr's family background?" "How did Mr. Dorr acquire his wealth?" "How did this one man successfully persuade individuals to donate land and money to the park?" "Did Mr. Dorr really swim in the Atlantic Ocean every day?" "What happened to Oldfarm and the gardens and grounds if indeed, in Mr. Dorr's own words, 'Oldfarm, more than aught else, led me along the way, step by step…to the founding of Acadia National Park'?" Inevitably, once familiar with the Dorr story and upon conclusion of the program, a debate was sparked with the question, "Why don't more people know about George B. Dorr?" It seemed very clear to people that this is a man who might compare to John Muir or Theodore Roosevelt for his vision for conservation and preservation of natural lands. Visitors would marvel at his dedication, perseverance, and passion for what became Acadia National Park.

Still, likely only a small fraction of Acadia's 2.5 million annual visitors have thought about the origins of Acadia or consider the man whose name graces one of its most beautiful mountains or know of that little corner of the park called Compass Harbor. As Ronald Epp has written, "Even in the present day, those who live on—or travel to—Maine's Mount Desert Island do not fully comprehend the scope of [Dorr's] achievements."

I learned that Dr. Epp was writing a biography of George Dorr, that Dorr's achievements might be more generally appreciated and that a wider public would have an understanding of the man who devoted the latter half of his life to ongoing conservation efforts. For me, personally, the summer season of 2011 was approaching and I was fortunate to have been hired as a ranger posted at the Village Green Information Center in downtown Bar Harbor. New responsibilities were required. Other rangers would have the opportunity to conduct the Missing Mansion program and praise the efforts of Mr. Dorr.

In May 2011, Ronald was in Bar Harbor to present a program to the rangers and park staff. To my great surprise, he offered to meet me at the Atlantic Eyrie Hotel in Bar Harbor to share his research and photographs—arranged in a multitude of boxes, files, and binders. He promised to make copies of any of the articles and photos I wished, which he later did. Many of these would have taken me weeks to find and procure, so this was a tremendous gift. We talked briefly about his manuscript, conceived in 2001 and begun in earnest in 2005. The manuscript was a rough draft at that point, and he had yet to find a publisher.

In retrospect, the day I met Ronald, along with his wonderful wife, Elizabeth, at the Atlantic Eyrie was pivotal to our shared objectives. We discussed at length our common admiration, respect, and knowledge of Mr. Dorr, and from this point on I became more involved on a collaborative level to energize and promote Ronald's research. The research was too vital, too important, too historically significant for it not to be shared. It occurred to me then that George B. Dorr's memoir had been published nearly seven decades prior to our meeting, and that Acadia was fast approaching its 2016 centennial year. Wouldn't Ronald's book on the origins of Acadia be a fitting and appropriate means of celebrating not only the park, but the man himself without whom there would almost certainly be no Acadia?

The goal of publishing *Creating Acadia National Park: The Biography of George Bucknam Dorr* was finally and appropriately realized with the decision by Friends of Acadia to publish this much anticipated work in conjunction with Acadia National Park's 2016 centennial celebration. It is thanks to this organization, and the support of countless islanders and amateur historians, editors, and contributors, that the world will now be introduced to the extensive scholarly research that Ronald has done. He draws on previously unearthed correspondences, administrative documents including monthly reports to the National Park Service, Dorr manuscripts preserved at the Bar Harbor Historical Society, the New England Historic and Genealogical Society, the Massachusetts Historical Society, and records uncovered from in-person visits to numerous libraries and archives including the Rockefeller Archive Center in Sleepy Hollow, New York, and the National Archives.

Once Friends of Acadia agreed to publish this book, I began to work on indexing the multitude of names representing acquaintances, public and political figures, literary giants and celebrated scientists, statesmen and government officials with whom George B. Dorr had been in contact during his lifetime. I helped to organize and choose photographs for this manuscript. Ronald sent me his manuscript for proofreading and editing, and I responded to his requests for feedback. Each chapter offered me a more intimate and historically accurate look into the life of George B. Dorr.

As I write these words in January of 2015, I cannot help but consider what was happening exactly a century ago in the years 1914–15, the years leading up to the unprecedented 1916 gift of these lands (as Sieur de Monts National Monument) to the American people. Mr. Dorr was anything but idle, and he was filled with keen determination and visionary motivation to seek acceptance by the federal government of the lands protected on Mount Desert Island by the Hancock County Trustees of Public Reservations. Mr. Dorr's months of shuttling back and forth between Mount Desert Island and Washington, DC with documents and deeds, titles and boundary studies, was a most critical period for the creation of the monument. Once this federal status was finally recognized, it was universally agreed that success was due, as the Honorable Luere B. Deasy stated, "to the energy, the persistence, the unfailing tact, the consecrated altruism of George B. Dorr."

In August of 1916, a meeting to celebrate the new national monument was held in Bar Harbor at the Building of the Arts, a magnificent Greek Renaissance performing arts center. Mr. Dorr later wrote about this auspicious occasion: "It was a fitting climax to the long labor, the difficulties and anxieties the undertakings had involved, and upon it we rested, well content." Adding their own eloquent remarks that beautiful summer day were luminaries including President Charles W. Eliot of Harvard University, the Honorable L. B. Deasy, and biologist Dr. Alfred G. Mayer. It is President Eliot's message, however, that suggests to me the significance of Mr. Dorr's vision for the future. Dr. Eliot speaks of himself as one of the many "old lovers of the island," who could now "expect to welcome many new lovers" of future generations.

And here we are today, one of those future generations to whom Mr. Dorr gifted this beautiful national park. We are those welcomed "new lovers," even if we are natives of this island, seasonal residents, employees of the National Park Service, day trippers from nearby Maine cities and towns, vacationers from urban areas escaping the stress of city life, seekers of nature, hikers, cruise ship passengers disembarking for a few short hours, or travelers from other states and countries.

In my work as ranger at the Village Green Information Center, I have met many extraordinary "new lovers" who have been changed by Acadia, and who in turn have changed me. I especially remember Heiko, a fifty-year-old German who spent one spring and early summer hiking the Appalachian Trail; upon his completion of this trek he arrived on Mount Desert Island, planning to stay for a week. Because of Acadia's natural beauty and its incomparable trails, Heiko ended up staying six weeks, each day asking for hiking recommendations until he finished every trail! I remember Richard, a septuagenarian from Massachusetts, married forty-nine years to his lovely wife; each year they vacationed and camped in Acadia together. Richard lost his wife a couple of years ago, but he faithfully returns to this island retreat each summer, camping still, hiking always, and reliving memories with his wife in each footstep he takes. And often I remember ten-year-old Hannah. She walked in to the Village Green Information Center with her family one day last summer with a look of fear and trepidation and the need to be encouraged to hike The Beehive. "Everybody in my family has climbed The Beehive, and I'm the only one who hasn't. I'm not sure I can, but I *really* want to." After a long discussion and a look to her parents for support, Hannah boldly declared she was going to climb it that afternoon. And she left with her family to do just that, promising to come back and leave me a note. I have that thank-you note still, and the photograph of a beautiful young girl who conquered her fear that day. She is one of the newest generation of "new lovers" of this park.

It is well established in previously published works the debt to which we owe George Bucknam Dorr. Obviously, Acadia National Park would not exist without his persistence and his decades of indefatigable dedication to conservation and preservation of this land we now enjoy. In the noted Building of Arts celebration speech, Dr. Eliot also remarked that "one of the greatest satisfactions in doing any sound work for an institution, a town, or a city, or for the nation is that good work done for the public lasts, endures through generations; and the little bit of work that any individual of the passing generation is enabled to do gains through association with such collective activities an immortality of its own.... The greatest element of satisfaction in looking back on that work is the sense that what I was enabled to do, with the help of many others, is going to last—as *good bricks* built into a permanent structure."

It is now, with the publication of *Creating Acadia National Park: The Biography of George Bucknam Dorr*, that we see another layer of "good bricks" added to the foundation of knowledge about the life of George B. Dorr. This book is solid and enduring, standing as a permanent record for generations to read. When visitors and readers alike better know and understand Mr. Dorr, then rooted in this understanding will be further commitment to love, preserve, and protect this "permanent structure," Acadia National Park. Furthermore, as it was "significant, proper and important, as a matter of history," for Mr. Dorr to write his own memoir for the public good, it is equally appropriate and essential, especially in this centennial year of Acadia National Park, that Ronald Epp's pages be read by any "lover" of Acadia.

We each have the opportunity through *Creating Acadia National Park* and Ronald's own decade-long labor of dedicated research and writing, to better understand from whence come our own passion and relationship with Acadia National Park. For the gift of this book, all lovers of Acadia may be grateful that we now have an enduring tribute to the "Father of Acadia."

Maureen Fournier

January 2015

Introduction

Beneath the jutting façade of Dorr Mountain on Maine's Mount Desert Island, local residents, visitors, and guests of the National Park Service gathered on a bright August morning in 2006. They intermingled at one of the most-visited stops on Acadia National Park's Loop Road: Sieur de Monts Spring and Nature Center, adjacent to the Wild Gardens of Acadia.

Usually few visitors pay close attention to a prominent three-foot-high granite memorial, adjacent to the site's springhouse. But on this day, the stone (relocated from atop Cadillac Mountain) with its tarnished and barely legible plaque was the centerpiece of a public celebration.

Ninety years earlier, on August 22, 1916, Acadia's founders had gathered nearby to celebrate the taking of nearly half the hills of the island. But on this day in 2006, the 1916 establishment of Sieur de Monts National Monument (which would be formally recognized as a national park three years later) shared center stage with the centennial celebration of the Antiquities Act. This legislation had authorized the President of the United States to assign national monument status to a site without congressional approval.

President Theodore Roosevelt had utilized this power to expand federal protection of some of the most scenic and historically significant landscapes in the American West. But by the end of his administration, there were still no national monuments or parks east of the Mississippi; in addition, the existing sites were administratively scattered among several federal departments.

Shortly after Woodrow Wilson's inauguration in 1913, Stephen Tyng Mather, a wealthy California industrialist, wrote to U.S. Secretary of the Interior Franklin K. Lane and argued that distinctive national landscapes were a source of great national pride that should be better served by the federal government.

With war raging in Europe, the threat of America's involvement was increasingly felt. Was it possible for Mather—who came to Washington in 1914 to serve as assistant to the interior secretary—to realize a conservation agenda at a time of growing threats to national security?

At the same historical moment, two proper Bostonians—George B. Dorr and Charles W. Eliot—were championing the creation of a federally protected public landscape in Downeast Maine with even more cards stacked against them. At this time, many Americans and their local, state, and federal representatives believed that all of the nation's natural splendors were west of the Mississippi River. With war in Europe and no national agency to represent the park idea for one of the original thirteen states, did it not fly in the face of reason to seek the establishment of a national monument on a small island in Maine?

Both efforts succeeded! On August 25, 1916, the National Park Service was created, just seven weeks after President Wilson accepted a 5,000-acre parcel on a coastal Maine island as the Sieur de Monts National Monument—the first parcel of what today is Acadia National Park. Federalizing this property was precedent-setting. Never before had the United States accepted donated property from what is now known as a land trust. Yet in a larger political context, decades would pass before the model of a land trust—as a third party between the donor and the federal government—gained popularity.

My own interest in the origin and early development of Acadia National Park was sparked by travel to the villages of that island over several decades. My wife, Elizabeth, and I repeatedly hiked the terrain, spoke with residents about island history, and collaborated during the fifteen-year inquiry that led to this publication. The fascinating Dorr family history provided answers to most vexing questions about the motivations of the "Father of Acadia National Park," situating this persistent gentleman within the history of the National Park Service and the American conservation movement. My career path in university teaching, scholarly publishing, and academic library administration was an asset for the archival research that stretched from Cambridge, Massachusetts, to Santa Barbara, California, and from Bar Harbor to Yorkshire, England.

Creating Acadia National Park traces the life of George Bucknam Dorr (1853–1944), the founder and first superintendent of New England's only national park and the central figure in Maine's land trust movement. Tens of millions have stood before the park memorial that characterizes the founder of Acadia National Park: "gentleman, scholar, and lover of nature." In a life that began in the decade prior to the Civil War and ended in the closing months of World War II, Dorr's most significant accomplishments took place in his last four decades. What were the family, personal, and social wellsprings of his late-in-life achievements? What character traits enabled him, in his passionate promotion of landscape preservation on Maine's Mount Desert Island, to secure the continuing support of the Department of the Interior, philanthropist John Davison Rockefeller Jr., and Harvard University president Charles William Eliot?

In the language of a late nineteenth-century tourist guide, the place where their interests intersected was "a gay watering-place," a remote island that attracted prosperous tourists from Boston, New York, and Philadelphia.[1] Mount Desert Island is situated in the Gulf of Maine, roughly 200 miles northeast of Boston. Its 110 square miles of soaring landscapes are barely detached from the indented Maine coastline by the narrow channel of Frenchman Bay. A lively geological history combining ancient volcanic activity with glaciation and the constant power of the sea produced the most prominent feature of the island: a range of granite mountains extending across its southern half. Here Somes Sound, a glacially sculpted, five-mile-long, very deep inlet (known as a *fjard*), separates the more severe eastern summits from the forested western peaks.

Harsh winters, frequent fog, plentiful rainfall, and warm summer sunshine envelop the spruce-fir and northern hardwood forests that lie beneath the rugged prominence of the highest mountain on the eastern seaboard from Newfoundland to Rio de Janeiro. These mountains are divided by valleys, gorges, lakes, streams, meadows, and quite inaccessible woodlands that end abruptly above brilliantly colored oceanside cliffs. Nearly fifty species of mammals crossed this channel from the mainland to populate the island, and the offspring of most survived into the present era. So too did the Native Wabanaki peoples, who lived for thousands of years in the area now called Maine. A mobile community of hunters, fishers, and gatherers, these "People of the Dawnland" came seasonally to this seacoast domain for the resources vital to their year-round survival.[2]

Since its European discovery in 1604 by Samuel de Champlain, the island's landscape was contested terrain in the struggle between two Old World powers: England and France. Widely traveled, Dorr could speak with expertise about the Continental traditions of the French and English descendants who lived in the island's villages where during "the first half of the nineteenth century Mount Desert Island still remained remote and inaccessible, except to coasting vessels, but fishing hamlets gradually sprang up along its shore, the giant pines…were cut and shipped away, town government was established, roads of a sort were built, and the island connected with the mainland by a bridge and causeway."[3]

Romantic mid-nineteenth-century representations of Mount Desert by nature writers and artists generated interest in the dramatic beauty of the isle. Following the Civil War, rapidly expanding rail lines brought affluent seasonal visitors who had heard of its distinctive landscapes. When the fashionable world became aware of coastal Maine's natural environment and scenery, the island's boardinghouses were replaced by grand hotels that met the expectations of inner-city aristocrats—or rusticators, as they were locally known—accustomed to the fineries of Newport and Saratoga.

Like the poet Henry Wadsworth Longfellow and the novelist Nathaniel Hawthorne, Dorr was born into a cosmopolitan community adjacent to the sea. Indeed, for more than six decades he lived first on Park Street at the foot of the Massachusetts State House and then beside the Boston Public Garden on Commonwealth Avenue. Some of Dorr's favorite haunts—the Boston Common, Beacon Hill, and Commonwealth Avenue—were close to the Atlantic Ocean. He never grew weary of revisiting these, nor of the mountain charms of the Berkshires, where in the two decades before the Civil War both sides of the Dorr family had been among the pioneering cottagers of Lenox.

The Dorrs and the Eliots were among the prominent Boston families drawn to Mount Desert Island. Prosperous merchant Charles Hazen Dorr and his two adolescent sons first arrived in 1868. The elder Dorr was so affected by the landscape that he purchased a large oceanfront farm. Charles W. Eliot and his eldest son, Charles, first visited a decade later. The Dorr family returned in 1878 to design, construct, and landscape their new Oldfarm residence, sited on a large parcel of land facing Frenchman Bay and featuring broad setbacks and a contoured driveway.

Few private homes in Maine have played a more central role in public affairs than the Dorr family estate. For sixty-four years, Oldfarm was a center of hospitality on the island, the operational center for the management of Acadia National Park, and the horticultural testing ground for the adjacent Dorr family commercial enterprise, the Mount Desert Nurseries. Mary and Charles Dorr indulged their son. The tall, lanky, walrus-mustached, scholarly Harvard graduate had uncertain plans and spent much of every day hiking the island's pathways, applying the keen observational skills of a naturalist—skills he had developed as a child when he explored the Massachusetts rural woodlands near Jamaica Plain, Canton, and Lenox.

The Eliot family resided in quiet Northeast Harbor, an hour-long buggy ride to the south. The younger Charles used the island as a natural resource for his Harvard College scientific studies. These formative inquiries aroused his enthusiasm for conservation. As a landscape architect, following his partnership with Frederick Law Olmsted, Charles Eliot would spearhead the creation in 1891 of the first American land trust, The Trustees of Public Reservations (today called The Trustees).

As the twentieth century approached, the island's cottagers worried that the choicest undeveloped landscapes were rapidly disappearing. Far too many new residents restricted access to their property, limiting the landscape available for exploration by foot. Moreover, there was increasing concern that these expensive properties would eventually revert to piecemeal private development. The island's forest itself was threatened as the technological innovation of the portable saw made resumption of commercial logging—and deforestation—appear inevitable.

Charles W. Eliot agreed with Dorr's more philosophic assessment of the situation: "We are passing into a new phase of human life where men are congregating in vast multitudes, for industrial purposes, for trade and intercourse; the population of the future must inevitably be many times the population of the present, and the need of conserving now, while there is time, pleasant, wholesome breathing places for these coming multitudes is great...[yet] it goes far beyond that and is deeply concerned with the inner life of men...to preserve in their openness, in their unspoiled beauty and the interest of their wild life, of their native trees and plants, their birds and animals, the places where the influence of Nature may be felt the most [or] observed and studied in its fullest."[4] In order to realize his conservation goals, George Dorr was no longer content to engage in community improvement activities, develop his new nursery business, and retreat into the rugged beauty of its landscape.

Late in the summer of 1901, the senior Eliot invited a dozen individuals to meet in Seal Harbor to discuss courses of action to conserve island land not yet threatened by the lumberman's saw or sequestered by the affluent few. Later, that meeting was described by Seal Harbor resident George L. Stebbins as arguably the most significant event in the history of the island.[5] Of those present, wealthy entrepreneurs like John S. Kennedy and George W. Vanderbilt could afford to own vast scenic tracts. Nonetheless, persuaded by Eliot's visionary language they aligned themselves with him "to acquire, hold and maintain and improve for free public use lands in Hancock County which by reason of scenic beauty, historical interest, sanitary advantage or for other reasons may be available." Eliot was selected as president; Dorr became first vice president. Modeled on the Massachusetts Trustees, the Hancock County Trustees of Public Reservations (HCTPR) was incorporated two years later by the state of Maine.

Eliot was unable to provide timely guidance from Harvard, so the HCTPR vested de facto executive authority in nearly fifty-year-old George B. Dorr, who now lived mostly year-round on Mount Desert. Eliot deferred to Dorr's mastery of the ebb and flow of local affairs—as is revealed in their extensive correspondence. He knew that Dorr would devise successful strategies—acquired from his Harvard University alumnus experience in urban planning—to guide land acquisition. Mount Desert Island was the right setting for Dorr to apply his post-graduate experiences as a Harvard University alumni fundraiser, drawing upon the practical lessons of philanthropy that tracked back to his maternal grandfather, banker and Harvard treasurer Thomas Wren Ward.

Ward was a member of that influential New England merchant class that gave liberally—often anonymously—to an array of worthy causes. Dorr learned "at his grandfather's knee" of this tension between private and public interests, later adapting his insights to landscape preservation. Grandfather Ward was a patrician "determined to carry out, in every sphere in which their interests lay, [his] duties as an American...to make Boston a model town...to make New England a model region."[6] Ward's children were much involved with the "Boston Brahmin" (so called by Oliver Wendell Holmes Sr., referring to members of Boston's traditional upper class) literary and social movements of the day, including relationships with Ralph Waldo Emerson, Julia Ward Howe, Margaret Fuller, and other literary notables of antebellum America.

Over the last half-century, historians have pointed to the writings of Henry David Thoreau, George Perkins Marsh, and Gifford Pinchot as forging a new paradigm about the relationship between nature and culture. The "scholars, poets, philosophers, scientists, writers, painters, clerics, and even the politicians of the settled, increasingly, urbanized East" first called for nature's protection.[7] Even though landscape architect Charles Eliot died prematurely in 1897, his conservation ethic had already inspired his father, Charles W. Eliot. In 1890, the senior Eliot completed a social science inquiry into "the common mode of life" for most Americans. Mount Desert Island was the locale for this empirical investigation into the conservation underpinnings of its residents' livelihoods.[8]

Eliot's research anticipated a recent argument for the origins of conservation as a grassroots phenomenon—based on the long-standing practices of farmers, fishermen, lumbermen, and craftsmen.[9] Dorr nowhere wrote in general terms about the genesis of landscape conservation; instead, he individualizes the wellspring of his conservation ethos in the landscapes improved through family gardening. His behavior embodies the characteristics of New England land conservation: an ethos that emphasizes self-determination, innovation, individual leadership, civic engagement, and an ethical concern for the future of this unique landscape.[10]

The first part of Dorr's memoir, *The Story of Acadia National Park,* described the protracted political process that led to the 1919 elevation of Sieur de Monts National Monument to national park status. Known until

1929 as Lafayette National Park, its admission into the rapidly evolving park system was based on a novel concept—that private land donated by a conservation organization was entitled to be federally protected public land. This decision irrevocably altered the concept of a national park.[11]

Nearly all national parks had been carved out of federal land quite distant from population centers. Consequently, there was limited sensitivity in the Department of the Interior to the local challenges that Dorr faced. Both summer and year-round residents frequently expected that they would participate in decision-making about the direction of park development. The Department of the Interior was frequently inattentive to the specific park development strategies that Dorr employed to resolve ambiguous and complex issues. To be sure, this inattention gave Dorr latitude but also contributed to pent-up hostility among residents who believed that they were negatively affected by the local agent of a distant bureaucracy.

From 1915 to 1935 Dorr routinely spent lengthy periods in Washington lobbying at the highest levels for approvals that benefited the park, conferring with officials at the Department of the Interior about matters both local and system-wide. This modest Bostonian earned a reputation as the most distinguished of the first generation of National Park Service superintendents. But would he be able to stand shoulder-to-shoulder with the son of an oil titan who had turned away from family business interests, acquired in 1910 The Eyrie—a 150-acre Seal Harbor estate surrounding Barr Hill—and was interested in acquiring contiguous property for the development of carriage roads modeled on family properties in Ohio and New York?[12] Both Dr. Eliot and Mr. Dorr saw quite clearly the conservation implications of the arrival of John Davison Rockefeller Jr., if officials in Washington could be persuaded to be flexible.

Dorr's unpublished correspondence with Mr. Rockefeller and his less restrained letters to and from Dr. Eliot provide key manuscript sources that underscore their complex relationships. Would their respective philanthropies align or collide? Would their perfectionist personalities aid or hinder their relationships with the HCTPR, the National Park Service, and local government authorities? Dorr and senior park service officials recognized that local government is the vehicle that private landowners use to protect themselves against more severe county, state, or federal restraints.[13] On Mount Desert Island a patchwork quilt of private and public lands provided the setting for disagreements. When Mr. Rockefeller's plans for road development came to public attention in 1924, opponents objected to the intrusion of carriageways into a primitive inner wilderness. Moreover, they suggested that the expansion of carriage and motor roads was an unseemly collusion between the park superintendent and Mr. Rockefeller.

Officials at the Department of the Interior renewed their support for the philanthropist's carriage road and innovative bridge construction designs, anticipating that in due course these features would become iconic. They also recognized that the philanthropist's new construction techniques and architectural styles were applicable to other national parks, especially during the New Deal years when the Civilian Conservation Corps improved park infrastructure in ways unimaginable in the preceding decade. Eventually there was public recognition that the carriage roads and bridges built by Rockefeller were among the cultural centerpieces of Acadia.

As park management responsibilities were delegated to Acadia staff, Dorr was charged with acquiring additional donations and deepening his involvement with Mr. Rockefeller, whose philanthropy was no longer limited to Maine. The rehabilitation of Colonial Williamsburg, development of both the Shenandoah National Park and Great Smoky Mountains National Park, and the acquisition of the Grand Tetons were conservation projects Rockefeller supported. Mather used the infrastructure lessons from Acadia as a model for the development of other national parks, including these new national parks in the eastern United States.[14]

Less well known is Dorr's acquisition of an extensive number of properties at his own expense, real estate cornerstones on which gifts from Mr. Rockefeller and others were erected. Dorr acted as the silent partner in Rockefeller's acquisition of Mount Desert Island real estate, not through financial investments but by serving as the acquisition agent for property later transferred to the New York philanthropist—all the while employed by the National Park Service. Like Rockefeller, Dorr understood the need for parks to be regulated by a plan, one "wisely and strongly following its main purpose." The Olmsted Brothers landscape architect Henry V. Hubbard reiterated Dorr's insistence that adhering to a plan was essential to conservation success, even when tourist interests were expressed as paramount. Park planning should not be "turned aside to inappropriate ends, however good they may be in themselves, or however much they may bear the sacred name of recreation."[15]

Despite the formality of his suited attire, Dorr was known for "rolling up his sleeves" in all operational aspects of park development. He inspired others to ally themselves with his objectives and always offered the hospitality of Oldfarm to promote the friendships that others identified as essential to both his and their well-being. He foresaw the potential of the new federal agency and demonstrated the qualities of the New England conservation ethic that could be applied elsewhere.

As with Rockefeller, the importance of genuine friendships was essential to Dorr's personal growth and professional success. Certain individuals regularly experienced a closeness in their relationships with Dorr—one that he characterized in a non-sexual sense as "intimate." Since Dorr was a bachelor, some might infer that cultivating relationships with others offset attachment to a family of his own making. The evidence suggests that he genuinely valued the counsel and affection these close friends gave and that they appreciated what he offered in return.

Many of Dorr's friends had great wealth and social standing: entrepreneurs John S. Kennedy, George W. Vanderbilt, John D. Rockefeller Jr., and Henry Lane Eno. Some came to Dorr's rescue when his acquisition of property to be donated to the government led him close to financial ruin. Other friends were academics who reshaped the intellectual fabric of American culture: William James and Josiah Royce, Harvard colleagues of President Eliot. Those committed to redesigning America's landscape were in this select circle as well: Beatrix Farrand, Frederick Law Olmsted Jr., and the foremost leaders in the U.S. Department of the Interior—Horace M. Albright, Stephen Mather, Franklin K. Lane, and Harold Ickes. Dorr's affection for his immediate family and those in his household staff cannot easily be separated from his attachments to others, such as physicians Robert Abbe and S. Weir Mitchell. Dorr's success was not dependent on summer residents "from away." Largely unrecognized are the contributions of attorneys Luere B. Deasy, John A. Peters, and A. H. Lynam, all Maine natives. Not to be omitted among this highly diverse company were friendships with authors Julia Ward Howe and Edith Wharton, geologist William M. Davis, and botanists Merritt L. Fernald and Edward L. Rand.

The National Park Service did not actively involve scientists in its development plans until the 1930s, when they could no longer ignore the NPS biologist George M. Wright's troubling findings about the status of national park wildlife. Yet more than a decade earlier, Dorr's promotion of scientific inquiry anticipated NPS interest in the management of natural resources.[16] Dorr's generative role in establishing the Mount Desert Island Biological Laboratory and the Jackson Laboratory would eventually yield internationally renowned institutions employing thousands of investigators—a derivative benefit beyond his expectations.

Dorr's writing style combines the force of artistic sensitivity with the precision associated with scientific pursuits. He speaks of the seemingly static elements of nature as enduring, as near permanent as anything conceived by man. A contemporary landscape architect captures the essence of his insights into the natural forces on Mount Desert: "Rock erodes to sand, cemented sand becomes stone, erodes to sand once again. Fire consumes plants and releases seeds, ashes mix with soil to nourish new seedlings.... materials are dynamic, constant but constantly changing, flowing, growing, decaying, transforming."[17] On a human scale, the durability of the island's landscapes exceeded the most archaic cultural remains that Dorr experienced during his extensive travels. Landscape offered a sense of permanence that residents and visitors found irresistible, as riveting as the "constancy" of the surrounding sea. Whereas the psychologist William James affirmed a passionate belief in human nature, Dorr adapted the thinking of his friend to suit his experience and affirmed belief in "the power of nature to mold, control, and create the world."[18]

In his memoirs, Dorr's faith in the durability of America shines through: "The present generation will pass as my own has done, but the mountains and woods, the coasts and streams that have now passed through the agency of the Park to the National Government will continue as a national possession, a public possession henceforth for all time to come. It never will be given up to private ownership again. The men in control will change, the Government itself will change, but its possession by the people will remain whatever new policies or developments may come."[19]

The park triumvirate—Eliot, Dorr, and Rockefeller—aspired to preserve scenery, to make it accessible, and where needed, to improve upon it. Following Eliot's death in 1926, Dorr further committed himself to securing the preservation of sufficient landscape to prevent fragmentation of habitat, one of the ecological goals of contemporary environmentalism. He accepted the reality that there would always be local apprehension—if not opposition—regarding land-management issues. And so at times, the superintendent was less than transparent in his planning.

Dorr was not a major historical figure. Nor was he recognized as an administrator jockeying for ever-more important positions of responsibility. Unlike John Muir, his published writings did not transform national policy. Yet this grand old man of the National Park Service on Mount Desert Island brought about a federal investment in the conservation of nearly half the landmass of the island. The resultant loss of property tax revenue was offset by the ever-growing number of visitors that clearly contributed to village prosperity. At the county level, Dorr extended the scope of Acadia National Park beyond Mount Desert Island, to other shorelines and islands within Hancock County. For many years Maine has benefited from park-fueled tourism and reveled in its status as having the only national park east of the Mississippi River.

Dorr's comfortable and cosmopolitan upbringing provided the foundation on which his passion for the natural world would be realized on Mount Desert Island. Dorr's alliances were essential to his success in advancing the historically unique argument that privately donated land from a conservation organization deserved federal protection. In the end, Maine's century-old national park remains a respite for urban populations drawn to an enduring seacoast preserve that reflects the Yankee values of self-determination, initiative, and civic engagement of its founder. Dorr's finest work, the creation and management of Acadia National Park, was his vehicle for promoting democratic values and the fruition of his transformation of an elitist social inheritance into an all-consuming commitment to conservation.

CHAPTER ONE

First Impressions

In the mid-century years following the catastrophic war between the Union and the Confederacy, many Boston merchants took pride in the fact that their city led all other regional communities in its rapid expansion. To be sure, its location had spared it the ravages of that conflict, enabling the population of Boston to quadruple—reaching about one million—in the years between 1850 and 1900, spreading out over thirty-one smaller cities and towns to form a true metropolis. The flow of German and later Irish immigrants continued unabated. They would later be joined by thousands of Italians and eastern European Jews.

The desperate new arrivals, including children and women, formed a vast pool of cheap labor for New England's textile mills, shoe factories, and ironworks.[1] Similar changes were affecting cities throughout the nation. The first flush of peacetime spawned the greatest industrial boom the United States had ever seen. This economic growth was fueled by the expansion of the railroads, the new oil and steel industries, and advances in technology that spurred existing enterprises.

Yet many in Boston—and to a lesser extent Philadelphia and New York—were striking out in search of scenic Northeast landscapes that showed no evidence of the impact of war and industrialization. Such jaunts had a higher purpose than mere sightseeing, although passive enjoyment certainly was part of the experience. The destinations they chose—the Adirondack Mountains of New York, the White Mountains of New Hampshire, and the New England seacoast—were inspired by trends affecting the nation as a whole.

One such trend was a new appreciation of America's vanishing wilderness, inspired by romantic literature and painting in the first half of the nineteenth century. Ralph Waldo Emerson and Henry Ward Beecher linked nature, spirituality, and moral character. Their publications provided an intellectual underpinning for both the reform and conservation movements that gathered force after the Civil War.

At the same time, Hudson River School painters led by Thomas Cole were traipsing the last of the Northeast wilderness and covering vast canvases with radiant landscapes. As art historian Pamela Belanger has observed, such paintings exposed the contradiction between national expansion—and the accompanying plunder of forests, animals, and minerals in the path of settlement—and the growing attachment to wilderness as a defining national motif. The wilderness became a new opportunity for artists to align their expertise with the economic potential of tourism and railroads.[2] Frederic Church was among the artists drawn to the rareified light and sublime scenery of Mount Desert Island, and helped popularize the island as a tourist destination.

Mirroring this current, social reform was deeply infused with the notion that "outdoor scenery" possessed physically and morally restorative effects. City life carried associations of overcrowding, pollution, dirt, disease, stress, and moral corruption. In urban settings, park design tended to follow the pastoral picturesque aesthetic of Frederick Law Olmsted, first expressed in Central and Prospect parks in New York City. Olmsted passionately embraced the notion articulated by landscape designer Andrew Jackson Downing—that outdoor scenery could shape individual character, and, on a public scale, civilization itself. Olmsted, enamored of the serene English countryside, designed tranquil scenes to soothe and refresh jangled nerves.

As interstate passenger trains fanned out during the period, new tourist accommodations sprouted along rail routes, including the northeast coast of Maine—known as "Downeast" to Mainers. A 110-square-mile island named Mount Desert, several hundred yards off the mainland south of the lumber-industry hub of Bangor, drew especially animated accounts. Since its European discovery in 1604, when bare summits were observed on the island's mountains, prompting French explorer Samuel de Champlain to name it "l'Isle des Monts-déserts," there has been ongoing disagreement about how to pronounce "Desert" in English. Naval historian Samuel Eliot Morison refers to the "Sahara School" as those who accent the penult; the "Ice Cream and Cake School" accent the last syllable (as in "dessert"). In Morison's day and ours, "the penult accenters are much in a minority."[3]

Frederic Church, Thomas Cole, Sanford Gifford, and Fitz Henry Lane had rambled the shoreline—drawn to its isolation, its dramatic landforms, and its unusual, rose-tinted granite. Forged in a violent succession of volcanoes and glaciers, these features also attracted early geologists including the Harvard naturalist Louis Agassiz, who documented Mount Desert Island in his book *Geological Sketches* (1866). But it was the vast, luminous canvases—especially Church's—that burned these places into the imaginations of thousands of Americans.[4]

Mount Desert Island came to the attention of the Dorr family of Boston. It was the third largest island off the coast of the continental United States and the highest point on the Atlantic seaboard between Newfoundland and Rio de Janeiro. For the first half of the nineteenth century, the island was only accessible to coastal vessels. The advent of the Boston and Bangor Steamship Line to Mount Desert Island in 1868, coupled with a rough roadway connecting the island with the mainland, led to summer life as we know it.

Word of mouth, artistic imagery, and the first-hand published narratives of Clara Barnes Martin and Benjamin DeCosta whetted cultivated appetites for coastal scenery and the challenge of wilderness exploration.[5] A historically significant journal of a monthlong stay in 1855 by the party of twenty-five accompanying Charles Tracy of New York City also fostered public interest. The temperate climate and varied topography nurtured an array of flora and fauna, rich in ecological and biological diversity. Villagers earned their living from the bounty of the sea. The intertidal zone harbored a profusion of invertebrate species. In an economy based on the success of seamen, few sailors lost sight of the striking, fine-grained, pinkish granite mountain range clothed in spruce and fir forests that touched the Atlantic shoreline. Broad valleys, deep gorges, clear lakes, and rolling meadows invited exploration.

As rail service expanded and new ports were opened with tourist accommodations Downeast, these northern destinations were increasingly visited by Boston's upper class. In the summer of 1866, the Dorr family left the comfort of their affluent Commonwealth Avenue townhouse and took rail service to Bangor en route to Mount Desert Island. Now in their forties, Charles and Mary Dorr were accompanied by their two teenage sons, William and George, on their first family adventure outside Massachusetts. After learning that no suitable accommodations were available in the town of Eden (later renamed Bar Harbor), the family headed west into the White Mountains of New Hampshire and then further north to Canada. Sixty years later the youngest son, George Bucknam Dorr, recalled in his memoirs the adventure of their steamboat running the famous Lachine Rapids before they turned south again into the Adirondack Mountains where "all as yet was very wild and primitive."[6]

Over the next two years the Dorrs heard more about the beauty of Mount Desert Island from old friends and neighbors. In 1868 they redoubled their efforts to reach a locale quite unlike familiar Massachusetts, traveling this time by steamboat and disembarking at the village of Southwest Harbor on the western shore of Somes Sound, the deep-channel, five-mile-long fjard dividing the eastern and western halves of the island. From there they boarded a stagecoach for Eden, jouncing over sixteen miles of "rough roads and long, steep hills."[7]

This was not a sightseeing trip. The family was sufficiently impressed with the grandeur of the landscape that Charles purchased hundreds of acres fronting Frenchman Bay, on Compass Harbor. This was not an impulsive decision, but one that resulted from land grant inquiries that Dorr's father had pursued prior to their arrival. The original Oldfarm grant, acquired by Charles H. Dorr, was less than a mile from Eden's village green and extended toward Newport (now Champlain) Mountain.[8]

Near the end of his life, in a letter to President Franklin D. Roosevelt, George B. Dorr emphasized the significance of his father's acquisition for the future development of Acadia National Park. For, "long before the park was established…its real history begins. In writing my history of the park beginning, I want this clearly recognized and established." Indeed, he would write in an official 1939 Department of the Interior publication that "it was from the impulse of that early summer life that the movement for public reservations and the national park arose, springing from pleasant memories and the desire to preserve in largest measure possible the beauty and freedom of the island for the people's need in years to come."[9] However, many years would pass before the Dorrs took advantage of the potential of this extensive and superbly situated landscape. Their attention had shifted back to Boston, where the memories of the war still dominated their thoughts.

Much earlier, following their marriage in 1850, Charles Hazen Dorr and Mary Gray Ward Dorr had moved from the urban residences of their parents adjacent to the Boston Common, into the rural community of Jamaica Plain, six miles to the southwest. Mary's father purchased for them a residence on the shore of Jamaica Pond. Each brought affluence, high social standing, and the intellectually progressive weight of their families to the union. That is, a "remarkable combination of concern for the 'self' and the integrity of one's position...with a concern for proper thought, appropriate action, tact, restraint, concern for the world at large."[10]

The Dorr residence stood on an acre of land at the end of Lakeview Place, directly across the seventy-acre pond from Sunnyside, the estate of the historian, horticulturist, and family friend, Francis Parkman. Parkman's studies of the French colonization of America would later loom large in Dorr's writings about the development of Acadian culture. The Dorrs appreciated the remarkable beauty of the Parkman property, the adjoining deer park of the Chickering estate, and the "rich landscape features" of nearby Bussey Woods—later transformed into the Arnold Arboretum of Harvard College, now Harvard University—as they routinely walked these grounds.[11] This early exposure to pastoral designed landscapes would only increase in the coming years, as George Dorr's relatives built their own country estates in the Berkshires, and George and brother William began spending summers at their grandfather Ward's property in Canton, Massachusetts.

For the time being, the Dorrs left behind the new markets for Boston's commerce, which rapidly transformed the city. The railroad had shifted the focus of trade away from the historical hub of the waterfront. Most of the 140,000 residents still found stability in Puritan ideals, though even here a dramatic shift was occurring. By mid-century, Unitarianism would become the dominant religion. The Dorrs further recognized and supported the increasingly prominent anti-slavery agitation.[12]

In its political activism, Boston prided itself as an intellectual center of public discourse—the nearby town of Concord, home of Emerson and Hawthorne, notwithstanding. Oliver Wendell Holmes expressed this community pride in his famous claim that the Boston State House is "the hub of the solar system,"[13] and later Cleveland Amory situated "The Hub" within the larger context of Boston's first families.[14] Yet for the Dorr newlyweds, the lure of the Jamaica Plain countryside proved more inviting than the State House environment off Park Street where Mary was born and matured.

Mary Gray Ward Dorr's family traced their origins to Miles Ward, who migrated from County Kent in England to Salem, Massachusetts, in 1640. George B. Dorr would be the ninth in line of descent. In all the generations between, no family member was revered more highly by George than his maternal grandfather, Salem-born Thomas Wren Ward.[15] Thomas's father, William, was an adventuresome youth who became a privateer, eventually captured by the British during the Revolutionary War. Imprisoned in the English seaport of Gosport until he was exchanged, he then served on many voyages to the West Indies, India, and China before becoming president of the State Bank of Boston.

As a boy of twelve, Thomas was taken to sea and by nineteen years of age became a Salem sea captain engaged in the risky transport of commodities to and from Canton and other international ports.[16] As Salem's prosperity began to wane, Grandfather Ward relocated first to New York and then to Boston, where he became a partner in the import-export firm of Ropes & Ward. The young merchant soon built a small fortune through his continuing involvement with Salem acquaintances. These included the family of Abraham Gray and sons Samuel Gray and William Gray, the largest ship-owner in America. Throughout the nineteenth century, the Gray family influenced the development of Harvard College both as graduates and faculty members, and through their philanthropic gifts.

Thomas Wren Ward (often referred to as T. W. Ward) also found in the Gray family an appealing young woman named Lydia, the daughter of Samuel Gray. Ward approached Samuel and asked for his daughter's hand in marriage.[17] Between 1812 and 1831, Lydia Gray Ward gave birth to eight children, of whom only Dorr's mother, Mary, and her brothers Samuel and George lived into the Civil War era. For nearly a half century—beginning in 1816—the Ward family resided at 3 Park Street, a four-story prestigious "Bulfinch Row" Federal-style townhouse, abutting the Boston Common and a stone's toss from the Massachusetts State House.[18]

Like many other successful entrepreneurs of that era, T. W. Ward was able to retire while still in his thirties. His friend Joshua Bates assessed Ward as "honest, meticulous, and with an encyclopedic knowledge of American business and businessmen." Bates also apprenticed with William Gray who later sent him to Europe as a general mercantile agent. In 1829, Bates suggested to his new partner, London financier Thomas Baring, that Ward was best suited to become the first American representative of Baring Brothers & Company, the most important British firm brokering with American businessmen and the United States government. Baring convinced Ward to come out of retirement and become the "pioneer credit reporter," evaluating the creditworthiness of American business houses and securing their loans. As a "financial ambassador plenipotentiary" for more than two decades, Ward significantly shaped the country's developing commercial institutions.[19] On a smaller scale, when the City of Boston negotiated with Baring Brothers in 1852, the establishment of a public library for Bates's adopted home prompted him to offer funds to build library collections—on the condition that the city provide sufficient funds for a building that would be an ornament to the city. In the year of his death, Bates was acknowledged as the founder and largest benefactor of the Boston Public Library.

But Ward was also called upon by Harvard College. Another Ward family friend from their Salem days, the navigator Nathaniel Bowditch, exerted as much power on the Harvard Corporation as he exercised in mathematics and navigation. He secured the 1828 election of Ebenezer Francis as college treasurer, and working together they put the chaotic finances of Harvard College in order. This set the stage for the 1830 election of another Salem businessman to the Harvard College "Salem Administration."[20] New treasurer Thomas Wren Ward sustained their progress over the next twelve years, one of a handful of men who guided the direction of the institution during the presidency of Josiah Quincy III—while fulfilling at the same time his responsibilities to Barings.[21] Nearly a century later, his grandson, George Bucknam Dorr, would adapt Ward's talent for philanthropic enterprise to the conservation challenges of the new century.

The eldest offspring of Thomas and Lydia Ward were starting their own families and setting their sights beyond Boston. Mary's elder brother, Samuel Gray Ward, married the wealthy beauty Anna Hazard Barker, an event attended by his friend Ralph Waldo Emerson. A few years later, in 1844, the couple surprised acquaintances and friends by relocating to rural Berkshire County.[22] They purchased Lenox farmland to create a Ward family residence and named it Highwood. The Sage of Concord was astounded that the intellectually gifted Ward would attempt to become a farmer, especially so far from cosmopolitan Boston.[23] At Ward's suggestion, Nathaniel Hawthorne would relocate nearby at the Red Cottage, where he penned *The House of Seven Gables.*

Siblings of Mary's husband, Charles Dorr, also established a country place in the Berkshires. Francis Fiske Dorr, a New York export merchant, purchased thirty acres on a Lenox hillside overlooking Laurel Lake.[24] In late 1853, Francis and his brother, George Bucknam Dorr, after whom Charles and Mary's younger son was named, set about creating a grand country estate called Highlawn. They were soon joined by their two sisters, Elizabeth Dorr and Martha Ann Dorr Edwards, who lived at Highlawn off and on. These four siblings, born out of their father's first marriage, would welcome their younger half-sister, Susan Dorr, and half-brother, Charles Dorr, to their Lenox home. Both Highwood and Highlawn would draw Charles and Mary Dorr and their family to the Berkshires for expansive opportunities to explore on foot, carriage, and horse its woods, hills, and valleys.

Highlawn's proximity to Highwood inevitably led to comparisons. Popular opinion held that Highlawn was the "more elaborate and symmetrical" of the two, due to the energy and time that the elder George B. Dorr had dedicated to the grand house and grounds. Highlawn had given him the opportunity to indulge his horticultural passion and hone his landscaping skills. His neighbor, the minister and social reformer Henry Ward Beecher, began his 1854 essay on "Dream-Culture" by noting that "it takes me but a second to run down that eastern slope, across the meadow, over the road, up that long hillside (which the benevolent Mr. Dorr is so beautifully planting with shrubbery for my sake—blessings on him!)."[25] Over the last two decades of his life, the elder George B. Dorr spent his summers transforming the grounds of Highlawn into a seat of unsurpassed beauty, which a local reporter described as "a place almost too perfect," where the views are complete and the grounds in perfect order.[26]

Close by at Highwood, Samuel G. Ward regarded the experience of farming as a "golden time." Yet after seven years, local acquaintances regarded the departure of the first Lenox cottager as "a public misfortune." Nonetheless, the failing health of Samuel's father, Thomas, obliged their return to Boston where T. W. Ward coached his eldest son in the skills necessary to assume the leadership of Barings.[27] Boston welcomed back Samuel as one of their own shortly before the establishment of the distinguished Saturday Club. Ralph Waldo Emerson conceived the idea that became that most prestigious of Boston's social clubs, but it was Ward who brought together the small, congenial band of historians, essayists, scientists, poets, and businessmen.[28] Samuel enjoyed sharing amusing tidbits from these stimulating encounters at family gatherings.

But the joys of the Berkshires were not so readily recalled as the winter of 1853–54 approached and Mary Dorr's second pregnancy came to term. Though Christmas was "sparely kept in the New England of those days," the Dorr and Ward families anticipated gathering around the Christmas tree at family friend Henry Ingersoll Bowditch's residence on Beacon Hill, surrounded by twenty-three grandchildren and other relatives.[29] Across the Common, Charles and Mary Dorr, with young William, stayed close to the Ward residence in consideration of Mary, then swiftly returned home to Jamaica Plain.

In his diary, Mary's father noted that a "violent snowstorm" commenced during the first minutes of December 29. Three hours later—with the temperature at six degrees—George Bucknam Dorr was born in the family's weather-besieged residence on the eastern shore of Jamaica Pond.[30] In recent years upper-class Bostonians had moved to this lovely recreational district, with its access to downtown Boston improved by the expansion of train and streetcar networks. Yet even rail transportation could be halted, as Grandfather Ward described how the neighboring homes on Beacon

Hill were not visible the day of his grandson's birth, hidden by the twelve-hour storm.[31] More than eighty years later, George B. Dorr expanded on his grandfather's account, stating that he arrived "at night in the midst of a wild snow-storm, through whose deep drifts my father ploughed his way [five miles] on foot the following day to carry the news to my mother's father in his Park Street home."[32]

According to the January 3, 1854 diary entry of George's aunt, Anna Barker Ward, Grandfather Ward arrived at her Beacon Hill home a few days later and took her and all the children to Jamaica Pond "to see Mary Dorr and her new born boy—all doing well."[33] Similarly, T. W. Ward wrote to his son John, announcing the arrival of his new grandson: Mary "has another fine boy and is as happy as possible."

George B. Dorr spent the first six years of his life beside Jamaica Pond, "a beautiful location fronting through tall trees the sunset view across the lake from the top of a steep bank."[34] Unfortunately, his memoirs contain no additional remarks on the landscaping of the site, the architectural style of the residence, nor the internal character of the residence as seen through the eyes of a young child. The late Ward family archivist Donald Fitch rightly summarizes three generations of Ward family history beginning with T. W. Ward through George B. Dorr. Namely, the enduring desire "to involve one's self culturally, politically, literarily and philanthropically, for the benefit of all. The basis of this humaneness resides…in family intimacy, harmony, and love."[35]

CHAPTER TWO

Dr. Eliot Sails into Frenchman Bay

In 1871, three years after the Dorr family's second visit to Mount Desert Island, an exceptional Harvard gentleman purchased a 33-foot sloop with four cabin berths. Named *Jessie*, this vessel sailed in a race of the Dorchester Yacht Club and the following month went on several excursions in Boston Bay. On July 8, 1871, *Jessie*'s five passengers sailed past the buoys and beacons of the bay and headed eastward and downwind of the prevailing winds (that is, *downeast*) toward coastal Maine. Four days later they safely arrived in Southwest Harbor, where the Dorrs had also disembarked.

Two years earlier, *Jessie*'s owner, Charles William Eliot, had become the president of Harvard College at thirty-seven years of age. His rise to the presidency was precedent-setting. In 1863, when his faculty advancement at Harvard appeared administratively blocked, he went abroad for nearly two years. During this time Eliot studied the organizational and pedagogical structure at a number of German universities; upon his return to Boston he taught for a while at the "pioneering" Massachusetts Institute of Technology. With his appointment to the top administrative post at Harvard, therefore, he was poised to reform the tradition-bound institution.

But for the time being he concentrated on sailing counterclockwise around Mount Desert Island. The crew passed the beach at the jutting Great Head landmark before they sailed between the Porcupine Islands, off Bar Harbor. Finally, they found suitable camping ground in Frenchman Bay on unoccupied Calf Island, a mile-long sliver of rugged land a nautical mile southeast of mainland Sorrento.[1]

Cruising the New England coast in sloops and camping on isolated islands were comparatively rare activities in the aftermath of the Civil War. After unloading cargo at their first camp on Frenchman Bay, Dr. Eliot sailed to Bar Harbor to retrieve his family. His wife, Ellen Derby Peabody, had died two years earlier on the day after the Harvard Corporation elected her husband president; the extended family of the widower included his sons, Charles and Samuel, and his three sisters. This location was the first site of five seasons of summer camping with routine excursions to Mount Desert and other Maine coastal islands. The younger Henry James, Eliot's biographer, reports that "these were small tent colonies…[where] Eliot ran the commissariat, arranged and led exploring expeditions and picnics, and was, in short, skipper, shore commander, housekeeper, host and organizer of entertainments."[2]

No standardized navigation charts existed for the eastern coast of Maine, making a coastal cruise more risky than one might suppose. In 1872, Eliot had a larger vessel, the 43½-foot sloop *Sunshine*, built to cruise the New England coastline. For the next five decades—with the exception of one year—Eliot would leave Cambridge every June to summer at the Asticou property, which his eldest son Charles had discovered for him in 1880 in Northeast Harbor village, across Somes Sound from Southwest Harbor. There, for several months each summer, sailing and family gatherings absorbed this yachtsman completely, as the sea had his ancestors.

The roots of the Eliot family of Boston can be traced to the early seventeenth-century seaside communities of Devonshire, England. By the early nineteenth century, Samuel Atkins Eliot had followed the Harvard family tradition.[3] Having graduated as well from the Divinity School, Samuel never preached but served the public in both legislative branches of the Commonwealth of Massachusetts and the U.S. House of Representatives. He was elected Mayor of Boston in 1837—three years after his wife, Mary Lynam, gave birth to Charles William Eliot, their only son.

The Eliot family resided at 31 Beacon Street, on the western edge of what is now the Massachusetts State House lawn and adjacent to the Boston Common. Nearby were other Eliot and Lynam relatives to comfort young Charles when either his poor eyesight or conspicuous facial birthmark made him the butt of malicious taunts by other children. Summers were spent in Nahant, situated on a long peninsula a dozen miles north of Boston, where Charles fished from the coastal rocks, sailed, and swam. His family taught him to "seek assurances of contentment in his own courage and his own right deeds, 'to look outward and not inward, forward and not back.'"[4]

This principle became a touchstone for Eliot throughout his life. It was reinforced by Reverend T. R. Sullivan, who held a school for boys in the basement of the Park Street Church, a mere block from the Eliot home. In walking to school at "Brimstone Corner" each day, Charles passed 3 Park Street, the home of banker and family friend Thomas Wren Ward. Proximity was not the only factor contributing to the social interactions of these two families: Samuel A. Eliot had recently succeeded Ward as treasurer of Harvard College, a post he held for more than a decade. Eliot retired four years before the economic panic of 1857 wiped out his investments. Seeing his father lose his home and his fortune, Charles, now a young man, stepped in and used his academic income and a $40,000 legacy from his father-in-law to buy a home for his parents and his three unmarried sisters.

George B. Dorr was not yet four months old when his Ward grandparents started seeking a rural retreat outside Boston for their expanding family. Although T. W. Ward had retired from Barings, he had been advised by his physician to find a country home where he could be temporarily "out of the atmosphere and anxieties of business."[5] For $7,600 Ward acquired twenty acres of partially developed property on Pleasant Street in Canton, a rural community fifteen miles southwest of the Boston Common.[6] This parcel adjoined Bywood, an estate purchased by his eldest son, Samuel, after abandoning country life in Lenox.

Shortly after making the Canton purchase, Grandfather Ward acquired additional acreage on the west and east sides of Pleasant Street, where he spent $40,000 to erect both heated and cold greenhouses, a grape house, and arbors situated among forest, fruit, and shade trees. His wife, Lydia, was delighted with the farm, and during that first summer Ward wrote to his son John, "She is having greenhouses made and a garden of an acre prepared for fruits and flowers and is to have all kinds of grapes, etc. She and Sam have both a natural taste for the Country."[7] Later, when business took Sam and his family to New York to live, Charles and Mary Dorr bought Sam's Canton residence. Until Lydia's death in October of 1874, the Dorr family would spend their weekends, holidays, and summer months at the Ward compound. There a rich natural environment provided young George with a strong sense of place and historical associations that would thereafter seed his imagination.[8]

George found his grandfather's property delightfully wild. The adjacent Reservoir Pond offered an enticing spot for sailing and fishing. A network of dirt roads drew the children deep into the countryside, where they could leave human habitation far behind. Grandfather Ward routinely rode several miles on horseback before breakfast and reported on what he saw during these outings. His stories around the breakfast table may have prompted the Dorr boys to seek out the more sizable Ponkapoag Pond to the north. Ponkapoag lay at the base of miles of rugged terrain, where the ledges, valleys, ravines, and other rugged features of the Blue Hills further aroused their curiosity.

As Dorr later recounted, these exploits in the wild gave him and his brother "a great education, teaching us to love the country and the wilderness about us without need of company…There, in real country, with woods and a lake for neighbors, dogs and horses for companions, my bother and I grew up."[9] While William sailed, George gathered wildflowers and collected bird eggs, identified birds by their song and appearance, and examined nest construction.

The Ward property contained one hundred pear trees, one hundred peach trees, fifty apple trees, nectarine and plum trees, and a wide array of produce including potatoes and cauliflower. As might be expected of an outdoorsman and horticulturist, Dorr recalled in his memoirs the grape house, which produced "the most delicious grapes I have ever known." Grandmother Ward had "a passion for gardening which her life in the city gave no opportunity for gratifying." He further remembered the "perfection" of his grandparents' peaches and that the Bartlett and juicy Beurres Bosques pears grew as well as those on the Dorr property at Lenox. Mrs. Ward entered her harvested produce and flowers in horticultural shows where she took many prizes, implanting in George's mind the notion that horticulture could not only be an avocation but perhaps a profitable vocation.

When summer heat became severe, both the Eliot and Dorr families traveled north to Nahant as well as the Cape Ann seashore, about forty miles northeast of Boston. But for nearly six decades the Berkshires exerted a greater pull on the Dorrs.[10] In his memoirs, George described Lenox as "real country…where my mother had stayed with my uncle and, as a girl, had ridden over the whole region—the most fearless horsewoman… save Fanny Kemble. There we spent delightful summers, driving about the country or exploring it—my brother and I—on horseback or on foot. This migratory habit of the family was to prove important afterward in leading us to Bar Harbor."[11] In later correspondence with John D. Rockefeller Jr. about landscape design, Dorr made the aesthetic point that "open grassy spaces like wild sheep pastures, are often better in contrast to continuous woods. I used to be familiar with them, wandering over the Berkshire country when I was a boy."[12]

Dorr provides few childhood recollections about his elders. He notes that he saw his uncle Francis Fiske Dorr "at Lenox during occasional visits that I made to Highlawn, the family estate, as a child where I recall him—a kindly old gentleman, he seemed to me then—pruning trees that bordered on the beautiful great lawn, while I stood beside him."[13] A contemporary and friend of George B. Dorr, Maud Howe Elliott, the daughter of Mary Dorr's friend Julia Ward Howe, observed somewhat trenchantly that "Children take grown people for granted, accept them as fixed facts like the earth, the heaven, and the stars. They do not analyze them as they do their contemporaries."[14]

Other family members appreciated the benefits of country life as well. Mary Dorr grew weary of city life and longed for her quiet country home, a comment that suggested her weakened condition and foreshadowed the consumption that would debilitate her when George was not yet two. The Ward family physician understandably held out little hope for Mary's recovery from a disease that had proven fatal to her sister and two brothers. Charles, "acting on his own initiative," took her to St. Augustine, Florida, where over the winter "the climate conquered and her life was saved."[15] The Dorr children were cared for in Jamaica Plain by the Welsh family nurse, Elizabeth Hind, who George recalled "was with my mother when I was born and cared for me thereafter as though I were her own," and who remained with the Dorr family until her death.

Impressed with the frailty of human existence, Mary accepted the realities of life in mid-century. She wrote to a relative that her boys "are fine promising lads. If they live I think they will be a pleasure and comfort to us," and that their Christmas tree was "all hung round with drums and trumpets and dogs and horses and six-penny whistles, and gay streamers," looking forward to Christmas day when they were to have a dozen other children to "merry-make and divide with, thereby learning the blessings of giving as well as receiving." Mary described her Jamaica Plain home as "comfortable and beautiful, and in perfect order." Her husband, by contrast, worried that "we have too many blessings...but we endeavor not to grow selfish in our happiness."[16]

Amid life's uncertainties, Dorr recalls the sense of permanence that the Park Street residence of his Ward grandparents inspired. Years later, as an elderly Bar Harbor resident, Dorr enjoyed gazing upon a library bookshelf that in his childhood was set "against the wall of the library of my grandfather's Ward's house on Park Street, Boston." In his memoirs, he described the impression made by delightful engravings in *Arabian Knights:* "I remember well climbing up on a chair to look at the back of the books on the shelves, for I could not yet read." Still adorned with "long, fair curls," he had not yet graduated into trousers when he received his grandfather's permission to borrow the book so that Elizabeth Hind could read to him while he perched "in a high chair."

As he grew, Dorr spent hours reading in his grandfather's Park Street library, pausing to glance out to the Granary Burial Ground, which lay beyond the back garden that his grandmother tended. With respect to the common belief in the disease threat of decaying bodies in the Granary and other inner-city church grounds, Ward and other Boston Brahmins became incorporators of Mount Auburn Cemetery, a landscaped rural garden cemetery founded by the Massachusetts Horticultural Society. Glancing to the left, the lad gazed upon the three galleried floors of the Boston Athenaeum.[17] More than two decades earlier, Grandfather Ward had served for eight years as treasurer of this distinguished cultural institution.

On the front side of 3 Park Street, the rooms "looked out delightfully over the Common with the sunlight streaming in the afternoon and throwing on the walls colored light from glass prisms hanging from a great chandelier in the center of the parlor."[18]

Thomas Ward died suddenly in March 1858, at the age of seventy-two. Lauded as "a man of strict integrity, of great enterprise and uncommon business capacity, and much respected in the community," he was buried in Mount Auburn Cemetery.[19] Although Dorr's relationship with his grandfather appeared to have ended at Thomas's death, it became increasingly evident over time that George fostered and developed that relationship—between the living and dead—in ways unforeseen by his relatives.

Harvard College received from Ward a bequest of $5,000 for library acquisitions, as did the Boston Athenaeum.[20] His executors were further directed to be conservative in their investments of his capital, adhering to the minimal risk principle that had profited him so well in life. The overarching goal was investments "in the safest manner, not caring for a high rate of interest, but rather for permanent security of the principle."[21] The Boston Athenaeum, the Boston Missionary Society, the American Peace Society, and his sister received portions of an estate that exceeded half a million dollars. The Park Street home and investment revenue were assigned to Lydia, and at her death in 1874 the property was equally divided among the three surviving children. Unusual for a document of this time, Ward 's will specified his concern for the fate of their two daughters. Quite progressively, Ward stipulated that their inheritance be "wholly free" from the debts, control, or entanglements of their spouses.

The wealth George Dorr inherited on his mother's death in 1901 was substantially derived from Grandfather Ward's enterprise and wise investments. As head of the largest British investment house in America, he was famous for his reliability in appraising—and profiting from—commercial ventures. In the years following his death, family conversations emphasized the importance of the broad constituencies and social networks that Ward established as director of "the Provident Institution for Savings, the Massachusetts Hospital Life [Insurance Company], the Boston Marine Insurance Company, the Boston and Worcester Railroad, and [as] a substantial investor in New England textile mills."[22]

As the years passed the usefulness of the strong foundation provided by his maternal grandfather would be amply demonstrated. George would slowly come to realize the importance of his cultural endowment and as an adult be of one mind with Charles W. Eliot. As Eliot's biographer, Henry

James Jr. observed, "Charles William Eliot was a great believer in 'stocks,' and thought that families whose men and women he had known and watched through four generations...had been serviceable and influential people."[23]

Both George and his father kept detailed genealogical records, now archived at the New England Historic Genealogical Society in Boston. Extracted from several hundred pages of documentation, information about the key figures in this line of descent begins before 1674 with Edward Dorr's arrival in America from Dorset, England, and his marriage to Roxbury-born Elizabeth Hawley. This union resulted in twelve children between 1680 and 1700. One son, Joseph, supported his son Joseph through Harvard College and later became a Judge of the Court of Common Pleas in Mendon, Massachusetts, from 1776 to 1801, and a Worcester County probate judge for eighteen years. The paternal great-grandfather of Acadia's founder, he married Catherine Bucknam in 1767, one of eight children of Harvard-educated Reverend Nathan Bucknam who preached in Medway for seventy-five years. Judge Joseph's son Samuel Dorr worked as a commission merchant, trading "West India goods" very profitably at 30 India Street on the Boston wharves; he retired from shipping and became a banker, serving for thirty years as Director of the New England Bank. His public service in the Massachusetts Senate and House of Representatives did not limit his financial acumen, and at the time of his death his estate was worth $400,000.

Samuel's first marriage yielded five sons and one daughter, but the line of descent to Acadia's founder is through Samuel's second marriage in 1815, to North End Bostonian Susan Brown. She was the first of five children of Susannah Adams and Joseph Lasinby Brown, later regarded as "among the most influential" of the prominent nineteenth-century residents of Emerson's Concord.[24] The youngest son of Samuel and Susan was Charles Hazen Dorr, who spent his childhood opposite the Common on Tremont Street in the company of Susan Elizabeth Dorr, his only direct sibling.

Consequently, in terms of Dr. Eliot's belief in the importance of family lineage (i.e., "stocks"), both the Ward and Dorr ancestry included prominent merchants, bankers, scholars, and culturally sophisticated individuals. Dr. Eliot, too, was indebted to his family line for certain blessings, even as he recognized that his facial scarring was especially difficult for him in his youth. Perhaps that is what prompted him, as a Dorr family friend, to be empathetic to young George's serious stutter, a disfluency that almost surely led to insensitivities on the part of his peers as well as concerns among his elders.[25] Dorr nowhere spoke of this stutter, and we would be unaware of it if it were not for Charles W. Eliot, who well understood the social consequences of being marked with a physical limitation. Two years before his death, Eliot referred to Dorr's speech in a cautionary letter to the secretary of the interior. He stated that his friend was beset with a stutter "since his boyhood...which was originally very pronounced and conspicuous... preventing him from uttering a word for an appreciable length of time."[26] In antebellum America there was considerable disagreement about the cause and preferred treatment for stammers and stutters.[27] Yet despite the physical and social afflictions of these men, the change that each experienced when the beauty of Mount Desert Island washed over them was transformative.

CHAPTER THREE

The Most Impressionable Years

This first public botanical garden in the United States had been the inspiration of philanthropist Horace Gray, a relative of Mary Gray Ward Dorr.[1] Over time the spacious landscape featured meandering paths, a shallow lake, and brightly planted Victorian flowerbeds. It formed the eastern terminus of the planned Commonwealth Avenue Mall—a broad, Parisian-style boulevard with a double allée of trees. In the words of architectural historian Bainbridge Bunting, Commonwealth Avenue "represents one of the country's first concerted efforts to create a homogeneous urban environment on a grande scale...the Back Bay is for Victorian Boston what Beacon Hill is for the city's Republican era."[2]

Residents in abutting neighborhoods, including the Dorrs, still living at 3 Park Street, no doubt enjoyed their front-row seat to these massive construction projects as Boston re-created itself in fashionable Victorian style. For the filling in of the Back Bay alone, twelve trains a day, each pulling twenty-five cars filled with gravel, chugged across the Charles River from Needham to deliver the necessary fill. By early 1861 the first four- and five-story Commonwealth Avenue residences were occupied.

George Dorr certainly had more than a casual interest in such expansion since his progressive uncle, Samuel G. Ward, decided to relocate his family from Beacon Hill's Louisburg Square to 1 Commonwealth Avenue, at the head of the new grand boulevard. As they had pioneered cottage development in Lenox, Sam and Anna Ward were "pioneer residents" of the reclaimed Back Bay. Sam had recently been involved in laying the cornerstone for the 1858 version of the Boston Public Library, a precursor to the Copley Square McKim Building of 1895.

In 1863 Sam and Anna received approval from London to relocate the Barings American office to New York City, where it remained until Sam's retirement in 1888. Sam's father, T. W. Ward, had taken a similar course of action, both convinced at the time that this much larger city "is the best place to thrive." Sam would serve as an incorporator of the American Museum of Natural History and of the Metropolitan Museum of Art; yet the Wards would remain "strongly centered in Salem and Boston by origin, religion, and social and business connections."[3] On the south side of Commonwealth Avenue, where architects Gridley Bryant and Arthur Delvan Gilman were constructing nine contiguous brick and sandstone residences, Sam acquired 20 Commonwealth Avenue for his mother, Lydia. Further west at 34 Commonwealth Avenue lived George Dorr's aunt, Martha Ann, and her husband Henry Edwards. By 1865, the Charles Dorr family had cut ties to Jamaica Plain and 3 Park Street and occupied the five-story brownstone next to Lydia Ward at 18 Commonwealth Avenue. This was George Dorr's principal residence for the next half century.[4]

As a teenager, Dorr paid close attention to the interplay between the Commonwealth Avenue central mall and its four parallel rows of trees and related plantings. He observed how vast empty lots were filled piecemeal over many years with scores of residences that would fit architecturally if relocated to an upscale Paris neighborhood. Unlike Bar Harbor, here the distinctive façade of each residence enhanced the entire avenue rather than directing attention to itself. In his planting decisions sixty years later, Dorr would apply this principle through the selection of distinctive flora that improved the scenic design of the coastal Maine park landscape as a whole. Curiously, he revealed little about the tenor of interior life in the family Commonwealth Avenue residence.

The Boston Common lay just on the other side of the Public Garden from the new Dorr residence. Here, George was drawn into urban realities more diverse and demanding than in the pacific Jamaica Pond neighborhood. Dorr's friend, future probate judge and novelist Robert

Grant, characterized the school days and recreation of Dorr's neighbors in his 1888 novel, *Jack Hall.*[5] The winters of Grant's youth involved fierce snowball fights and year-round skirmishes with hordes of boys from other localities, who bore names like the "Round-pointers and the Nigger-hillers, and the North-enders and the South-enders, and the Charlestown pigs." About this place Dorr's contemporary, Henry Cabot Lodge, recalled the vigorous outdoor life of his playmates, who "played all games assiduously—football, baseball, hockey, and the rest, varied in winter by coasting, skating, and savage snowball fights on the Common with boys from the South End and the back of Beacon Hill, whom we called 'muckers.'"[6] In the early 1860s, however, the tense buildup to the Civil War pre-empted everything else in the Dorr household.

Dorr's memoirs were largely written in the final two decades of his life, and yet the Civil War years were described as "the most impressionable in [my] life.... Everywhere the war was in our thoughts.... [It was] slavery that made the Civil War for us and our friends in Boston a holy thing." Although Dorr was only seven years old when Confederate forces bombarded the Union garrison at Fort Sumter, the memory of his grandmother bringing the newspaper account of the barrage was forever etched in his memory. Spending a warm spring at the lakeside residence that his parents still owned, Dorr recalled the "sun streaming into the parlor where [the family] sat across from the lake, the leaves not yet out upon the trees.... [It] was the end of our life at Jamaica Plain."[7]

The family quickly recognized that their lives would now be centered on the Boston Common even as Dorr's father, "deeply stirred, at once enlisted, arranging to serve as a major in a Massachusetts regiment." During strenuous military drills on the Common, Charles was stricken with typhoid fever. As he recovered, he resumed training prematurely and suffered a relapse that nearly killed him; this time it took years for his health to be restored. The family traveled to sedate Newport, Rhode Island, where Charles recovered in the home of Mary Dorr's childhood friend Julia Ward Howe and her husband, Dr. Samuel Gridley Howe.

Mary had been engaged to Julia's brother, Henry Ward, when he died of typhoid fever in the fall of 1840.[8] Julia had found solace in Mary's comforting words and her encouragement to respond to the romantic overtures of Dr. Howe, the patriarch of the New England Asylum for the Blind. The Howes repeatedly visited the Dorr residence in Canton, where the youngest of their three daughters, Maud, was a playmate of George.[9] When the family returned to Boston the reality of the Civil War was displayed for them ceremonially on the Common. While the military gatherings there proved "of special delight to the juvenile members of the population," the Common emerged as "a place of poignant association with the ardors and the pathos of the war-time…a rallying point of soldiers departing for actual battles or returning from it." William and George saw the troops assemble, among them the older brothers of their friends; they heard of the battles and losses sustained by these troops; they saw them return with torn banners and depleted ranks.[10]

Others dealt with the pain of prolonged civil strife by removing themselves from its path, seeking solace in foreign lands. A few embarked on adventures fraught with uncertainty, as was the case with Dorr's lifetime friend, his cousin Thomas Wren Ward Jr.[11] Tom was part of the Thayer Expedition, a highly successful specimen-collecting expedition team led by Harvard scientist Louis Agassiz. Tom spent the better part of 1865 in the uncharted territory of Brazil with his "chum" and relative William James, later widely regarded as the father of American psychology and philosophy.[12] Dorr's memoirs corroborate the closeness of the two families when he notes that "William James's father had been an old family friend and William and Henry had been familiar figures at our house while I was growing up."[13]

Less clear is Charles W. Eliot's response to the war. He had recently been promoted to assistant professor of mathematics and chemistry, shortly before his engagement to Ellen Derby Peabody. As the war worsened, the health of both his parents deteriorated. While his mother was recuperating, his father died. Samuel Atkins Eliot succumbed just prior to Charles's promotion to acting dean of Harvard's Lawrence Scientific School. Charles was offered a military commission when his Harvard contract expired in 1863, but he declined after considering his own nearsightedness and his extended family responsibilities. Shortly thereafter the Eliots sailed for Europe, where they remained for nearly two years.

From the slim evidence available, the Dorr boys' elementary schooling was likely private and secular, much in the mode of Charles W. Eliot. Shortly after the Confederate defeat at Gettysburg in July 1863, George enrolled in the most eminent private preparatory school in Boston. Founder and headmaster Epes Sargent Dixwell was a Harvard graduate who had resigned the headmastership of Boston Latin to open his own school. Dixwell's became the best-fitting school for those who were Harvard-bound. George studied there under Dixwell, as Eliot had, for the next six years.[14] Military drill became the order of the day during the war years, and according to another classmate the Dixwell School "was formed into a military company. Twice a week they drilled under the supervision of an army officer."[15]

The school accepted fifty boys, divided into six classes. Dorr acknowledged that "there was no choice of studies; all was definite and fixed and the goal was Harvard." The curriculum "was of the old, traditional stamp under which we learnt lessons and recited them—Latin all through the six-year course; Greek the last two years. It was a training in memory, not in the power to think, and took little or no account of individual character and needs."[16] Robert Grant corroborated Dorr's recollection when describing his own education under Dixwell: "...all we learned was to memorize and that the reasoning faculty was [to be] kept in abeyance."[17]

The larger issues of national peril were brought home to eleven-year-old George on the morning of April 15, 1865 when the country's cultural bearings were irrevocably altered. Dorr recalled that "Father came up to where we were dressing for breakfast, the morning paper in his hand and tears in his eyes, to tell us, in a broken voice, that President Lincoln had been shot. Great tragedy as it was to North and South, it was a fitting end to a great drama."[18]

In the lighter-spirited years after the war, a lively intellectual atmosphere prevailed, with Boston's literary celebrities—Henry Wadsworth Longfellow, publisher Thomas G. Appleton, diarist Annie Fields, and others—frequently seated at the finely orchestrated dinners at 18 Commonwealth Avenue.[19] Mary Dorr, whose standing in Boston society freed her from the subordinate feminine role, presided over gatherings noted for their wit and high spirits. With Julia Ward Howe, she enjoyed planning and performing costumed drawing-room charades to widespread amusement. One member of the Howe family recalled a dinner at which Mary entertained "sixteen at table and the room was [heated] like the black hole of Calcutta but the company was very brilliant."[20]

As Cleveland Amory points out, with the social standing that Mary Dorr had achieved she advocated liberally for social reform, assumed a leading role in church activities, and was emancipated from playing "the yes-dear second fiddle to her merchant-husband[;] even in the domain of ordering meals and hiring servants, she soon fought fire with fire and became an executive in her own right."[21] While Mary is center stage, Charles Hazen Dorr is more often offstage—no less admired by George but elusive in the historical record.

On the occasion of Charles Dickens's five-month American tour in 1867, that foremost writer of the day read *A Christmas Carol* to the paying public. Privately, his Boston hostess, Annie Fields, served up a Christmas dinner at her home at 37 Charles Street for Dickens, who had the month earlier dined there with Ralph Waldo Emerson.[22] According to Dickens, the renowned publisher's wife prepared a Christmas feast of roast turkey with "plum pudding, brought on blazing, and not to be surpassed in any house in England."[23]

In her diary, Annie Fields wrote that Dickens's fellow guests were James Russell Lowell, his daughter Mabel, and Charles and Mary Dorr. "It was really a beautiful Christmas festival, as we intended it should be for the love of this new apostle of Christmas. Mr. Dickens talked all the time, as he always will do, generously, when the moment comes that he sees that it is expected.... We played games at the table afterward, which turned out so queerly that we had storms of laughter."[24]

According to historian Samuel Eliot Morison, "In the year 1869, America was in the midst of the most roaring, spectacular material development that she had ever known. Exploitation and expansion were the order of the day.... A golden spike forged the last link in the railway chain from Atlantic to Pacific.... Steel mills in Pittsburgh were running full-blast; cotton and wool mills in New England were hanging up new annual records of production...everyone was making money and expecting to make more."[25] And into this dynamic milieu stepped the new president of Harvard College, Charles William Eliot.

The Harvard over which he presided had changed little during the prior decade. Its roughly one thousand students and thirty faculty members had little inkling of the changes that the new president would champion. The leading dignitaries of the day—James Russell Lowell, H. W. Longfellow, and

Ralph Waldo Emerson among them—listened attentively on the autumn afternoon that President Eliot gave his inaugural address, outlining an agenda for the new culture that would challenge the Harvard community.[26]

Eliot knew that there would be hostility to his educational reforms. Faculty opposition greeted his ultimately successful establishment of the Graduate School as well as the elective principle that let students choose their own course of study. Indeed, the eminently quotable Oliver Wendell Holmes would say of Eliot that he "turned the whole University over like a flapjack." Eliot was determined to introduce a new spirit of learning and study into Harvard's venerable halls.

One of his early innovations was to establish a set of lectures in philosophy, and he approached Ralph Waldo Emerson to promote its development as a department of the college. Emerson, then in his late sixties, was reluctant to accept, largely because he had never authored three lectures a week.[27] Also, Emerson's relationship with his alma mater had been uneasy since his famous "Divinity Address" of 1838, in which he had, among other things, essentially charged organized Christianity with spiritual bankruptcy.[28] But Eliot's heartfelt entreaties prevailed. Emerson's lecture series, "The Natural History of the Intellect," proved popular and well attended.[29] Having secured a genuine American luminary to advance at least part of his reforms, Eliot next enlisted an emerging intellectual powerhouse: William James was offered an instructorship in physiology.

George B. Dorr was part of the earliest cohort to breathe the air of this newly invigorated culture. In late June of 1870, he sat for the Harvard Class of 1874 entrance examinations. These took place over three days and presented a wide range of intellectual challenges involving the demonstration of proficiency in Greek composition and grammar, Latin grammar, translating English to Latin, arithmetic and algebra, plane geometry, history, and geography.[30] Dorr was sixteen when he was formally admitted to Harvard College on the first day of October 1870.[31]

Dorr was one of 190 students admitted; of these, 158 would receive their degrees four years later. Unitarian belief dominated the class, though Dorr would indicate at the close of his senior year that he was an Episcopalian. Quartered at 18 Harvard Block, his roommate was David

Sears of Boston, a member of a family with long-standing ties to Harvard. Dorr undeniably felt himself a part of the illustrious institution that counted fifteen members of his family among its alumni.[32]

Despite President Eliot's agenda—fewer required courses, expanded academic options, and new faculty appointments—longstanding rituals and customs persisted with few changes from Eliot's class of 1853, the year of Dorr's birth. Each class of two hundred was divided alphabetically into groups of thirty to forty men. As a freshman, George saw his entire class assembled at roll call for lectures and prayers. Class spirit ran high as students formed new bonds.[33] Robert Grant, who entered Harvard in 1869 as a classmate of William Ward Dorr and Edward Wharton (the future husband of novelist Edith Wharton) sketched this account of college life outside the classroom: "There was much sociability among the students in my day. There was considerable loafing in one another's rooms, and sitting around doing nothing...[and] the classes were still small enough for a man to know all his classmates by sight, and the majority of them pretty well...Though we were boyish, we were, as a rule, right-minded and eager at heart to do well, and thoughtful withal when no proctor's vicinity catered to our taste for mischief."[34]

As a freshman, Dorr had no say in the selection of his courses or of his instructors. Many of the courses were more advanced versions of those George had taken at Dixwell's school, including elocution, ethics, Latin, Greek poetry, Greek composition, and advanced French. A complicated ranking system balanced grades received for themes, recitations, and orations against deductions for absences from class (and prayers) and violations of gentlemanly conduct.[35]

President Eliot initiated changes in the pedagogical infrastructure as well as physical changes to Harvard's external shape and dimensions. Campus facilities were expanding with the addition of Thayer, Mathews, and Weld halls—in part as a response to a rapidly expanding student body. A large residence hall at the corner of Harvard and Holyoke streets was under construction. Yet none of these changes in the physical environment could compare with the symbolism attached to Memorial Hall. The distinguished structure would not be completed for four years; between these bookend dates the Class of 1874 witnessed the construction of a massive memorial honoring Harvard's sacrifice during the Civil War.

In the spring of 1871 Dorr completed his first year, best described as a qualified success: he placed 94th out of a class of 176.[36] That summer, he and William embarked on their first transatlantic voyage, eventually meeting their parents in Europe. The brothers anticipated not only the novel sights and sounds of unexplored lands but temporary freedom from academic rigors. After stops in Liverpool and Chester, they luxuriated in the refined atmosphere of London; crossing the Channel, they landed in Belgium and steamed up the Rhine, where they joined their parents. The Dorrs next traveled to Heidelberg, Dresden, and Nuremberg—arriving at last in the heart of the Bavarian Alps. While in Switzerland they made forays into Italy's Lake Como region.

George Dorr increasingly fell under the spell of the rarefied air of ice-capped mountains and became enchanted by the high mountain passes, the craggy peaks, and the countryside that stood in such stark contrast to his familiar urban haunts. His memoirs suggest that it was here he became smitten with hiking, especially the adventures of following new trails and exploring unmarked territory that would dominate his activities on Mount Desert Island. And it was here that he first noticed how much he had become "interested in nature…the development of life and the development of landscape."[37] The renowned writer Henry James, brother of William James, captured this spirit when reflecting on his "love of the long, again and again of the very longest possible, walk which was to see me, year after year, through so many of the twists and past so many of the threatened blocks of life's road."[38]

With a summer of memorable sights and impressions behind him, George Dorr began his sophomore year in the autumn of 1871. His brother decided to withdraw from Harvard and remain in Europe with maternal relatives. Perhaps the most notable aspect of George's second year in college was his membership in the Institute of 1770, a speaking club that emphasized student facility in "declamation, composition, and debate."[39] Otherwise, his days were filled with required courses. He relocated into the new, five-story Holyoke House, which contained "forty-seven elegant suites of rooms that comprise a study, two bedrooms, bath room, and clothes closet."[40] Living alone in luxury quarters on Massachusetts Avenue across from the Harvard Yard, Dorr applied himself to course requirements in chemistry, physics, rhetoric, natural history, and modern and classical languages. As his sophomore year came to a close, his class ranking improved to 69th out of 169.

One of the most admired Harvard scholars, Francis James Child, the Boylston Professor of Rhetoric and Oratory, made a lasting impression on Dorr.[41] Later known for his complete critical edition of *The English and Scottish Ballads*, Child's influence resonates through the robust narrative that Dorr employed throughout his life. But for the moment, with William returned from the Italian Riviera, the Dorr family again headed to Mount Desert Island for the summer.

President Eliot also embarked on his second summer there and with his newly acquired sloop, *Sunshine,* again ba sked in the natural beauty of the island. The Eliots and Dorrs may have been stimulated anew by the lead essay, "On the Coast of Maine," in the widely distributed *Picturesque America* (1872), which featured descriptions of "forests crowded with evergreens, and the furs and spruce trees marshal in such array on the hill-sides that, with their slender, spear-like tops, they look like armies of lancers."[42] Similar sentiments were moving Americans all over the country. That year, Congress took the unprecedented step of reserving the Yellowstone country in Wyoming and Montana territories "as a public park or pleasure-ground for the benefit and enjoyment of the people."[43]

In September of 1872, William Dorr and his father embarked from the port of New York aboard the White Star Line *Baltic*, for London. William's ultimate destination was Paris, where he planned to study architecture at the École des Beaux Arts. George Dorr later recalled that his father expressed concern about the effect of the work and climate upon William's health. Before returning to Boston, Charles lingered in Paris to enjoy the companionship of Harvard's Smith Professor of Modern Languages, James Russell Lowell, a lifelong family friend. A man of letters, Lowell composed for Charles in 1869 a lengthy poem of appreciation for a delicious gift received from his friend. The poem is a celebration of Stilton cheese, and we can infer that such was the gift, as well.[44]

William withdrew from the École after a few months, ostensibly because he found the European educational system at odds with, as he termed it, "our American way of thought." He wended his way south along the Mediterranean coast to Genoa and Rome. He reappeared in New England in 1873 still casting about for a career, finally arranging to study law in New York City.[45]

George, by contrast, dutifully returned to Harvard to begin his third year. With his solid grounding in arts and sciences, he took more advanced courses in physics, political economy, French, and German. He also demonstrated a keen aptitude in the logical rigor of both forensics and rhetoric. College life ticked predictably through the crisp autumn until the evening of November 9, 1872, when sparks from a steam boiler in a warehouse in downtown Boston quickly ignited the piles of merchandise and engulfed the surrounding neighborhoods.[46] The flames raged over two days and panic-stricken residents of Boston feared that the entire city could be lost.

A Dorr family friend, eighteen-year-old Maud Howe—daughter of Julia Ward Howe—viewed the mounting destruction from a relatively safe vantage point and later recounted the scene. She "watched the terrible conflation from the window of the room in the Institution for the Blind, where eighteen years before I first saw the light...as I sat at the open easement watching the flames devour whole blocks of the city...[and] the white spire of Park Street Church was often threatened...I caught a glimpse of that white finger pointing heavenward, fresh hope sprang up; so long as the steeple stood, we knew that the fire had not crossed the Common, and that Beacon Hill and the State House were safe."[47] The Great Boston Fire destroyed the Summer Street Trinity Church, where the Dorrs worshipped, and much of the city's financial district, leaving more than sixty-five acres smoldering in ruins. George Dorr had witnessed the fire's destructive fury, and he commented in his memoirs how saddened he was at the devastation inflicted upon the neighborhoods of his youth.

Studious immersion required long bouts of reading, which began to take a toll on his vision. This "trouble with my eyes" recurred periodically throughout his life, resulting in episodes of blindness that became longer and more persistent as he aged.[48] But by the summer of 1873, these progressive ocular difficulties had temporarily resolved, allowing George and William to journey to London and spend the summer rambling over the British countryside. The brothers toured Oxford and then embarked on an Irish Sea voyage to the Isle of Man. There, in an incident that presaged George's adult regime of daily year-round ocean swims on Mount Desert Island, the brothers assayed into the sea *au naturel.* Having miscalculated Victorian Britain's tolerance for nudity, the two scrambled back to shore and dressed in the presence of curious bystanders.

Next, they continued on to northwest Wales. The brothers visited cherished literary landmarks and climbed to the summit of Snowdon, the highest mountain in Wales, as their father had done years earlier. Traveling back into England, they hiked through the Lake District, seeing first-hand the landscapes that their mother had told them of since they were children. Dorr described it in his memoirs as "one of the loveliest in the world." He began to appreciate more deeply the role that landscapes of exceptional splendor could play in the life of a man. After a summer steeped in the literary associations and outdoor charms of England, he was poised to begin his senior year.

Advanced courses were the order of the day, and Dorr chose courses in forensics, history, philosophy, and German.[49] By the end of the fall term, Dorr had received instruction from nearly two dozen members of the Harvard faculty, many just a few years older than he was. These younger instructors included George Herbert Palmer, instructor in philosophy. An 1864 Harvard graduate, Palmer's appointment signaled a shift toward presenting philosophy as a secular discipline rather than a course in spiritual and moral edification. It was later said of Palmer that, "philosophy as an autonomous division of instruction in the university is largely the work of his thought and labor."[50]

In its new secularized version, the growing ranks of philosophy faculty paved the way for Harvard to offer the discipline at the graduate level. William James, the American philosopher whose name is nearly synonymous with "practicality," was appointed instructor in anatomy and physiology shortly after Palmer accepted his new position. For Dorr, the discipline's new orientation gradually took root. He began to ally himself intellectually with this approach to openness and innovative thinking. Dorr was also uncharacteristically mindful of shaping his own education into something outwardly coherent. He concentrated in history and languages, both classical and modern, complementing these subjects with equal ardor in elocution, oratory, and rhetoric.

Meanwhile, that autumn the United States economy had started to teeter. Major financial reverses that had begun in Europe in the summer reached the shores of America by September and heralded the Panic of 1873. Unregulated postwar industrial growth had led to the overbuilding of railroads, among other problems. When the large investment firm Jay Cooke and Company failed in the fall, a chain reaction of financial disasters plunged the country into a five-year economic depression. In Dorr's memoirs there is no indication that the failing economy influenced the family decision to spend most of the next five years abroad.

Dorr returned to Europe with his father for his final semester, having been granted permission by the Dean, for health reasons, to complete his studies abroad and to take his exams when he returned. Dorr again experienced bouts of what he later characterized as an "unexpected lack of muscular convergence of the two eyes." In Paris, he read extensively in history and near the end of winter 1874 spent several weeks alternating hours of reading with long walks, venturing into what he described as "the high, mountainous interior" of Europe.[51] On his return to America, he successfully completed his examinations.

Despite the disappointing weather on Senior Class Day, the private journal of Harvard librarian John Langdon Sibley documents the offering of prayers at Appleton Chapel, the fellowship of lunch at faculty residences, and the festive music and dancing campus-wide.[52] Harvard's Commencement that year inaugurated Memorial Hall as the location for that annual rite of passage. On June 23 hundreds of students, faculty, alumni, and military officers entered the impressive structure, which became "packed full of humanity."[53] The event was significant not only because of the grandeur of this Civil War monument—a massive, ornate building in High Gothic style—but also because it was the first time that Harvard "physically and architecturally...attempted to express its coming status as a great university."[54]

The following day, George Bucknam Dorr graduated from Harvard College. His handwritten note in the Harvard class book referred to his immediate plans "...to study abroad for a couple of years. And, for after that, my plans are undecided."[55] With a Harvard diploma in hand, Dorr possessed a recognized, socially accepted grounding for life. Now he was ready to begin what his successor at Acadia National Park would call "his real education."[56]

CHAPTER FOUR

The Long Journey to Mount Desert Island

During four years of immersion in the culture of Harvard, George B. Dorr had grown accustomed to a life in which intellectual pleasures were yoked with the companionship of like-minded men. It was with this genial attitude that he set out with his father in the fall of 1874 on what would become a four-year odyssey around the British Isles and continental Europe. Charles Dorr's mission was to locate ancestral sites, pay homage to his Puritan forebears, and impart to his son the importance of such a spiritual and intellectual quest. The sensory richness of the journey prompted George to reflect anew on what the Puritans believed and why they held their most cherished principles.[1]

In his memoirs, Dorr devoted a singular amount of attention to these travels, which stood out as possibly the happiest—and most influential—years of his life. The journey began in southwest England where Dorr and his father confirmed that their ancestor, Edward Dorr, had sailed to New England from the shire of Dorset in 1674. Their intense engagement in this quest, not surprising for members of the "grandfather-on-the-brain" generation, enhanced George's excitement in such discoveries.[2] "One must travel with others, and with others thoroughly sympathetic with ourselves to get the full value and enjoyment out of travel," Dorr wrote in his memoirs.[3]

Although he had trekked with William through the Lake District and visited other parts of Great Britain steeped in literary and familial associations, this time George felt emotionally transported by what he saw and experienced. Meandering through the lush vales and breathing the dank air of ruined abbeys, he was overtaken by upwellings of feeling. George and his father walked the countryside with books in hand, enriching their immediate impressions with the dimensions of history and literature. The history of the region and the genealogy of their family were continually alive to them as they sailed rivers and lakes familiar from English verse and prose. Without explaining himself, George later claimed that these explorations of English landscape and culture led "directly on our return to the building of our old home at Mt. Desert and the establishment of the first true pleasure garden on MDI...for without this interest the work I later did at home would never have been done nor Acadia National Park come into existence."[4] Consequently, Dorr reminds us that the genesis of the coastal Maine park concept is not isolated to thought and action within these United States.

Wanderjahr experiences were common for young men of George Dorr's class and generation, for whom extended travel sometimes served as a both effective and face-saving strategy to avoid adult responsibilities. Theodore Roosevelt, who graduated from Harvard a few classes behind Dorr, made a similar observation when he spoke to the Harvard Union in 1907. Roosevelt expressed the fear that elite colleges like Harvard produced men "too fastidious, too sensitive, to take part in the hurly-burly of the actual work of the world...[who stood] aloof from the broad sweep of our national life in a curiously impotent spirit of fancied superiority."[5] Dorr's memoirs provide no evidence that this characterization applied to him, nor do they offer insight about his parents' intentions in accompanying him on his travels. Mary Dorr arrived in England in the winter of 1875, following her mother's death. She joined Charles and George with an eye to scrutinizing country residences as models for their proposed summer home in Bar Harbor, then called Eden.[6]

The festivities ceased in May 1876, when Charles and Mary Dorr received news in England that their son William had fallen seriously ill. William had been studying law in the New York City offices of attorney Lewis L. Delafield. Charles immediately sailed for America, but did not arrive in time; during the passage he received word that his eldest son had died. George recalls that William contracted "the terrible Typhus fever, then more or less endemic in New York," and despite "the heroism and devotion" of Mrs. Delafield, he succumbed. As the citizens of the United States prepared for the nation's centennial, on May 18, 1876, Charles and family friends stood beside William's grave as he was interred in Mount Auburn Cemetery.[7]

Meanwhile, Mary and George remained in England as guests of one of the great families of England. Months earlier while in Rome, the Dorrs had met George Howard—who would become the ninth Earl of Carlisle—and his wife, Rosalind Francis Stanley Howard.[8] On learning of William's death, the Howards insisted that their new friends accept temporary refuge at their London townhouse on Palace Green, which overlooked Kensington Park. Married for twelve years, the Howards—despite the demands of their six children—welcomed George and Mary Dorr into their inner circle. Thus began a relationship between the two families that was to last for more than thirty years. Their extensive correspondence provides more information about personal matters than any other historical source.[9]

When Charles rejoined George and Mary, the Howards escorted the Dorrs to one of their ancestral properties, Naworth Castle, near the Scottish border. There the Dorrs experienced a level of opulence rare by Boston standards. Woodlands and wild gardens gave Rosalind Howard singular pleasure, and she took pride in showing off her landscape gardens and the new paths she was developing on this two-thousand-acre estate.[10] It is also likely that as a diversion the Howards took them to see the extensive gardens and woods at their well-known family estate at Yorkshire, Castle Howard. That palatial house and picturesque landscape both date from the early eighteenth century, the result of a collaboration among Charles Howard, third Earl of Carlisle, and architects Sir John Vanbrugh and Nicholas Hawksmoor. Although both residence and landscape had evolved significantly over three centuries, Castle Howard encapsulated the period's picturesque landscape features: a serpentine lake, winding woodland paths, streams and bridges, follies, fountains, temples, and classical sculptures.[11]

In her grief over the loss of her elder son and mother within eighteen months of one another, Mary Dorr turned away from her Episcopalian faith and explored Spiritualism, a movement popular between 1840 and 1920 that promoted the belief that it was possible to contact spirits of the dead.

In the years immediately following their deaths, Mary attempted to contact their spirits through automatic writing, in which the spirit purportedly communicated by controlling the handwriting of a living person.[12]

The Howard family's cultural and intellectual interests may have offered more worldly distractions. George Howard was not simply a member of one of the great Whig aristocratic families, but also a patron of Pre-Raphaelite artists and a talented painter in his own right. His watercolors and oils attracted Mary and her son. At the newly opened Grosvenor Gallery, where George Howard exhibited, Mary met Pre-Raphaelite painters including Edward Burne-Jones and Frederick Leighton.[13]

Rosalind Howard was described by one of her sons-in-law as "impetuous and formidable," and her hospitality was surely of great interest to Mary.[14] In Rosalind, Mary met her equal both intellectually and socially, and like Mary, Rosalind filled her dining room with famous artists and writers of the day, vigorously argued her opinions, and encouraged her guests to do the same.[15] More importantly, the recently uncovered cache of Ward–Howard letters reveals that Mary found in Rosalind a friendship that was remarkably similar to the youthful Mary's relationship with Julia Ward three decades earlier. While Mary believed that her son's death had "broken [her life] beyond all cure," her self-absorbed correspondence with the future Countess of Carlisle provides little evidence of Mary's interest during this time in the activities of either her husband or her sole surviving son.[16]

During their stay with the Howards, the Dorrs' grief was compounded by the news that Charles's brother, George's namesake, had passed away. A portion of his estate was directed to Harvard College, and the family also learned that the Dorr property at Lenox had been divided into shares. The two surviving paternal aunts had provided that their sole surviving nephew, George, could purchase their interests in the estate after they died.[17] Just two years after graduating from Harvard, twenty-three-year-old George B. Dorr found himself the last of his generation, and the sole heir, on his father's side. Assuming that Charles Dorr shared his sisters' wishes with George at the time, this knowledge would have influenced his future plans.

Departing England, the Dorrs began a series of seasonal migrations throughout the Continent. While no detailed account of this travel survives, their whereabouts can be traced through the frequent letters between Mary Dorr and the Howard family. Mary often traveled in the company of Julia Ward Howe as well as other friends and relatives.[18] Her husband's agenda was dictated by business interests while George moved throughout Europe driven by the scholar's desire to explore language, landscape, and history. Through these letters alone we learn that Charles, Mary, and George would often travel separately for weeks on end. During these years abroad, Mary studied frequently with George Howard's mentor, Italian landscape artist Giovanni Costa.[19]

As Mary immersed herself in her aesthetic interests at this time, her son George roamed the Italian landscape, and during the winter of 1876–77 he had an uplifting encounter with a ravishing young widow, Mrs. Craig Wadsworth (née Linda Peters). Picnicking at an ancient volcanic lake in the Alban Hills, east of Rome, he met "one of those rare beings who seemed afterwards to have disappeared completely from our world, a beautiful woman, beautiful like some Greek goddess of the olden times."[20] In the following weeks, as they became better acquainted, Mrs. Wadsworth confided to George that she had become accustomed to male adoration. Only a scholar of ancient culture like George would have associated her beauty with a philosophical ideal of the classical age. Decades later he wrote that "women do not seem to stand out in these days as some did then, and the world is the poorer as I think for it. For it means the loss of an ideal, the loss of something that does not enter into the world of fact."[21] These romantic associations were not coincidental, given that the lake where they met was known as "Diana's Mirror" because its reflection of the moon was visible from a nearby temple dedicated to the goddess. One unfortunate result of Dorr's report of his encounter with Linda Wadsworth is the simplistic popular conclusion that unrequited love caused him to remain a lifelong bachelor.[22]

George also consulted European ophthalmologists about his recurring visual difficulties. Mary implies in an 1877 letter to Rosalind that George may have also been beset with clinical depression.[23] Yet the young scholar also recognized his mother's protracted grief, and wrote to Rosalind to thank her for being "a good Samaritan" to his mother, "whose life had been broken and made desolate" by William's death.[24]

The death of George's namesake contributed to the Dorrs' prolonging their stay in Europe. So too, with Bar Harbor reeling in the aftermath of a typhoid outbreak in 1876, they felt no imperative to return there or to Boston, where memories of William and Lydia would surely haunt them.[25] With ample financial resources they continued to live abroad, corresponding with architects about the location and design of their country home.

George Dorr's years of intimate companionship with his parents spawned a deep understanding and appreciation of their finer qualities. His father, he wrote, was "what Chaucer would have called 'a verra parfait' gentleman, with constant thought for others, broad human interests, and no thought for self, though full of the capacity for great enjoyment in all things beautiful and good." His mother, he observed, was highly intuitive, a quality rooted in an inherently social and artistic nature. In his memoirs, George extolled a gentler side of Mary Dorr that ran counter to her reputation in Boston society: in her "warm interest in human life...she was remarkable; people came to her always for sympathy and help in their times of trouble for she was strong to lean upon."[26] Neither Charles, Mary, nor George seemed to lean on anyone else. Each cultivated personal independence and privacy. This reflexive emotional reticence may account for the omission of Dorr's responses to situations he later chronicled in his memoirs.

In the autumn of 1878, Mary wrote to the Howard family, lamenting that her "heart is heavy" at the thought of returning home. She recognized nonetheless that her interests, hopes, and fears were as changed as if she had journeyed "to some other planet."[27] Returning to their residence on the westward-expanding Commonwealth Avenue, Mary was called upon to provide comfort for the housekeeper who had been employed by the Dorrs since the birth of William. Mary sadly confided to Lady Carlisle that Elizabeth Hind "died in my house, under my care." An indication of their closeness is that she was buried in the Dorr family plot at Mount Auburn Cemetery.[28]

During the fall of 1878 and the winter of 1879, the Dorr family was very involved in the building of their country home on a dramatic clifftop site in Bar Harbor. Their expansive property faced northeast to the mainland Gouldsboro Hills, across the long reach of upper Frenchman Bay. They would name their estate "Oldfarm," recalling its heritage as an old farm during the area's agricultural heyday. During their earlier summers on Mount Desert Island, both the Dorr and Eliot families had made use of the accommodations of resident families. Still later in the 1870s they had the option of staying in numerous hotels that had been constructed to satisfy the expanding tourist trade. Shortly thereafter, the "rusticators" pioneered a new mode of tourism. The clergy, professionals, and academics "from away" now acquired undeveloped property on which they constructed private residences, taking their pleasure in exploring the so-called wildness of the island.[29]

Of the architects who had submitted plans to Charles Dorr while they were abroad, Henry Richards, a son-in-law of Julia Ward Howe, was selected.[30] Richards was not far removed from Mount Desert Island. With his wife, Laura, and their three children, the family had recently relocated from Boston to Gardiner, Maine, to help manage a paper mill owned by the Richards family. Eager to extend his limited success as a Boston architect, Richards began working closely with the Dorr family to execute his design of a large Queen Anne Shingle-style residence. The shingles, hewn from California redwood, harmonized with the warm, reddish-pink, two-foot-thick granite foundation.

The foundation, one hundred and thirty-two by fifty-two feet, supported a year-round residence of eleven thousand square feet. The first and second floors—of oak, birch, and maple—contained more than a dozen rooms for family and servants, including six bathrooms. The drawing room, den, library, dining room, and bedrooms were outfitted with new furnishings and familiar pieces from their Boston residence, including paintings by John Singleton Copley and William Morris Hunt. George Dorr's third-floor Sea Room contained, in more than five hundred square feet, a huge fireplace, a large window seat, full-length wall-to-wall bookshelves, and small swinging windows that opened to the landscape and seascape. Atop an oriental rug, Dorr placed a writing table, an eight-sided pedestal table, and several walnut rocking chairs.[31] Though he slept in a bedroom across the central hallway, it was in this study—surrounded by books—that his reflective activity took place. Within ten years the house would be electrified, easing the visual strain of late-night reading; town water and telephone service were added to keep abreast of the times. A few feet away there was a side porch with views of Champlain Mountain, where Oldfarm's granite foundation had been quarried.

Richards took keen interest in his architectural work and followed the project closely throughout. Laborers on Mount Desert Island could be hired at this time for a dollar a day, skilled laborers for three dollars. Even at these rates, the residential and landscape expenses were $70,000. Richards also oversaw the erection of several outbuildings. During this construction Charles, Mary, and George resided several hundred feet distant at Storm Beach Cottage.[32] This thirty-six- by fifty-four-foot, eight-room, gambrel-roofed clapboard structure, which still serves as a park residence, was designed in 1879 by Charles Dorr to accommodate the family while Oldfarm was under construction. Over its lifetime, Storm Beach Cottage would serve as George Dorr's second home since Oldfarm would frequently be leased—as a revenue source—in the summer.

Oldfarm exposed Henry Richards to the challenges of managing client expectations, especially since these clients had close family ties. Decades later he wrote of the "many delightful and some very difficult interchanges" with "Molly" Dorr (as Mary was known to many friends). In his autobiography, published four years before George Dorr's death, Richards was not the first to characterize Mary Dorr as "a noted character in Boston, charming when talking intimately, but masterful, arbitrary, and dictatorial in social relations." Richards wrote uncharitably—if not bitterly—that "Mrs. Charles Dorr... looked so like a witch that the cottage was known locally as the Witch House."[33]

Molly Dorr would prove to be a formidable social force as Bar Harbor rapidly changed from hotel to cottage life. Eliot's son Samuel Atkins Eliot II later recorded that—despite the island's romantic associations—the precipitous rise in land values had unanticipated landscape consequences when streets were laid out, sewers constructed, and "smooth lawns painfully developed from the rocky pastures and steep hillsides."[34]

During the winter of 1880, the Dorrs resumed their social life in Boston. George Dorr's memoirs contained no hint that, once re-established in the familiar social scene of Boston, his parents expected him to pursue either a career or marriage; the correspondence of Mary and Charles nowhere suggests impatience. In the years that followed, however, they all came to realize that the landscape of Mount Desert Island provided more than a retreat from urban life. Its natural beauty began to inspire the twenty-eight-year-old George with new purpose and direction. He would strive throughout the 1880s to answer the questions that had gathered in his mind during the physical and intellectual journeys of the last decade.

Recently returned from the diversions of Europe, the Dorrs were now buoyed and energized by the design and construction of their new summer residence in Bar Harbor.[35] For the next decade, Mary and Charles—now in their sixties—would focus their lives on Oldfarm and draw into it persons of substance who enriched their lives. Mary describes her son in a letter to Rosalind Howard as "quite well, and has been so since the first year after our return." Specifics are not mentioned, but clearly the visual problems had persisted and grief attending his brother's death may have led to a depressed state of mind. Yet now "after thirteen years of illness, and almost despair, the reward of all the waiting has come. He has eyes too! The entire use of them—thank God—and he has been working hard ever since."[36] The future of their only surviving son, however, was more determined throughout the 1880s by the actions of others than by the force of his own hand. And the dominant force continued to be Mary Dorr.

In the Eliot family, the feminine influence led to decisions that would change the character of another island village. After eight years at the helm of Harvard College, widower Charles W. Eliot married Grace Mellen Hopkinson in October of 1877. As his eldest son, Charles, adjusted to the challenges of student life at Harvard College, it soon became evident that the outdoor tenting life that the Eliots had enjoyed would not be suitable for Mrs. Eliot. While the newly married couple spent the summer of 1880 in Europe, Charles Eliot set in motion a course of events that eventually resulted in dramatic changes for his father, for George B. Dorr, and for Mount Desert Island. He suggested to a dozen of his undergraduate Harvard friends interested in natural history that they undertake an adventure on a remote Maine island. Accompanied by his younger brother, Samuel Atkins Eliot II, Charles also scrutinized possible family home sites between Somes Sound and Seal Harbor.

Over seven weeks, the Eliot brothers and their colleagues carried out field research on the natural history of Mount Desert Island—its botanical, geographical, and historical features—at a camp established on the east side of Somes Sound opposite Dog (Flying) Mountain. A brief visit by the young Harvard geology instructor William M. Davis—who much later would play a significant role in Dorr's conservation research in the American West—gave added credibility to their enterprise. Naming themselves after the famous French explorer, the Champlain Society conducted research of such high quality that publications by its members have standing to this day.[37]

Following their late-September return from Europe, Charles showed his father and stepmother favored home sites, focusing on the sparsely settled Northeast Harbor coastline where there were as yet no summer cottages. Northeast Harbor clergyman Reverend Henry Wilder Foote II described his community at that time as a "very small community. There was no village street lined with shops, only a road through the woods…[requiring] an all-day round trip over rough roads to Bar Harbor to mail a letter, or send a telegram, or consult a doctor…. It was indeed 'a quiet place apart' for those who came to find relief from 'the madding crowds' ignoble strife.'"[38]

The property selected was a one-hundred-twenty-acre site, fifty feet above water level, offering a commanding view and a suitable anchorage.[39] High land lay to the north, and to the west lay another property being developed for Boston landscape engineer Joseph Henry Curtis: Thuya Lodge, with granite stairways and rustic architecture surrounded by *Thuya occidentalis*, eastern white cedar. Mainer Augustus C. Savage had owned both properties; he and his son Fred Lincoln Savage built the Eliot family a Shingle-style cottage designed by Dr. Eliot's brother-in-law, the renowned Boston architect Robert Swain Peabody. A thousand feet of beach fronted the residence, and the property extended one mile inland to the top of Asticou Hill (Eliot Mountain).[40]

Twenty-year-old Fred Savage's "unusual ability in wood-carving and cabinet-making…[quickly] attracted the attention of the summer colony."[41] Dr. Eliot was sufficiently impressed that he arranged an apprenticeship with Peabody. In due course the younger Savage became a close family friend, and to this day he is regarded as the premier architect of Mount Desert Island. Until Charles W. Eliot's death in 1926, the residence that Savage crafted—the Ancestral—was occupied by the Eliot family every summer save one. The Ancestral's *Visitors Record* contains the names of a pantheon of luminaries, including conservationists John D. Rockefeller Jr., George B. Dorr, and Frederick Law Olmsted Jr.

After returning to Cambridge, Champlain Society members continued discussions about the data they had collected and what further investigations should be pursued. Charles carefully planned activities for the following summer, recognizing his abilities, in the words of his father, to "plan and perform executive work, exercise authority over a considerable party... and do business and give orders in a manner which satisfied the interested persons."[42] Eliot's meticulously detailed notes survive and document scientific progress that was unprecedented—even for Harvard students. Most importantly, the Champlain Society records are the earliest surviving documents advocating the protection of the local landscape of Maine. Society secretary Edward L. Rand—who later achieved international standing as a botanist—proposed three possible agencies to protect the natural beauty of the island: the State of Maine, island residents, or private parties. It was the third course of action that Rand thought best.[43]

It would take another two decades before this process began in earnest. For the moment, both the Dorr and Eliot families invested in Mount Desert Island and saw their future tied to this place. Natural splendor may have lured them to this coastal island, but they were now poised to energetically contribute to its culture, sharing with other island residents the bounty of their worldly travels and new educational philosophies imported from Harvard.

CHAPTER FIVE

Restless Indecision

While little is known about their more constrained lives in Boston on Commonwealth Avenue, the Dorrs appear to have taken advantage of the relatively relaxed island culture in Bar Harbor, inviting guests who would be companionable and yet spontaneous in these less-formal social interactions.[1] Benjamin Hadley, Dorr's successor as superintendent of Acadia National Park, reflected on more than half a century of family hospitality when drafting Dorr's obituary in 1944. He characterized Oldfarm as "a place of great hospitality. Beneath its roof-tree have slept the great and near great of America and Europe...a veritable cross section of contemporary professional, political and social life of a day now gone."[2]

A vivid sense of the island is documented in the family papers of a grandson of Nathaniel Bowditch. A close friend of Thomas Wren Ward, Bowditch was a Salem mathematician widely regarded for his *New American Practical Navigator*. His grandson, Charles P. Bowditch, was an accomplished Mayan archaeologist at Harvard and a major benefactor of the Peabody Museum in Salem.[3] Though a decade older than George Dorr, they were friends and travelers together. During an 1888 stay at Oldfarm, Bowditch's twenty-year-old daughter Cornelia informed her father that Mrs. Dorr is "determined that we young people shall see everything, and she plans our days for us, so that they are full of everything entertaining." Charles Dorr escorted the Bowditch daughters on excursions up Newport (Champlain)

Mountain, put them at ease during visits with established summer residents, and engaged them in tennis tournaments with other cottagers. George emphasized in his memoirs that younger and older Oldfarm guests mingled "without formality. No dinner parties but teas and suppers only and no dress suit, no telephone as yet, no electric lights, my mother at the center of it all."[4]

Cornelia Bowdich was effusive about Oldfarm: "Mr. Dorr's place is the most beautiful on the island...about fifty acres in the house lot, though he owns a good deal more land. The grounds are very well laid out, with a great many flower beds—and the house is very attractive, covered with vines in many places, and having inside, a great-many [sic] very beautiful things they have collected abroad. Altogether it is a very attractive place, and the view of the harbor is wonderfully fine."[5]

In the context of a description of the bird life that vitalized its gardens, the psychologist, playwright, and ornithologist Henry Lane Eno provided topographic detail about the Oldfarm home of his fellow conservationist: "Inshore from the house lie wood-encircled gardens, the nearest of which, deeply sheltered with a riotous tangle of old-fashioned bloom and high edges, is the favored resort of all creatures who love sunshine and flowers. Beyond this garden a broad grassy swale flows gently down between tall evergreen forests from a rocky knoll to a small cove bordered by steep and lofty cliffs.... Here, therefore, within the brief compass of a few acres, are found all the varied conditions of ocean shore, upland glade, and steep hillside with their rocky dells and ancient forests."[6]

Two of the most frequent guests at Oldfarm were the emerging titans of the Harvard faculty during the years 1880 to 1910: psychologist William James and philosopher Josiah Royce. Dorr was certainly conscious of the fact that these two intellectuals were at the center of American philosophy. No other Harvard department rivaled philosophy during this golden era. American philosophy itself grew in no small way through the tension between the empiricism of James and the idealism of Royce.[7]

James and his family visited often over the next two decades, while Josiah Royce was the most frequent Oldfarm guest between 1889 and 1896. Mary and Charles were fully aware that the presence of such luminaries would elevate casual conversation into the grand world of ideas. Those who knew William and Josiah recognized that philosophical questions and arguments were the unavoidable consequence of even the most mundane talk. Moreover, James's intellectual gymnastics had a practical force that appealed to George. After all, was it not Mary Dorr's son who had said nearly a decade earlier that he would pursue philosophy following his graduation? Was Mary Dorr's choice of houseguests a deliberate ploy to further her son's education through the art of philosophical conversation—just as her own intellectual development had been shaped as a young woman by conversations with transcendentalists Margaret Fuller and Mary's dearest friend, Julia Ward Howe?

It is difficult to believe that the talented William James was unaware of Mary Dorr's motives. America's novelist-in-exile, Henry James, was informed by his elder brother in the late 1880s that William had returned from a twelve-day visit with the Dorrs, during which time he spent eight days with "loathsome fever attacks." A year later he recalled Oldfarm with longing for "that wondrous sunrise view of the Porcupines out of my sickroom window." Nonetheless, he found Mary Dorr "as restless and imperious as ever, but a woman of first rate conversation, and I believe of fundamentally warm heart."[8]

The quality of the interior life of Oldfarm rarely equaled what the island landscape had to offer. The Dorrs recognized this attraction and first encouraged guests to explore their own property. Casual walks along woods roads and pathways often began by descending several dozen steep steps that led from the hilltop residence to a broad lawn set atop cliffs that rimmed Frenchman Bay. Since property owners were concerned about the threat of fire to shore homes, guests would likely be shown the cistern dug by Charles and his son, more so to relate an interesting anecdote about the museum-quality shells of now extinct sea life that they had uncovered in the process. Many years later George would recall that such a chance discovery sparked his growing interest in geological phenomena at a time when the evolutionary claims of Charles Darwin were relatively new.

Strolling guests would become aware that family tradition and sensitivity to the natural conditions guided the selection of plantings. Native species were retained when they served to bring the native woodlands into an aesthetically appealing relationship with the new structures. In some instances the now-controversial introduction of non-native species was attempted, including an experiment to determine which could prosper within a woodland dominated by red spruce and balsam fir. Given Mary's attachment to flora propagated at their Jamaica Plain home, her responsibility for at least some of the varied flower gardens at Oldfarm likely went uncontested.

While no detailed property descriptions survive from this early era, Dorr described Oldfarm as the first "true pleasure garden on Mt. Desert Island and, so far as I know, on the whole Acadian shore from the Penobscot east."[9] But other cottagers were arriving in increasing numbers, and the Dorrs kept an eye on other island "pleasure gardens" established throughout the last two decades of the nineteenth century. One of the most highly regarded twentieth-century gardens was about to be established just two miles north of Oldfarm.

New York entrepreneur Frederick Rhinelander Jones and his wife, Mary Cadwalader Rawle Jones, first visited Bar Harbor soon after the completion of Oldfarm. Accompanying them was Frederick's eighteen-year-old sister, Edith Newbold Jones, and Frederick and Mary's daughter Beatrix, age eight. The teenaged Jones (who would mature into the writer Edith Wharton) was accompanied by "Trix" and others, who enjoyed "canoeing and rowing on the enchanted mountain lakes…[and] fishing and bicycling and looking for odd-shaped rocks along the shore."[10] Both girls found the environment and conversation invigorating, and much less formal than Newport, Rhode Island, where they had previously summered.

In the small enclave of Bar Harbor cottagers, George B. Dorr would surely have taken notice when a large plot between Hancock Street and Atlantic Avenue, fronting on Frenchman Bay, was purchased in 1882. The buyer was Frederick Jones; when completed, the Joneses' Reef Point residence, a modest structure that was one of twenty-two Bar Harbor cottages designed by the Boston firm of Rotch & Tilden, provided their daughter Beatrix with an environment strikingly different from New York City. In due course she would secure her reputation as the pioneer landscape gardener—long before her 1916 marriage to Yale University historian Max Farrand. Not until 1917 would the mother of Beatrix Farrand sign over Reef Point to her daughter, enabling the Farrands to begin "building a personal institution that married their scholarly and horticultural interests."[11] Here they would promote ecological objectives that today are deemed intrinsic to the conservation of landscapes.

Landscape concerns had already captured the interests of Charles Eliot when he graduated from Harvard in 1882.[12] Charles was six years younger than George and thirteen years older than Beatrix, and had resolved to become a landscape architect. Charles enrolled in graduate programs at the Bussey Institution in Jamaica Plain, where Harvard University offered courses in farming, horticulture, agricultural chemistry, economic zoology, and entomology. Plant specimens were collected and studied at the Arnold Arboretum.[13] In the spring of 1883 architect Robert Swain Peabody introduced Charles, his nephew, to Frederick Law Olmsted, America's first landscape architect.

At sixty years of age, Olmsted was renowned for "rough-hewed green spaces [that] constitute perhaps the finest public art ever created in North America."[14] Young Eliot was invited, in his own words, to "go about with Mr. Olmsted and am expected to gather the principles and the practice of the profession in the course of this going...making working drawings from preliminary designs, plans, etc."[15] While Boston had promoted holding certain features of the urban environment landscape (e.g., the Common and the Public Garden) as legally permanent landscape features, throughout America a culture of change was sweeping the land. Olmsted and his adopted stepson, John Charles Olmsted, challenged Charles Eliot with varied parkland projects—few more protracted than Boston's Emerald Necklace, a linear park design stretching along the Muddy River from the Boston Common through the Back Bay to the Arnold Arboretum and ending at the necklace's greatest jewel, Franklin Park. Eliot fully invested himself in this opportunity.

Charles Eliot's interest in landscaping and conservation was not narrowly confined. As we know from his professional scrapbook, he showed great interest in pioneering land preservation developments throughout the United States.[16] In 1885 Eliot finished his internship and traveled along the eastern seaboard of the United States, then spent a year in the U.K. and traveling on the Continent recording his observations on natural history, horticulture, and landscape design. While abroad, Eliot clipped newspapers and kept abreast of efforts to apply democratic principles to the management of land. In June of 1886 Olmsted asked Eliot to join his firm, but the young man declined and opened his own Boston office, following Olmsted's earlier advice to use his writing skills to advance their common agenda through publications in the popular and professional media. Eventually, however, an all-too-brief Olmsted, Olmsted & Eliot partnership (from 1893 to 1897) was realized.

In Maine, the Eliots and other Mount Desert Island summer residents were becoming increasingly aware of threats posed by residential development. The Mount Desert and Eastern Shore Land Company in the late 1880s offered hundreds of lots in a large tract on the eastern edge of Jordan Pond and the western flank of Green (Cadillac) Mountain. Earlier, the Green Mountain Railway Company had negotiated leases for two hundred acres atop Green Mountain and a ninety-six-foot-wide strip from base to summit. The cog railway opened in June of 1883, an easy conveyance to the highest point on the eastern seaboard. Ridership declined after 1886, however, and by 1890 it ceased operation.[17]

The spirit of development persisted as Bar Harbor merchants organized the Green Mountain Carriage Road Company to purchase or lease land from the base of Green Mountain to its summit. Their objective was to locate, control, and operate a toll road to the scenic splendors visible from the summit. The poorly constructed seasonal roadway opened in July of 1888; when it failed to attract the profitable clientele its builders envisioned, the road to the summit closed.

Prominent families watched the scarring of the landscape resulting from such commercial development. In 1919, Bar Harbor's most prominent attorney, Associate Justice of the Supreme Judicial Court of the State of Maine Luere B. Deasy, remarked that conservation first came to the level of public consciousness nearly thirty years earlier, when the only thing on the island dedicated to public use was dirty or muddy roads. At that time no man, woman, or child had a right to stand in any place—or sit in any place outside their own home—and view the island landscape.[18]

Deasy's comment was radically different from the new tourist-manual narratives about Mount Desert Island and accessibility to its scenic attractions. Indeed, his remarks help us better understand the rationale for the 1888 incorporation of the Bar Harbor Village Improvement Association (BHVIA). In the absence of effective town planning, the association was organized to provide "better regulation of the village pertaining to health, cleanliness, and public convenience…[and] to secure the best results in preserving the natural beauties of the place."[19] The association tended the town cemetery, designed the village green, and lobbied town officials for a sewer system, garbage incineration, and qualified inspection of water and milk quality.[20]

Charles Hazen Dorr became a BHVIA charter member. Mary and George later figured prominently in committee activity concerning finance, entertainment, roads and paths, sanitation, and trees and plantings.[21] By the early 1890s Bar Harbor "captured from Newport one of the largest lions of the day in the person of the sixty-three-year-old Philadelphia physician and author S. Weir Mitchell," when he remedied his Newport-induced "intestinal neuralgia" by hiking the mountain trails of the island with companionable outdoorsmen like the bishop of Massachusetts William Lawrence, George Dorr, and Josiah Royce—the last of whom described Dorr as my "captain in many well-planned and wisely directed walks."[22]

In Boston and Cambridge, Royce's reputation as a conversationalist "made him a darling of the Bostonian grandes dames…chief among these ladies was Mrs. Charles Dorr…Molly, as Mrs. Dorr was known to her friends."[23] Royce approached George Dorr for suggestions as to how the philosopher might secure the funds necessary for the new house he was building beside the William James residence on Irving Street in Cambridge. When George confided to his mother about Royce's financial difficulties, she set about organizing "some lectures for him on the history of philosophy, its men and problems, to be given in different private houses in Boston."[24] At the encouragement of Mary Dorr, Royce gave two ticketed series of weekly lectures in 1889 and 1890, titled "Some Noteworthy Persons and Doctrines in the History of Modern Thought."

Now in her late sixties, Mary Dorr saw Royce's lectures as an opportunity to influence religious discourse. She offered to sponsor the series, aimed at a Boston audience made up of women who moved in her social circle. Royce expressed some concern about the suitability of academic content to this audience but was urged by Mary Dorr to retain content rigor. After all, she had been asked by Royce to critique his presentations, which he rewrote and enlarged for presentation to the Harvard faculty. George Dorr learned that he intended to dedicate this publication to Mary Dorr. George's advice was solicited on the language of the dedication since, Royce declared, "the lectures are so largely hers."[25]

Royce dedicated *The Spirit of Modern Philosophy* to "my friend" Mary Gray Ward Dorr, "as a token of affection and veneration in recognition of the wise counsel that suggested its preparation and of the thoughtful advice that accompanied and aided its growth."[26] Reviews by fellow philosophers were positive, recognizing that the chapters were delivered in "a simple and non-technical fashion" before a circle of friends.[27]

Royce's acknowledgment of Mary Dorr was no mere formality. In the final decade of the nineteenth century many emerging leaders were coming to realize that a very distinctive generation of elder New England women was passing. Their intellectual, political, and social influence could no longer be ignored. Judge Robert Grant devoted a chapter of his autobiography to this "group of fashionable women who stood out from the rest by mental agility or aesthetic culture as tacitly acknowledged leaders—leaders in the realm of ideas, yet not always with coquetry."[28]

These society matrons included Julia Ward Howe, Annie Fields, Sarah Orne Jewett, Edith P. Wolcott, and—of course—Mary Dorr, whom Grant described as a "woman of cultivation and great energy, [who] managed Society with a capable but slightly heavy hand, for at her bidding her guests—of whom as a young man I was often one—had to change seats at dinner halfway through to suit her fancy." Furthermore, all these women "bore a cousinly resemblance in their mental suppleness to the no less fastidious, but more elegant and more widely cultivated, women of France of a century earlier. Unconscious as this ambition might be, it aimed at all events at getting near to refined truth as possible."[29]

William James, too, was interested in the pursuit of truth. He was part of a community of prominent social and natural scientists involved with organized investigations of paranormal—or occult—phenomena. His interest was motivated by a prevailing scientific attitude that ignored facts that did not accord with the existing theoretical structure of nature. Methodologically, science aims at universal propositions that can be upset by proving one instance to the contrary (e.g., all crows are not black if you discover one that is white). For James, a spiritualist named Leonora Piper was his "white crow," a person whose knowledge threatened the accepted system.[30]

One of Harvard's men of letters, Barrett Wendell, a friend to Dorr and James, recalled in a 1919 letter that he "dabbled in [the occult] thirty years ago...[yet] I dropped it...[for] in general, I have thought occult experiment dangerous to critical intelligence and to strict sense of truth; both William James and Richard Hodgson—pretty intimate friends—unwittingly went, as I saw them, a bit to pieces. So far as I remember, only one friend whom I have known well bore the full moral test of this exploration without harm and on the whole with benefit. This was old Mrs. Dorr, George's mother, a woman of such remarkable quality that I have no better name for it than genius. With her the magic seemed white; elsewhere I have found it at best grayish."[31]

The unconventional psychic inquiries of James and others may have proved helpful to the resolution of a threat to George Dorr in the early 1880s. Contained in Dorr's memoirs is a brief essay on his "long illness with a complete break-down of nervous vigor and energy." Family physicians were unable to diagnose the affliction and it "looked as if I might not live." The chance discovery of the hypnotic power of suggestion led Dorr to consider a variety of hopeful options. Offering no specific details, Dorr went on to state that once a therapy was selected, he was cured after a few weeks by a form of "mental healing."[32] In this era before Freud, Dorr later credited his recovery to the workings of "the unconscious mind." Both James and Royce complained frequently of their own "nervous disorders"; at a time when diagnostic measures were ill defined, James acted prudently when he reserved judgment about the success of Dorr's "mind cure."

The nineteenth-century renaissance of American letters was fast fading as the industrial age loomed ever larger in the thought and actions of men and women of every social class. Henry James published in 1886 his masterful fictionalized portrait of American life, *The Bostonians.* Readers who appreciated James's insightful characterizations still balked at his descriptions of the local street scenes, residences, and the personalities, especially those who were dedicated to diverse reform movements. Irving Howe noted in his introduction to the novel, that "not one of the people in *The Bostonians* has a secure sense...of what his culture expects from him.... All of them are displaced persons, floating vaguely in the large social spaces of America."[33] One would be hard pressed to argue against the claim that George B. Dorr—now approaching middle age—fit this characterization.

Few, however, would characterize Arnold Arboretum director Charles Sprague Sargent as displaced. As a botanist well established in scientific circles, he took a step in a new direction when in 1888 he launched an innovative serial publication that marked the beginnings of specialized disciplines. At a time when horticulture still "piggybacked on agriculture," *Garden and Forest* ranged over the domains of botany, horticulture, forestry, and a loosely defined newcomer, landscape design. *Garden and Forest* roused public interest in forest preservation and broadened awareness of the importance of establishing new national parks that would conserve distinctive American landscape. No other horticultural reference is cited more often in Dorr's memoirs; referencing *Garden and Forest* became obligatory for publications with related content.[34]

Could a publication influence Dorr's future direction? Since his graduation, fourteen years earlier, Dorr had not found a suitable vocation or career path. Or could the growing family relationships with professors Royce and James re-energize his interests in academic matters? In his memoirs, Dorr speaks of his mind "bent toward the study of philosophy. But my aim was practical; not the study of dialectics and past systems of thought leading nowhere but to get light on human nature and the problems of existence." Nonetheless, he arranged to read privately with Royce the systematic thoughts of the seventeenth-century rationalist Benedictus de Spinoza. What prompted Dorr's interest in the last major representative of medievalism was Spinoza's efforts to bridge the gulf between traditional religious problems and the emerging new sciences.

In pursuit of this goal, Dorr enrolled in Harvard's Graduate School of Arts and Sciences in 1888, just shy of his thirty-fifth birthday.[35] The Harvard archives document that Dorr enrolled in five graduate courses in chemistry, physics, and mathematics. In each case he either dropped the course or received no grade. Instructors in these disciplines simply recorded that Dorr was absent from examinations; circulation records show that he did not borrow library resources.[36]

That Dorr was unable to sustain his academic focus for these subjects may have had to do with the pull of family expectations, which were strong. Perhaps George—who had mastered classical and modern languages as an undergraduate—could not relate to the methodologies of these rapidly developing sciences. We do know that early that year he had been drawn back to Lenox, where family bonds were being both tightened and yet paradoxically expanded through a marriage.

The October wedding of Sam and Anna Ward's granddaughter Louise Thoron at their Oakwood estate received elaborate preparation. It was "the most acclaimed social event of Oakwood's brief history."[37] The groom was the son of Grover Cleveland's recently appointed Secretary of War and bore his name, William Crowninshield Endicott of Salem. The deep New England roots of the Endicott family trace back nine generations to John Endecott and the founding of the Massachusetts Bay Colony.

Marriage into the Endicott family for a Ward family descendant was to prove significant for Dorr; for the next half-century he remained more closely attached to the Endicotts than to any other Dorr or Ward family relatives. When Dorr received news of Louisa's engagement, he told the bride-to-be that he felt "unalloyed pleasure" on hearing the news. George knew William C. Endicott Jr. through their common friends, writing to cousin Louisa that he "likes him well, already. And how pleasant to think of what we here must all look upon as your homecoming to New England. I have no near cousins here now—you will be doubly welcome, here, to me."[38] The Ward, Dorr, Thoron, and Endicott families were joined at the wedding by Lenox friends, the wife of President Cleveland, and other Washington dignitaries.[39]

Over the next decade, the relationship between W. C. Endicott Jr. and George B. Dorr matured into an enduring friendship based on shared values. Not only did they genuinely enjoy each other's company, but they shared convictions about the importance of conserving the landscape and history of New England. After Endicott's death, his biographer, Walter Muir Whitehill, noted that "it was not merely that he believed in the old ways and the old standards; he was the embodiment of them."[40] In the course of his career Endicott had official responsibilities with the Society for the Protection of New England Antiquities, the Isabella Stewart Gardner Museum, the Massachusetts Horticultural Society, the Essex Institute, the Museum of Fine Arts, and the Massachusetts Historical Society—serving as its president for twelve years. Later, Endicott's influential circle proved to be of conspicuous advantage to Dorr as he gathered support for his conservation objectives.

The expansive Dorr residence had been generously shared with family and friends after they relocated from Storm Beach Cottage to Oldfarm in

1880. Whether they interacted socially with the Eliots during those first few summers in residence at Oldfarm is unclear, but the fragile Dorr Guest Book on exhibit at the Bar Harbor Historical Society Museum witnessed the signatures and remarks of hundreds whom they entertained over more than two decades. In quiet moments, the family likely recalled those visits as they read the poems, anecdotes, and musical passages left behind by notables including President Chester B. Arthur, Oliver Wendell Holmes, Julia Ward Howe, and others with whom the Dorr family socialized.

One of the most memorable entries was the singular characterization of the Oldfarm landscape left in August of 1888 by the autocrat of the breakfast table, Mr. Holmes:

> *La Maison d'Or*
> From this fair home behold on either side
> The restful mountains or the restless sea
> So the warm sheltering walls of life divide
> Time and its tides from still eternity.
>
> Look on the waves: their stormy voices teach
> That not on earth may toil and struggle cease.
> Look at the mountains; better far than speech
> Their silent promise of eternal speech.[41]

CHAPTER SIX

Between Boston and Mount Desert Island

By 1890, landscape architect Charles Eliot had completed three landmark essays for Sargent's *Garden and Forest,* which were followed the next year by the establishment of the nation's first land trust. In the long term, these lucid essays and the experience in Massachusetts were seminal to his father's proposal for the incorporation in Maine of the Hancock County Trustees of Public Reservations.

Eliot's first essay was a seemingly modest proposal. On the basis of their stature, age, and site uniqueness, he argued in "The Waverly Oaks" for the preservation of twenty-three large oaks and one large elm growing on a three-acre terminal moraine in Belmont, Massachusetts. Within walking distance of Boston, this then-rural area was threatened by rapid commercial and residential development. Eliot called for the "establishment of a small public park" to protect "so many large trees… not often seen now anywhere in eastern America."[1]

A longer companion essay, "The Coast of Maine," richly described the Pine Tree State's coast, topography, botanical uniqueness, and cultural history. President Eliot's son explained that since the Civil War, this picturesque environment had been overwhelmed by "the flood of humanity." Specifically, it had been exploited by land companies and speculators who profited from the sale of the most desirable real estate. Unchecked, such free-wheeling behavior robbed coastal Maine of "that flavor of wildness and remoteness which has hitherto hung about it, and which in great measure constitutes its refreshing charm.... The readers of *Garden and Forest* stand in need of no argument to prove the importance to human happiness of that refreshing antidote to city life, which fine natural scenery supplies, nor is it necessary to remind them that love of beauty and of art must surely die, if it be cut at its roots by destroying or vulgarizing the beauty of nature."

Echoing writings from his Champlain Society days, a decade earlier, Eliot proposed that sites such as Great Head on Mount Desert Island could be preserved for public use by local, county, or state authorities. He contended that the "material prosperity" of the citizenry would be improved if legislation were passed to encourage the formation of "associations for the purpose of preserving chosen parts of her coast scenery." This brief and underappreciated article demonstrates clearly that it was Charles Eliot who provided the vision for the trustee organization that his father would formally establish eleven years later.[2]

The final essay drew attention back to Massachusetts. Bearing the same title as the first essay, it is an ambitious conservation plan not only for the Waverly oaks but for other areas of natural beauty within the borders of his native state as well. Eliot then realistically acknowledged the protectionist philosophy of communities that resist spending local funds for conservation if access is not restricted to their own constituents. It was an ambitious plan. To offset such parochialism, he insisted that what all Massachusetts residents thirst for are the surviving fragments of the primitive New England wilderness, "bits of scenery which possess uncommon beauty and more than usual refreshing power." In the final two paragraphs Eliot mapped out a powerful analogy. "Just as the Public Library holds books and the Art Museum pictures—for the use and enjoyment of the public...an incorporated association, composed of citizens of all the Boston towns, and empowered by the State...[should] hold small and well-distributed parcels of land free of taxes." Once established, Eliot believed that "generous men and women will be ready to buy and give into its keeping" sites of superior natural quality just as others buy and donate to museums' fine works of art.[3]

Eliot carefully orchestrated the movement that over the next fifteen months made his vision a reality. He used his authority as an officer of the

Appalachian Mountain Club Council to invite a mix of fellow councilors and nonmembers of stature—Charles S. Sargent, Francis Parkman, and the writer, minister, and famed abolitionist Thomas Wentworth Higginson—to develop further the framework for a conservation organization that reached beyond the parochialism of community interests. From the larger council, he secured the general endorsement of the idea of a statewide organization. Protection of historic structures was added as a trustee responsibility. A judiciary meeting of the Massachusetts State Senate considered Eliot's plan for preserving natural scenery, and within two weeks the precedent-setting legislation was approved by both houses and Governor William Eustis Russell. The Trustees of Public Reservations, the nation's first statewide conservation and preservation organization, became a reality on May 21, 1891.

Charles Eliot was appointed secretary of the Trustees of Public Reservations and chairman of the Standing Committee, the organization's governing body. At a time when no academic department of landscape architecture existed, few realized that Eliot had pioneered a new profession: one that consciously analyzed "landscapes as entities composed of layers of systems—cultural, economic, and ecological—while devising scientific methods for recording them, and implementing political measures to conserve them."[4]

Other important conservation efforts would be initiated during the early 1890s. John Muir founded the Sierra Club on the West Coast. Modeled on the Appalachian Mountain Club, it had the boldest of agendas: protection of America's natural environment. On the East Coast, the New York State Adirondack Park was established by its legislature as the nation's largest forest reserve; its landscape "shall be forever kept as wild forest lands." In New England, the Trustees of Public Reservations published "The Province Lands Report," which revealed human abuses on the sand dunes of outer Cape Cod and resulted in a state management plan for four thousand acres of terrain.

The young landscape architect was not the only family member drawing public attention to the coast of Maine. In the widely circulated and highly regarded *Century Magazine,* President Eliot published an important empirical study that should have received greater attention by public officials who decided matters of social policy, including protection of land for public use. He presented a statistical inquiry into "the mode of government, mode of life, and general social condition of the people who make up the sparsely settled town of Mount Desert," one of several towns and villages that comprise Mount Desert Island.[5]

Dr. Eliot reminded readers that the "cruelest of industrial practices, the most revolting human habitations, and the most depraved modes of life which anywhere can be discovered—in miner's camps, factory villages, or city slums," are not the norm. Instead, in the last decade of the nineteenth century three-quarters of the American people remained scattered in communities where people "live comfortably and hopefully, and with as much contentment and gladness as can be expected in people of their rather joyless lineage." With exacting precision, Eliot presented comparative data to demonstrate that "this sequestered, wholesome, and contented community [of Mount Desert] affords a fair type of the organization of basal American society."

"The Forgotten Millions" was interpreted by some as a conservative defense of the status quo, mostly serving to reassure the leisure class with the false belief that the "forgotten millions" are content with their lowly existence. Instead, this revealing essay showed the Brahmin president of Harvard University in an unexpected light—displaying a man with heightened sensitivity and a deep understanding of the circumstances of those millions. Eliot did not willfully ignore or unconsciously accept the servitude of native island residents. His arguments for the character of the habits and conditions of the local population were based on more than a wide array of empirical data drawn from local town records. He had years of experience with hardy and humble neighbors who taught him about the lasting and changeable facets of land and sea. He saw them as a microcosm of American life—even if they regarded him with suspicion since the Eliot family was, after all, "from away."

Eliot's essay can also be seen as championing a conservation concept that was deeply traditional in outlook, invoking preservationist ideals to defend a relatively egalitarian Jeffersonian-style society—prioritizing men who make their living on the land and other such folk—and the resources on which it was based. Dr. Eliot and his son were not naïve. They recognized that, in the face of surging recreational interest in coastal Maine, its landscape "offered a new commercial potential, distinct from traditional land uses and those of corporate industrialists."[6] Corporate-industrial developers and resort proprietors in their own ways sought to reorganize the natural landscape. Railroad and steamship entrepreneurs, hotel and resort proprietors, and recreational travel agents promoted rusticity as an important commercial resource. Tourism "offered new markets for produce, real estate, and rural craftsmanship, and new life for villages suffering from the collapse of northern New England's agricultural base."[7] These changes also threatened the social fabric, the relationship between neighbors near and far.

Mary Dorr expressed neighborly feelings as she wrote to Rosalind Howard in 1890, referring to their summer Oldfarm home and inviting—almost begging—the Howard family to visit. The island abounds with "delightful people, charming and representative...[surrounded by] sea and inland bays...like Naples. Sailing. Yachting. Mountain climbing, rocks and shore such as you will see almost nowhere. Climate for the summer months I know nothing like it—with all, there is quite enough of the roughness and primitiveness of a new settlement to give [your] boys and girls all the outings they can devise."[8]

Nonetheless, after a decade of summers in Maine, the Dorrs arranged with the phenomenally successful London travel agency, Thomas Cook & Son, for an eight-month eastern Mediterranean adventure. As a student of ancient languages, George Dorr was delighted that after departing Venice in late 1891 the tour would proceed to the Greek Isles, then turn south to the Nile before completing the adventure in the Holy Land the following spring.[9] At this time "everybody who wanted to be thought a bone fide traveler went to Egypt and the Nile and most of them traveled on a Cook's Tour...[their passenger lists] read like a Who's Who of late nineteenth-century royalty, commerce and the arts."[10]

Chaperoned by tour agents, travelers were largely insulated from the daily life of the native population. They were far more likely to converse with an acquaintance last encountered at an Edwardian country house than a slum dweller or beggar. In 1891 Lord Randolph Churchill had covered the same territory as the Dorrs, and informed friends at home that he enjoyed "good food, hock, champagne, Pilsner beer, Marquis chocolate, ripe bananas, [and] fresh dates" as he floated the Nile.[11]

Yet no organization could fully protect travelers. The Cook agency offered secure steamers like the recently commissioned floating hotel, *Ramenses the Great.* The Dorrs, however, chartered a specially built steam-powered, steel-hulled vessel called a *dahabeah,* which the Cook's organization outfitted for smaller parties.[12] Written aboard the *Dahabeah Hathor,* Mary's lengthy letter to her brother Samuel is the only surviving documentation of these eight months of what Mary describes as "wanderings."[13] Her letter expresses concern about personal security, having encountered passengers with "small purses, short educations, ill health." At some length she recounts an incident in which the ship's captain was attacked by a knife-wielding "perfectly frenzied idiot," who was finally overcome by the crew.

Mary took this all in stride, finding dahabeah life on one of Cook's "best and newest" vessels a "first class" experience. This much-traveled family adapted well to foreign ways. It is something of a stretch, however, to accept Mary's claim—in this twenty-page letter—that "we are as much at home here as we could be at Oldfarm." Notable is the inclusion of but one passing reference to husband Charles and son George. The absence of references to the activities of her family is consistent with Mary's self-absorbed letters to Lady Howard and reinforces George's generous remark in his memoirs that the three Dorrs customarily behaved independently. She summarized the judgment of all, however, when describing their voyage through the Aegean Sea as "one of the most wonderful and beautiful experiences of our lifetime."[14]

While abroad, the Dorrs were saddened to receive news of the death of their close friend, Harvard professor of belles lettres James Russell Lowell. They would likely have agreed with the assessment by family friend T. W. Higginson that: "His death took from us a man rich beyond all other Americans in poetic impulses, and in readiness of wit; sometimes entangled and hampered by his own wealth; unequal in expression, yet rising on the greatest of occasions to the higher art; blossoming early, yet maturing late."[15]

On their return to Massachusetts in early summer 1892, Mary wrote to Samuel from Oldfarm, apologizing once again for her "long silence." She had taken ill in Lenox and was "barely able to muster the strength to come [to Oldfarm for]...my trouble has been as most of my later troubles have been—fever and eye sensitiveness with a necessity of almost total abstinence of the use of the eye, and this time it has been accompanied by a good deal of prostration and pain—but I am already much better."[16]

Mary's optimism was overstated; she soon learned that surgery for her acute and painful glaucoma was required. The unfortunate result was the loss of sight in one eye. Politely, Oldfarm guests did not comment on this misfortune. The still-smitten Josiah Royce, however, informed William James several months later that "Mrs. Dorr is very loving now, and very gracious, but has reached such a spiritual height since she saw Egypt that I can but grovel in her presence, and weakly babble a little about hypnotism to please her."[17]

The family's season of misfortune was destined to continue. On the heels of Mary's partial loss of sight, her husband Charles died of pneumonia on January 28, 1893. Many throughout the nation were already in a state of bereavement following the death five days earlier of Boston's influential Trinity Church preacher, Episcopalian Phillips Brooks. George Dorr's memoirs contain but one brief reference to his father's death: "My father had passed on the winter following our return from Egypt, along with Bishop Brooks, the greatest preacher I have ever heard who left all doctrine behind to get to the heart of things."[18]

Dorr eulogized the life of Reverend Brooks, yet in contrast he barely mentions his father's death in comments that are free of emotion and implication. Dorr's restraint in characterizing his loss was consistent with the behavior he attributed to his father more than four decades later: "My father was more reserved...for of his inner self I never heard him talk."[19] The body of Charles Dorr was interred January 30 in the modest Ravens Path family plot at Mount Auburn Cemetery in Cambridge.

Following her stay at Oldfarm in 1887, Laura Richards, the wife of Oldfarm architect Henry Richards and daughter of Julia Ward Howe, had been inspired by a "distant lighthouse" in Frenchman Bay to write the first of eighty books she would eventually pen. *Captain January* became a classic of children's literature, made Laura a wealthy woman, and inspired two films. In her family papers, however, she deposited documents intended solely for family eyes. Recently made available to researchers is Laura's unguarded eight-page characterization of Mary Ward Dorr. "When her husband died, [Mary] was inconsolable for a long time. My mother went to the funeral, which was a little reception room...there were only a half dozen people... [Mary] came into the room and gave us one glance and changed us all round. 'Fannie, you sit there; Julia, you sit so; George, you sit there.'"[20]

Six letters of condolence also survive. Predictably, they convey sympathy and more than a hint of hyperbole. Nonetheless, two are notable. Mrs. William Hunt, wife of the artist and one of Charles's oldest friends, wrote to George that she had been a "life-long admirer of the beautiful character and accomplished mind of your father." Francis S. Watson, M.D., a schoolmate and friend of George, refers to his father's "extraordinary patience, pluck and cheer at the time when I operated on him at Bar Harbor. In all my experience of courageous and enduring people in sickness, I have never known his conduct on that occasion equaled.... He had a quality of endurance and of readiness to meet and accept whatever might be in store for him which was entirely apart from anything I have ever seen in anyone else."[21]

The will of Charles Dorr assigned to Mary Dorr "all my property real, personal or mixed." If she had not survived Charles, then the same would apply to his son George B. Dorr.[22] If both had predeceased him, a charitable trust ensured that the revenue from the principal would be used "for the benefit of the New England States and especially of Boston...[to] make the general life of the people more vigorous and healthful, mentally, morally, or physically without being in their character specifically religious or political." Family friend Robert Grant probated the will.[23] On his death, Charles's personal estate totaled $19,151.11—not a modest amount. Nonetheless, the wealth of this family appears to be largely derived from the Ward family line.[24]

Writing to Rosalind Howard two weeks after the death of her husband, Mary remarks that "George and I are now alone, with only one another. It is a great sudden...blow. There were only us three, and how close we were, how absolutely one, it is difficult in words to say. A very noble...absolutely unselfish life, devoted to the highest aims, and wishing only to serve and to do good. Full of true manliness and of fine spiritual quality—we thank God who gave him to us [for] so long."[25]

Not only was the Dorr family experiencing a difficult transition, the nation was struggling economically due to a sharp decline in industrial productivity. For both, the spectacle of a world's fair that celebrated the quadricentennial of Columbus' discovery of the New World served as tonic.

Dorr was one of more than twenty million visitors who experienced the Chicago World Columbian Exposition from April through late October 1893. Fair promoters promised to "show the enormous strides in cultural achievement since the [1876] Centennial, to set to rest forever the quibbles about American cultural inferiority.... By overshadowing the latest spectacles at Paris in 1878 and 1889, [the exposition] would conclusively demonstrate the passing of world leadership from the Old to the New World."[26] Despite the nationalistic agenda, it was commonplace for visitors to be overwhelmed by the sixty-five thousand exhibits representing fifty-one nations.

Exposition visitors were affected by the giant Ferris wheel, the Midway, and all the distracting sounds and sights—including, most likely, a well-dressed young gentleman from Cleveland, Ohio. Perhaps more so than any other visitor, it was this Brown University–bound nineteen-year-old "who was to have a profound influence on the future of America for the next half century."[27] With an upbringing confined by the zealous Baptist faith of his parents, it is not surprising that this serious and unsophisticated son of the richest man in America was impressed by the vastness and immensity of the Exposition. John Davison Rockefeller Jr. brought to the world's fair a deeply ingrained appreciation for the natural world—developed at his father's Forest Hill estate outside Cleveland—that would ally him with Dorr and President Eliot when their paths crossed nearly twenty years later on Mount Desert Island.

In the face of the optimism of the fair, Mr. Rockefeller's biographers explain that "a financial panic was emerging that that would lead to three hard years of economic recession. From the top of the Ferris wheel one could see the areas of Chicago that would bear the brunt of this latest downturn.... Here dwelled the growing underclass of immigrants from Europe and distant prairie provinces, a dispossessed and landless peasantry laboring under appalling conditions in the city's factories and stockyards."[28]

Meanwhile, Dorr's distant cousin, the "dean of American horticulture" Charles Sprague Sargent, would make the thirty-two-hour trip from Boston to Chicago with his wife, Mary. Accompanying them was their Holm Lea estate guest, twenty-one-year-old Beatrix Jones, whom Sargent had encouraged to study landscape gardening. Of course they knew in advance that horticulture would be prominently featured at the Columbian

Exposition, but that did not diminish the impact of the lavish space given to it. Horticultural Hall was a 67,000-square-foot structure containing eight greenhouses that filled one of the fourteen great buildings. Horticultural Hall proved of great interest to George B. Dorr, who visited the fair in the summer months. It is no coincidence that less than three years later he would open the Mount Desert Nurseries, his first business venture.

Immediately prior to her departure for Chicago, Beatrix Jones had found much "to admire and emulate" in Mary Dorr's Oldfarm gardens. She used one of the newest pieces of technology, her Kodak camera, to take images of gardens planted more than a decade earlier. In her five-hundred-word journal entry for October 12, 1893, she records in part that "the fashionable eulalia, lyme grass, if planted in a sheltered spot would survive the island winter; that a generous planting of hollyhocks and larkspur looked wonderful against the 'solid background' of the arborvitae…hedge," and so on. We know that two small lilac bushes flanked Oldfarm's front doorway while a larger lilac sheltered the kitchen. Jones was critical of Mary Dorr's "unfortunate" weakness for magnolias and other exotics that were contextually out of place.[29] Credit is due to Ms. Jones for preserving the fullest surviving characterization of this striking garden.

During the winters, life continued much as before at the Dorrs' Boston residence on Commonwealth Avenue. There was a new opportunity for the forty-year-old gentleman who resided there, one that would constructively involve him in the life of his alma mater in ways that were unanticipated. As a Harvard alumnus, however, Dorr had done little to keep his classmates informed of his activities. Twenty years after graduation, he reported succinctly to his classmates that Boston remained his home and that he had recently returned from travels to Egypt and the Holy Land.[30]

But following the death of his father, George showed a growing willingness to contribute his time and energy (and sometimes his capital) to Harvard University, should the opportunity present itself. His growing closeness to Josiah Royce, William James, and the Eliots certainly figured into his receiving an invitation that fall to serve on a new Harvard committee. In order to remain more attentive to the faculty-driven activities of academic departments, visiting committees had been established to be the eyes and ears of Harvard's governing Board of Overseers. Alumni were appointed to evaluate the quality of academic departments and empowered to investigate every activity at the department level. Departments were expected to comply with all committee requests, and committee chairs were expected to produce periodic written reports for the board.

In Dorr's selection, the eminent William James carried great pedagogical and administrative weight. The anti-systematic unconventionality of James as a thinker was by now a mainstay of Harvard culture, and his cultivation of talent would not have been regarded with suspicion. Put somewhat differently, James found ways to promote self-esteem in those whom he deemed worthy.[31] Following the death of Charles Dorr that January, it is probable that James situated Dorr's son where his leadership potential could be fostered close at hand.

Dorr accepted appointment to the new Philosophy Visiting Committee and within a few years ascended to the committee chairmanship.[32] What he did not anticipate was being charged with responsibility for raising the funds necessary to erect the first academic building in the United States devoted to the discipline of philosophy. That imposing structure ultimately bore the name of a family with whom the Wards and the Dorrs had a long association: Emerson.

The pace of Dorr's life had quickened, the focus of his interests had sharpened. After so many years of searching for some larger purpose, he at last felt the internal sense that this goal was on the near horizon. Momentum was building toward the conservation objectives that we today associate with his name.

CHAPTER SEVEN

Landscape as Our Common Heritage

Pulitzer Prize–winning historian Van Wyck Brooks has captured New England's regional spirit in the last decade of the nineteenth century: "The old New England was slipping away. The rock bound coast was stern no longer; its villas, lawns and gardens suggested the Hudson river or the Isle of Wight.... The old public spirit was fading...[and the New England mind] seemed to be exhausted, and its mood was sad, relaxed, and reminiscent."[1] On Frenchman Bay, Dorr was not convinced that the days of Yankee ingenuity and public philanthropy were numbered. He was confident that Mount Desert Island held untapped resources that could be turned to public purpose. With cautious optimism, he began to purchase parcels of undeveloped land; he set his sight on properties that possessed characteristics meriting protection—along Cromwell Harbor Brook and the Great Meadow—or were contiguous with more impressive landscapes.

Dorr was less attracted to remote mainland country than to the underappreciated—and presumably less familiar—world of coastal Maine. A lengthy tenancy had led both Dr. Eliot and Dorr to this preference. Each trekked the island year after year, becoming increasingly familiar with the seasonal strengths and weaknesses of its landscapes. In effect, they opened themselves to the environment, enabling the island to educate them about its distinctiveness. Through repeated exploration of the land and seascape, Dorr came to realize that "The earth is our common heritage. It is both right and needful that it should be kept widely free in the portions that the homes of men, industry, and agriculture do not claim."[2]

Dorr did not deny the value of wilderness. However, his family heritage, education, and travel had well prepared him to pursue on the coast of Maine, on lands historically contested by the English and French, the enduring natural features that had been shaped by those recurring conflicts. Dorr focused on acquiring natural landscapes that had been overlaid by human landscapes—and where the character of the landscape inspired humankind to realize new heights.[3]

A 2004 study by the Olmsted Center for Landscape Preservation shows that Mount Desert Island today has four sets of historic trail networks: Native American carry paths; straightened, narrow logging routes constructed by European settlers; challenging and sometimes precipitous paths and commemorative trails developed after 1890 by village improvement societies; and Civilian Conservation Corps trails developed and improved during the 1930s. Maps, trail guides, improvement society annual reports, trail logs, paintings, and photographs provide abundant evidence for what might be called an "Acadian" style of trail making, "characterized by a high level of construction that is clearly evident to trail users; it includes split granite steps, coping stones, graded graveled paths, and iron work."[4]

In contributing to this Acadian style of trail architecture, Dorr allied himself with Bar Harbor Village Improvement Association Roads and Paths Committee chairmen Herbert Jacques, Waldron Bates, and Edward Rand. The BHVIA initially led the way in developing path-making techniques, stabilizing path conditions, erecting and standardizing signs, building footbridges, and publishing sophisticated island maps.[5] Dorr collaborated with Jacques on a half-mile connector path for pedestrians and carriages, through a heavily wooded area from Schooner Head Road to the base of Champlain Mountain and around to the Otter Creek Road.

Over the two decades spanning the turn of the century, such "connector trails" enabled residents and visitors to design their hiking adventure, accessing a rapidly growing number of new trails within reach of nearby villages. Moreover, connector trails appealed to Dorr the horticulturist, for the routes could be designed to draw the saunterer's attention to what

Dorr called "hardy herbaceous plant" exhibits, an essential feature of the plan from which the park resulted.[6]

Dorr used his wealth to protect a landscape that was not fully healed from damage done in earlier generations. Each outing on the footpaths acquainted Dorr with continuing threats to land wrecked by logging and fires (in addition to lightning, fires set by humans to clear land or burn waste were significant). One prominent tourist guide described the island environment in the years following the Civil War: "The forest primeval is gone; but huge stumps and scathed trunks show what the axe and the fires have done. The three western mountains...are covered with a second growth, but the other summits are bleak and bare."[7] In acquiring property, Dorr weighed commercial applications as well. Of course, quarrying granite was an island tradition, but Dorr appears to have anticipated the need for granite to build park roads and bridges as he purchased and later quarried the favored pink-hued granite sites.

What Thoreau called "bare and pathless rock" forced Dorr and others to judge carefully where to plant the next step, a difficult decision when the bare granite stretched for hundreds of feet. Thoreau's "favorite mode of walking was 'cross-lots' on a compass line," a strategy that trespassed private land. When Dorr instead followed the island topography and the limits imposed by the surrounding sea, he surely recalled his countryside walking experiences in England, where footpath rights-of-way were deeply engrained in common law.[8] The sheer joy of exploration and of recovering one's bearings after getting lost was balanced by Dorr's persistent effort to commit to memory exacting details of his journeys. This reservoir of detail proved critical in planning future trails, acquiring conservation properties, identifying biological resources and geological features—not to mention the importance of this stored experience for later recommendations to park officials and John D. Rockefeller Jr.

In planning trails that wend their way through the island landscape, Dorr applied some advice contained in an *Atlantic Monthly* essay published a month after he entered Harvard College. Therein, T. W. Higginson extolled the benefits of footpaths: "Instead of striking across the natural lines, [the footpath] conforms to them, nestles into the hollow, skirts the precipice, avoids the morass. An unconscious landscape-gardener...there are a thousand concealed fitnesses in nature, rhymed correspondences of bird and blossom, for which you must seek through the most hidden paths."

Higginson claimed that well-designed footpaths provided intimate knowledge of both nature and the walker. "It is only in the footpath that our minds, like our bodies, move slowly, and we traverse thought, like space, with a patient thoroughness."[9] The summer after that essay was published, while hiking footpaths in Italy's Lake Como region, Dorr experienced what Higginson had described. Even earlier, in 1868, when the Dorr family first visited Mount Desert, island footpaths had responded to the pressure of Dorr's boots. Higginson wrote that "he had never experienced so much, existed so thoroughly, lived so truly, and been so wholly himself, as during his travels on foot." Dorr clearly felt the same.[10]

Dorr and Waldron Bates, "the island's two pre-eminent path makers," believed that Native American footpaths frequently provided the best guidance for trail direction. In his correspondence with National Park Service officials, Dorr often referred to these pre-European paths as single-lane footways only wide enough for one person. A central principle adhered to by Native Americans—and that Dorr promoted—was that the "earth led the path, not human inclination to 'challenge' the landscape." Path refinements were not intended to manipulate landscape but to adapt to it.[11]

Dorr's explorations were efforts to decipher the power of place. Each new hike enlarged his consciousness of that power implicit in the extraordinary natural variation within the island's one hundred square miles: that is, seascape, coastline, rugged headlands, mountains, valleys, freshwater lakes and ponds, watersheds, wildlife, and the three hundred species of plants.[12] What would be the consequences of residential development, of increased footpath use, of landscape segregated from public access? Might not the best response to the dizzying consequences of industrialization lie beneath Dorr's feet? After all, had not Olmsted shown that landscape possesses the power to transform human aspirations?[13] Might it be feasible to develop natural reservations to restore and sustain historic and indigenous conditions?

William James grasped the melding of the natural forces that Dorr experienced, the "strength" and "character" of Mount Desert. He wrote to his wife, Alice, that his "Mt. Desert visit was a success, especially yesterday with its fine weather, which we spent on a big walk over the Mountains. I had no idea of the strength of that Island."[14] On that same day, in a letter to experimental psychologist James M. Baldwin, James referred to "a glorious day yesterday—steam launch to Seal Harbor then over Sargent's Mountain.... I never saw so much *character* in so few miles."[15]

The island landscape was also personified by the daughter of Dorr's cousin Thomas Wren Ward Jr., the son of George's uncle, Samuel G. Ward. Vacationing at the Northeast Harbor Kimball House, Elizabeth Howard Ward described an ecclesiastical atmosphere following a memorable experience as her vessel neared Mount Desert Island: "I was oppressed all the way up the Harbor, by noticing a striking resemblance in one of the mountain profiles to Aunt Mary [Dorr] in her best cap. There she was watching me from the top of the Island. She became less terrific on a nearer view."[16]

Cottage development during the last two decades of the nineteenth century accelerated. From his various footpath perches, Dorr saw the loss of landscape as prominent families "from away" rapidly developed the shoreline. Eden's village area now included George W. Vanderbilt's Pointe d'Acadie, and John S. Kennedy's Kenarden Lodge. Northwest of the village—on the corridor to Hull's Cove—the new estates of Bournemouth, Bogue Chitto, and Brook End privatized the coast.[17] Residential and commercial expansion was evident elsewhere on the island, especially in the Shingle-style designs of Fred L. Savage, whom Dorr would enlist in Oldfarm improvements.[18] No other resort could offer the 'walk and talk' seasonal residents with anything comparable, where a "person's social prestige depended on the number of pedestrian miles accomplished up and down [the torturous trails] each summer."[19]

As the close of the nineteenth century neared, new path development as well as the marking of established paths attracted larger numbers of island residents, seasonal residents, and tourists. Eventually, more than three hundred miles of trails bisected the island. Village improvement societies examined and recommended upgrading public roads, paths, and village greens, and the Dorr family contributed to the process. For several years, Mary Dorr chaired the BHVIA Committee on Trees; her son served with Beatrix Jones on both the Roads and Paths and the Trees and Plantings committees. In 1897, Dorr and two physicians accepted appointments to a new Sanitation Committee, charged with establishing standards and securing expert assistance in dealing with contagious diseases.

Two years earlier, as chair of the BHVIA Bicycle Path Committee, he completed construction of a nearly mile-long path around the Beaver Dam Pool on Bear Brook Valley land. This site, a lovely sheltered sanctuary on the flank of Champlain Mountain, held special significance for Mary Dorr. Summer resident Marian Lawrence Peabody described Dorr's path as "heavenly smooth with pine needles and the sun just flickering through."[20] The Roads and Paths Committee recognized "the work done by Mr. George Dorr on the roadsides and contrast it with the horrible eyesores with which our [eyes are] met on most of the roads on the island."[21]

Some time later, Eden selectmen accepted Dorr's offer to construct a road around the western side of Strawberry Hill and the northern end of Great Meadow, connecting Otter Creek county road with the town road to Harden Farm. The intent was to avoid village congestion for "my mother and our friends and neighbors" on the eastern shore, who wished a short and pleasant route to the western side of the island. Dorr financed half the cost of this civic gesture.[22]

Year after year Dorr traversed this island, retracing his steps countless times, climbing one more peak even though he had been there too often to keep count. New observations, photographed images, and questions received attention later, when he consulted specialized publications in his extensive libraries at Oldfarm and Storm Beach Cottage. Whether on the trail or in the village, neighbors and acquaintances easily identified this very popular man, described by Cleveland Amory as "a scenic wonder himself—a tall, lean man with shaggy eyebrows and a striking down-sweeping mustache."[23] Whether on the trails or in Boston's swankiest socials clubs, Mr. Dorr was recognized as a stately gentleman dressed in tweeds, shirt, tie, and hat, befitting the customs of the day. He was, however, someone who appeared to have too much on his mind to give much thought to the propriety of his attire. In his later years he would have been described as slightly rumpled.

These "wanderings," as Mary Dorr described his island journeys, were often in the company of relatives, friends, and village improvement acquaintances. Even in their company, her son scrutinized trail conditions, paying attention to the effects of erosion, glaciation, distinctive landforms, water level fluctuations, and the ways in which trees and plants responded to human intrusion by overuse or logging. New trail routes were mapped and routing consultations with others took place, then closely supervised work crews constructed the trail. Years later, Dorr would draw upon these experiences with the island's forest, its wildlife, and the surrounding sea when crafting articles for a twenty-three-title series he established in 1916, *The Sieur de Monts Publications.*

The pull of unfamiliar places still vied for Dorr's attention even three years after his family's return from abroad. In October of 1895, he took a two-week canoeing and camping trip in the company of a local guide and his wife, describing it in a five-page memoir. They paddled through the northern Maine wilderness, from Moosehead Lake north through Chesuncook Lake and ending on the second longest river on North America's Atlantic coastline, the Saint John.[24] The adventure followed a route familiar to students of American literature—through the wilderness described by Henry David Thoreau in 1846 and 1853. Dorr's accounts (in contrast to Thoreau's more scientific descriptions) previewed the values that much later were more fully developed in discussions with National Park Service officials, Charles W. Eliot, and John D. Rockefeller Jr.[25] Regrettably, the only autobiographical documents to have survived from Dorr's first forty-two years is this travel summary and the one-page, handwritten personal profile that was required of all Harvard students prior to their graduation.

Of the woods seen from his canoe Dorr wrote, "...even if they be very fine in themselves are monotonous when one sees them stretching on unbroken by civilization, unrelieved by open ground or any sign of human homeliness...[for] if the woods be open, one should walk *in* them, under and among the individual trees to realize their beauty and grasp the feel of their charm." One core landscape value articulated here is that "individual features of the landscape and its play of light and shadow" must not be "swallowed up in an unbroken sea of mixed foliage."[26]

Dorr's years of European travel, immersed in both formal and picturesque aesthetics, informed his belief in an aesthetic superiority of landscape that included open space, cultivated terrain, or human habitation. His emerging conservation philosophy was both pluralistic and cumulative. Dorr's uncle, Samuel G. Ward, expressed this view as well within the context of European culture: "Painters' mountains must be varied with peaks and hollow curves and associated with human habitation or occupation to relieve their austerity."[27] Dorr saw varied terrain elements as necessary for the sake of the larger whole, suggestive of the ecological philosophy that would be developed by the scientific community a half-century later.

As winter arrived, Mary and George Dorr headed back to Commonwealth Avenue, where social invitations awaited them. Professor William James invited George to another "Philosophical Conference" at his home in early January 1895, suggesting that Dorr attend in "his official capacity" as a member of the Philosophy Visiting Committee.[28] Such invitations were always welcomed, especially as Dorr knew that these events were unpredictable and always enlightening. Dorr also knew that, unlike his Harvard acquaintances, both he and James came to the discipline of philosophy without the constraints that are often the consequence of graduate studies.

Educated by tutors, James had acquired facility in French, German, and Italian that qualified him for entrance into medical school abroad, where he received his medical degree. The limitations of the scientific method, however, prompted him to apply the clinical perspective to the emerging discipline of psychology and the traditional problems of philosophy. It quickly became apparent to colleagues—and to Dorr—that James infused static philosophical issues with a dynamic perspective rooted in the biological sciences. He was increasingly compelled by empirical evidence to experiment with ideas and to find the meaning of these concepts in the practical difference they made. Even though James's pragmatic philosophy was still not fully formed, Dorr drew from his example as he took steps toward a profession that itself was rooted in the biological sciences.

Dorr later recalled that the Mount Desert Nurseries "sprang directly from my mother's Oldfarm garden, the first pleasure garden on Mount Desert Island."[29] Without acknowledging the horticultural impact of the Columbian Exposition in Chicago, Dorr declared in his memoirs that "my own interest in public reservations had an ancestry different from that of President Eliot and his son, for it had its root far back in old Salem and Medford gardens and the England from which they came." Indeed, his business would have pleased his horticultural-minded maternal grandfather.

Public demand for nursery stock also figured into the establishment of this commercial enterprise. As Dorr recounted, "the stream of visitors increased…and summer residences, simple or costly, were springing up on every available site along the shore. Flowers were in demand to make the bare hotel rooms beautiful and gardens around the new summer homes were everywhere in the making." Established in 1896, the nursery occupied twenty acres of Oldfarm property, well sited on lower Main Street on the heavily used road leading to Seal Harbor. The nurseries would initially focus on what Dorr called "old-fashioned" flowers that made the Massachusetts North Shore gardens, like their English counterparts, famous. Dorr's memoirs, unfortunately, provided more historical detail about early English gardening than about the four decades of his commercial venture. Nonetheless, he offered $50,000 of stock to capitalize the business and attracted highly qualified staff such as nursery manager William Miller to a year-round enterprise that had no rival on the island.[30]

Nursery plant stock was not limited to what customers expected from nurseries in Boston and Philadelphia. Summer residents might be partial to non-native species, but like his cousin Charles Sprague Sargent, Dorr offered for sale locally tested species appropriate for the rugged environment. This year-round operation achieved standing throughout Hancock County, and in due course customers from throughout New England would ask that a range of hardy herbaceous perennials, evergreens, vines, fruit trees, and deciduous trees and shrubs be shipped from Maine to their addresses.

In Cambridge, Dorr's service on the Harvard College Philosophy Visiting Committee demanded more of the new businessman. He was now committee chairman, a position he held for more than a decade. Professor Royce later asked Dorr to "look into our Philosophy work...[since] I know nobody, other than yourself, whose sympathy and criticism I should equally value as I should yours."[31] The committee provided the Harvard Overseers with a well-organized, thorough, and clearly articulated departmental analysis based on years of fruitful interaction with faculty and students.[32] Finding that the department "is doing work of great value...work wisely planned and well carried out," Dorr's committee recommended expanded roles for students in not only the selection of coursework but in the formalized sharing of the results of their inquiries. The objective was that "men hear their own work and that of their companions read, appreciated, criticized, and discussed not by their teacher alone but by one another."

This educational prescription would be generally accepted today although it certainly disturbed some Harvard faculty, many of whom at first resisted President Eliot's changes to the comfortable status quo. Nonetheless, philosophy faculty increased pressure on the university for new classrooms, laboratories for psychological research, and office accommodations befitting their academic standing. These expectations did not appear unwarranted at the close of the century, when the department was professionally without peer—a judgment reiterated three decades later by Harvard professor Bliss Perry: "By the tests of productivity and interesting personalities the leading department at Harvard, in 1900, was that of Philosophy."[33] In this unrivaled 'philosophical menagerie,' as senior professor George Herbert Palmer termed it, Josiah Royce and William James were now allied with Spanish aesthetician George Santayana and the German-trained psychologist—and department chairman—Hugo Münsterberg. He pressed the case that overcrowding conditions required a new facility dedicated to his discipline—a concern that was repeatedly filtered through Dorr and his committee.

In recent years President Eliot's son Charles had been successful in enlisting the support of the Trustees of Public Reservations and the Metropolitan Park Commission (MPC) in conserving open spaces throughout the urban and rural environments of greater Boston. Surveys of forested areas were undertaken and presented to the MPC, later published as *Vegetation and Scenery in the Metropolitan Reservations.* Eliot's research enabled community planners to identify specific sites and describe their environmental values. Other conservationists outside the United States had taken notice of the trustees. In Britain in 1895 the National Trust for Places of Historic Interest and Natural Beauty was established. The National Trust history credits Eliot's organization as "...the senior body...[whose] constitution deeply influenced that of the Trust."[34]

Beginning in 1895, Charles Eliot represented the Olmsted firm in development of a system of parks in Hartford, Connecticut, the birthplace of Frederick Law Olmsted. The firm of Olmsted, Olmsted & Eliot assisted the city in development of a planned system—a ring of parks like that in Boston. At nearly six hundred acres, Keney Park was the largest holding within the system, and Eliot's task was to draft general plans and prepare detailed drawings. Two years later, in March of 1897, as he finalized the course of the main road through a tract called Ten Mile Woods, he felt poorly and returned to his family in Brookline, Massachusetts. He had been stricken with cerebrospinal meningitis and within a week the thirty-seven-year-old Eliot died, leaving behind a wife and four children. As Henry James remarked in President Charles W. Eliot's biography, "the shock of this blow which fell without warning was almost prostrating to Eliot…[and] it was apparent that Charles's death submerged him in grief." No death among his family and friends had been "such a heavy loss and calamity as this one."[35]

In their sincerity and depth of feeling, the responses of faculty, family, and friends surprised him and signaled his arrival at "a truly cordial relationship with his associates at Harvard." Later, others would credit to President Eliot the establishment of The Hancock County Trustees of Public Reservations. At the 1916 ceremony celebrating the establishment of the Sieur de Monts National Monument, Judge Luere B. Deasy honored President Eliot for the land trust concept that led to "taking nearly half the hills of the island as a National Monument." Charles W. Eliot immediately set the record straight: The Trustees of Public Reservations model adapted for Hancock County, Maine, "my son not only conceived, but carried into effect."[36]

Within two years, Eliot began to organize and assemble his son's professional correspondence, public reports, landscape plans, diaries, travel writings, and other documents. Much of the detailed landscape content was unfamiliar and challenging, even to an exceptional administrator who was well accustomed to evaluating academic content. He found that he could not work on it in Cambridge; consequently, much of "Charles's book" was drafted in Maine. It contains the publication record of the landscape architect as well as a discrete and clear account of the life of the first-born son of Charles W. Eliot. The name of Harvard's president nowhere appears on the title page of the 1902 publication. The central claim of the seven-hundred-page tome, *Charles Eliot: Landscape Architect,* is that his son was the "perfect model for the young profession."[37]

CHAPTER EIGHT

Fin de Siècle

In 1962 Rear Admiral Samuel Eliot Morison completed the autobiographical *One Boy's Boston.* The Pulitzer Prize–winning historian vividly captured momentous events six decades earlier, describing his childhood memory of watching "the ceremonious ushering in of the new century from the balcony of the State House. We owed that privileged position to friendship with a gallant figure of the closing century, Governor Roger Wolcott. The Reverend Edward Everett Hale recited the Lord's Prayer in a sonorous voice…a cannon on the Common announced midnight, and every church bell in the city pealed forth. It was a high moment of hope and glory—peace and prosperity everywhere."[1]

In retrospect, Morison knew that dark clouds loomed on the horizon. In 1900 the first quantity-production automobile factory was built in Detroit. For the country as a whole no less than Mount Desert Island, "the internal combustion engine turned our economy upside-down and placed our society on a completely new basis. Life would never be the same again."[2] New towns were carved out of the forests, the course of rivers and streams were altered, and the landscape was flattened as wilderness regions were opened to more intensive logging.[3] At the same time, from Kittery to Bar Harbor the coastline offered the economic potential of summer resorts. Fueled by both the frenzy of development and a certain unease about it, railroad, steamship, and resort entrepreneurs celebrated Maine as the "true poetical conception of the wilderness in all its wild beauty, unpolluted by the march of modern progress."[4]

Romanticizing the rustic landscape was not at the forefront of the Eliot or Dorr families' concerns at this time. As Mary Dorr neared her eightieth birthday, she became more interested in an important preservation project undertaken by her son's sole surviving uncle, eighty-two-year-old Samuel Gray Ward. Despite the infirmities of his advanced age, Sam had recently begun to gather family memorabilia, intending to write an autobiography modeled on the one completed in 1825 by Sam and Mary's grandfather, William Ward. Sam remembered his grandfather's "Letter to my Grandchildren" as a vivid account of William's risky life as a privateer in the service of the rebellious Colonials and the voyages that led to his imprisonments in Wales by the British during the Revolutionary War.

In post-war years, William Ward's alliance with the phenomenally successful Salem ship owner and merchant William Gray led to Ward's prosperity—and later the marriage of his son, Thomas Wren Ward, to Gray's niece, Lydia Gray. Sam's objective was to merge the historic document with the one he intended to write, placing them in the hands of family members and friends following publication. That goal was driven by the value he attached to legacy. Sam hoped that his "son and grandson" would be enriched by this family history and continue it, adding "chapters of the story in their turn."[5]

Sam's strategy appears straightforward and commendable, yet he was unaware of the extent of family documentation that Mary possessed; since only Mary and Sam survived of the eight children of Thomas and Lydia Ward, if grandfather Ward's ancestry remained within the family it must have been with her. As he was no longer strong enough to travel from Washington, D.C., to New England to examine Mary's family manuscripts, she provided him with family documents that he requested, and apparently only these. Strangely, he played a game of charades—at which Mary was a known master—by downplaying the significance of the autobiographical letter: "In arranging my papers and notes it occurs to me that I always meant to have a copy of Grandfather Ward's little memoir. I believe there is a copy but I forget who has it." Surprisingly, Mary put it in the mail.[6]

Samuel Gray Ward's biographer described Ward's circumstances: "Writing from a sickbed at the age of 82 at the rate of only two pages a day... Ward was accurate enough in what he told, but he chose to be silent about important matters... [for] in his memoir there is no mention whatever of any critical writing, of any of his good works (including his vital help in launching the Metropolitan Museum of Art), and only the slightest mention of any of his success as American agent for Barings."[7]

In less than a year, Sam completed a 137-page autobiographical letter to his grandchildren. The twenty-nine chapters detailed his childhood, education, travels, marriage, careers, and friendship with Ralph Waldo Emerson, an important cultural profile by one of the last Puritan aristocrats. Published in 1900 at his own expense, *The Ward Family Papers* included the "letters" of William and Samuel G. Ward, genealogical details, correspondence, and family photographs.[8] Only three first-edition copies survive, one being a gift copy deposited in the Harvard College Library in late December 1900 by Samuel Ward's friend, Harvard professor of art and Dante scholar Charles Eliot Norton. From 1869 to 1907 Ward had sent no fewer than 130 letters to Norton. The year before *The Ward Family Papers* appeared, including Ward's own account of his relationship with Ralph Waldo Emerson, Professor Norton had midwifed publication of letters from Emerson to Ward covering the early years (1837 to 1853) of their relationship. Norton was convinced that these letters were historically significant in illuminating the nature of friendship.[9]

In the final days of the nineteenth century, Thomas Wren Ward Jr. had informed the Mount Auburn Cemetery superintendent that his mother, Anna Hazard Barker Ward, had passed away on October 28. His father, Sam, wrote to Mary a week later that "No one but you [is] left who can look back over the sixty years of our married life, which you knew from the beginning."[10]

But at another time, Sam expressed concern to Mary about the "ultimate disposition" of Ward family manuscripts, genealogies, correspondence, memoranda, and photographic images. He stated his conviction that family treasures should be transferred "while we are here to the next generation of the Ward name." Such foresight is commendable but it was also paternalistic and self-serving. There was only one male Ward descendant, his son, Thomas Wren Ward Jr. How Mary reacted to the exclusion of her own son is unknown. When *The Ward Family Papers* were published, Sam failed to acknowledge the contributions of other family members.[11]

Beyond such family squabbles, what attracts historians even today to *The Ward Family Papers* is the continuing historical relevance to Anglo-American business history of Thomas Wren Ward, Samuel G. Ward, and George C. Ward as the American agents—for sixty years—of the great banking family, the House of Barings.[12] Yet the publication contains only incidental financial and political information about Barings. Despite the urging of family friends, Sam states that "there were good reasons" for omitting an account of his business career.[13] But the omission of the professional activities of his father, himself, and his brother remained unexplained.

Dorr had the advantage of hindsight and offered an explanation, having spent years studying his ancestry and producing, by the 1930s, annotated typescript biographies of family members.[14] In one such *Dorr Papers* entry, he records that following his grandfather's retirement, Thomas Wren Ward planned to use his extensive correspondence with the Baring Brothers "in writing a history of his time.... But he unwisely mentioned it in a letter to one of the Baring firm."[15] Delayed by family travel abroad, the autobiographical project was nipped in the bud by his death in 1858. Fearful that elements of the thirty years of record-keeping might not serve their interests, Barings asked his successor, Samuel G. Ward, "to burn the whole, which he did, without ever examining the contents for historical material."

Dorr explained that this destructive act was brought to his attention in the late 1930s by no less an authority than Sam's son, Thomas Wren Ward Jr. Both men were by this time in their eighties and each had preserved family documents, in Dorr's case more than a dozen document boxes. The Ward family content spanned nearly two hundred years, an impressive collection of family correspondence, diaries, genealogies, and business correspondence. Of special importance are thirty years of Thomas W. Ward's correspondence with his close friend and Baring Brothers partner Joshua Bates. In addition to nine T. W. Ward diaries covering the Barings years, there are two decades of correspondence with Daniel Webster, who served as legal counsel to Barings in America.[16]

Though we primarily associate Dorr with the conservation of nature, it is significant that the conservation of cultural artifacts has been a largely unrecognized part of his legacy. He legally ensured that after his death this archive would be preserved *and* made accessible to the public. Within a mile of his Boston home on Commonwealth Avenue, his executors deposited Ward family papers with the Massachusetts Historical Society and a larger cache of Dorr family papers with the New England Historic Genealogical Society. As Cleveland Amory had said, the "grandfather on the brain" phenomenon persisted into the twentieth century—and Mary Ward Dorr's son surely was one of its practitioners. Yet there was a new element in the philanthropy of George B. Dorr—preservation was always linked with public accessibility.

Meanwhile, Mary Dorr was aging but still socially powerful. One of the final descriptions of Mary late in her life resulted from the three-day visit of poet John Jay Chapman and his wife Elizabeth, frequent Oldfarm guests for nearly a decade. Chapman's 1898 book *Emerson and other Essays* included passages in which Chapman attributed radicalism to the Sage of Concord, claims that must have aroused historical associations from Mary's youth. In his unpublished "Retrospections," he describes George's mother in the spring of 1900 as "one of the original transcendentalists, a friend of Emerson and Margaret Fuller. She gave large dinners and caused her guests to change places in the middle of the meal, called all women by their first names and all men by their last names. She had a low-pitched, authoritative voice, and was a tyrant; but dear me, what social talent!" Moreover, she "was highly educated, had lived in Europe and known the *literati,* great prelates, scientists, British countesses who drove about in phaetons. She loved fine bindings, religious essays, old Roman prints, good china, India shawls, and rosewood. Her pose was that she had known everybody intimately. Of course, all salons arise out of the ambition of clever women and the vanity of clever men whom they subtly flatter."[17]

Though her health was failing, Mary traveled with George to Lenox "after an absence of some seasons" (likely around 1898 or before) to look after the rented Highlawn residence, her last contact with the property that her son now owned.[18] George eventually chose not to retain Highlawn; by 1902 it had transferred to Robert Warden Paterson, a Scottish-born turpentine broker. Within the year, Highlawn was demolished and an extravagant new Tudor mansion stood amid the towering elms, copper beeches, and black walnuts planted decades earlier by the Dorrs' uncles, Francis and Albert.

Dorr's tie with Lenox, however, was not permanently severed. For the next six years, he would correspond with and visit a new Plunkett Street property owner he had first met in Bar Harbor in the 1880s, when the Rhinelanders first occupied their Reef Point shoreline cottage. New Yorker Edith (née Jones) Wharton purchased farmland in Lenox to experience "the joys of six or seven months a year among fields and woods of my own."[19] She designed her new Laurel Lake home, The Mount, and in the years ahead Dorr provided much-appreciated professional advice on the location and naming of gardens and paths.

In November 1902 Dorr left by train for Asheville, North Carolina, where he would celebrate the holidays with another Bar Harbor neighbor, George Washington Vanderbilt. In 1889 the intellectual and romantic twenty-five-year-old bachelor millionaire had purchased Watersmeet, the Gouverneur Morris Ogden residence near Oldfarm, which he renamed Pointe d'Acadie. But in the winter Vanderbilt resided in the milder mountain climate of the Great Smoky Mountains. Recently married to Edith Dresser, the family was celebrating the August birth of their daughter, Cornelia. Mr. Vanderbilt had also extended an invitation to Edith Wharton, who arrived on November 26, 1902, at the largest private residence in America—the Biltmore Estate—the day before Dorr himself arrived.[20] Surrounding this magnificent 250-room château was the 100,000-acre Biltmore Forest, where Dorr and Wharton surely shared their interest in the gardens and woodlands. The forest conservation efforts here began in 1889, when Frederick Law Olmsted reforested the valleys and mountains of this massive estate as part of his overall estate-landscaping plan.[21]

In August 1901, an unnamed acquaintance had written about Mrs. Dorr's condition to Boston artist Sarah Wyman Whitman. The news gave Whitman "a sad little pang, for I see how little can be done, and yet that vital spirit is so cabined by the persistent flesh. Ah well, I try to remember that she may be free from suffering in any such sense as this, and only waiting for the new freedom under a new sky." Two months later, in a letter to novelist Sarah Orne Jewett—best known for her novel *The Country of the Pointed Firs*—Whitman again referred to liberation: "Yesterday Mrs.

Dorr was set free after so long a captivity, and now one may believe walks freely in that sky at which she has sat looking for these months past."[22]

Louisa Endicott, Dorr's cousin (once removed), records in her diary that she saw George in early October 1901 after he and his mother returned to Boston from Bar Harbor. On the twenty-first, "Aunt Mary Dorr died quietly—in the afternoon—at her house, 18 Commonwealth Avenue."[23] Louisa reached Boston by train the next day and went to see cousin George, who took "LouLou"—as she was affectionately known—to Mary's room to see her remains. That same day a permit for burial was issued by the Boston Office for the Board of Health certifying "old age" as the cause of her death.[24]

More than two decades later one of Julia Ward Howe's daughters, author Laura E. Richards, felt strongly enough about Mrs. Dorr to compose an eight-page "sketch of this remarkable woman"[25] in which she described Mary's husband, Charles Dorr, as "one of the gentlest, sweetest, most amiable of men." In striking contrast, Mary "felt that she occupied the highest position in Boston or wherever she came or went. Arrogance is the word. She was the most arrogant person I have ever known. Brilliant, kindly, hospitable—all these to a high degree. People loved her and detested her, and everybody wanted to go to her house."[26]

Julia Ward Howe recorded in her *Journals* the timeliest commentary on Mary's death. "I am today in much confusion of mind. My friend in early youth and of many years, Mary Dorr, died on Monday, 21st.... Mrs. Dorr's death is a relief from much weakness and bodily infirmity. We were once very intimate but have grown apart, although I have regretted her seeming neglect of me in these last years. She was much interested in spiritualism and mind cure, both of which I eschew. Other and younger people have gathered around her, of which I am glad, yet a little jealous for the old friendship."[27]

Two days later Julia "went with dear Maud to Mary Dorr's funeral.... At the Dorr house found a wreath of laurel and violets over the usual crepe. [MIT English professor] Arlo Bates helped me up stairs, where George Dorr took me affectionately by the hand and seated me next to Thomas Ward, his uncle [sic, his cousin]. Rev. Frank Peabody was the minister.... Mary's old coachman, Bennett, stood beside George, at, I suppose, the foot of the casket, which was closed. Many old friends were there; no indifferent acquaintances I should think."

The next day, Julia "thought much about Mrs. Dorr's life and death. This last event opened to me such a panorama of retrospect—Mary's visit here in 1839, her engagement to my brother Henry, my visits to her in Boston, Henry's death, our intimacy of many years and her singular estrangement from me, during say the last five years. She always met me affectionately, but never sought me nor sent any greetings when I was ill or at other times. Remembering now the delight which I once had in her society, I am sad that our record closed with no postscript regarding the old affection. Of this she once said to my Maud: 'Your mother and I were once like hand in glove, but *I* have grown.'"[28]

Two weeks later, Charles Eliot Norton wrote to Samuel G. Ward: "The death of your sister has removed what I presume to have been one of the strongest motives for your coming [to Boston]. Her [death] deprives me of a very kind friend, and almost the only one who had many familiar memories in common with me of persons and places dear to us both in childhood and youth. I was very much at Ticknor's and the Guilds' in those days, and your sister's intimacy with my cousins led to our meeting frequently. She was a grown girl, I a little boy, but she treated me so pleasantly that I became much attached to her. What a worthy set of people lived on Park Street then, before Abbott Lawrence disturbed its tranquil dignity with his big new house!"[29]

George B. Dorr petitioned the Massachusetts Judicial Courts to probate his mother's 1897 will. Because George survived his mother, she assigned to him "all my estate, real and personal and I appoint to him all property" in which she had authority.[30] One important stipulation in Mary's will had significant consequences for historical inquiry into the inherited wealth of her son. Namely, Mary insisted that "no inventories or accounts" be undertaken at the time of her death. This concern for financial privacy was not uncommon. Rumors have persisted, nonetheless, over the last century that Mary Gray Ward Dorr left an estate valued from one to ten million dollars, claims that cannot be verified.[31]

Fortunately, Julia Howe's *Journal* offers important insights into how Dorr dealt with the death of his mother—and the historic consequences of the resolute advice Julia offered. Between 1901 and 1908 the two met on four occasions. Nearly two months after his mother's death, Julia—who had been inconsolable at the death of her father and brother—writes that

George called on her for "a long talk about the long past, and especially about my brother Henry who was engaged to George's mother. It seemed like getting into a crypt to recall the scenes of that distant time. He asked leave to call again tomorrow [when] he called again and brought a great number of letters to his father from my father and many other people. We had a good sitting together." As George shared more about Mary's unfulfilled engagement to Julia's brother in 1840, "which he had heard from his mother, the tears came and his voice faltered. As he rose to take leave, I said: 'Dear George, I love to go over the past with you, but you must not dwell on it too much. The future is before you; you must think of it.'"[32]

The death of Mary Dorr marked a new beginning for her son. The scholarly, middle-age gentleman so attracted to the world of ideas, who had been generously supported by his parents for nearly forty-eight years, must now chart his own course. His mother had been the steward of nearly two centuries of Ward family history. If George had not embraced this weighty responsibility, the depth and breadth of his later conservation of other cultural and natural resources in the years ahead would surely have been diminished. Fortunately, George B. Dorr heeded Julia Ward Howe's stern counsel to not be constrained by the past. Instead, her resounding imperative moved him to seize the opportunities now before him.

To be sure, Mary had been sufficiently prescient to recognize that the audience for the Ward family history was much larger than her immediate family. Over the last two decades she had also become mindful of her son's growing appreciation for the landscape of Mount Desert Island—and the forces that threatened it. Despite her lofty objectives that resonated with transcendental themes, Mary framed her renowned "hospitality" narrowly—confining it to the social circles of the aristocracy of her day.

For this small island to meet the challenges of the new century, Dorr recognized that elements of Mary's highly regarded hospitable skills should be adapted and applied to a new environment. George had been more than an observer of his mother's social networking skills. His later life would provide abundant evidence that the apple had not fallen far from the tree. But with her death, financial resources were put in his hands to shape Mount Desert Island's natural and cultural resources to benefit a far broader constituency than its aristocratic seasonal residents.

The late Ward-Perkins family archivist Donald Fitch captured the relevance of this privileged class when he wrote that the Wards, Dorrs, and others of their standing are of continuing interest because of their specific desire "to involve one's self culturally, politically, literarily and philosophically for the benefit of all."[33] Preserving family papers, conserving the island landscape, and shaping the development of new cultural institutions were forms of public service aimed at providing access—regardless of class, religion, ethnicity, or gender—to worthy objectives.

Dorr now set himself the task of championing the Brahmin principles of philanthropy and universality. As he described it in his memoir, *The Story of Acadia National Park*, the origin and development of Acadia began with an invitation from Harvard president Charles W. Eliot to extend the legacy of landscape architect Charles Eliot along the coast of Maine.

CHAPTER NINE

The Birth of the Trustees

After an unusually warm spring and early summer on Mount Desert Island, Charles W. Eliot sent invitations to a dozen island residents to join him for a meeting at Caroline Bristol's Music Room—still standing today on Rowland Road—on August 13, 1901. This familiar Seal Harbor meeting place was just a few miles east of Eliot's home in Northeast Harbor. In Bar Harbor, Dorr received an invitation and brought his neighbors George W. Vanderbilt, physician William J. Schieffelin, and railroad investor John Stewart Kennedy. This group arrived aboard Kennedy's yacht, but buggies were the means of transportation for Bishop William Lawrence and six others representing village improvement organizations. The far-reaching and historic consequences of this gathering were not anticipated.

Eliot's surviving son, Samuel Atkins Eliot, said that his father's discovery of Charles Eliot's 1889 "Coast of Maine" article motivated this gathering to further consider the feasibility of acquiring and maintaining public nature sanctuaries.[1] Now that his memorial biography of Charles was about to be published, his father wanted to practically apply his son's recommendation for the coast of Maine. Landscape historian Robin Karson argues that Harvard's president for the previous thirty-two years had fully grasped that his son had been first "to analyze landscapes as entities composed of layers of systems—cultural, economic, and ecological—while devising scientific methods for recording them, and implementing political measures to conserve them."[2]

Eliot's two decades of summering at Northeast Harbor convinced him that public use of private land had been curtailed by the new summer population. On the other hand, the philanthropy of some influential and gifted individuals contributed to improvements in the local infrastructure. Summer residents provided leadership in sanitation, road and trail development, and town beautification projects—not to mention support for churches, libraries, and community parks. Private ownership of land was "both the cause and remedy for the preservationist problem" that the new corporation would face.[3]

After extensive discussion, those gathered endorsed Eliot's vision to create the Hancock County Trustees of Public Reservations (HCTPR), dedicated to preservation of the wild beauty of the island. Eliot became the HCTPR president, George Dorr its vice president and executive officer, mineralogist Lea M. Luquer its secretary, and realtor George L. Stebbins its treasurer. These officers represented the Northeast Harbor, Bar Harbor, and Seal Harbor communities.

The conservation concept—as applied in Maine—largely originated with people "from away." Its implementation within the legal realities of Maine, however, was championed by three local attorneys. The Bar Harbor legal firm of Deasy and Lynam was chosen as counsel for the Hancock County Trustees.

A recent Boston University School of Law graduate, Luere B. Deasy had opened Eden's first law firm in 1884, and served as President of the Bar Harbor Banking and Trust Company from 1893 to 1929.[4] His partner, Albert Harry Lynam, mentored with attorney John A. Peters of nearby Ellsworth before admission to the Maine Bar in 1896. Attorneys Deasy, Lynam, and Peters played essential roles in HCTPR property acquisition as well as the founding and development of Acadia National Park.

On August 29, 1901 the eight charter members (or incorporators) of the HCTPR signed a legislative proposal for incorporation for "social, charitable and benevolent purposes."[5] Following additional discussion they added language to their draft that recognized the need for improvements such as "laying out and building roads and paths." On the same day that Theodore Roosevelt assumed the office of the president following President McKinley's assassination, the incorporators met again. The beginnings of the land trust movement in Maine thus dovetailed with the national inception of the Progressive Era. With its roots in the Populist politics of the late nineteenth century, progressive thinking was now united with a national conservation movement—and became a cornerstone of Roosevelt's domestic policies.

In the words of the second director of the National Park Service, Horace M. Albright, Roosevelt "glamorized conservation, emphasizing it at every turn. He got out into the woods.... He traveled extensively through the national parks and the national forests. No president before or since [had] been so active personally in covering the territory involved in conservation, nor in understanding and even participating in the use of its resources."[6]

By 1902 the village improvement societies of Bar Harbor, Northeast Harbor, and Seal Harbor had endorsed this new organization and were considering Luere B. Deasy's draft petition to the Maine Legislature, amended to include a statement that trustee lands shall be exempt from state, county, and local taxation. Added as well was a provision that the criteria for selection of land were "scenic beauty, historical interest, sanitary advantages, or other reasons."[7] A corporate charter was secured (Private Acts of 1903, Chapter 369) at the January 1, 1903 convening of the Legislature. Nearly forty years later, trustee treasurer Stebbins insisted that the "most important development in the history of the island was the establishment of the Hancock County Trustees of Public Reservations."[8]

This conservation commitment did not immediately result in systematic activity to secure donations of Hancock County property. The incorporators believed that opportunities would naturally arise. Consequently, a half-century later local author Sargent Collier would write that during these early years "...the corporation slept. No gifts were bestowed, no efforts made to acquire them, no toes stepped on."[9] Historical evidence shows, to the contrary, that membership did more than quadruple to fifty-five members during the first year. In 1903 two small parcels were donated—a hilltop site overlooking Jordan Pond and a twenty-four-and-a-half-square-meter site in Seal Harbor, set aside for a Champlain memorial plaque. The membership did not increase further until the first substantial properties were acquired, five years later.

Despite the general interest in the purposes of the conservation body, when Eliot returned to the island in 1903 he found roadways once bordered by trees and shrubs "now defaced by telephone poles bearing wires," the beauty of roadsides and bordering woods newly degraded by clear-cut areas, and the hillsides eroded "by heavy rains without the protection of good-sized trees [impairing] seriously the uses of the island for all summer residents."[10]

As a corrective to this state of affairs, in late 1903 Eliot published a widely circulated municipal planning document, *The Right Development of Mount Desert.* It reaffirmed the Hancock County Trustees' responsibility for holding *and* improving land in Hancock County for free public use—limited to property that had scenic, historic, or other distinguishing characteristics. Moreover, Eliot ambitiously argued that landscape principles, embraced by residents and codified in town statutes, should guide development throughout the entire island! Taking a cue from Frederick Law Olmsted Sr., Eliot outlined the restorative, re-creative influences of natural landscape on urbanites—what author William H. Wilson has called "a benign instrument of class reconciliation and democratization."[11]

Eliot understood that the appeal of the island as a resort was due to no fewer than four factors: "the cool and equable climate, the beautiful conformation of the island itself, the availability for sailing and fishing the waters that surround it, and the roughness and wildness of its hills and shores." In this slim fourteen-page community advancement tool, he cautioned that recent economic prosperity could only be increased—or at worse maintained—if one understood the "wants and wishes" dynamic; that is, the tension that exists between summer and year-round residents, a theme explored earlier in "The Forgotten Millions." Local residents should not take for granted their current status, he reminded them, for "it is hard to establish a successful summer resort, and easy to impair or degrade one already established." To promote "right development…the whole island ought to be treated by every resident, and by the body of voters, as if it were a public park."[12]

Implicit here is the conviction he shared with Dorr that the island's future must rest on something more secure than the flux and flow of man-made innovations. Although the trustees were mostly strong personalities with impressive accomplishments, Eliot recognized the dangers of unrestrained individualism. He had succeeded in uniting the incorporators in pursuit of a common good, as he wrote in *The National Geographic Magazine* a decade later: "Within the last 40 years a different form of liberty, the liberty of association and collective action, has begun to check some of the evils fostered by individualism, and so improve the human environment."[13]

Eliot, Dorr, and other trustees increasingly became aware that even as distant a place as Mount Desert Island was not exempt from the consequences of the quickening pace of life. Innovations were making distant locations more accessible. Marconi wireless radio transmitted signals across the Atlantic in 1901; cable laid across both the Atlantic and Pacific oceans in July 1902 enabled a message to be sent around the Earth in nine minutes; and the Wright brothers, five months later, accomplished the first controlled, sustained, heavier-than-air flight at Kitty Hawk.

It was the horseless carriage, however, that posed the greatest threat to the rustic tranquility of the island. Most residents initially opposed the intrusion of automobiles. By 1903 automobile opponents secured passage by the state legislature of ordinances to exclude these vehicles from specific highways in each island town. Local businessmen saw this legislation as a threat to their livelihood, and persisted for more than a decade to lobby for the repeal of these restrictions. Toward the end of the decade, Dorr began to speak publicly about the inevitability of this new mode of transportation, suggesting a compromise that enabled motorized access outside the borders of Bar Harbor.[14]

Far removed from Bar Harbor, Dorr's home on Commonwealth Avenue provided well-worn comforts, family associations, and convenient access to Harvard, where the urban pull of Cambridge on both him and Eliot remained powerful. Growth of the Harvard curriculum, student body, and faculty required consideration of enlarging the campus footprint. A few months after the establishment of the HCTPR, Dorr became secretary and treasurer of an alumni committee that aimed to raise sufficient funds to secure properties that, when gifted to Harvard, would enable the construction of an impressive Harvard Yard boulevard connection to the Charles River. The muddy banks of the Charles were to be transformed into an academic landscape that conformed to the urban vision of the City Beautiful Movement.[15]

The Harvard Board of Overseers resolved in 1894 to develop plans for the university's growth onto the unattractive Charles River waterfront.[16] Since Harvard had been slow to take an interest in this blighted area, an alumni committee letter bearing Dorr's signature was sent to Harvard graduates. It called their attention to the merits of constructing "a wide, park-like street connecting [Charles River] parkway with Quincy Square," providing a "dignified and suitable approach" from the Harvard Bridge to Harvard Yard.[17]

President Eliot insisted that external funds needed to be secured to cover the cost of property acquisition. Alumni contributions quickly reached $50,000 for the redesign of DeWolfe Street into an eighty-foot-wide boulevard to the Charles River; supplemental funding would still be needed from the city, state, and Park Commission. Dorr aroused the interest of Ralph Waldo Emerson's grandson, Edward Waldo Forbes, who rallied others to envision a more comprehensive plan that included all properties between DeWolfe and Boylston streets.[18]

For more than a decade, Harvard Overseer and attorney Francis R. Appleton Sr. worked with Dorr, Forbes, and his elder brother, banker W. Cameron Forbes, to raise sufficient funds to justify Harvard's acquisition of scores of properties that separated the Yard from the Charles River. In early February 1907, Dorr opened his home to Governor Curtis Guild, Cambridge Mayor Walter Wardell, and other prominent individuals who were receptive to discussion of the Boulevard Plan.[19] A Catholic school objected to the plan, but it was Cambridge politicians who balked at the expenses that would be borne by the city despite the $40,000 offered by Dorr's alumni associates. Appleton reported that Mr. Dorr "and I did everything we could think of to push the matter along and we guaranteed the $50,000...[but as a result of] opposition at the various hearings before the City of Cambridge Council... the project became politically impossible."[20]

Appleton then headed a new alumni group, the Harvard Riverside Associates (HRA), which succeeded in raising more than $400,000. Yet a decade would pass before the HRA acquired all but 22 of the 115 properties needed for the creation of this new Yard.[21] In 1913, the Associates would turn over their land holdings to the University, and construction of freshman dormitories would begin shortly thereafter. In several years a second Harvard Yard eventually emerged after Dorr's DeWolfe Boulevard model was altered by the new Harvard administration of President A. Lawrence Lowell, who would succeed Eliot in 1909. Dorr's vision for the quality of student accommodations, the aesthetics of the property, and its access corridors would ultimately be realized, and his leadership experience in the practical realities of institutional advancement proved useful elsewhere. The lessons learned through town planning negotiations with Cambridge government officials and the evaluation of urban roadways and construction of campus structures would soon be tested on Mount Desert Island.[22]

Another form of campus expansion made demands on Dorr's talents. In the opening years of the new century, the internationally celebrated Philosophy Department faculty were frustrated by the fact that their practical needs for office and classroom space—scattered throughout the Yard—remained unaddressed by the administration. In 1901 Philosophy Department Chairman Hugo Münsterberg escalated pressure on the university to address the needs of its most highly regarded faculty. Backed by Dorr's committee, approvals from President Eliot and the Harvard Corporation were secured.[23]

With building cost estimates ranging from $150,000 to $250,000, Albany legal scholar—and later federal judge—Learned Hand responded to the challenge by becoming the first donor in June 1901. In contrast, Massachusetts Supreme Judicial Court Justice Oliver Wendell Holmes declared that he would not "fork out for the philosophy department," nor would he ask others to contribute.[24] As one might expect, there was much discussion about an appropriately distinguished name for the building. Philosopher George Herbert Palmer (who had come to Harvard to teach in the same year that Dorr began his studies there) offered both a name and a persuasive rationale that quickly gained near-universal acceptance. In his view their new structure should commemorate a philosophical model peculiar to Harvard and New England. "Who other than the Sage of Concord, whose hundredth birthday was near, could aptly characterize the New England tradition and give an appropriate name to the home of philosophy at Harvard!"[25] Since college officials knew that extensive planning for the 1903 Ralph Waldo Emerson Centennial was underway throughout the country, they strategized how best to use the celebrations to expand—if not complete—their fundraising.[26]

One Concordian did not take the naming of a Harvard facility for his mentor in a singularly positive light. It awakened in journalist Franklin Benjamin Sanborn long-standing resentments about Emerson's earlier mistreatment by Harvard authorities following his famous 1838 "Divinity Address," wherein he challenged theological orthodoxy. Having received an invitation to a planning meeting at Dorr's residence, Sanborn's response emphasized that "the movement" at Harvard to establish Emerson Hall brought to mind another related mistreatment. Sanborn referred to the "paralysis of speculative philosophy which existed under [Professor Frances] Bowen in 1853–54" when he was one of Bowen's pupils; two decades later Dorr listened to Bowen's lectures on civic responsibility and moral philosophy.[27] Sanborn praised the Committee for the "wiser spirit [now] prevailing in his University. Much time has been lost...but we may now hope that the wider range and opportunity of the Department in which you have an official place will in some measure atone for the defects of past years."

Dorr's cordial response to Sanborn's "interesting letter" sidestepped Sanborn's criticisms entirely. Instead, he stressed the "high appreciation of Emerson's deep and ennobling influence" that were expressed recently in addresses by Eliot, Palmer, and Higginson. Dorr closed with the assertion that a sign of the vitality of the department was shown by its recognition that Emerson is "...the best exponent of its spirit. I trust our building may become his monument."[28] Two days earlier, William James had invited Dorr to hear physician Edward Waldo Emerson—then an art anatomy instructor at the School of the Museum of Fine Arts—read a paper on his father's philosophy. Due to family associations, it would be expected that these efforts would have drawn Dorr deeper into the spirit of the Emersonian Centennial.

Yet, following the credo of President Eliot, Dorr looked outward. A new educational opportunity that Harvard University promoted at this time—the use of scenic natural wonders as classrooms for instruction and research—attracted Dorr's attention. University faculty at Columbia, Chicago, and Harvard took their students and interested parties out West to examine the geology of proposed and existing national park sites.[29] Through his connections, Dorr learned that the Sturgis-Hooper Professor of Geology, William Morris Davis, was assembling a team of researchers. Since Dorr lacked first-hand experience of western flora, he was attracted to the opportunity to examine not only bedrock but what grew over it as well. He wondered whether the western parklands had biological and geological commonalities with the island landscapes that the HCTPR was intent upon conserving. Prior to his July 1902 departure for the Southwest, he asked the Curator of Harvard's Gray Herbarium for botanical advice, specifically for "studying the flora and forest growth of Arizona and Utah" as well as Oregon, Washington, and the Canadian Rockies. In the spirit of Julia Ward Howe and her imperative to seize the day, the esteemed geologist encouraged Dorr's involvement, and in Dorr's memoirs he notes arrangements "to meet Professor Davis in southern Utah and join him in an expedition down the western side of the Grand Canyon."[30]

A 1903 letter survives from Eugene Lusk Roberts, then a college-age expedition member, written to Dorr six months after the completion of the Davis Team's geological field work. Roberts credits Dorr with the motivation for his new scholastic efforts and elevated ideals. Among his vivid memories: "the sun-set we witnessed while riding together into Kanab after the Buckskin trip."[31]

Years later, in an unpublished autobiography, Roberts spoke again about Mr. Dorr's appreciation for a natural environment quite unlike that of New England. Dorr "called my attention to the beauty of the desert landscape, the purple hazes, the brilliant sunsets, the savage grandeur of barren mountains sculpted into grotesque shapes. He led me to observe the fierce struggle going on between desert plants and desert animals fighting for life sustaining moisture. I shall always be grateful to the Boston bachelor… for guiding me into a new world."[32] Eugene's father was sufficiently moved by the positive effect of this fieldwork on his son's character that he visited both Dorr and Davis in Boston to express his appreciation.

In Dorr's mind, the educational objectives of the Davis expedition were fully realized. This fieldwork provided him with models of landscape preservation at the national scale. A more important asset of the Sawtelle Research Center is a copy of "Two National Monuments," his published 1916 memoir of Zion National Monument. Like Eugene Roberts, Dorr was awed by "the immense solitudes of that region…a region of strange contrasts of sterility and life in the plant world. The land that water reaches blossoms like a garden; what water fails to reach is desert."

Dorr used the language of the naturalist, infusing the observations of the field biologist with personal anecdotes—as was his habit. His essay also contained a biographical anecdote about the onset of a sudden illness that resulted in his becoming separated from his traveling companions. He described his solo meanderings for the next two days in a highly hostile environment, "a stranger who had lost his way." Yet there was a positive result, "one memory that I have always cherished." The discovery of a spring of water where the "rich color-contrast of the fronds and rock, the fresh green hue and splendid vigor of the fronds themselves, and the delight of the water dripping quietly down made an impression on me in that arid region which is as fresh today as then."[33] The deep attachment Dorr felt for the Sieur de Monts Spring site on Mount Desert Island resulted also from encounters with other natural springs on his European travels. None, though, were as vital to his survival as the Zion spring.

During that same year, Professor Davis and Dorr joined five other charter members in the establishment of the Harvard Travellers Club, to promote intelligent travel and exploration. Under Davis's presidency, an international cast of speakers addressed members on foreign sites from the Andes to Abyssinia, discussing themes as varied as the Byrd South Pole expedition and the economic value of plants. Dorr was involved in managing the direction of the club, arranging for the second club gathering to take place at his 18 Commonwealth Avenue home, the first such meeting held in a private residence.[34] For three decades, he remained involved with the club and his colleagues. They shared their philosophy with Homer's Ulysses: to strive, to seek, to find, and not to yield.

Just prior to Thanksgiving 1902, Dorr and Davis traveled to North Carolina. Frederick Law Olmsted Jr. joined them in Asheville "to climb Mt. Mitchell and to see something of the forest region round about it."[35] The summit of Mount Mitchell, at 6,684 feet, the highest peak in eastern North America, was a challenging climb made riskier by the seasonal lateness of their ascent. Following the descent, on Thanksgiving Day, Dorr was one of eighteen formally attired guests served up to ten courses on the twelve-foot-wide oak dining table in America's largest private home.[36] In the fifteen years since his friend George Washington Vanderbilt had first visited Asheville, Vanderbilt's 250-room French Renaissance château had been erected, the Biltmore gardens had been developed by Frederick Law Olmsted Sr., and a vast, impoverished landscape was replanted under the supervision of Gifford Pinchot, a forester who would later serve as the first chief of the

U.S. Forest Service. On this second visit to the estate, Dorr encountered his friend Edith Wharton, who sent him a letter on his forty-ninth birthday expressing hope that she "might claim that dinner you were kind enough to promise us if we came to Boston for a few days before sailing."[37]

Despite his success in such social encounters, Dorr was having trouble securing pledges for Emerson Hall. One committee member reported to President Eliot that donations had stalled.[38] Unknown to the committee and Eliot, the clergyman who had presided at Mary Dorr's funeral, the Reverend Francis G. Peabody, was at that time in New York City visiting a friend who eventually provided the needed cornerstone gift.

For more than two decades, Peabody taught a highly popular course in social ethics at Harvard. The dominant theme of this Progressive theologian was that the wealth produced by an increasingly industrialized society was being abused. "They have learned to get, but have not learned to use... ownership involves obligation. Service is the only way to freedom. A rich man may be worth having if he use his peculiar faculties for benefiting society."[39]

The philanthropist and real estate developer Alfred T. White was Peabody's host in New York. White was a Brooklyn engineer-turned-merchant whom Peabody had known since 1880, when the Harvard theologian visited the real estate developer known for his innovative construction of the most advanced tenement villages. Today "tenement" has deep negative connotations, but in White's era such villages included fireproof construction, outside stairways, interior parks, and playgrounds; and were exceptional working-class communities where infant mortality was halved.

Peabody and White shared not only the articles of their Unitarian faith but Progressive values that stressed social reform. Peabody, however, took ethics in a new direction by combining it with empirical studies of social movements. He dramatically altered the discipline of ethics from a theoretical classroom exercise into a social science that connected ethical inquiry to the social life of the individual.[40] His course work required that students study, analyze, and compose papers on such topics as slums, settlement houses, temperance problems, and workforce exploitation.[41]

White wondered aloud what he could do to make social service easier for others than it had been for him. He asked Peabody how he might help young men in Harvard College address contemporary social problems. Peabody's self-serving response was that White might leave an endowment at Harvard for social ethics instruction.[42] Unknown to Dorr's committee, White pledged $50,000, the largest single Emerson Hall benefaction. The donor attached three conditions: that by Commencement Day, Harvard must raise the remaining funds, space in Emerson Hall must be assigned to "a department of social questions" in proportion to the donation, and there must be assurances of White's anonymity.[43] These lessons were not lost on Mr. Dorr.

President Eliot and the Harvard Corporation immediately accepted these terms, despite the change that the conditions of White's gift would bring to the intellectual scope and physical character of Emerson Hall. Dorr further realized that success would be achieved by optimizing circumstances unanticipated by the best-laid plans. What had been a personal and temporary effort had, through White's gift, been institutionalized and made permanent.[44] With the Emerson Centennial only a month away, Dorr was further buoyed by the news of Münsterberg's success in securing a $12,000 gift from industrialist and philanthropist Andrew Carnegie.[45]

Despite a shortfall of $8,500, Eliot was heartened. He informed Dorr that he would report to the Harvard Corporation that the Emerson Hall subscriptions would be completed. University planners began the process of locating the site and removing the Quincy Street home of the renowned geology professor Nathaniel Shaler, which was aligned to the west with Sever Hall in the heart of the campus. Architect Guy Lowell was engaged as the institution took the necessary preparatory steps. Lowell was married to a daughter of Dorr relative and Arnold Arboretum director Charles Sprague Sargent; he had recently designed Harvard's Lowell Lecture Hall.[46]

Dorr kept active the relationship that the Ward family had established seven decades earlier with mathematician Nathaniel Bowditch. His grandsons were firmly entrenched Harvard professors roughly a decade older than Dorr. Physician Henry Pickering Bowditch and his younger brother Charles, a Mayan archaeologist, planned with Dorr a spring vacation that overlapped the Emerson Centennial. Without mentioning the celebration, Dorr informed President Eliot in May 1903 that he was about to embark on an "eight or nine day riding trip" through the Shenandoah Valley and Blue Ridge mountains.[47]

On May 11 rail transportation took them to Charlottesville where a carriage transported the threesome to Lexington, the Natural Bridge, and on to Hot Springs. There the allegedly curative baths relaxed their sore limbs before the return to Boston, arriving two days after the centennial events.[48]

Dorr's absence from this celebration is perplexing. Of course, he was not needed to quietly solicit funds since in this context it was a Philosophy faculty responsibility. Given the closeness of his uncle Samuel Gray Ward to Mr. Emerson, Dorr certainly would have been welcomed by historically centered Concordians, even if he were not a Harvard alumni advocate for Emerson Hall. Grief over the death of his mother a year and a half earlier might have prompted him to continue to pursue new travel opportunities. Nonetheless, for reasons that are not disclosed, the self-effacing Dorr removed himself from the limelight.

The May 25 celebration was about Emerson the man, after all, not Harvard the institution. Even though funds were still needed to cover the internal outfitting of the structure, Chairman Münsterberg's address at Concord made clear that the necessary Emerson Hall funds had been secured through the efforts of Dorr's committee. Elsewhere, churches of varied denominations celebrated Emerson's life. Dozens of lectures were given between Boston and Concord alone. National publications reprinted selections from Emerson's works, and essayists assessed his accomplishments. Even the Handel and Haydn Society praised his life in Boston's Symphony Hall.[49]

Standing in the shadows of the Concord celebration was Herbert Wendell Gleason, who had been employed as event stenographer by the Social Circle of Concord. Gleason's medium of communication, however, was photography. His Merrimack Valley landscape photographs had recently achieved regional recognition. These graphic images were the result of Gleason's resolve to identify and photograph the physical locations for narrative passages in the writings of Henry David Thoreau. Gleason's main energies, however, would be devoted to graphic documentation of the scenic splendors of the national parks, and to that end he would spend many months on Mount Desert Island.

Intrigued with Gleason's approach—and desiring to improve marketing appeal—Houghton Mifflin & Co. proposed that a selection of his hundreds of Merrimack Valley photographs be integrated into the twenty-volume 1906 Walden edition of *The Writings of Henry David Thoreau*.[50] Prior to that publication date, Dorr and Gleason likely befriended one another at meetings of the Boston Camera Club or at Gleason's highly successful lectures on travel and nature study, which were illustrated using lantern slides hand-colored mostly by his wife. Over the next two decades he would travel the country offering his "National Parks of America" slide show as one of more than thirty topics available for audiences.[51]

Nearly a hundred miles west of Concord, Edith Wharton was developing her gardens at The Mount in Lenox, Massachusetts. In midsummer 1904 Dorr visited Lenox at Wharton's invitation to help her resolve "landscape gardening" problems. Following his departure for the West Coast, Wharton sent the second of eight surviving letters to his Commonwealth Avenue home informing him that after his departure she found one of his books on the terrace. She thanked him for his help with landscape design problems, flattering him by stating that he left behind "so many fruitful ideas that I often feel that you are not gone, and must be somewhere about, ready to answer the new questions."[52]

Most importantly, Wharton informed him that "...your path is finished, & the task of planting its borders now confronts me; & we are just about to attack the laying out of the path from the flower-garden to the little valley which is to be my future wild garden." These letters demonstrated Wharton's sincere appreciation of Dorr's horticultural counsel. Since "the Dorr path" was the only physical feature of her estate named for a person, it is reasonable to conclude that this was at the very least an explicit acknowledgment of the value of his counsel.[53] She also referred in this letter to Dorr's trip west, hopeful that "you may be able to spare us a day or two on your return" when the autumn work will be nearly over and future plans can be discussed unless "my pigmy [sic] planting will quite vanish from your mind among the giant boles of the redwoods."

In late August of 1904, the fifty-year-old bachelor arrived by rail in the Sierra Nevada Mountains. Unlike the Southwestern exploration two years earlier with the research team of Professor Davis, on this adventure Dorr would travel alone or in the company of a guide. Immediately upon his return to Bar Harbor, he typed a forty-page memoir, "A Trip through the California Sierras," and sent it off to his neighbor and close friend, attorney

David Ogden. With the exception of correspondence, this is the earliest sustained narrative by George B. Dorr that has survived; it is preserved in the Acadia National Park archives.[54] Fortunately, philosopher Josiah Royce had anticipated what his friend would encounter in his native California and had arranged for Dorr to first visit the University of California. At Berkeley, president Benjamin Idea Wheeler, a comparative philologist whose disciplinary interests were shared by Dorr, welcomed his Boston visitor. Because of Royce's connections, Dorr was then introduced to faculty who were members of the Sierra Club.[55]

From Berkeley, Dorr first traveled south by rail along the California coastline, using his horticulturist's eye to assess the cypress of Monterey prior to stops in Santa Barbara, Los Angeles, and Santa Catalina Island. Dorr set out on a remarkable journey into territory rarely seen by those of European descent. Dorr's sole companion was a packer, who coincidentally was a "Maine man originally, and of my own name [Frank Dorr]." Contemporary Sierra packer and historian Raymond DeLea Jr. writes that Dorr's adventure was "quite unique…[and did not become] commonplace until the 1930s and 1940s when the park service began constructing trails for pack animals."[56] They headed north for 220 miles through Visalia to Sequoia National Park and territory that in 1940 would be designated Kings Canyon National Park. George was intrigued—perhaps even mesmerized—by the scale and diversity of the landscapes at hand. Though he nowhere stated the motivations for this trip, as he traveled he read naturalist John Muir's descriptions of the remote areas. Dorr's unpublished letter to Ogden is significant for it details the exploration of a demanding landscape, a vast and little-visited wilderness, through the eyes of a man—like Muir himself—with national parks ever-present in his thinking.

Over the next three weeks, Dorr experienced the natural splendors of both Sequoia and General Grant national parks (the latter now absorbed within Kings Canyon National Park) which "were practically one, separated only by a few miles of trail…[and] there was nothing but a local camp to which the people from the valley below came up for refreshment in the heat of the summer."[57]

Their route east from the Giant Forest through Mineral King and along the Kern Canyon would take them on repeated ascents and descents of five thousand feet. Dorr's account includes extended descriptions of the local flora, including an arborist's conjectures about climate, moisture requirements, and species competition. Distracted, on more than one occasion he was unintentionally separated from his guide for hours. Finally they intersected the new pack trail up the east side of Mount Whitney. As Dorr later reported in his letter to David Ogden, they once again "lost the trail completely, buried in the snow which was up to our knees."[58] Finally, they reached the summit!

Two years earlier Dorr had climbed the highest mountain east of the Mississippi River. He had now conquered the highest mountain in the contiguous United States; at 14,500 feet it was twice the height of North Carolina's Mount Mitchell. They traveled eastward and reached "one of the most magnificent scenes I have ever looked upon, the Owens Valley." Over many days, the two men traversed the rim of the Owens Valley, which lay six thousand feet below. In due course they left the mountains behind and spent time with the ranchers, talking to them "about the limitations they have run up against, the difficulties and drawbacks and faults of climate."[59] Leaving Independence, they traveled west and north of their route to Mount Whitney, finally ascending trails just south of Yosemite National Park. Another week of trekking southwest returned them to the Giant Forest. After a brief visit to Yellowstone National Park, a rail journey east then took Dorr back to Boston.

Dorr's impressive account reveals that his interests were botanical, centered on the character of the ancient forest and the life cycle of the giant sequoias that clustered together in groves and soared skyward for 275 feet. Their sheer height, however, reduced the available sunlight for herbaceous garden plants—gentians, penstemons, and columbine—that lay "along the banks of streams alone, or here and there in patches upon slopes kept moist by soaking down from the springs above."[60]

His memoir includes episodes reminiscent of Muir's writings, as when he fell asleep following a lengthy trek and when awakening felt "a delightful sense of absolute repose and far away detachment from all earthly things."[61] As with Muir, small natural splendors soon wrested him back to reality. Always partial to swimming, Dorr joined a large trout swimming in a bitterly cold Sierra pool. When separated from Frank Dorr—in this instance in the Kings River Canyon—Dorr emotionally recounted the anxiety and frustration of his plight until he wandered back into familiar foothills where their journey had begun.

In the span of two years, Dorr had explored landscapes incorporated into Zion, Grand Canyon, Kings Canyon, Sequoia, Yosemite, and Yellowstone national parks. Only the latter three were formerly established prior to his arrival; the remainder he experienced in their formative stages. At the time, these two trips could be seen as ends in themselves. Nonetheless, exposure to geological, botanical, and climatic conditions were also the means of informing his thought and action for the remaining four decades of his life. Dorr's modesty prevented his speaking about the western adventures to anyone—except those who later would champion the establishment of the National Park Service. As he journeyed east by train, taking notes for his memoirs, he surely thought about how the "majesty, sublimity, order, stability, cleanliness, [and] complete absence of humanity" emphasized by John Muir could be applied to Mount Desert Island.[62]

CHAPTER TEN

Gatherings

During the first decade of the new century, buildings were being added throughout the villages of Mount Desert Island. Fifty-three commissions were undertaken between 1900 and 1909 by local architect Fred Savage, the majority being new private residences.[1] Combining these projects with those undertaken by other architectural firms, landscaping became more profitable.

One indication of this prosperity was the opening of a downtown-Eden branch store for the nurseries. From its inception in 1896, horticulturist William Miller had managed the Mount Desert Nurseries, sharing with Dorr a "vision to build one of the best plant collections in the Northeast."[2] *The Bar Harbor Times* would report in 1912 that Arnold Arboretum arborist A. E. Thatcher would succeed Miller and that contractors planned to carry out Savage's plans for a forty-eight-foot-long photograph exhibition gallery at the nursery, to display Dorr's "unrivaled collection of [garden images as well as] photographs of the Wild National Parks of the West."[3]

During the winter of 1905 Dorr was working in Boston on the itinerary for a trip to Oregon and Washington when an unexpected opportunity arose. William James asked Dorr to travel with him aboard *The Romantic*, bound for Naples and then Greece. Perhaps with an oblique reference to the absence of motherly constraints, James says: "Now's your chance! I have a stateroom which you can share, if you like, an inside; only $90 to Naples. Pray come." But several afflictions forced James to delay the trip for two months.

In mid-June, Dorr departed for Mount Desert Island following another stay with Edith Wharton at The Mount. He found the Eliot family settled in for another Northeast Harbor summer.[4] One topic of discussion was the just-published *Mount Desert: a History* by the recently deceased New Hampshire Congregational minister George E. Street. As the publication was still in a very rough state at the time of Street's death, his family asked President Eliot's son, the Reverend Samuel A. Eliot, to complete the work. "Eliot thereupon radically altered the format of the book…into a continuous historical narrative," resulting in acclaim that resonates to this day.[5]

A half-century later that Unitarian cleric's wife, Francis Hopkinson Eliot, delighted *The Atlantic Monthly* readers with her reminiscences of early twentieth-century Mount Desert Island family gatherings—to which Dorr would occasionally be invited. These "patriarchal" picnics that took place during the summer months were usually full of guests and relatives, especially the grandchildren. Dr. Eliot passionately wanted the children to spend their summers learning how "to swim and sail and ride and explore the woods and the mountainsides." He "was the prime mover, the organizer, the enthusiast." As Francis described him, the public thought of Harvard's president as "awesome and unapproachable. His children and grandchildren did not find him so…. He was a man of action rather than words."[6]

All who summered with the Eliot family felt great attachment to the natural landscape. Their outdoor gatherings were more often than not vigorous excursions. Three generations of Eliots and their guests would climb aboard a carriage that took "the cavalcade" to the foot of a mountain. Disembarking, they then plodded up steep slopes. Francis recalled that "a climb in those early days was one of dogged determination, decorum, and sweat. Once on the mountaintop, the elders would nap, the young people would pick blueberries, and everyone enjoyed the beauty all around….Once, I remember, when picnicking on Flying Mountain, a small hill with open pastures down to the sea, the elders staged a race. At seventy [in 1904], President Eliot sprinted down the hill followed by a bevy of stout, well-corseted ladies holding up their skirts, with veils flying as they dashed to the bottom."[7]

Returning to the more formal confines of Harvard Yard, in October 1905 Eliot delivered an address of lasting significance to the students on how they might profit from the values that guided his life. Now in the thirty-sixth year of his presidency, Eliot's concern for the public good became more pronounced as he aged. A profoundly private man, life experiences convinced him "that there were some things that lasted, that endured, that were worth keeping." These self-described "durable values" had shaped his entire life and profoundly influenced his landscape aesthetic.

In the essay "Great Riches," Eliot showed that there was a rarely recognized flaw in the use of wealth to maintain and improve private estates. "In this country it is difficult to pass down to another generation large holdings of lands, at least with any assurance that the holdings will be kept...[for] estates inherited through three generations are rare in the United State[s]."[8] This was a cold, empirical fact that Eliot, Dorr, and other trustees—in both Massachusetts and Maine—employed in discussions with prospective donors. Its currency was underscored by Eliot's friend, the Reverend Francis Greenwood Peabody, who noted in his biographical essay on Emerson Hall donor Alfred T. White that "a still rarer trait in the wise use of wealth is persistency. Much giving, even by generous people is occasional, spasmodic, and transitory. An object is temporarily interesting, but the giver soon passes to the next benefaction."[9]

Eliot continued, "In the neighborhood of large cities almost the only way to make sure that an estate...will remain in good condition is to get the estate converted into a public domain...[where] chances are that all improvements will be maintained and that care will be taken to preserve all its landscape beauties." Dorr may have been foremost in Eliot's mind when he concluded that "it is only a generous and public-spirited man, however, who looks forward with satisfaction to this fate for fields and forests which have become dear to him."[10]

Surely Eliot must have wondered what Dorr had done to preserve the "landscape beauties" of Oldfarm. In late summer 1905, Dorr touched on that issue when he wrote that he was "straightening out my boundaries from time to time, by exchanges with my neighbors and by purchase."[11] Though it was likely an inconsequential matter to Eliot, Dorr brought to his attention the fact that abutting Oldfarm were two acres of undeveloped land with no road access; property that was part of a recent bequest to Harvard College.[12] Dorr then offered to purchase the Harvard property to secure a protective corridor against the building plans of a new owner.

Real estate attorney David B. Ogden agreed to evaluate Dorr's proposal and after careful study reported to Eliot that the land "in itself [is] of no intrinsic value, considered alone."[13]

Dorr's offer of easements through his land for water pipes, sewer, and electrical utilities to the Harvard property would have made the property marketable, yet by the by the fall of 1906, the institution having deemed it too isolated to serve a timely purpose, Dorr had purchased it.[14] Nothing in the documentation suggests that the sale of the property rewarded Dorr for his service to Harvard.

Yet again, returning to Boston for the winter, Dorr received two invitations. Philosophy Chairman Hugo Münsterberg thanked him for his "generous energy" in making Emerson Hall a reality, inviting him to a full day of activities on December 27, 1905.[15] Similarly, Josiah Royce asked Dorr to the philosophical and psychological meetings on the 29th, Dorr's fifty-second birthday. Unfortunately, an unexpected private controversy erupted, undermining the high spirits that should have characterized these proceedings.

After the formal opening, the first use of Emerson Hall was for the two-day joint meeting of the American Philosophical Association and the American Psychological Association. The most prominent national and international figures in both disciplines passed the impressive bronze figure of Ralph Waldo Emerson in the main corridor. They were attracted to this celebration in large part because of the incomparable stature of Harvard's philosophy faculty and the formal institutional recognition given to both disciplines.[16]

Hugo Münsterberg presided over the event and made the introductions. In the audience, Dorr's friend, poet John Jay Chapman, was displeased with the behavior of the chairman. Chapman later recalled that the program speakers were poorly served by Münsterberg's introductions: "Of course, he made a self-glorifying harangue between each one of them. He danced upon the lid of Harvard, while all the professors gripped their umbrellas and ground their teeth. [William] James, on leaving the hall, went home and wrote to Münsterberg such a letter as made the retirement of one or the other of them inevitable."[17] A copy of the letter also went to President Eliot. James accused the chairman of behavior inconsistent with the previously agreed upon event roles for philosophy faculty. The intent was that no voices "save the President's and Edward Emerson's should be heard."[18] To ignore the threatening implications of this disagreement was not an option for either Eliot or Dorr's alumni committee.

Professor James was scheduled to leave for California the next day. He had arranged with Stanford University president David Starr Jordan to spend a semester organizing Stanford's new philosophy department. In the wake of the Cambridge conflict, speculation arose over whether James might choose to remain on the West Coast. Münsterberg responded to James by immediately submitting his letter of resignation.[19] James defended his "irritation" with Münsterberg's "excessive prominence" throughout the celebrations, yet told Eliot that he was remiss in not being more directly involved in the preparations. He urged Eliot not to accept Münsterberg's resignation, the president agreed, and the controversy quietly died. This untimely academic conflict signaled more than the clash of forceful personalities. The historical tensions between the "queen" of the rational sciences and the empiricism of its psychological offspring had come to a head during an event celebrating their intellectual kinship.

President Eliot had already stated that the new building did not bear Emerson's name because he was a psychologist or a philosopher. Eliot explained that these were systematic disciplines and Emerson was more than that, "a poet and a prophet many of whose prophesies have already been fulfilled. He was a political, educational, and religious seer...a genuine New Englander, but also an American in the broadest sense. Hence the University has found his work and character eminently fit for commemoration."[20]

Edward W. Emerson, the son of the Sage of Concord, gave the keynote address, extending his appreciation to Dorr's committee for the invitation to speak. Dr. Emerson elaborated Eliot's thesis, offering a surprisingly frank portrait of the intellectual development of one who "could not follow systems," who was lauded for his Phi Beta Kappa speech and shortly thereafter "condemned by most of the faculty of the College" for his Divinity School remarks. His father's life, after all, could not be contained by celebrated local recognition inasmuch as he "obeyed a higher call, to be, in his country, a teacher-at-large for life, of the theory and practice of Philosophy for the People."[21]

After this academic disruption in Cambridge, Dorr welcomed the opportunity to open his residence for "good talks on horticulture, free-will and predestination" with Edith Wharton. But the visit was postponed and instead the witty John Jay Chapman was his houseguest for more than a week. As always they enjoyed each other's company, especially Chapman, who wrote to a friend that "I've been here for a week staying with George Dorr and revisiting the glimpses of the moon—Porcellian, Somerset, and Tavern etc. Really I have enjoyed myself. What a world it is—of friendship and tie. There are twice as many people about here that I know and care for—ten times as many—as there are elsewhere all over…."[22]

Chapman was referring to the Boston clubs that Dorr was very much attached to throughout his adult life, especially from 1905 to 1935. As Dorr drifted away from his biological family, he nested within the habitat of these congenial urban male enclaves. As he grew older, these familiar haunts provided him with delightful company and (when he sought it) solitary relaxation. In this buffered environment, he could think through a particularly vexing problem, draft letters outlining his position, and discuss possible implications with those who had no vested interest.

More than a hundred social men's clubs had been organized in Boston since the antebellum era. Some attracted individuals with specific interest in literature and art (e.g., St. Botolph's) or book collecting (The Club of Odd Volumes). Drawn to listen to brief papers on topics of diverse interest, the members were the sons of Brahmin families, Harvard-educated, and leaders in their respective areas of competence.

Club facilities—mansions, really—were usually not far removed from members' homes, and many included accommodations for temporary or permanent residence. Custom dictated that it was "bad form to introduce oneself (one is supposed to *know*), and actually offensive to identify one's job or standing in the world." The physical character of the mansion, its décor, comfortable chairs, library, and staff demeanor were not the only incentives for membership. Partaking of fine French fare, sipping the choicest of brandies, and enjoying the after-dinner smoke in congenial company, all had the effect of binding members—perhaps as much as anything they had in their homes—to a common world of things that were believed to endure.[23]

The Dorr precedent for membership had already been established by grandfathers, fathers, and uncles on both sides of his family. Upon graduation from Harvard, Dorr became a dues-paying member of the Somerset Club, widely regarded as the most prestigious of the Boston clubs—the hub of The Hub.[24] For sixty-four years Dorr renewed his membership in large part because of its enduring qualities that harkened to an earlier era. Its collegial ambience suited his temperament as he reflected on what was needed to change the culture on Mount Desert Island. Relying heavily on the Somerset Club after he sold his Commonwealth Avenue residence, he finally allowed his membership to lapse when he was eighty-four years of age and living year round in Bar Harbor.[25]

In his thirties, Dorr had begun long-standing memberships in the Union Boat Club and the University Club. At fifty, he accepted an invitation to become a member of the less-formal Tavern Club, "made up of old and young, distinguished and undistinguished, artists, actors, musicians, literary men, amateurs, and professionals."[26] There, Dorr was often found in the company of Henry and William James, John Jay Chapman, Oliver Wendell Holmes, Robert Grant, and George Santayana. And in the years ahead when consultation with National Park Service officials required extended stays in the nation's capital, Dorr would become a member (from 1921 to 1934) of the most celebrated Washington club for public-policy intellectuals, The Cosmos Club.[27]

At the 1905 annual meeting of the Tavern Club, Dorr enthusiastically involved himself in a presentation by landscape photographer Herbert Gleason. He invited Harvard's Gray Herbarium faculty and staff to view Gleason's images of wildflowers and scenic splendors taken in the Canadian Rockies. President Eliot was "sorry to miss the pleasure you offered me" since he had seen Gleason's photographic work and knew "its merit."[28] Whether Dorr was in the audience of a thousand that attended Gleason's April 1908 Huntington Hall lecture before Appalachian Club Mountain members we cannot say. However, the "Glories of the Sierras" illustrated lecture surely would have interested him, following his exploration of the region four years earlier.[29] He could not anticipate how vital would be Gleason's role in advancing public appreciation at a national level about the landscape of Mount Desert Island.

By the spring of 1906, the James family had not yet returned from California. William's wife, Alice Howe Gibbens James, sent a letter to

Dorr recounting at length "the most terrifying experience" they had witnessed the preceding week: the catastrophic San Francisco earthquake. She described the physical condition of the university but reserved the remainder of the letter to quoting—in confidence—from a letter recently received from her son "Harry" (also named Henry James) regarding Dorr's behavior at society gatherings. The society in question is the American Society for Psychical Research, which William James founded in 1884, one vehicle that James used—in the words of Eugene Taylor—to bring "together the newest insights into the field of suggestive therapeutics with those from psychotherapy, medicine, and psychology."[30] Harry James stated that "I very much like and admire G.D. I've seen him very much tired and he's behaved handsomely. I don't grudge a bit the time which this S.P.R. situation has taken me. I've long wanted to have some acquaintance with the business and I've learned more, and in a more interesting way, than I could in any other. Besides which, it's worth some sacrifice to be on hand and see anybody get hit as hard and ring true as G.D. has, especially if you are on hand cementing a friendly relation."[31]

Forms of spiritualistic belief had been part and parcel of Dorr family history for more than a half century, despite formal affiliations with Episcopalian and Unitarian religious belief system. On the one hand there was his mother's enthusiasm for making "contact" with the spirit of her eldest son and later her husband; in contrast was her son's attitude (markedly similar to that of William James) toward a phenomenon that defied scientific explanation.[32]

In his memoirs written three decades later, Dorr affirmed with even more skepticism than James—the physician and psychologist—that we know "literally nothing of consciousness…neither where it is seated nor how it operates."[33] Moreover, even if we have provocative "facts" about paranormal phenomena we can't begin to formulate a theory on which to hang such "data." In our own day, it is difficult to imagine that intellectuals of the highest academic standing were drawn into such inquiries. Like Dorr and James, they were fascinated by phenomena "hard to accept but difficult to dis-credit." Dorr labored for several years at what he described as the "exceedingly hard job" of completing Hodgson's inquiries and managing the accumulated documentation.[34]

Following his return from a trip to Greece in 1907, Dorr undertook a series of interviews in Bar Harbor that would become part of the published work of William James.[35] Medium Leonora E. Piper and her daughter stayed at Oldfarm in 1907 as Dorr's guests. William James described Piper as a "white crow," an exception to the universality of black crows. Dorr was asked to corroborate whether she possessed factual information that she could not have had access to through empirical channels. These "sittings" were documented by a scribe, annotated by Dorr, and included unique historical details regarding Dorr family life.[36] Mrs. Piper typically fell into a trance whereupon the "control" guide, separate from the medium, allegedly acted as a conduit to those present.[37] The findings that resulted from Dorr's sessions with Mrs. Piper were credible enough that James integrated the "Oldfarm Series" narrative content into his writings and addresses—consequently, Oldfarm became known to an international audience. The Oldfarm inquiries became yet another example of how diverse were the varieties of religious experience. As he expanded his pragmatic philosophy, James argued against the view that objectivity was fixed and maintained instead that truth was a relationship between ideas and their consequences.

William James continued to encourage Dorr's interest in such matters, suggesting that collaboration with the president of Clark University, the psychologist G. Stanley Hall, would be worthwhile for it would "pay him [Hall] to see the Temper in which *you* work at the phenomena."[38] The immediate issue was the worthiness of spiritualistic trance claims made by Mrs. Piper at Oldfarm. Between April 14 and May 29 of 1909, more than a dozen letters reveal Dorr's efforts to facilitate Hall's interest in meeting with Mrs. Piper. How would her utterances fare when pitted against scientific methods? Hall praised Dorr for the "very great assistance" provided and when Hall exhausted the available funds to pay for the Piper sittings, Dorr covered expenses.[39]

William James was kept abreast of these matters, but they pale in comparison with his concern about his worsening heart condition. In the summer of 1910 William and Alice returned from Quebec following a trip to England. On August 26, William James died at their country home in Chocorura, New Hampshire. Years earlier, William James had written to his wife that he wanted Dorr to be one of his pallbearers; so it was that Dorr stood beside the coffin several days later in Harvard's Appleton Chapel, standing beside President Lowell, George H. Palmer, and Henry L. Higginson.[40] With the death of his dear friend, Dorr's interest in psychical research ended—but not the involvement of Harvard University. As a memorial to Dr. Hodgson, the university accepted in 1913 an endowment fund for psychical research, officially recognizing the merits of earlier inquiries by their faculty and alumni.

Dorr's interest in the empirically elusive character of our inner life did not distract him from public service. One expression of this was his involvement in establishing a public library in Bar Harbor. Books and reference works at this time were predominantly held in private, fee-based, collections. The public library movement in America had not yet secured the necessary political support, even though—most conspicuously with Andrew Carnegie—there was a growing movement toward private philanthropy for the benefit of public literacy.

Two years after the 1906 incorporation of the Bar Harbor Village Library, Dorr approached a new widow whom he knew from social interactions in Lenox. He outlined for Mrs. Maria van Antwerp DeWitt Jesup the social benefits to be derived from purchasing land near the village green for a public library, in memory of her husband, banker and philanthropist Morris Ketchum Jesup.[41] The facility was to serve both general education and "the higher life of thought and feeling" that we associate with a scholar's library.[42] She agreed with Dorr's objectives and offered $20,000, but as construction costs escalated she asked Dorr to step in and oversee the completion of the building. Applying lessons learned at Harvard, Dorr further secured from Mrs. Jesup a $50,000 endowment. The Jesup Memorial Library was dedicated August 30, 1911. At that ceremony, attorney Luere B. Deasy remarked that the community was indebted to Mr. Dorr for the completeness and careful attentiveness to detail now manifest in the inviting facility.

Another ally, financier and HCTPR incorporator John S. Kennedy, had died the year before William James. In 1900 Kennedy and Dorr had joined with others in funding the establishment of the Bar Harbor YMCA and in that same year Kennedy acquired the several acres of undeveloped land at Park and Main streets. In 1907 Dorr, Kennedy, and other investors had proposed that this property become the transit destination for a trolley line from Ellsworth to Bar Harbor.[43] That goal had not been realized, and the HCTPR suggested to Kennedy's widow that she donate the property to the town. However, Dorr secured her agreement to an alternative proposal: that a private corporation administer the property as a public athletic field. Following her death in 1934 the athletic field became town property, and is still a popular location for sporting and community events.

The population of the island had increased in recent years and so too cosmopolitan expectations among its highbrow summer residents. Bar Harbor took the lead in promoting a facility for the performing arts. In 1905, five summer residents—including Catherine Amory Bennett Abbe, the wife of New York surgeon Robert Abbe, along with George W. Vanderbilt and George B. Dorr—resolved that a structure in a commanding setting was needed to provide a venue for artistic talent: music, theater, and dance. The structure would represent Bar Harbor's contribution to the City Beautiful Movement.[44] This unprecedented Mount Desert Island cultural institution was substantially financed by the Building of the Arts Founders Committee. As its president, Dorr purchased land with donated funds on the outskirts of Bar Harbor adjacent to the putting green at the Kebo Valley Club, well sited on the slope of a hill against a background of cool groves beneath the island's bare-topped mountains. By recommending this specific site, Dorr mingled nature and culture—a blending process that would guide his development of Acadia National Park.

Emerson Hall architect Guy Lowell was selected to design a structure that would "increase not only the love for music but the desire for whatever is excellent in art."[45] Despite the lofty aspirations of the committee, completion of this facility was demanding, as Dorr confided to Charles W. Eliot: "…the responsibility, financial and architectural, for the new 'Building of the Arts' has been on my shoulders and I have not felt that I could leave it."[46]

The building was a rectangular structure, Classical in design, with Greek Ionic columns flanking the entrance to an auditorium where gatherings of up to four hundred could witness performances on the stage at the east end of the building. *The Century Magazine* review described the establishment as the "first conspicuous effort [in this country] on a large scale to crystallize the diverse elements that form, the summer colony into a real society, having as its objective the highest aesthetic and intellectual stimulation...to contribute to self-education and to the helpful mingling of city and village life."[47] The Building of the Arts had its début performance on June 13, 1907.

While it had been many years since Edith Wharton walked the island shoreline, ten days after the opening she responded to Dorr's invitation. Her letters suggest that, for the Whartons, Downeast Maine had become a touchstone, and only through discussions with Dorr did they pursue their hopes for a "Bar Harbor Revisited."[48] Nonetheless, Dorr was encouraged to join them at The Mount within the next two months to see "the George Dorr path, the new pond, and other improvements."

This is the last surviving correspondence between Dorr and Wharton. Wharton's letters show her sincere appreciation for Dorr's gardening counsel. Wharton's persistence in developing a relationship with Dorr was not restricted to horticultural matters as is evidenced by Dorr's repeated acceptance of invitations from the Lenox couple, known for being very selective of those they invited to their home. Dorr and Wharton relished their Bar Harbor associations but also the ease with which each moved in the stimulating world of ideas.[49] Shortly after that final letter, Wharton pursued a new life abroad, and for personal reasons those all-too-brief Lenox years came to an abrupt end.

Lenox would be on Dorr's mind in October of 1906 as he welcomed George Howard, now the ninth Earl of Carlisle, and his daughter Dorothy for a short stay at Dorr's Commonwealth Avenue home. Thirty years earlier, on the death of William Dorr, Howard and his wife Rosalind had opened their London home to the grieving Dorr family. Now on their first American visit, the Earl and his daughter were entertained by Dorr and provided with introductions and encouragements to visit the Berkshires, where Dorr had made arrangements for them. Later, Howard wrote to George that "the hospitality [in Lenox] is as incessant as at Boston...[where] you made our visit [as] delightful as it could not otherwise have been.... I fear to lose myself in superlatives but they are not prompted by gratitude or civility. The same thing applies to my visit here." A few days later Dorothy Howard wrote that she had imagined American towns as lacking stimulation and now feels "so absurdly ignorant...[and] quite ashamed."[50]

As the end of the first decade of the twentieth century neared, Julia Ward Howe recorded her final words about the Dorr family. She invited "George Dorr for a tête-à-tête dinner and evening, devoted to the reading of old family letters, mostly of Samuel Gray Ward to George's mother, Mary Dorr." Two months earlier, atherosclerosis had claimed the life of Samuel, Dorr's most celebrated living relative—and the only surviving offspring of his maternal grandfather, Thomas Wren Ward. Dorr and William James were present at the service. Julia wrote in her *Journal* that this was "a rather ghostly evening. G is too much enwrapped in the story of past times, especially that of his mother's engagement to my brother Henry. He should make haste and marry, probably will not."[51]

Howe's assertion about Dorr's bachelor status was not a topic that she commented on again. She died in October of 1910, two months after the passing of William James. The public record contains no explanation for Dorr's unmarried status—and there is nothing in the surviving documentation to suggest he was homosexual.[52] Despite Julia Howe's repeated insistence that George look to the future, she clearly was not fully aware of what he had indeed achieved in the six years between the death of his mother and that of his uncle, Sam.

CHAPTER ELEVEN

Trustee First Steps

In the early years of the twentieth century few Americans were unaware of the dramatic shift in the administration of natural resources that transpired with great speed under President Theodore Roosevelt (1901 through 1909). At the phenomenal rate of eighty-four thousand acres per day, during both his terms, the Roosevelt administration placed under public protection five national parks, one hundred fifty national forests, eighteen national monuments, four national game preserves, and fifty-one federal bird sanctuaries.

The Department of the Interior had formerly acted as a clearinghouse to dispose of public land for individual or corporate exploitation. But conservationists increasingly advocated wise decision-making through government use of scientific principles and reliable information, aimed at benefiting society at large. Professional organizations like the American Association for the Advancement of Science and the Archaeological Institute of America drafted legislative proposals to protect prehistoric artifacts against commercial exploitation, much taking place on federal land. More ambitiously, some argued that federally controlled natural resources should be preserved indefinitely or until future conditions justified their use. This was not the conviction of the forceful new federal forestry chief.

On February 1, 1905, President Roosevelt established the United States Forest Service (formerly the Bureau of Forestry) and appointed his close friend Gifford Pinchot as chief forester. Since Pinchot's appointment in 1898 as chief of the Department of Agriculture forestry programs, he had built his bureau into "one of the most potent bureaucracies in American political culture."[1] Many interpreted this elevated bureaucratic stature as a shift in focus from preservation to scientific forestry, albeit with a commercial focus. At Bar Harbor, George Dorr and Pinchot had become acquainted and found they shared certain conservation principles; Pinchot also entertained Dorr at Grey Towers, the Pinchot family estate in Milford, New York. Roosevelt gave considerable independence to the Yale-trained forester whose Progressive principles now were opposed to the preservationist values of Sierra Club founder John Muir, whose convictions had shifted with the turn of the century.[2]

Muir wanted to stop the commercial devastation wrought by short-sighted men who wielded economic power, whether in the guise of the lumberman's axe or the public utility's dam (as with the ruination of Hetch Hetchy Valley to supply water to San Francisco). On the other hand, Pinchot argued that national forests were a utility—a useful commodity subject to restrictions that ensured the permanence of the natural resource. Muir was convinced that there was a fundamental conflict between the values of preservation and those of forestry conservation as practiced by Pinchot. In the fray, many issues were not addressed. How do water, soil, and atmospheric dynamics relate to forest health?[3] MIT professor of landscape architecture Anne Whiston Spirn emphasizes what was then ignored: What constituted a forest "and whom it is for? Is it for plants, animals, or people?" Which ones? Native oaks or Norway maples? English sparrows or bluebirds? Hikers or hunters, naturalists or lumbermen?[4]

Formalized notions of "conservation" existed, but there was no legislative or institutional structure to implement or sustain such a concept.[5] Iowa Representative John Lacey advanced the arguments of archaeologist Edgar Lee Hewett through congressional legislation and enabled the executive branch to quickly respond to the conservation counsel of scientific experts.[6] Lacey's legislation broadened the definition of national monuments to include archaeological, historical, and scientific sites and structures because of their commemorative, scenic, or inspirational associations. The Antiquities Act of 1906 enabled Theodore Roosevelt and his successors to quickly achieve—through the establishment of national monuments—a system of preservation without congressional consensus. Historian Hal Rothman put it rather bluntly: "No piece of legislation invested more power in the presidency than the Antiquities Act."[7]

Pinchot prepared bills for Congress that would have shifted control of the National Parks Bureau from the Interior Department to the Forest Service. Lacey opposed this veiled effort to economically optimize national park resources. The Forest Service saw a new bureau as a resource competitor whose domain would be carved out of lands under its authority.[8] Although Pinchot's efforts to shift the parks bureau into his domain failed, his initiative catalyzed a movement to establish a permanent, separate bureau within the Interior Department to administer the growing number of national parks.

By May of 1908, with only six months until the next election, President Roosevelt convened at the White House the first Conference of Governors—a commission that he dominated. It produced a declaration supporting the conservation of natural resources. In an era before the term "environment" had much clout, conservation issues were further brought to the forefront of public consciousness when thirty-eight states initiated conservation commissions as offshoots of Roosevelt's conference.

Public awareness of conservation issues was further raised when the First Conservation Conference was held in Seattle four months later. At the request of the Bar Harbor Village Improvement Association (BHVIA), Dorr arranged for Gifford Pinchot's forestry address to be delivered at Bar Harbor's exclusive Casino before the Forest Service chief departed for the West Coast gathering. There he maintained that through the use of "foresight, prudence, thrift, and intelligence" Americans could practice conservation. Pinchot adapted the Utilitarian principle of British philosophers, affirming that conservation "means the greatest good to the greatest number for the longest time."[9] The Utilitarian credo had not included the phrase "for the longest time" and its inclusion signaled growing public concern about sustainability. Much later, Roosevelt would attach poignancy to this principle: "The 'greatest good for the greatest number' applies to the number within the womb of time, compared to which those alive form but an insignificant fraction. Our duty to the whole, including the unborn, bids us to restrain an unprincipled present-day minority from wasting the heritage of these unborn generations."[10]

Roosevelt's expansive reference to "the heritage of these unborn generations" was complicated by events that quickly developed a few months after the March 1909 inauguration of William Howard Taft. Gifford Pinchot was carried forward but immediately was at odds with former Seattle mayor Richard A. Ballinger, the new secretary of the Department of the Interior. When Ballinger revoked a Roosevelt-era conservation regulation that prevented the sale or lease of federal land for waterpower development, the "press-feeding frenzy" led first to Taft firing Pinchot, and then Ballinger's resignation a year later; this was the consequence of public disclosure of Ballinger's anti-conservation beliefs during questioning by Congressional committee counsel Louis D. Brandeis.[11]

In a new political environment where conservation goals were threatened by many forces, Pinchot enlisted James R. Garfield, the son of former President Garfield, who had been the interior secretary under Roosevelt. They met with conservationists Charles W. Eliot, Henry L. Stimson, and Walter L. Fisher to create an organization to educate the public about conservation and to lobby for legislation supportive of their agenda. With professional staff and a location near Congress, this "watchdog" National Conservation Association would quickly attract fifty thousand dues-paying members under the leadership of its first president, Charles W. Eliot.[12]

Another organization with deep connections to the public park movement was the American Civic Association, led by J. Horace McFarland; among its objectives was the quantitative expansion of federal lands apart from their perceived utility. At the American Civic Association's Seventh Annual Convention held in Washington in 1911, a presentation of "Some Picturesque Features of Our National Parks" by landscape photographer Herbert Wendell Gleason was followed by unsettling remarks from ACA President McFarland. His key point was the jarring statement that "the parks have just happened; they are not the result of such an overlooking of the national domain.... [For] nowhere in official Washington can an inquirer find an office of the national parks, or a desk devoted solely to their management."[13]

Indeed, historically the parks were government orphans. They lacked oversight and often were victimized by financial interests that stood to profit from federal neglect. The second director of the National Park

Service later described the underappreciated McFarland as a "giant among conservationists," whose leadership—outside government circles—to establish a single agency to protect and administer the national parks has too often gone unrecognized.[14] Even the phenomenal popularity of the automobile contributed to the need for centralizing national park authority. Railroad entrepreneurs responded to this new vehicular competition by promoting a separate park bureau, convinced that park administrators would favor use of rail service as a less-disruptive intrusion than roadways on the public landscape.

Conservation developments on the coast of Maine cannot be directly credited to land preservation innovations on the national stage, but these federal achievements did not go unnoticed by the Hancock County Trustees of Public Reservations. For the time being, however, they implemented—with surprising success—alternative strategies for conserving thousands of acres of the island and for protecting the watersheds that were vital to the well-being of the Mount Desert Island villages.

In May 1908, President Eliot received a deed from Mrs. Eliza Homans for parcels of land that began in earnest the HCTPR's activity in assembling landscapes that became Acadia National Park. The trustees "had received their first important gift…a gift singularly appropriate to the trustees' purpose, beautiful, unique, and wild."[15] For four decades the Homans family of Boston had been island summer residents; Dr. Charles Homans, a prominent Boston surgeon, died in Bar Harbor in 1886. His widow, Eliza, was the daughter of a New Hampshire cleric, Reverend Samuel Kirkland Lothrop, later the head of Boston's Old Brattle Street Church. In 1868, the Dorr and Lothrop families had been drawn closer together. Charles Dorr and Eliza Homans's brother had purchased the substantial Higgens Tract, which fronted on Frenchman Bay. A decade later Thornton K. Lothrop sold his portion of the property to Dorr's father enabling development of the Oldfarm estate.[16]

During the HCTPR's early years there had been speculation about the signature donation that would be needed to energize subsequent donations. The friendship of Eliza Homans with Charles W. Eliot—cultivated on Mount Desert Island—provided the context for her precedent-setting philanthropy. Mrs. Homans offered the trustees their first sizable tracts of land, including landforms of singular historic and artistic interest.

In conveying the deeds, Eliza informed Eliot that she had not put any restrictions in the deed. In light-hearted manner, she recognized that she ran the risk that "my grandchildren may find a 'Merry-Go-Round' established there!" On a serious plane, it was her intent that this gift in May of 1908 would be "a bright example," albeit an anonymous one. She asked Eliot to publicize the gift but to do so "without bringing my name in."[17] Eight years later, Dorr had a Homans family memorial path constructed, a challenging ascent up granite steps and graceful stone archways on the steep face of a mountain that would later bear Dorr's name. This was one of six memorial trails added to the system from 1913 to 1916, an accomplishment that pathmaker Rudolph Brunnow attributed to Mr. Dorr, who "envisioned the memorial trails as part of a plan to enhance the public reservation and improve its eligibility for designation as a national monument or park."[18]

By accepting this first gift to the Hancock County Trustees, Eliot and Dorr had acted not merely as agents of opportunity. Each had historical associations with the Homans family, and realized the promotional value of such gifts.[19] The property lay on the south side of Newport (now Champlain) Mountain. It held a glacial cirque historically known as The Bowl. The site was contiguous with a 520-foot granite crag, prosaically named The Beehive. From its rounded summit overlooking Sand Beach and Great Head, those who completed the Beehive ascent took in expansive views of Frenchman Bay and Otter Cliffs to the east and south.

Hudson River School painters including Thomas Cole, Frederick Church, Fitz Henry Lane, Sanford Gifford, and Aaron Draper Shattuck had represented landscape features like The Bowl and The Beehive in the nineteenth century, creating near reverential public interest in the natural history of the island. Indeed, in the marginal notes to his 1844 "Sand Beach Mountain, Mt. Desert Island," Cole gazed from Schooner Head toward the Beehive precipice and wrote in his marginal notes: "This is a very grand scene. The craggy mountain, the dark pond of dark brown water—The golden sea sand of the beach and the light green [sea] with its surf altogether with the woods of varied color—make a magnificent effect such as seldom seen created in the sun."[20] In the words of Farnsworth Art Museum curator Pamela J. Belanger, "the enshrinement of Mount Desert as one of the nation's most exclusive 'sacred places' was, in its initial stages, a product of the cultural work of landscape painters who were also 'enshrined' for their genius in representing the place."[21]

How might Dorr add to Eliot's success? Dorr turned his thoughts to the acquisition of the most prominent island landmark. He immediately informed Eliot that he "would see what I could do to get the summit of Green [Cadillac] Mountain." It was a moment of immediate and unifying recognition, a secular epiphany! Dorr knew that the goals of conservation would be best served if he could secure the most topographically significant landscape on the island—the summit of the highest mountain on the eastern seaboard.

Dorr's quiet acquisition of island property over the last decade now escalated strategically to focus on the active pursuit of "the one outstanding tract upon the island or the whole neighboring coast." These eighty-five acres of Green Mountain were selected for one particular reason: their landscape quality.[22] Wasting no time, Dorr explained to Dr. Eliot that land speculators intended to purchase the summit, on which they held a lease. Vehicular summit transportation was not a new idea. Between 1883 and 1891 the Green Mountain Railway transported passengers from Eagle Lake to the Summit House before diminished passenger interest forced the cog railway to cease operations. During the same period, an existing stone and dirt summit road was improved by the newly formed Green Mountain Carriage Road Company. Both ventures were short-lived. The purpose of the 1908 syndicate was to convey paying sightseeing passengers on "an automobile stage up and down the mountain," and possibly subdivide the acreage for sale to interested parties.[23]

Before the end of the summer, Dorr repeatedly walked the summit of the highest island peak with A. H. Lynam, "tracing out the boundaries of the land I sought." Dorr triumphantly derailed the syndicate plan with John S. Kennedy's financial backing and Lynam's legal counsel. He quickly purchased from the estate of Daniel W. Brewer—a descendant of early Hulls Cove settlers—the eighty-five-acre "Mountain House Lot" where the Brewer family had earlier entertained guests at their inn at the end of the rough summit road.[24] Dorr explained that the distinctiveness of this exceptional property "lies in its all-round view," which he characterized three decades later as critically important, for this new acquisition included "every commanding view upon the whole broad summit, the highest and boldest on our oceanfront, from Maine to Florida, and the central feature of Acadia National Park."[25]

Of secondary importance, Dorr stopped the summit road entrepreneurs at a time when the growing popularity of the automobile generated island-wide speculation—and heated controversy—about the benefits and risks of this new vehicle to island culture. The HCTPR acquisition delayed public motorized access to the summit for the next twenty-four years. Only later would he realize that his success atop the Cadillac summit had made "this Park's creation my major interest and work."[26]

By 1907, at fifty-three years of age, the intellectual and emotional melding that had eluded him at last gelled. The "ghostly" historical excursions that had so concerned Julia Ward Howe would now be turned to another purpose—unfolding the rich history of the contested landscape of Mount Desert Island. In 1909, even Eliot acknowledged that "...the encouraging success of the Corporation in acquiring reservations of land for public use was due principally to the work of Mr. Dorr and the cooperation of Mr. Kennedy."[27] Eliot downplayed his own role and altruistically pushed Dorr to center stage, a characteristic behavior for Dorr's strongest supporter.

Dramatic change on the island paled by comparison with a fateful decision reached in Cambridge by Charles W. Eliot. On December 12, 1908 *The New York Times* reported that the Overseers of Harvard College accepted "with reluctance" the resignation of their president. Historian Samuel Eliot Morison summarized Eliot's impact over forty years as Harvard's president: "Eliot kept his finger on the pulse of every department.... His essential qualities did not change; he retained all his confidence, resourcefulness, energy, vitality, patience, scrupulous fairness, uncanny judgment of men, and relentless pursuit of the goal of making Harvard a fit instrument to serve the cause of learning and civilization."[28] Many wondered where Eliot would direct his undiminished energy once his retirement took effect. In the decade after his departure from the Harvard administration, Eliot would publish more than sixty articles on the larger issues facing America and the world community: the unscrupulous use of capital, employment practices, labor conditions, education, social inequalities, and wealth management in the service of philanthropy.

HCTPR issues came to his attention as a result of recent donations. For example, the forty-acre donation of Fawn Pond by longtime Bar Harbor resident Charles T. How—just south of the Crooked Road in Bar Harbor—resulted in spirited correspondence between the Bar Harbor Village Improvement Association, physician S. Weir Mitchell and Dr. Eliot.[29] The Fawn Pond issue concerned the breadth and depth of the trustees' responsibility to protect donated land. Open to interpretation was the concept of responsibility. Phrased differently, what constituted stewardship of said lands?

If we accept the silence of the HCTPR minutes about this issue, such questions implied other more vexing issues that may have been discussed but were apparently unresolved: Was it a responsibility of the HCTPR to provide identifiable points of access to its properties? To develop trails that encouraged public use? What action could be taken against interlopers who might log the land? Could a neglectful citizen who knocked out his still-lit pipe on trustee property be held legally responsible for destruction of acres of land by the ensuing fire? Would the public be permitted to hike, hunt, fish, and recreate on donated property?

Urgency again prompted a significant property acquisition in the spring of 1909, a site that Dorr later described as "one of the foundation stones on which the future park was built." A. H. Lynam learned that land speculators were on the verge of securing title to a parcel of land that was well sited just south of Oldfarm, and which contained a commercially profitable, "magnificent" spring. Set beneath the mountain that would later bear Dorr's name, Lynam knew that Dorr had secured an option on the site. Without giving Dorr advance notice, the owner decided to sell it and with Dorr's agreement his attorney took title in Dorr's name for the handsome sum of $5,000. The site was subsequently shaped into a shell-like concave basin. Over the spring itself, an octagonal structure was raised and topped by a Florentine-design tiled roof. A glass plate placed over the spring protected water quality while visitors could freely drink from the spring water that flowed to a nearby pool.

Dorr named the spring location after the late-sixteenth-century military leader and the governor of a Huguenot city of refuge in southwestern France, to whom Henry of Navarre—whom Dorr regarded as the greatest ruler of France—had entrusted in December 1603 nothing less than the establishment of the French dominion in America. This new charter encompassed all lands from the Atlantic to the Pacific oceans between the fortieth and sixtieth degrees of north latitude, roughly the longitudinal distance between present day Philadelphia and Montreal. This territory was designated *Lacadie*, or Acadia, and Pierre Dugua, Sieur de Monts (or Lord of the Mountains) represented Henry IV and to the present day is regarded as a founder of New France.[30]

The 1604 discovery of Mount Desert Island by Dugua's cartographer, Samuel de Champlain, was but one result of this exploration and colonization. Dorr described this most famous of French mariners as "first among recorded white men [to] set foot upon Mount Desert Island and explore its shores." Dorr's scholarship on the ancestry and career of Pierre Dugua was unrivaled in his day and anticipated what Pulitzer Prize–winning author David Hackett Fischer recently wrote in *Champlain's Dream*: "For the Sieur de Mons, Champlain and their friends, Acadia was not merely a place. It was an idea, and even an emotion. They thought of it as a place of natural abundance, with many resources in fish, fur, timber, and soil." Both fresh and sea water too, Dorr would add as he took this first step in educating others about the historical contributions of Pierre Dugua, Sieur de Monts.[31]

Dorr placed beside the Sieur de Monts springhouse a granite marker stone etched with the phrase "Sweet Waters of Acadia." This was not an impulsive act. Dorr had deep affection for spring-fed waterways, based on experiences with Mediterranean fountains and springs visited with his parents as well as his own investigations of the literature on the topic. After the springhouse was completed Dorr would publish a series of essays titled "Sieur de Monts Spring Papers on Water." Most contributions to the series resulted from armchair scholarship, but the locations ranged from England to Syria, Austria to China.[32]

Not all trustee acquisitions involved the type of urgent action or the attaching of signatures to legal documents. Dorr described a "precious" memory involving yet another funding request to financier John S. Kennedy. Negotiations had taken place with the owners of real estate on Picket Mountain (now Huguenot Head) adjacent to the Bear Brook site where he had built a bicycle path for his mother's enjoyment. Wishing to make the land where "she had found such happiness" a gift to the Hancock County Trustees, Dorr again asked Kennedy for financial assistance. His friend willingly agreed and a handshake struck the deal. Sadly, just as boundary issues were being sorted out in 1909, Kennedy suddenly died.

The purchase appeared doomed since "no papers passed between us; for his word was enough.... But it happened, most moving to me, that the last words his wife heard him utter, as she bent over him to hear what he might say, were: 'Remember...that I promised Mr. Dorr...to help him get that land.'"[33] Kennedy's executors were not legally bound by this verbal commitment. Still, during the following spring Dorr received a check for the verbal pledge.

A quite different conservation issue came to the fore at the same time. A tract along the eastern shore of Eagle Lake was purchased by Philip Livingston for a new residence. Unfortunately, the wastewater would drain into Eagle Lake, which supplied water for Bar Harbor. Trustee William Lawrence had anticipated residential development four months earlier and now asked Eliot to appoint a committee to look into the "whole subject of MDI water supply protection."[34] His concern was a sanitary issue: residential wastewater drainage into a public water source.

Anxious that the proposed Livingston residence would establish a precedent for subsequent residential development, the Bar Harbor Water Company Board met in New York City. Following deliberation, the board asked a respected citizen (not himself a member of the board) living closer to the Maine coast to travel to Mount Desert Island to "look the situation over." Mr. Dorr responded, but when he arrived in Bar Harbor he heard from realtor Fred Lynam, the president of the water company, that it was too late to stop the Livingston construction. Dorr's characteristic preparedness proved to be more than the board had expected. He pulled from his pocket a letter from Dr. Robert Abbe, chairman of the BHVIA sanitary committee. Abbe instructed Dorr to have the strongly disapproving letter printed in *The Bar Harbor Record* should the project move forward. Concerned about adverse publicity, the alarmed Lynam agreed to contact Livingston to determine his willingness to abandon the project.

When Livingston became aware of the extent of local concern, he abandoned his plans and the water company compensated both property owner and contractor. The trustees then developed a comprehensive plan to protect the watershed and safeguard the future purity of the lake. It prevented "others from making similar development plans…[since] the water company would finance the purchase of land it wished to protect, but the actual title would be placed in the hands of the Trustees."[35] Dorr and his fellow trustees learned "a valuable object lesson on the importance of anticipating other undertakings of the kind as now were likely."[36]

The development of land bordering Eagle Lake continued to concern the Bar Harbor Water Company and the trustees. The safety of the water supply was not yet secure—any lakeshore landowner could threaten to build on his site and extract the highest price from the water company. Here again, Dorr contrived a solution that required the precedent-setting involvement of the Maine Legislature. With the "solid support of the great body of summer residents and taxpayers of Mount Desert Island eastward from Somes Sound," a bill was entered in the legislature to grant the trustees the power to condemn all island land that threatened the public welfare. Though the scope of Dorr's request was not fully realized, "what I got [from the Maine Legislature] was the power granted to our Trustees to condemn, on evidence of importance shown, the connected watersheds of Eagle Lake and Jordan Pond."[37]

Later, one of the trustees of Dorr's estate praised Dorr's "brilliant idea," the use of the power of eminent domain. In one bold stroke, the trustees had combined "the protection of Bar Harbor's health…[and] its mountains."[38] In the name of the HCTPR, Dorr then purchased (with $65,000 of water company funds) all lands within the drainage basin of Eagle Lake. He had successfully established in the public mind the interrelatedness of two environmental forces—the hydrological and the geological.

Seal Harbor residents remained concerned about development of the mountains enclosing Jordan Pond "and the green, rounded Bubbles which separate its basin from that of Eagle Lake."[39] The trustees residing in that community finally secured a financial commitment from their water company that "made quite as much as a contribution toward the trustees' work in conserving the attractiveness of the island as to ensure the purity of their water product."[40] That a public utility contributed to "conserving the attractiveness of the Island" or the protection of landscape was precedent-setting.

Yet in terms of HCTPR land holdings, the highlight of 1910 was yet to come. Seal Harbor resident and fellow trustee George L. Stebbins became aware that title could be obtained for more than 3,600 acres in the center of the eastern half of the island. Prompt action was again needed due to increased market demand for lumber and improved harvesting access in the previously inaccessible forests. The new portable sawmills had made this both possible and profitable.[41]

The combined donations of seven Seal Harbor residents were pooled to purchase the western slope of Green Mountain, Pemetic Mountain, and South Bubble. The massive property agreement stipulated that 1,600 acres would be sold to Dorr for $3,000—later to be donated to the HCTPR. One thousand acres were lowlands that the Seal Harbor consortium retained while the Pemetic Mountain tract was donated to the HCTPR directly. The mountains sheltering Jordan Pond—and its water supply—were further protected in 1912 when the executors of the estate of Charles T. How, who had donated the forty acres at Fawn Pond, offered a two-thousand-acre tract that included Jordan and Sargent Mountains. These were purchased for less than $10,000 by John Melcher and George L. Stebbins, protecting the Seal Harbor watershed.[42]

The HCTPR's earliest land acquisitions were the result of either donated funds that were used to purchase desirable properties or donated family holdings given during the donor's lifetime or as an estate provision. The trustees were learning that, of these models, Dorr favored acquiring parcels as gifts made during the donor's lifetime. He also developed the strategy whereby trustees worked with a public utility, both to acquire new holdings and to protect natural resources that remained under the protective arm of the utility. Island community leaders also spent their own funds in response to opportunity and environmental threats, forming temporary holding companies that purchased property worthy of preservation. In the four years since Eliza Homans's gift, these land-trust strategies secured nearly three thousand acres of land, including the core properties that would eventually become Acadia National Park. And the momentum was still building.

CHAPTER TWELVE

Mr. Dorr Goes to Washington

As Dorr approached his sixtieth birthday, he continued to be attentive to the horticultural facilities adjacent to Oldfarm. The Mount Desert Nurseries entrance was now flanked by heavy stone posts cut from Dorr's quarry. The focal point was a new 200-foot-long greenhouse. Ever attentive to new markets, in 1913 Dorr published *Hardy Plant Descriptions,* printed by the venerable Riverside Press in Cambridge. This fifty-page catalogue, sent to American and foreign clients, included plant photographs accompanying fulsome characterizations of his nursery flora.[1] Harvard University utilized Dorr's horticultural expertise through his service on yet another visiting committee, assessing the Arnold Arboretum.

It is not clear from the historical record how deeply Dorr was involved with horticultural research. As with many of his interests, he often sheltered them under an umbrella of generalist concerns. For example, he was a member of the Boston Society of Natural History, which covered a wider range of scientific disciplines than the more specific botanical interests of the Massachusetts Horticultural Society (MHS). He was a long-standing participant in several of its committees, and his nurseries received professional recognition including successive prestigious MHS gold medals. Acknowledgment was not limited to a few choice plantings; displays of irises, peonies, astilbe, wolfsbane, foxtail lilies, ferns, and herbaceous flowers were honored by Dorr's colleagues; the MHS

Committee on Gardens visited the Mount Desert Nurseries and published a glowing account of its findings.[2] Medals and certificates of merit were awarded by the North Shore Horticultural Society of Massachusetts and the Society of American Florists for plant hybrids that were listed among the nursery trees, shrubs, vines, hardy perennials, bedding plants, and roses. Exhibit awards were not valued just for their own sake. As the park took shape, nursery manager A. E. Thatcher recalled that these awards promoted interest in Mr. Dorr's conservation efforts.[3]

Events unfolded so quickly in the 1913 Maine Legislature that Dorr had little opportunity to continue a high level of personal involvement in his nurseries. Bar Harbor residents—mainly realtors concerned about land development—had found support for a legislative bill to annul the charter of the Hancock County Trustees of Public Reservations. With the survival of the organization at stake, Dorr left Boston on the fastest Augusta-bound train. There he rallied support from the Speaker of the House, Ellsworth attorney John A. Peters. Over the final ten days of the legislative session, they secured sufficient votes to ensure that the proposed legislation would not survive committee review.

Yet his success was unsatisfying. As he journeyed back to Boston on the Maine Central sleeper, he lay awake, weighing alternatives and pondering insoluble questions as was his nature. The evidence, however, was unavoidable: the trustees' properties were "unstable." Their corporate charter was vulnerable to ever-changing Maine political currents and the shifting agendas of men of influence. Dorr's confidence in the authority of the law, however, was not shaken.

Where could he turn for a more secure legal foundation? Was there precedent for the donation of land to the federal government? If so, what process was involved in securing federal acceptance of HCTPR property? How should that property be characterized: as a sanctuary, a reserve, a park? And perhaps the most vexing question of all: would the trustee organization relinquish their authority over the land trust properties, in whole or part?

Galvanized by the clear threat, the very next morning Dorr traveled to Cambridge and met with Dr. Eliot, who "knew nothing of the matter nor the danger that had threatened."[4] There is no indication that Eliot believed that Dorr's prompt action in Augusta had exceeded his trustee authority.

As Eliot approached his eightieth birthday, he relied even more heavily on Dorr, especially since the demands for his own involvement in public service had increased since his university retirement.

Eliot had long thought that the trustees could address each new assault. He had joined the Massachusetts Trustees of Public Reservations—the original land trust, founded by his son—in 1900 and was elected to its presidency in 1904.[5] Dorr had become a member in 1908; he had read Eliot's description of HCTPR achievements in the 1910 Massachusetts Trustees' *Records of the Standing Committee.* Unlike the Massachusetts land trust, the resources of its Maine counterpart were severely limited. However, as he confidently pointed out to Eliot, the federalizing of the HCTPR's properties would provide the security that they currently lacked. Eliot thought a while, then exclaimed, "I believe you are right! When will you go on to Washington?"

Public support was a key component in effecting political change. What steps needed to be taken to increase public awareness of the benefits of a public sanctuary, especially on the remote Maine coast? Arriving in Washington, Dorr met with men of influence who did not immediately grasp the significance of his proposal—yet some were intrigued. The editor of a popular serial publication approached him about HCTPR developments. Dorr sent a lengthy telegram to President Eliot in late May informing him that the popular *National Geographic Magazine* had requested a model plan for establishing an "Appalachian and Atlantic Coast system of wild life bird and plant preserves." Moreover, the publisher asked him to discuss whether the Mount Desert Island model could be expanded to a national scale.[6]

Dorr enlisted two scientists to develop a proposal that appeared in the July 1914 issue of *The National Geographic Magazine.* Titled "The Unique Island of Mount Desert," it first outlined the natural and cultural history of the island, including the rationale for the establishment of the Hancock Country Trustees. While assembling contiguous tracts of land remained incomplete, the trustee objective was creation of "a wild park of remarkable beauty, unique character, and great variety of landscape feature." This was the first published document by a trustee that referred to the establishment of a federally administered "wild park," demonstrating Dorr's intent to pursue national park status more than two years prior to the establishment of the National Park Service.[7]

Dorr crafted the first third of this article. Massachusetts State Ornithologist Edward Howe Forbush followed Dorr's essay with arguments that the island could be a model for restoration of the abundant variety of over-exploited bird species. And "the leading authority on the flora of eastern North America," Harvard's Gray Herbarium curator Merritt Lyndon Fernald, completed the article with evidence that the island contained a greater diversity of plant life than any other area on the eastern coastline.[8] A park on the Maine coast would prompt others to consider how they might provide similar blessings "for themselves and their children in other parts of the country."

In the same issue Charles W. Eliot offered a more philosophical contribution: "The Need for Conserving the Beauty and Freedom of Nature in Modern Life." He advocated "the creation, preservation, and enlargement for human enjoyment of mountains and valleys, hills and plains, forests and flowers, ponds and water courses, spring blossoms and autumn tints, and the wild life of birds and other animals in their natural haunts." Eliot urged "these beneficent powers" within the federal government to act in a geographically just manner, to set aside on Mount Desert Island and elsewhere on the East Coast "inviting sanctuaries" within reach of those who live in dense population centers beset with the evils of city life.[9]

The most immediate task was to secure in unfamiliar Washington, D.C., a base of operations; then, contacting those individuals with whom Dorr had personal history or family acquaintances, obtaining letters of introduction from Dr. Eliot, and confirming appointments with the appropriate public officials. In the winter of 1913 Dorr arrived in Washington on the heels of the presidential inauguration of Woodrow Wilson. He accepted the invitation of Gifford Pinchot to stay at 1615 Rhode Island Avenue, an impressive "political hub" built by Pinchot's parents as a staging ground for their son's career.[10] Pinchot was about to host a reception for members of President Wilson's cabinet. These fortuitous circumstances provided Dorr with the opportunity to meet key leaders in the new government. Two months later Pinchot left for Loggerhead Key, Florida, responding to an invitation of marine scientist Alfred G. Mayer to see the Tortugas research facility of the Carnegie Institution.[11] Dorr returned to Bar Harbor in the spring of 1914 to organize the proposed gift of HCTPR lands. Dorr was unaware that, within three years, Mayer's research skills would prove crucial to realizing another one of Dorr's goals for Mount Desert Island.

Dorr now made the difficult decision to sell his family residence in Boston. For a half century, 18 Commonwealth Avenue had been his home. In the future, when called to Boston he would reside in the familiar Somerset Club. The new thrust of activity in the nation's capital was the catalyst for Dorr's downsizing. With each passing year, the number of days spent on the coast of Maine or in Washington had greatly increased. He was now truly centered on Mount Desert Island, the site of his business, the location of his residence for more than thirty years, and the place where he was able to initiate and take advantage of timely opportunities. Moreover, the expenses associated with Oldfarm and his purchase of properties later gifted to the Hancock County Trustees surely weighed in his decision. His only written words on this transition were that maintaining the high social standards set by his parents was difficult for an unattached gentleman: "I have lived in it alone a dozen years, carrying on the old traditions of hospitality and friendly living, a tradition for which the house had gained a reputation during my parents' lifetime."[12]

Later in that spring of 1914, the tenacious Dorr returned to Washington with deeds, maps, and abstracts of titles for nearly five thousand acres of HCTPR properties. His co-author of the forthcoming *National Geographic Magazine* article, Edward Howe Forbush, accompanied him. Dorr arrived at the old Patent Office Building, where the Department of the Interior was housed. There, he met a director of the future National Park Service, the young Horace M. Albright. Albright later described his visitor: "A distinguished-looking gentleman quietly but rather timidly entered the office. He introduced himself as George Dorr of Bar Harbor, Maine. He wished to see [Interior] Secretary Lane.... He looked like the Washington heat had worn him out, so I suggested he sit down while I went for a cool drink...He gratefully drank several glasses and then related his reasons for wishing to see Lane. It was a fascinating story.... I was most impressed by the man and the ideals for which he stood. I made an appointment for him to see Lane when he returned. Apparently Lane was also impressed, as were many influential people in the government to whom I introduced Dorr."[13]

Several months prior to Dorr's first trip to Washington, the foremost figure in the history of the National Park Service had just begun to make his name known throughout the city. Stephen Tyng Mather, celebrated by those in his trade for creating the advertising slogan "20 Mule Team Borax," was widely known for marketing the mineral borax as a water-softener, eyewash, and household cleanser. An "energetic, backslapping, high-minded extrovert," Mather was a Sierra Club member committed to Muir's preservationist philosophy.[14] Greatly disturbed by the condition of the national parks and the wasteful practices of timber companies motivated to harvest Sequoia National Park's tall trees, this "human whirlwind," as his biographer described him, drafted a letter to Secretary Lane expressing his concerns.[15] According to Horace Albright, a luncheon meeting between Lane and the "high-voltage idea" man was arranged in Chicago.

Lane emphasized to Mather that the time was ripe for a person who really cared about national parks to get them "united in a strong, separate bureau, and get America acquainted with their own scenic and historic sites."[16] Mather adhered to the core value reaffirmed in 1909 by Sierra Club secretary William Colby, "that our National parks shall be held forever inviolate."[17] Mather insisted that this elevation of the national parks into a strong and separate bureau be based on this principle of inviolability. Additional meetings led to Mather's decision in January 1915 to come to Washington as assistant secretary of the interior. Mather's timing was opportune. Lane's special assistant in charge of national parks—his University of California chum Dr. Adolph C. Miller—had just departed but left behind his highly resourceful, University of California–educated clerk, Horace Albright (though his value to Mather was in question as Albright planned to complete law school on the West Coast).

Before President Wilson tapped him for his cabinet, Secretary Lane had been a journalist, served as San Francisco City Attorney, and was a political reformer and candidate for Governor of California. Known as a "Roosevelt Democrat," he was appointed by that president to a seat on the Interstate Commerce Commission; he had been reappointed by Taft."[18] Following the San Francisco earthquake of 1906, Lane became a supporter of the effort of water-rights advocates to secure federal permission to dam the Tuolumne River in the Hetch Hetchy Valley, a majestic portion of Yosemite National

Park. John Muir and the Sierra Club had led the legal struggle to prevent the creation of a dam and reservoir out of national park land.

A study by historian Robert W. Righter shows "no evidence that Woodrow Wilson had ever met Franklin Lane or even heard of the Hetch Hetchy controversy" during the presidential election of 1912.[19] Wilson deferred to the new interior secretary and his water development agenda. Secretary Lane supported California congressman John E. Raker's successful legislative effort, which resulted in the construction of O'Shaughnessy Dam and the flooding of Hetch Hetchy.

That precedent-setting outcome caused great concern about the future protection of federalized public land. Many in the conservation movement feared that other national park lands might suffer a similar fate. The presidential records of Charles W. Eliot in the Harvard Archives contain a file on the efforts to wrest away from Yosemite National Park its northern water—and hydroelectric—resources.[20] Well aware of the outcome of this controversy, how could Eliot support Dorr's federalization proposal? Was Hetch Hetchy but another example of influence and shifting political agendas that could overwhelm the inviolate principle of federal land protection? Committed to the Progressive agenda, aware of the unprecedented conservation achievements of Theodore Roosevelt, and knowing that there were renewed efforts to bring about a strong National Park Service within the Department of the Interior, the HCTPR leaders optimistically pressed forward.

Secretary Lane also faced the formidable task of imposing a new set of relationships on a federal department that was historically regarded as an unmanageable collection of bureaus, institutions, and field offices scattered about the city of Washington. Lane's support, however, was critical to the trustees' immediate goal to secure federal protection.[21] Becoming more familiar with federal politics, Dorr realized that a new federal agency was needed to define the meaning and mission of national parks and defend them to the hilt. Increasingly, Dorr saw the trustees' interests intertwined with a new conception of the national parks within the Interior Department.

Congressional resistance was formidable. According to Stephen Mather's biographer, during the early years of the Mather era "giving things to the federal government was almost as suspect as making bank deposits to the account of a Cabinet officer." When Mather drafted provisions authorizing the interior secretary to accept donations of money, land, and rights-of-way for the national parks, an appropriations committee member tore up the provision, convinced that "only a black-hearted briber would want to donate something to the government."[22]

Following unsuccessful meetings with the Coast and Geodetic Survey and Smithsonian Institution officials, on Dorr's return to the Interior Department Horace Albright did, in his words, "what little I could do to help him."[23] His understated assistance involved the perceptive suggestion that it might be possible for Dorr to secure Woodrow Wilson's support. Under provisions of the Antiquities Act, the president could accept land as a national monument, avoiding the Congressional approval necessary for national park status.[24]

Hal Rothman rightly argues that without the Antiquities Act "too many areas of outstanding scenic significance would have been lost to congressional inertia and indifference."[25] They were not necessarily second-class sites. The proposed Sieur de Monts National Monument was clearly recognized for its monumental features, and its advocates were not alone in earmarking it for national park status in large part because—as Rothman argued—it was "a remote natural area on the Atlantic seaboard [that] had a built-in constituency, the affluent residents of coastal Maine and of a railroad that made it easily accessible."[26]

In 1905 California congressman William Kent and his wife had purchased more than six hundred acres on Mount Tamalpais, a tract that contained an impressive ancient redwood forest. Following the San Francisco earthquake, a private utility offered to purchase Kent's property to create a water reservoir—after harvesting the profitable timber. Kent anticipated that the water company would invoke eminent domain. In late December of 1907, he mailed the deed for the land most coveted by the utility to the interior secretary and asked that the president declare it a national monument under the provisions of the 1906 Antiquities Act. Two weeks later Theodore Roosevelt established Muir Woods National Monument.[27]

Secretary Lane, aware of this precedent-setting public donation from an American citizen, pledged his support for Dorr's request for national monument status. The White House, however, remained unresponsive. Dorr received advice from Public Lands Commission officials that his goal would be more likely to receive the necessary endorsements if he accomplished three further objectives: secure two more tracts of land to delineate a single boundary line, obtain additional deeds and titles to ensure compliance with exacting government standards, and develop a land acquisition prospectus for the further consolidation of trustee holdings.

Complicating the matter even more, Dorr knew that influential political leaders in Maine were then pressing the Washington establishment to give national protection to wild and isolated Mount Katahdin. Congressman Frank E. Guernsey had introduced legislation in 1911 for a Katahdin forest reserve and national park, a proposal that never made it out of committee. Three years later, it was reintroduced as Dorr advanced the trustees' plan in Washington. Was there now competition between the two proposals? To the contrary, Dorr did not view Katahdin advocacy as competitive with trustee interests. Instead, he sent a letter to the *Boston Herald* supportive of the Katahdin bill.[28]

Even now, it is popularly believed that there were only incidental costs attached to the donated land that comprised Sieur de Mont National Monument. Dorr knew that there were due diligence expenses that could be insurmountable. "Until then," he writes modestly, "all survey and legal expenses connected with my work I had borne myself, but this new requirement.... I felt it only fair that others, cooperating with me, should assume." President Eliot agreed and initially thought that some of the university foundations with which he was associated since his retirement might come to the rescue. However, neither the HCTPR nor these "great public trusts" provided the necessary capital.

Enter the Rockefeller family. Standard Oil Company titan John D. Rockefeller and his wife, Laura Spelman Rockefeller, first visited Mount Desert Island in 1893 with their four daughters and one son, John Davison Rockefeller Jr. being the youngest. In 1908, the junior Mr. Rockefeller and his pregnant wife, Abigail Green Aldrich Rockefeller, returned to Bar Harbor so that Abby could be close to her physician, who summered in nearby Blue Hill. The family was impressed with Mount Desert Island's beauty—returning there in 1909 and 1910—but in the words of their youngest son, David, they thought "Bar Harbor too flashy and ostentatious, and spent little time there." Nine miles distant they purchased the sixteen-acre Clarke property on Barr Hill, which included a ninety-nine-room mansion known as The Eyrie, overlooking the "quieter and more conservative" Seal Harbor.[29] These were pivotal years during which the very wealthy businessman redirected his life's work, severing his relationships with his father's business interests and committing himself to philanthropy.

John D. Rockefeller Jr.'s development of parkland did not arise solely because of an appreciation for the scenic beauty of Mount Desert Island. The senior Mr. Rockefeller had been educated in the Cleveland public schools and in 1873 purchased several hundred acres in Ohio on a knoll called Forest Hill, where a Victorian mansion named The Homestead was built. On this summer estate he "improved the land with miles of winding gravel roads, bridle trails, foot paths, a race track for his horses and a nine-hole golf course."[30] The father provided outdoor tutorials to his son that emphasized the importance of preserving natural beauty as well as the best techniques for designing footpaths and carriage roads. By 1913 "the Park" surrounding Kykuit, the family's new Colonial Revival residence in New York—northeast of the village of Sleepy Hollow—was completed. Located on the Hudson River's eastern shore in the hamlet of Mount Pleasant, the private gardens and woodland of this 3,400-acre Pocantico Hills estate were seminal to Mr. Rockefeller's concept of a park—not only as a private place but as a public asset.[31]

Ann Clark Rockefeller Roberts is convinced that shortly after her grandparents' arrival on Mount Desert Island for the summer, Dorr's written invitation of September 11, 1914 initiated private conversations with Dr. Eliot and Mr. Rockefeller about the scope and character of conservation on Mount Desert Island. Each had closely monitored the impact of the automobile and the seesaw legislative process of restricting and then permitting motorized vehicular traffic on the island. Carriage road development arose in large part so that Rockefeller family and friends could continue the pleasures they knew from the New York and Ohio estates. If the philanthropist was to have his island carriage rides along the shoreline of Frenchman Bay, he would have to acquire sufficient contiguous properties to accommodate the scope of his interest. To that end, Ms. Roberts has explained, Mr. Rockefeller lost no time in contracting the services of Bar Harbor attorney Albert H. Lynam and realty expert George Stebbins to initiate inquiries about—and often purchases of—properties adjacent to Barr Hill, where he could extend his carriage roads.

Mr. Rockefeller joined the Seal Harbor Village Improvement Society in 1910. No objections were voiced in 1913 when carriage road construction began on the east side of Barr Hill and the perimeter of Little Long Pond. Some paths were converted to carriage roads, and his congenial neighbor—and Path Committee chairman—Joseph Allen appreciated the roads as connectors to the growing footpath system. Within two years of starting carriage road development, "Rockefeller envisioned a much larger carriage road system that would extend throughout the mountains," connecting distant villages. This could only be accomplished "if he gained approval from the trustees to build roads over HCTPR property at his expense with no legal rights."[32] Charles W. Eliot and George Dorr made sure that trustee approval was quickly secured. Conservation was not solely motivated by the desire to protect mountaintops from being lumbered. Instead, Ms. Roberts explains, her grandfather's goal "was about creating something much larger.... And Eliot and Dorr were the other great figure(s), the other great visionaries at that level."[33]

In partnership with these two men, the emerging national park became Mr. Rockefeller's first major conservation project. This echoed an idea recently put forth in the second edition of Roberts's *Mr. Rockefeller's Roads:* "The beauty of the island, its magnetic appeal as a summer retreat and resort, the existence of public reservations with George Dorr as its charismatic director, and the advent of the automobile—all conspired to invite the creation of Acadia National Park, and the masterpieces known as 'the Rockefeller Roads.'"[34]

Dr. Eliot, Mr. Dorr, and Mr. Rockefeller—sometimes referred to as "The Triumvirate"—would not immediately be recognized as the champions of a new model for establishment of national landscape reserves.[35] Unlike the Muir Woods precedent, the trustees' model in Maine was derived from a corporation established explicitly to protect land at the county level. Moreover, HCTPR holdings were not limited to a single private tract; instead, the scope of these private donations was still evolving. Given that these donations were on the Maine coast, the trustees' offered gift implicitly advocated a truly *national* park system that was not limited geographically to landscapes west of the Mississippi River. The following year, a series of eight illustrated lantern-slide lectures on "The National Parks in America" was presented, to large audiences, by photographer Herbert Wendell Gleason. These further magnified federal inattention to the preservation of the distinctive landscapes of the eastern United States.

Dorr's letters at that time to newly elected U.S. Congressman Peters were full of optimism at the prospects for establishing the national monument.[36] Dorr explained the challenges that the trustees faced, especially the stringent requirement that "its main tract shall be compact, well-knit together in a landscape way and capable of enclosure by a single line." Most importantly, he identified the specific benefits of federal ownership that the trustees had not provided: the "prestige, assured development and good control which ownership by the Federal Government alone can give."[37] These benefits were Dorr's counterpoint to the Hetch Hetchy concessions.

The final steps in establishing the national monument were at hand. Following months of exacting historical research, attorney Luere B. Deasy and his partner, A. H. Lynam, assembled six hundred pages of documentation "supplemented by larger sheets exhibiting inheritance lines after the manner of genealogical tables." Imperfect property histories were checked and rechecked, a time-consuming process that stretched into the next year.[38]

What Dorr and Lynam were up against was well described by the late Bar Harbor historian and fellow trustee Richard W. Hale Jr.: "There was...the usual complexity of county land titles, which has been a constant stumbling-block to those who try to put deeds in order to fit Department of Justice standards. Oral wills, undivided property passed on through various subdivisions, unrecorded deeds, warranties given by men long dead, all complicated matters...[back to] the original grant of Douaquet to Cadillac, and all the complexities of the ownership of Acadia."[39] That the talents of this small island community could rise to the challenges of the established Washington bureaucracy has historically been under-appreciated.

In late February 1915, Eliot and Dorr met to sort out the level of funding necessary to complete the transfer process. Dorr itemized the expenditures to date, in excess of $50,000 on the eastern half of the island alone.[40] Eliot incorporated the details into his own lengthy appeal to Mr. Rockefeller. Privately, Eliot emphasized to Mr. Rockefeller that their Oldfarm ally had already "put more money into this enterprise on behalf of the public than he should have done; and that his estate was seriously embarrassed in consequence…[and] that he could not ask his friends that have hitherto contributed at his request for further gifts."[41] Eliot did not state in this letter what he likely believed, that a full accounting of Dorr's role in property acquisition would likely never be forthcoming.[42]

Eliot raised the stewardship issue to the new island resident, pointing out that that the creation of a public reservation was "really the work of men and women who love the Island…. They do not, however, imagine that they are doing anything more than starting a large public benefaction. They expect the coming generations to do their share."[43]

Recognizing that Mr. Rockefeller, at this early stage of his involvement, preferred to "hold such purchases himself, and to pay taxes on them, rather than give them to the Public Reservations," Eliot nevertheless sent Dorr news of a qualified success. The new Seal Harbor resident promised to contribute $17,500 to cover two land purchases and the associated title expenses if two conditions were fulfilled: that other persons provide Dorr with funds to purchase an important tract on the Gorge Road—between Dry [Dorr] and Green [Champlain] mountains—and that all these lands be conveyed to the trustees "in case the Monument project falls through."[44]

Dorr had anticipated the philanthropist's reciprocity requirements. Several days earlier he sought support from "one of my friends in New York and fellow summer-residents at Bar Harbor," advising Eliot that if Mr. Rockefeller should balk "it seems to me that the next step should be to ask him if he will not contribute this on the basis of an equal or similar contribution, given or pledged, from summer residents upon our side [of the island]."[45]

By early April the arrangements were finalized. "In 1915 and 1916, JDR Jr. made his first substantial contribution, in two pledges, which enabled the HCTPR to complete the documentation necessary for acceptance by the Government as a National Monument. The total payment to George Dorr was $34,500"—twice the amount of the original request.[46] The careful documentation and persuasion exercised through the partnership of Dorr and Eliot proved successful. They had convinced Rockefeller to convert a small part of his capital into a landscape asset that was on its way to becoming a new national park. The partnership of the Triumvirate was secured.

CHAPTER THIRTEEN

Monumental Achievement

Steady progress was made in 1915 to fulfill federal requirements for documenting the complicated land history of the properties that the Hancock Country Trustees of Public Reservations proposed to give to the nation. Its confidence in the Interior Department, however, was more a matter of faith than the result of careful historical analysis. The department had jurisdiction over twelve national parks and nineteen national monuments, a 4.6-million-acre domain that received only minimal custodial care and had no coordinated administration. Only two federal officials were budgeted as full-time staff responsible for national parks and monuments.[1]

The prospects for establishing a National Park Service—to say nothing of creating new national monuments and parks—became less promising in late spring of 1915, after the Cunard ocean liner, RMS *Lusitania*, was torpedoed and sunk off the coast of Ireland by a German U-boat. The isolationism of an earlier day gave way to growing support for United States entry into World War I. Every branch of the federal government was affected by war preparation, including the Interior Department. In pressing forward with his effort to secure national monument status, Dorr faced the challenge of an American public that found it difficult to talk of anything but war. Nonetheless, Dorr's optimism was undiminished.

The demands of Dorr's horticultural business and the national monument initiative left little time for other endeavors. Those familiar with

Dorr's priorities were therefore surprised when he threw his hat into the local political arena and was elected in 1915 as an Eden (now Bar Harbor) selectman (he was subsequently re-elected for two additional one-year terms). Dorr's memoirs are silent on this unexpected behavior, though privately he confided to Charles W. Eliot that he was motivated to run for office because of the pressing need for a new system of accounting for the Town of Eden, perhaps one that fostered his private interests.[2] Following his election, a Portland accounting consultant was engaged to explain to town officials the strength and weakness of the proposed system—which the Board of Selectmen quickly adopted.[3]

In retrospect, several personal objectives made his public office useful for the sixty-one-year-old horticulturist. First, Dorr could use this office as a bully pulpit to encourage support for a Mount Desert Island national monument administered from Bar Harbor. Local support could be rallied for Dorr's efforts in Washington to secure federal interest in this remote island community. This leadership position further enabled him to influence cultural development beyond the circles of the summer residents.[4] In 1916, he deeded to the Town of Eden fourteen acres of real estate. This donation expanded the golf links at the Kebo Valley Club, which was largely exclusive to summer residents. Selectman Dorr cannily insisted that the town had an aesthetic responsibility "to so develop [this recreational area] as to make them not only the first class links to which they naturally lend themselves, but an object of beauty and interest in the town's surroundings," which included the adjacent Building of the Arts.[5]

The most convincing explanation for his involvement in town governance, however, is that Dorr anticipated the dramatic social changes that would occur when the HCTPR properties were federalized. The advantages of local political experience could aid a federal administrator in responding to local reactions to this new political force on Mount Desert Island. Historian Judith S. Goldstein has identified this larger cultural shift: "It was the beginning of a close and fruitful relationship among Dorr, Eliot, and Rockefeller. As they moved through intricate negotiations into the larger public domain of the federal government, the triumvirate took over the leadership of the island. Slowly, they stretched their concepts of public access far beyond the privileged boundaries of the small Protestant summer colony."[6]

The restrictive winter weather forced Dorr to find refuge in the physical and spiritual warmth of Oldfarm, where a growing array of intellectual resources eased his pursuit of scholarly projects. There he incorporated a new land trust, the Wild Gardens of Acadia.[7] The geographic range of this organization exceeded the scope of the Hancock County Trustees in that its mission was to acquire—by gift, purchase, or lease—parcels of Maine habitat that drained "into Penobscot Bay and River, the Bay of Fundy, and the sea lying between said Bays."[8] Its ecological focus was to identify habitats that contained trees, shrubs, herbs, and other plants that with proper administration could illumine for the public their "scientific, educational and artistic value."[9] Not surprisingly, the ambitious Acadian plant sanctuary agenda—to observe and study plant life, gardening, forestry and landscape art—went largely unrealized. The federalizing of geographically limited Hancock County Trustee property, however, did result in the integration of elements of the Wild Gardens of Acadia into the evolving national park.[10]

Wintertime scholarship led to the publication of a private edition of documents relating to the 1605 attempt by the French to colonize what would later be known as New England. Drawing on his familiarity with French language and culture, Dorr's introductory notes described the legal authority for the activities of Pierre Dugua, Sieur de Monts.[11] Aided by Samuel de Champlain, in December of 1603 Dugua seized vast territories of northeastern America, which "resulted in permanent settlement on the American continent." Dorr thus provided the rationale for the naming of Sieur de Monts National Monument. He also advanced the unpopular thesis that, had this well-conceived commission been fully realized, "France, not England, would have controlled the destiny and development of our northern country, and possibly North America itself."

It is no small matter that Dorr chose the Sieur de Monts as his paradigm, risking his own public endeavors by applying the name of a figure important to French history but little known to the English-speaking community. *Sieur de Monts* was not only attached to this first national monument east of the Mississippi River, it also was used to recognize the French heritage of the picturesque natural spring where seven recently developed memorial trails converged.[12] It has been claimed that "Dorr and his family were Anglophiles who looked to the gracious country living of the English gentry…as a model of behavior."[13] To the contrary, from his college days through his final years, the importance of French culture on the American experience dominated his thinking and provided the rationale for the names he assigned to park landscape features.

To be sure, Samuel de Champlain had achieved greater fame. Dorr would be drawn to Pierre Dugua because of "the value of his work and the greatness of his ideas." Those words were spoken by Civil War hero Joshua Lawrence Chamberlain at the three-hundredth anniversary of the landing of the explorer at St. Croix Island. His brilliant discourse should remind future generations that "…we must think back to de Monts when we consider the long sharp struggle for possession of these Acadian shores, and the tenacious hold which France maintained for more than a century, and which is not wholly yet unfelt."[14]

After Chamberlain's death in 1914, Dorr conceived of another way to promote the goals shared with Chamberlain. He prepared a series of publications that explained the cultural, historic, and natural distinctiveness of Mount Desert Island. Reserving some topics for himself, Dorr asked scholars of wide renown to draft articles intended for a general audience on carefully considered conservation themes that were related to the Acadian landscape. The brisk publication schedule for *The Sieur de Monts Publications* yielded more than twenty booklets in the years between the achievement of national monument status and elevation to national park status three years later.[15]

At the national level, the development of a cadre of promoters for the National Park Service concept was based on an outdoor adventure—and publicity event—of Mr. Mather's design. In the summer of 1915, he led a twelve-day mountain-packing trip that covered the Sierra Nevada territory that Dorr had trekked eleven years earlier—from the Giant Forest to Mount Whitney and finally to Lone Pine. Mather and Albright showed the distinguished participants—including publishers, newsmen, and railroad entrepreneurs—"the beauties and potential of Sequoia National Park," awakening in them an appreciation for the splendors of other national parks and persuading them to apply their expertise to move "forward the campaign for a National Park Service." As Albright later recalled, "To a man the Mather Mountain Party of 1915 took his words to heart and contributed far beyond his expectations."[16]

During the fall and winter, Mather's colleagues drafted versions of National Park Service legislation. They were guided by Mather's pioneering study, *Progress in the Development of the National Parks,* "the first comprehensive look at the condition of national parks as a system. With common purposes and goals."[17] Of the dozen individuals involved, it was landscape architect Frederick Law Olmsted Jr. who drafted the fundamental purpose statement: "to conserve the scenery and the natural and historic objects and the wildlife therein...by such means as will leave them unimpaired for the enjoyment of future generations."[18] Albright and his colleagues redrafted legislative language and codified the national park concept in such a way as to separate it from national forests. The National Park Service Organic Act attempted to balance the seemingly contradictory goals of resource preservation and visitor use. Some argued that the parks should be developed and promoted as luxury vacation resorts. They were convinced that once affluent Americans discovered the scenic wonders of the park and their plush, railroad-financed lodges, the public would follow their lead. Another cohort wanted parkland left as primeval as possible. Should one side prevail? Was a healthy balance feasible? Mather had "no formula to fall back on, no scales for weighing out use against preservation. The problem was permanent and, with travel increasing, aggravative."[19]

This so-called "contradictory mandate," however, was not based on inconsistent principles, according to the widely published Yale University historian Robert W. Winks. In his view, "the primary goal of the new Service is to 'leave' the parks and monuments unimpaired, placing clear priority on protection as opposed to restoration of landscapes and by implication arguing for the presumption of inaction in the face of any request for what may be viewed as 'impairment.'"[20]

Moreover, the NPS advocates were not in agreement about the future geographical distribution of the park system. Horace Albright reported "open" disagreement with Mather about additions to the park system. Mather was initially indifferent toward national monuments. The "twenty-three orphan monuments" were not funded and some thought them substandard to national parks. Albright later wrote "I also thought that we shouldn't overlook the East. I told him I had become acquainted with a Mr. Dorr who was trying to create a national park along the coast of Maine....[Don't] people in the East deserve some parks without having to travel thousands of miles to get to the great western [ones]?... Mather gave me a steely eyed look and sharply said, 'Nonsense! The wonderlands are in the West.'"[21] Albright would repeatedly exert pressure to change this perception.

National publications did not report such internal discord. They stressed instead the aesthetically unique character of park scenic splendors, a natural landscape that most Americans had never experienced. Western railroads saw potential profit in promoting the ever-enlarging national park system west of the Mississippi. At the 1915 dedication of Rocky Mountain National Park, Stephen Mather spoke of the need for a Yellowstone highway linking the new "gateway" park with the national park to the immediate north. He repeatedly urged the public to take to the highways to sample the recreational opportunities available in what he hoped would be expanded parklands.[22]

Even before the NPS was established, Mather arranged for a national parks superintendents' conference to take place in Washington in January of 1917. The meeting would draw attention to the splendors of the parks, reinforcing the message of Gleason's national parks lecture tour. A National Museum exhibit of forty-five paintings of park scenes by twenty-seven artists, including luminaries Thomas Moran and Albert Bierstadt, was planned to coincide with the superintendents' conference.

Dorr carefully scrutinized the political techniques of Mather and Albright, comparing and contrasting their strategies, weighing their effectiveness. All three were in Washington in the spring of 1916. Mather sought the company of fellow guests at the Cosmos Club, Mr. Dorr's primary residence in the capitol.[23] Not much time was available for Dorr's concerns as Albright and Mather were preoccupied with testimony before the House Public Lands Committee regarding park legislation. Two bills had been introduced, one by congressman William Kent and another by his colleague John E. Raker, the American Civic Association "having taken an immense amount of interest" in Kent's version of the park bill.[24] Kent's H.R. 8668, "A Bill to Establish a National Park Service," was passed and sent to the Senate, where amendments involved extended negotiations.

Regarding Dorr's disposition during these critical months, a September letter from Charles W. Eliot to his niece, Ellen Bullard, provides some insight. She had privately faulted Dorr for never "finishing anything."[25] Eliot explained that some of Dorr's undertakings were incomplete because of their scope and the necessity of support from "many persons of liberal disposition." Nonetheless, Eliot impressed upon Bullard the recently completed projects of Mr. Dorr: the Jesup Library, the Building of the Arts, construction of "first-rate" roads and footpaths, and his "distinct horticultural achievement," the Mount Desert Nurseries.

Eliot's letter referred to Dorr's scholarship: his current work on a manuscript on famous springs in the ancient and modern world, and yet another project delineating the literary use of allusion to flora and fauna in Western culture. Eliot concluded his letter, which found its way into Dorr's memorabilia, with one of the most expressive statements recorded concerning Dorr's character: "Dorr is an impulsive, enthusiastic, eager person, who works at high tension, neglects his meals, sits up too late at night, and rushes about from one pressing thing to another; but he is very diligent, as well as highly inventive and suggestive…and what he needs from his friends is sympathy, support, and furthering in his undertakings, and good advice in regards to the care of his health and moderation in work."

Armed with A. H. Lynam's fully researched deeds—dating back to the earliest title from the Province of Quebec—Dorr finally secured the House Public Lands Committee's approval for the documentation of his proposed national monument. Letters of support from Secretary Lane, Stephen Mather, and other government officials were then attached by Dorr and other members of the Maine delegation and delivered in person to President Wilson. Highly pleased with Wilson's interest, Dorr's hopes soared when the president discussed the proposed national monument more fully than anticipated.[26]

As Dorr explained in *Acadia National Park,* his concerns escalated when several weeks passed and there was no response from the president's office. Inquiries disclosed that Secretary of Agriculture David F. Houston had sent a memo to Wilson opposing the new monument—ostensibly because of the expense.

Administration of the three dozen national monuments was divided between the War, Agriculture, and Interior departments. The issue of management authority for the proposed Sieur de Monts National Monument defied the conventional policy apparatus dictating that national monuments were managed by the agency that administered the land; the Hancock County Trustees' donation was exceptional in that it gifted private—not public—land. Within the Department of Agriculture, the chief of the Forest Service, Henry Graves, resisted efforts to transfer its management of national monuments.[27]

Dorr met with Secretary Houston and assured him that he would manage the proposed national monument at the lowest federal salary—a dollar a month! Dorr, the Boston Brahmin, was too politically astute not to recognize the territorial issue at the heart of the matter—that the Interior Department would maneuver the Sieur de Monts National Monument into its fold and that other national monuments would follow suit. Doubtful that his words were convincing, Dorr asked Eliot to intercede with Houston, who had been a Harvard colleague.[28] Whatever transpired between the two, the secretary then informed Wilson that he thought the president should accept the Hancock County Trustee deeds. On July 8, 1916 President Woodrow Wilson signed the proclamation (No. 1339–19 Stat. 1785) creating the Sieur de Monts National Monument—seven weeks before the establishment of the National Park Service. The Department of the Interior assumed authority over 5,000 acres on Mount Desert Island.

It had taken the trustees fifteen years to achieve much more than the protection the incorporators had envisioned and thought necessary back in 1901. Those who knew Dorr well realized that this achievement was but the first step in his vision. Not every trustee grasped Dorr's conceptual shift from membership exclusivity within a local land trust to the inclusiveness of the federal government.

Yet in early summer of 1916 there remained uncertainties, and serious concern about the outcome of National Park Service legislation. If established, how would this new agency apply its authority? The central issue revolved around opposing principles—the parks' use and enjoyment by the public versus their preservation in an unimpaired state. Since these principles had been recognized in the establishment of Yellowstone and other early national parks, Mather and Albright wisely treated them as standing policy that required little elaboration. In committee hearings prior to the House vote on establishing the Park Service, congressmen representing western cattlemen were concerned about whether livestock would continue to graze on national parkland. Mather agreed with the principle of selective grazing, surprising many conservationists. Later, when colleagues asked him about this concession, he said that ideals had to be stretched to reach immediate goals. Moreover, Mather argued consistently that grazing was already the standing policy in Mesa Verde, Yosemite, and Sequoia—though his colleagues blanched when pragmatism trumped idealism.[29]

In due course, however, the Park Service legislation (39 Stat. 535) quietly moved through the congressional process and on August 25, 1916 President Wilson signed the National Park Service Act (16 U.S.C. Sect. 1,2,3, and 4). Secretary Lane appointed Stephen Tyng Mather as NPS director; he then appointed Horace M. Albright as assistant director.

The National Park Service Act was significant for no fewer than three reasons: First, it created a new conservation agency to protect and improve the administration of the national parks. Second, "it marked the emergence of aesthetic conservationists—the so-called 'nature lovers'—as an effective, organized force within the national conservation movement…[and it] forecast the end of Gifford Pinchot's domination of national conservation affairs and the decline of his strictly utilitarian conservation philosophy."[30]

Dorr's conservation effort at the micro level paralleled the larger efforts of Mather and Albright. Both movements charted new territory within the conventions of the Interior Department. They evolved organizationally within a political climate charged by looming fears of America's entry into the Great War. Also, they were championed by men of principle and tenacity. For the first time in his life, Dorr was constrained from afar by his new position as a federal custodian. Would the self-directed Boston Brahmin be able to work with the distant and untried NPS? How would his new federal role affect his organizational commitments and personal relationships? Would other trustees—most notably Charles W. Eliot—relate to Dorr differently now that he was accountable to Washington?

Before departing for Bar Harbor, Dorr summarized in a memorandum for Secretary Lane his most immediate objectives: to expand the landlocked monument's boundaries to the ocean's edge and acquire the mountains on either side of Somes Sound; to secure adequate monument access by developing roadways to select valleys, mountains, and meadows; and to acquire additional contiguous tracts that lent themselves to the purposes of a "biologic reservation" where students could be taught how to best conserve and exhibit the region's native flora and fauna.[31]

The specific means whereby these objectives would best be realized were left unstated. The central issue was Dorr's understanding of what measures would politically position Sieur de Monts to be upgraded to national park status. Hal Rothman's formidable study of *America's National Monuments* emphasizes that Sieur de Monts "was established to facilitate later attempts to create a national park....[it] was earmarked for eventual park status from the moment it was created. Its main features were scenic and recreational and it was not likely to remain in the monument category for long."[32]

Historians would later characterize the Sieur de Monts National Monument as "a way-station national monument." What Dorr and his colleagues would quickly achieve was nothing less than the precedent-setting modification of the scope of new National Park Service standards. This new federal property "changed the national park criteria...[for it] offered the agency what no western park could—a balanced geographic distribution of American national parks and monuments.... [This] strategically far-sighted move...[was] the first step toward making the national parks and monuments truly national." [33]

This bold vision pervaded the opening celebration of the Sieur de Monts National Monument, which took place at the Building of the Arts on August 22nd, just three days prior to the establishment of the National Park Service. The audience heard Judge Deasy repeatedly refer to the establishment of this "park" —rather than this "monument." The celebrated lawyer was not a man to be fuzzy in the use of language. Yet on this historic occasion his brief speech contained eight uses of the word "park." This was clearly an affirmation of the national significance of the day when portions of Mount Desert Island were rescued by the federal government "from the indignity of constant division and development for profit in private hands."[34]

In his remarks, Eliot identified Mr. Dorr as the "principal worker" whose "wise and far-reaching vision...persistent enthusiasm and devotion to...the public good," brought his vision into reality. Mr. Dorr, however, spoke not of the historic record. Instead, he drew upon Deasy's words and stressed the opportunities and challenges that faced the trustees and friends of "this park." Dr. Alfred G. Mayer—whom Gifford Pinchot had visited in the Tortugas research facility—outlined how further expanded federal property might attract "men of science working in Government bureaus, in the museums and universities." Dr. Mayer had been invited to speak by Mr. Dorr, and his presentation was a call to fulfill the third objective—the development of a "biological reservation"—that Dorr had detailed a month earlier in his memorandum to Secretary Lane.

In a few years, Mayer would be instrumental in furthering that objective. In 1907, Dorr had purchased a 14.5-acre parcel of Mount Desert Island property in Salisbury Cove that had looked promising as a wharf for a proposed transit line to the mainland; a project gone sour.[35] In 1914, he and summer resident Dr. Robert Abbe had raised funds locally to honor the memory of physician S. Weir Mitchell—one of America's foremost neurologists—for his public service to Bar Harbor.[36] While some favored a memorial on the village green, Dorr and Abbe thought that a living memorial in the life sciences would be more fitting to Mitchell's scientific achievements.

Dorr had earlier approached Dr. Mayer, to seek his counsel on the suitability of the Salisbury Cove site as a marine biology research station. Mayer, a former student and colleague of the distinguished Harvard Professor Louis Agassiz, was widely known for his findings at the marine zoology research laboratory in Florida. Dorr reasoned that Mayer's ten years of experimentation might help him, as custodian to the new monument, fulfill the Bar Harbor community's desire to memorialize Mitchell and also set into motion the promise of marine biological research on Mount Desert Island.

News of Mayer's public endorsement of Dorr's idea prompted in the late summer of 1916 a letter from one of Mayer's former Tortugas collaborators, Ulric Dalgren of the Harpswell Station in Casco Bay.[37] The marine laboratory there faced a "severe setback"—America's entry into World War I in May of 1917 had depleted faculty ranks of this economically marginal facility, threatening its continued existence. The wealth associated with the summer residents of Mount Desert Island and the prospect of generous donors was irresistible to the trustees of the Harpswell Station, who speculated that biologists would mingle "with the owners of great estates at fund-raising teas and receptions."[38]

Following the end of the war, a letter from Dorr to Mr. Rockefeller modestly stated that Dorr would "be going down to Bar Harbor in a couple of weeks' time with reference to the establishment of a marine biological laboratory this summer at Salisbury Cove."[39] In 1922, eighty acres of adjacent land was purchased and named the Weir Mitchell Station. Documentation suggests that donors believed that the property would in time be incorporated into the national park—though that would not be its fate.[40]

In late 1923, Dorr offered to deed the leased tract, subject to several conditions. The most notable caveat was that ownership would revert to one of his corporate entities—the Wild Gardens of Acadia—if active biological research was discontinued for a period of three consecutive years. This caveat was intended to impress upon the Harpswell trustees the serious interest of Dorr and his associates in the success of this new scientific endeavor. Plain-speaking J. Wendell Burger, laboratory director from 1947 to 1950, called the WGA "a dummy corporation…to hold land for cultural uses, outside the Park." Moreover, the laboratory Dorr envisioned was "a spin-off of the formation of Acadia National Park" executed by one who was "no administrative fool, full of only philanthropic motives. He laid down strictures for [the new facility] whereby if the enterprise failed 'he' could recover the tract."[41] The Harpswell trustees accepted the terms of the man whom Berger described as a "political genius," the property renamed the Mount Desert Island Biological Laboratory on November 10, 1923. Within several years the laboratory's financial goals were realized largely through significant and sustained contributions by John D. Rockefeller Jr.[42] Dorr's interest in the capacity of the laboratory to further public and scientific understanding of the Frenchman Bay marine life did not wane—he continued to serve as a trustee of the organization until 1938.

In our own day, researchers at the Mount Desert Island Biological Laboratory investigate vertebrate physiology, the membrane transport mechanisms in the kidney, and the processes whereby genes, chemicals, and disease interact within humans and their environments. After more than ninety years of operation, the results of such investigations are due in no small part to Dorr's ability to envision this research facility as a strategic component of island-wide development. Nevertheless, Dorr was clearly not content with what could be realized with local and island-based applications of marine research. Ever mindful of the larger context, Dorr pointed out to his superiors that this first seacoast national park provided a foundation for marine science research in the National Park Service as a whole.

It was not unexpected that Dorr would take his responsibilities as monument custodian seriously—and proactively. His authority was initially ill defined. This mattered little to someone with a clear set of priorities about what needed to be done at both the local and national level. Without a budget that first year, the new "custodian" was dependent on support from island trail chairmen and their volunteers. Aware that the new National Park Service was committed to system-wide standards—including criteria at odds with local conventions—Dorr boldly informed village improvement society trail chairmen that "the trails committee ought not… lay out new important trails over federal lands," establish new routes, or make new connections without "due consultation" with himself and with the chairman of any other path committee whose trails intersect. Dorr also delineated preliminary policies for landscape uniformity, fire safety, and wildlife management.[43] He also continued memorial trail construction "as part of a plan to enhance the public reservation and improve its eligibility for designation as a national monument or park."[44] Between 1913 and 1916 Dorr worked on the Sieur de Monts Spring area as a nexus of trails to downtown Eden and the mountains surrounding the area. Utilizing memorial funds donated by residents, six memorial paths were undertaken in these critical years leading up to federalization.

Throughout the early months of 1916, Dorr studied the natural and cultural history of the mountains traversed by these paths. He was preparing to challenge the suitability of long-standing mountain nomenclature, a risky move that began with a thorough investigation into the historical associations of each federally acquired geological feature. Where the historical roots were shallow, Dorr developed alternative historical arguments for a topographic renaming that would be adjudicated by the United States Board on Geographic Names, a federal authority that met not far from Dorr's D.C. lodging at the Cosmos Club.[45]

In the fall of 1916, before departing Mount Desert Island for Washington to lobby for an adequate appropriation for maintenance and administration of the new national monument, Dorr composed a strategic memorandum for the new National Park Service officials. In preparing for national park status, he claimed that the size of the federal property could be quickly doubled through additional donations and trustee acquisitions in order to "take in the whole mountain range and its adjoining valleys, together with good wharfages and sea approaches, and a considerable extent of shore." Dorr then advocated a "costly" and "intensive" acquisition of "certain noble [ocean-front] features" where the appropriate "landscape effects" availed by the vegetation and geological structures could be optimized for their scenic impact on tourists.

In addition, for the first time he also proposed that the park ought to become "one of the great health resorts [and] recreative areas of the county," centered around its inviting and expanding path system. Furthermore, its potential as "a great biological station" for scientific research in diverse areas awaited full realization. Finally, he reminded Albright that the monument had a historic mission to "enrich the national life with memories and associations" that were slipping from its grasp, implying that the *Sieur de Monts Publications* would be a key cultural enrichment tool and further support the NPS effort to promote park themes.[46] Dorr could not anticipate that during the next three years his publicity efforts would be dwarfed by "a total of 1,050 magazine articles [with diverse agendas and points of view] published on national park subjects."[47]

In the seven years since the donation of The Bowl and The Beehive by Mrs. Charles Homans, the objectives of the trustees had been transformed through a successful campaign to secure federal protection for lands on Mount Desert Island. Establishment of Sieur de Monts National Monument was secured as the National Park Service labored through its birth pangs. Mather, Albright, and other key officials would quickly learn that the character of Mr. Dorr's leadership required innovative strategies on their part—and that the effectiveness of the National Park Service improved as a result of Dorr's wise counsel.

Boston Common. Detail of an 1814 map of Boston by John Groves Hale, showing on the left the Charles River prior to filling in of the Back Bay. On the opposite end of the Boston Common is Park Street, where Dorr's grandparents would reside beginning in 1816. *From the Boston Public Library, via Wikimedia Commons.*

Thomas Wren Ward, maternal grandfather of George B. Dorr. *Portrait by William Page, courtesy of Harvard Art Museums.*

Ice skating illustration of Jamaica Pond, where on the eastern shoreline (to the right) Dorr was born at home on December 29, 1853. West Roxbury, MA. *1859 lithograph from Library of Congress Prints and Photographs Division, via Wikimedia Commons.*

Park Street in Boston, 1868. The Boston Common, on the left, ran one block north to the Boston State House. On the right is the Park Street Church; the third residence beyond is that of Thomas Wren and Lydia Ward, grandparents of George B. Dorr. *Courtesy of the Boston Athenaeum.*

The Dorr family's Boston residence at 18 Commonwealth Avenue (on right). George B. Dorr resided here at least seasonally for more than a half century, from 1863 to 1914. After 1878 he spent May through October on Mount Desert Island. *Courtesy of the Boston Athenaeum.*

First agents of Mount Desert Island conservation, 1881. The Champlain Society was begun by Harvard University student Charles Eliot, who in 1880 first brought scientifically minded college chums to research and conserve the native habitat. *Courtesy of the Mount Desert Island Historical Society.*

St. Joseph School children visit Sieur de Monts Spring, circa 1918. *Courtesy of the National Park Service, Acadia National Park.*

Audience departing from the Building of the Arts, circa 1918. *Courtesy of the National Park Service, Acadia National Park.*

Hancock County Trustee of Public Reservations president Charles William Eliot. Photograph taken by George B. Dorr at Asticou, 1919. *Courtesy of the Northeast Harbor Library Archives.*

George B. Dorr and Charles W. Eliot beside Jordan Pond with Penobscot Mountain in the background, circa 1919. *Courtesy of the National Park Service, Acadia National Park.*

Descendants of newspaper entrepreneur Joseph Pulitzer enjoy the spring and park information office at Sieur de Monts, circa 1919. *Courtesy of the National Park Service, Acadia National Park.*

John Davison Rockefeller Jr. This 1920 image shows the philanthropist as he expanded the carriage road system from The Eyrie in Seal Harbor into the new national park. *Library of Congress photograph, via Wikimedia Commons.*

The Honorable John A. Peters, in front of the Sieur de Monts springhouse. This unattributed photo originally appeared in a 1920 supplement to the *Bar Harbor Times* titled "Lafayette National Park, Bar Harbor, Maine," in which the photo caption noted that "Mr. Peters, influential Member of Congress from this district, has been active in securing for his native state the first National Park east of the Mississippi and the first in the country bordering upon the sea."

Dorr welcomes to Bar Harbor friends of long standing: the Rev. William H. Carnegie (Dean of Westminster Abbey), Ellen Peabody Endicott, and her daughter, Mary C. Endicott Carnegie, circa 1920. *Courtesy of the National Park Service, Acadia National Park.*

Judge Luere B. Deasy on a path near Sieur de Monts Spring, circa 1921. *Courtesy of the National Park Service, Acadia National Park.*

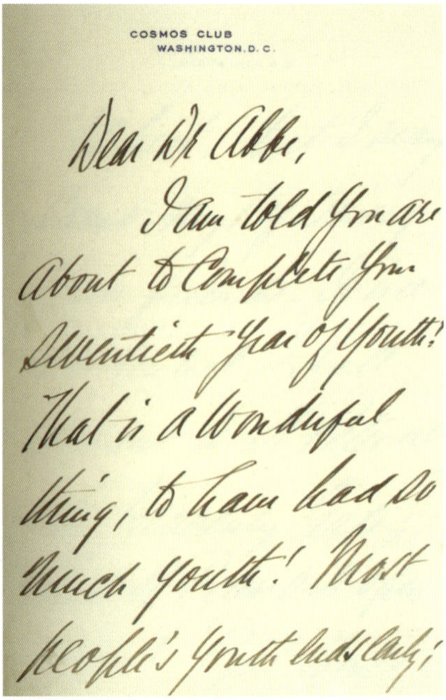

COSMOS CLUB
WASHINGTON, D. C.

Dear Dr Abbe,
I am told you are about to complete your seventieth year of youth! That is a wonderful thing, to have had so much youth! Most people's youth ends early;

The distinctive handwriting of George B. Dorr is evident in his February 16, 1921 letter to Robert Abbe, congratulating the physician on his seventieth birthday and a life "that is rare, beautiful and fine." *From the collection of the Abbe Museum, Bar Harbor, Maine.*

Oldfarm, the Bar Harbor residence of the Dorr family, circa 1923. This rear view of the building shows the steps leading from the veranda to Dorr Point on Frenchman Bay. Superintendent Dorr's bed chamber was the "Sea Room," on the peaked third floor. *Courtesy of the National Park Service, Acadia National Park.*

Entrance foyer at Oldfarm, 1922. Herbert W. Gleason, photographer. *Courtesy of the National Park Service, Acadia National Park.*

Bar Harbor attorney Albert H. Lynam in front of the park office located at Main and Park Street, Bar Harbor, circa 1922. *Courtesy of the National Park Service, Acadia National Park.*

NPS Director Stephen T. Mather (third from right) and his party on Champlain Mountain, overlooking The Bowl, in June 1922. Superintendent Dorr is seated in front of Mather. Herbert W. Gleason, photographer. *Courtesy of the National Park Service, Acadia National Park.*

Iconic H.W. Gleason photograph of leaders from four Mount Desert Island village improvement associations, at Jordan Pond in 1923. From left, Joseph Allen, Walter Buell, Fred Weeks, Charles H. Grandgent, William Turner, Thomas McIntire, and George B. Dorr. *Courtesy of the National Park Service, Acadia National Park.*

Mount Desert Nurseries greenhouse, circa 1923. *Courtesy of the National Park Service, Acadia National Park.*

NPS Director Stephen Mather stands on ladder immediately beneath George B. Dorr at the Cliff Palace in Mesa Verde National Park. Park service staff and their families gathered there in October 1925 for the Eighth Superintendents Conference. James V. Lloyd, photographer. *Courtesy of the National Park Service Historic Photograph Collection.*

Suspendered George B. Dorr (left) hikes with Maine Governor Ralph Brewster (center) and the Hon. Willis E. Parsons atop the summit of Katahdin, July 1925. *In the Maine Woods*, 1926. *Courtesy of Colby College Special Collections, Waterville, Maine.*

California newspaperman Ralph O. Yardley's delightful caricature of the park superintendent, circa 1925. *Courtesy of the National Park Service Historic Photograph Collection, Harpers Ferry Center for Media Services.*

Sixteen members of the Acadia National Park staff, circa 1940. Assistant Superintendent Benjamin Hadley is to the right of Mr. Dorr. *Courtesy of the National Park Service, Acadia National Park.*

George B. Dorr (seated, third from left) entertains a congressional party on the Oldfarm terrace, June 12–14, 1937. House Naval Affairs Committee members from Minnesota, Oregon, Virginia, and three New England states participated. *Courtesy of the National Park Service, Acadia National Park.*

A dozing George B. Dorr, circa 1942, at Storm Beach Cottage, the modest home he and his father built before Oldfarm was completed. *Courtesy of the National Park Service, Acadia National Park.*

Acadia National Park rangers flank the Dorr Memorial, Sieur de Monts Spring. Dedication ceremony, August 29, 1947. *Courtesy of the Woodlawn Museum, Ellsworth, Maine.*

CHAPTER FOURTEEN

The First Eastern National Park

Scribner's Magazine published in April 1917 Beatrix Farrand's "The National Park on Mount Desert Island." This well-crafted description of the island's geology, flora, and fauna by the esteemed landscape architect supplemented Dorr's efforts—in recent issues of the *Sieur de Monts Publications*—to promote the idea that the new national monument was truly a national park in every sense but in name and should be elevated to full park status. Similar reasons sparked Dorr's publication six months later of "The Sieur de Monts National Monument and the Wild Gardens of Acadia" in the inaugural volume of *The Journal of the International Garden Club.*[1]

Farrand's article contained a brief history of the Hancock County Trustees, an outline of the development of the path system, and praise for the "far-sighted devotion" of Mr. Dorr in enlarging park boundaries and establishing the Wild Gardens of Acadia. "Everyone who comes, either now or in the future, should remember that [he or she] owes a large share of [their] enjoyment to the clear vision, the wise development, and the self-sacrificing enthusiasm of the first custodian of the park."[2] What escaped public scrutiny was the inaccurate use of "national park" in the title. We might suppose that Farrand was intentionally prescriptive; she would not have been alone in that mission.

Four months earlier and on another stage, national park proponents had mounted a significant publicity event—the Fourth National Parks

Conference, which Mather planned prior to the establishment of the National Park Service. On January 2, 1917, park superintendents gathered in the auditorium of the Museum of Natural History in Washington, D.C. Interior Secretary Lane and Assistant Secretary Mather presided. The "much misunderstood" concept of a national monument was subsequently addressed in the *1917 Report of the Director of the National Park Service,* in which Mather affirmed that national parks and monuments are "practically identical." Information about this gathering came to Mr. Dorr second-hand, since he was not yet a park superintendent. The new national monument on Mount Desert Island, nonetheless, had been a topic of conference discussion inasmuch as it was described as "unexcelled by any of the other monuments…in accessibility, opportunity for experimental work, and as a field for botanical and zoological study."[3]

Following this strenuous conference, several days later Mather suffered a nervous breakdown at the Cosmos Club. According to his biographer, "two years of unrelieved high tension had broken Mather down as he had broken down in 1903."[4] Within six months of its formation, the National Park Service faced its first crisis: Could the NPS move forward as an organization under the interim leadership of Horace M. Albright? Mather's true condition was shielded from the public eye as he received therapy in a Pennsylvania sanitarium. One month after the April 1917 declaration of war against Germany, Albright was appointed acting director. He beefed up his staff, centralized the administration, formulated uniform policies, and applied them consistently, system-wide. Albright insisted that Mather would rally from his manic-depressive state. Twenty-one months would pass before the director resumed his NPS responsibilities.[5]

On Mount Desert Island, Dorr discreetly turned his attention to the study of possible conservation properties in Southwest Harbor. It was only later, in the fall of 1919, that Dorr fully revealed that in 1917 he had received "in trust certain funds from Mr. Rockefeller to employ [Mr. Schuyler R. Clark of Southwest Harbor] in acquiring lands for reservations and inclusion in the park."[6] Clark was selected as an agent so that the names of Dorr and Rockefeller would not appear in a public listing of land transactions. John D. Rockefeller Jr.'s quiet financial arrangement with George Dorr to acquire conservation properties had begun. Dorr ranked the most important properties and Clark proceeded to acquire with great discretion those that were available, well aware that the price would inflate should the involvement of the philanthropist become known.

That fall, Mr. Rockefeller donated to the HCTPR one hundred acres on Beech Hill Cliff and another hundred adjacent acres on Echo Lake, the first of many Rockefeller land donations that eventually became federal property. By Dorr's own admission, he was working "under considerable difficulties, having the park lands included in the national monument [with] no appropriation from Congress to take care of them or for obtaining clerical assistance."[7] He certainly was further challenged by Franklin Lane's acceptance of the invitation to visit Mount Desert Island for a first-hand inspection of the new national monument; at the same time, Horace Albright was preparing to tour several western national monuments. Dorr pointed out to Secretary Lane that access to the island's mountains had improved with costly new trails through Otter Creek Gorge, and via the construction of a demanding path to the summit of Dry (now Dorr) Mountain. Lane was sufficiently impressed that he encouraged Dorr to request $50,000 for the first year of federal appropriations. Due to America's entry into the war, however, Dorr later admitted to Eliot that there was "no chance of getting any appropriation…at the present session" of Congress.[8]

On August 23, Dorr and Lane left Oldfarm for lunch with Mr. Rockefeller at The Eyrie estate, atop Barr Hill in Seal Harbor. This was the first interaction between the philanthropist and the most senior Interior Department official. Discussion focused on plans for an extended road system. Sensitive to development issues involving carriage roads adjacent to park lands, Rockefeller received Lane's approval to begin the expansion with an understanding that the government would prohibit automobile access to the carriage roads.[9]

Lane's recollections of that first visit to Mount Desert Island were highly positive. In a letter to philanthropist Henry Lane Eno, a friend of Dorr's who had also been on hand during Lane's visit, Lane remarked that "there are not many weeks in a man's life of which he can say that one was without a flaw, that it could not have been improved upon in company, comfort, or surroundings. And all these things, my dear Mr. Eno, I can affirm of the days spent with you… As I look back I think of but one good thing that gives occasion for regret—we had too few good, mind-stretching talks, you, Dorr, and myself. But those we had were certainly not about affairs of small concern. We indulged ourselves as social philosophers, psychologists, war-makers, and international statesmen. The world was ours, and more—the worlds beyond.... I am sending a line to Dorr, noble, unselfish, high-spirited, broad-minded gentleman that he is."[10]

Shortly thereafter, Lane wrote to Dorr that political figures were always looking for a place to retire. After this visit, "if I could have an extended term of exile on your island with you and your friends, I would feel reconciled to banishment from politics for life, provided however...that we had time and money to make the park what it should be—a demonstration school for the American to show how much he can add to the beauty of Nature. A wilderness, no matter how impressive and beautiful, does not satisfy this soul of mine.... It is a challenge to man. It says, 'Master me! Put me to use! Make me something more than I am.' So what you have done in the park—the Spring House and the Arts Building, the cliff trails and the opened woods, show how much may be added by the love and thought of man. May the gods be good to you...that your dreams may come true, and that you may give to others the pleasure you gave to yours sincerely."[11] Four years later, Lane—son of a Canadian preacher from Prince Edward Island—died at fifty-seven, too soon to see his wish come true.

Over the winter of 1918, Eliot and Dorr both expended considerable energy educating members of the House and Senate about the importance of elevating the new national monument—and of securing appropriations for its management. Dorr urged Eliot to enlist the support of the influential Winthrop Murray Crane, the former junior senator from Massachusetts and fortieth governor of Massachusetts. Crane responded positively, communicating to the ranking Republican on the House Appropriations Committee, Massachusetts congressman Frederick Huntington Gillett. Within the month, Dorr secured a meeting with Congressman Gillett. Following productive discussion, Dorr informed Eliot that Gillett "said there was no question as to the justice and reasonableness of our [appropriation] claim."[12]

Congress apparently agreed, granting an initial appropriation of $10,000. This level of financial support implicitly recognized the national-park-worthy character of Sieur de Monts National Monument. Congress had conceptually bridged the gap between monument and national park, enabling Dorr to enlist administrative staff. Secretary Lane appointed Princeton University's Henry Lane Eno as park ornithologist, New England Botanical Society secretary—and Champlain Society member—Edward L. Rand as park botanist, and Boston Natural History Museum researcher Charles W. Johnson as its entomologist. When the national park on Mount Desert Island was established in 1919, attorney A. H. Lynam became assistant superintendent. Whether these were salaried appointments is uncertain. Confidentially, John A. Peters assured Dorr that the House Land Committee would take up the matter of the monument's status following the summer recess.[13] A park office was established in July 1918 at the corner of Main Street and Park Road, leased from the Wild Gardens of Acadia.

In spite of Dorr's success, his collaborators had some concerns about his behavior and habits, which they expressed openly as well as privately. He was about to leave for Washington to press his case for monument appropriations—and more importantly, full national park status—when he received a letter from Dr. Eliot, who stopped just short of demanding an immediate and full accounting of all land acquisition activity with which his name was associated as president of the HCTPR. No explanation was offered for this urgent request for information about land negotiations and transactions: "Before you leave home again I hope you will make a list of all pledges given by you, all projects concerning the monument and the Wild Gardens which you have actually entered on, and your visions which have not yet been put on paper. This is the piece of work which should take precedence [over every] other. It ought to be done today, or tomorrow at the latest."[14]

Mr. Rockefeller was aware of Eliot's concerns about Dorr's entrepreneurial approach to land acquisition, the absence of shared documentation about the status of complex negotiations, and the extent of Dorr's indebtedness. Eliot confided to the philanthropist that "nobody knows what the lands are which Mr. Dorr has established some kind of claim on," a concern that was likely felt by other trustees. Eliot was clearly frustrated at his inability to motivate Dorr "to write down the information he has in his head about lands on this Island which ought to go either to the National Park or the Wild Gardens." Moreover, Eliot was concerned because Dorr's familiarity with the island human and natural history "ought to have been written down years ago [but] he has on paper only scattered memoranda that nobody else could make anything out of, and he himself cannot find when he wants them. I fear that the situation is a hopeless one....[for] he lives in such a preposterous way as respects the care of his health, and takes so many absurd risks in rushing about this Island that we are likely to lose him any day by disease or accident."[15]

This is a startling list of concerns. On the one hand there is the claim that Dorr had failed to document activities and decisions in ways that are intelligible to others; then the assertion that "he lives in such a preposterous way" that his mortality is at risk. But the source of this criticism is a man in his late eighties surrounded by a large family, having lived within the largely risk-free environment of academia. The lifestyle contrast is conspicuous. Admittedly, surviving first-hand documentation of Dorr's first four decades of life is shallow at best; the managerial evidence of Mount Desert Nurseries is marginal; Dorr's letters for the first fifteen years of the Hancock Country Trustees are contained in the papers of Charles W. Eliot and others. A case could be made for Dorr being inattentive to the importance of "historical associations" when applied to documenting his own life.

Two issues bear on the accuracy of this interpretation. Possessing phenomenal retentive powers, Mr. Dorr lived in his head and was unwilling to devote time and energy to passive organizational efforts; moreover, he lacked the supportive apparatus of Dr. Eliot. Yet most importantly, the recently uncovered records of Albert H. Lynam in the archives of the firm's successors demonstrate that at this time in his life Mr. Dorr provided his attorney with a wealth of documentation that would have likely satisfied Dr. Eliot and Mr. Rockefeller—had they only known of its existence.

Many years later, Horace Albright wrote that "the most important issue" he faced in late February 1918 was the Sieur de Monts National Monument. "It was the first national park area east of the Mississippi, created only a year and a half before." That he refers to the federal land on Mount Desert as "a national park" demonstrates its standing in the minds of the senior-most NPS officials a full year before its elevation received congressional approval. In contrast to the practical, political, and principled concerns of Dr. Eliot and Mr. Rockefeller, Albright makes clear that above all "this particular monument was close to my heart because of George Dorr."[16]

On May 30, 1918 the House Committee on Public Lands (HCPL) initiated questioning of Mr. Dorr about "Mount Desert National Park," a fascinating fourteen-page inquiry that included twenty-four pages of supportive testimony. What was brought to the table by the Hancock County Trustees of Public Reservations was a donation of 5,000 acres to be added to the original 5,000 acres of the national monument—a doubling of acreage of what was then referred to as Mount Desert National Park.[17]

Secretary Lane attached four arguments for creating a national park with these lands. Specifically, he argued for (1) the historic value of the island, (2) the aesthetic distinction of combining sea and mountains unrealized elsewhere in the National Park Service, (3) the conservation value of its geology, flora, and fauna, and (4) its merits as a recreational asset easily accessible to the major population centers on the eastern seaboard. Following an April 1918 lunch with Dorr at the Colony Club in New York, Theodore Roosevelt also urged favorable action by the HCPL, for he had "watched with keen interest the work that has led to the creation of this Park," stressing both its recreational and wilderness appeal.[18] Thirteen additional letters of support were submitted to the committee by distinguished attorneys, clerics, ornithologists, geologists, public servants, and businessmen. To secure national monument status Dorr had relied on the credibility of local agencies and regionally notable persons; once the Park Service was created, his strategy shifted to the national stage coupled with the published findings of scientists of national and international standing.

Elsewhere in Washington, Albright made use of many of Mather's ideas to draft "a creed, a framework of ideological guidelines to which the National Park Service could aspire and grow in the future as time and conditions might change." This so-called Magna Carta of the national parks was circulated to a top tier of conservation advocates before it was presented to Secretary Lane. Three broad management principles were delineated: first, all system units "must be maintained in absolutely unimpaired form for the use of future generations as well as those of our time; second, they are set aside for the use, observation, health, and pleasure of the people; and third, the national interest must dictate all decisions affecting public or private enterprise in the parks."[19] As to the manner of its distribution, Albright suggested that the May 13, 1918 document with its two dozen policy standards should come from the interior secretary as a directive to Mather. And so it was accomplished, masking for some time the authorship of this foundational document, a technique often employed in developing Acadia National Park.

At the same time, Albright faced "a concerted effort…to make adverse use of the parks, excusing it as patriotism but, in reality, attempting to open them once and for all for commercial and money-making projects alien to the park service's Organic Act."[20] Commercialism was being directed at something other than the war effort as the fighting neared its end; there were national feelings of a new beginning. Yet on Mount Desert Island and elsewhere throughout the country the public was alarmed by public health announcements about the rapid spread of Spanish influenza. In late August of 1918 sailors stationed in Boston reported symptoms of the grippe. Throughout September the disease spread, and by early October hundreds of Americans died daily in metropolitan areas. From Asticou, Eliot wrote that "influenza has attacked Northeast Harbor severely; and is likely to go far."[21] Only later would health statisticians document the catastrophic dimensions of the pandemic—more than twenty million deaths worldwide, including 675,000 Americans. In such an environment, it is not surprising that three months later Dorr would finalize his earliest extant last will and testament.[22]

In this unstable environment, two identical bills were introduced in the 65th Congress for the creation of Mount Desert National Park; one (S. 4569) sponsored by Senator Frederick Hale and another (H.R. 11935) by Representative John A. Peters, both of Maine. These bills sought to resolve HCPL confusion about the park's name and location, the landscape character of the area (due primarily to the word "desert"), and the intent of its supporters to connect the park to its French heritage as well as the events of the current war.

Some suggested that Mount Desert National Park or George B. Dorr National Park were the most appropriate names. But according to a September 27, 1918 press release from the Interior Department, the "magnificent frontage [of the proposed park] on the great ocean highway which our troops are traversing to France's aid and for whose freedom we are now contending, no more striking expression of national regard and amity could be conceived than the creation…of our first eastern national park."[23] Eliot thought that Lafayette was "a good name for the Park, although he was never much of a hero in France."[24] Nonetheless, the official Interior Department announcement stressed that the name was chosen for our first eastern national park as "a symbol of international friendship between America and France."[25] Horace Albright later remarked that "Dorr and I really didn't approve of the name [Lafayette], but we went along with it until I became director of the service in 1929. Then I pushed through the name that we had chosen years before, Acadia National Park."[26]

The Senate passed its bill (S. 4957) in early October 1918, and it was referred back to the HCPL. Conservation pioneer Theodore Roosevelt died on January 6, 1919. As the nation mourned, Stephen Mather resumed his responsibilities, the political process moved forward, and the House approved the park legislation unanimously on February 17.[27] In appreciation, Dorr sent Peters several of his dramatic Lafayette National Park landscape photographs, which the congressman proudly displayed in his Washington office.

President Woodrow Wilson prepared for peace talks. In Paris, he visited the tomb of Lafayette, leaving behind a wreath and his card, writing on it: "In memory of the great Lafayette, from a fellow servant of liberty."[28] Well publicized was Wilson's promotion of the League of Nations in the face of the horrific outcome of the war. As Wilson's biographer emphasizes: "The Great war had taken the lives of 16.5 million people, roughly a third of them civilians.... 116,000 brave Americans would not see Hoboken, and another 700,000 would return to the United States wounded."[29]

Despite Wilson's disinterest in conservation and the national parks, when he returned to Washington he quickly signed the Lafayette National Park bill on February 26, 1919. Horace Albright recalled that the new national park "could have been named George B. Dorr National Park, for if ever a park was achieved by the inspiration and determination of one man, it was this one."[30] This legislation also established Grand Canyon National Park, the two parks tying for seventeenth place in the growth of the national park system.[31]

Besides Dorr's continuing use of the *Sieur de Monts Publications* to promote the park, he also supported the efforts of writers to reach a much larger constituency than this specialized series. An editor for *Munsey's Magazine* had written historical and nature-centered articles for the mass-marketed serial—one of the first of its kind. As early as September 1919,

William S. Bridgman's eleven-page article on "The Lafayette National Park" was being seen by tens of thousands of readers, who also viewed the nine superb black-and-white uncredited photographs by the park superintendent, Mr. Dorr.[32]

Conspicuous in hindsight is the absence of any mention of Mr. Rockefeller's carriage roads in the Farrand and Bridgman articles. Of course, the carriage roads were private and not to be included in park promotion. But, in the long run both they and the bridges would become known to the public and become much celebrated park features. The first bridge, constructed in 1917, was distinguished by being faced with smooth cobblestones concealing a reinforced concrete structure. The Cobblestone Bridge, crossing Jordan Stream, connected the Jordan Pond House to carriage roads surrounding The Eyrie in Seal Harbor. Mr. Dorr criticized it as "artistically" inappropriate even as it became a most popular destination; it is the only bridge that was never transferred to the park, remaining restricted to carriage, horse, and pedestrian use.[33]

Two other bridges also designed by architect William Welles Bosworth—Little Harbor Brook and Jordan Stream—were completed as the national monument formally became a national park. Carriage road expansion necessitated seven additional bridges designed by Bosworth; the final seven bridges built between 1928 and 1938 were designed by Charles W. Stoughton. All of the bridges, excepting Cobblestone, are made of native rough-cut granite on modified Gothic or barrel arches, thirteen being single arches. The Amphitheater Bridge is the longest at 235 feet. Designed to be sited in the deep woods, only three are close to motor roads.[34]

Following an inspection of Rocky Mountain National Park and advocacy of an enlargement of Sequoia National Park, Horace Albright returned from the West Coast as father of a baby boy—named Robert Mather Albright. Director Mather had known for the last three years that Albright intended to return to a private law practice. Now Albright had new offers from a San Francisco firm, and his letter of resignation was submitted in early March. Within a month Mather offered a plum: a new position as both superintendent of Yellowstone National Park and field assistant to the director.[35] Albright accepted.

To fill the Washington vacancy, Mather reached outside the bureau to Arno B. Cammerer, who had been secretary to the Public Buildings Commission of Congress. With Albright gone, Dorr's efforts in Washington in the ensuing months depended substantially on the good will fostered with Mr. Mather and his new assistant director.

Throughout this national park gestation period, Dorr pursued research into the names of its prominent landscape features. He initiated correspondence with Frank Bond, who had been chief clerk of the General Land Office and had evaluated national monument proposals, drafting twenty-eight proclamations establishing national monuments between 1906 and 1911. Now aligned with the U.S. Board on Geographic Names (USBGN), Bond reviewed Dorr's rationale for his proposed renaming of a number of mountains within the park, each endorsed by the National Park Service.[36] Acadia, Bernard, Cadillac, Champlain, Huguenot Head, Mansell, and Norumbega were substituted for existing nomenclature, a decision that critics characterized as arbitrary. Dorr's motives for renaming these natural features were complex. Yet his most common complaint was that the existing names (Brown, Dog, Green, etc.) were undistinguished.[37]

Dorr did not, however, substitute names for all local nomenclature. To the contrary, Dorr, Dr. Eliot, and Samuel Eliot had recently completed some studies of the local Native Americans. In a letter to the USBGN, Dorr wrote at great length of his research into the Penobscot and Passamaquoddy tribes and his culture-based rationale for "changing the name of the mountain mass...whose northern and southern portions are now known as Sargent and Jordan Mountains respectively, to Penobscot Mountain."[38]

Furthermore, early island settlers often provided "excellent descriptive names" to the seacoast and harbored waters, where names like Egg Rock and Otter Creek suggest their own interesting ancestry. His guiding rationale was that "mountains and paths, woods, and lakes, must all have names for sake of distinction and as points visitor reference." This would not be the last instance where Dorr sidestepped public discussion, relying on his scholarly expertise in referencing a more ancient lineage than was customary on Mount Desert Island.[39]

Such action did not diminish his local popularity. At the 1919 annual town meeting in March, a unanimous resolution was passed: "That [the] inhabitants of Bar Harbor extend [their] most appreciative thanks to George

Bucknam Dorr for his tireless, persistent, intelligent work, carried on under the most adverse circumstances. He has overcome obstacles that no other friend of the [island] would have commanded the courage to overcome, and has finally secured for us and for our posterity the Lafayette National Park on Mount Desert Island. We regard the achievement as a crowning event in a life, so much of which has been devoted to the interest of Bar Harbor."[40]

Dorr had predicted the advent of a cultural shift, which became evident when the Town of Bar Harbor departed from its convention by appropriating $6,500 to "making known the town's newest asset in the Lafayette National Park."[41] Dorr credited this appropriation of public relations funding to Benjamin L. Hadley. This Bar Harbor native had recently been discharged from military service as commander of a tank corps. When he applied to the National Park Service he very much impressed Dorr, who offered him—after completion of Civil Service examinations—a position as clerk-stenographer.[42] He quickly advanced through the ranks—and nearly a quarter century later became Dorr's successor as superintendent. But for the time being, Dorr expressed his hope that this was but the beginning of a "permanent attitude...and of a sympathetic comprehension by [the Town residents] of the Park Service aims and plans." Similarly, Bar Harbor insurance agent Fred C. Lynam confided to Representative Peters that the village wished to cooperate with the park in promoting island resources, concluding that "the park will not only be a great thing for Bar Harbor but for the whole island and the county as well.... [And] I realize how much the success of this enterprise has depended upon the help that you have given to Mr. Dorr."[43]

Still, there were miscalculations. Well known at the time was the effort to erect a religious artifact atop Flying Mountain, modifying the natural landscape with a cultural icon. Seven years before the Pilgrims landed at Plymouth, the first European settlement on the island was at Jesuit Field on Fernald Point in present-day Southwest Harbor. In a follow-up letter to Mather, Dorr explained that the destruction of the settlement was not the result of Native Americans, who actually had befriended the Jesuits. Instead, "a hostile expedition from Virginia under the charge of Sir Samuel Argall" committed this "lawless and unjustifiable act" that killed or imprisoned the missionaries.[44]

Dorr continued, saying that three centuries later "a long time resident of Northeast Harbor [Mrs. Winthrop Sargent] and an old friend of my own, consulted me in the summer of 1917 with regard to commemorating the Jesuit settlement by the erection of a cross on Flying mountain." Ever attached to "historic associations," Dorr was part of a local committee that aimed to secure sufficient funds to erect on Flying Mountain a "stone cross—a 'Celtic' one." This memorial would inform those trekking to the summit about the significance of the French colony seeking a foothold in the New World. In his report to Washington, Dorr went so far as to state that this cross would promote the idea of a pilgrimage to a shrine.

With the approval of Secretary Lane, a thirty-foot temporary wooden cross designed by prominent Boston architect Ralph Adams Cram was erected on the proposed site. As the fall of 1918 approached, Dr. Eliot brought to Dorr's attention the fact that the cross "is objected to by a considerable number of persons, including most of the residents on the easterly side of Somes Sound."[45] Some were unsure what the cross was intended to represent, while others objected to its conspicuous visibility against the landscape.

Six months later the cross was removed at the direction of an unnamed member of the committee. The cross had been erected on private land, but if that land were to be transferred to the federal government, volatile issues relating to the separation of church and state would have come to the forefront. Moreover, the incident highlighted questions regarding a federal employee's involvement in private ventures. The erection of a temporary cross, after all, was the result of input from HCTPR members with the approval of the secretary of the interior. Nonetheless, the incident was instructive in reminding the new park superintendent that local sensitivities must be carefully weighed, and his administrative compass must always be referenced to the impact of his decisions as viewed from the nation's capital.

Shortly after the end of the Great War, a hundred people gathered in late July 1919 at Sieur de Monts Spring. A prayerful ceremony took place, centered on the planting of two young trees dedicated to lasting peace.[46] Benjamin Hadley joined Eliot and Dorr as they broke ground to plant two saplings provided by the Mount Desert Nurseries: a sequoia from Yosemite National Park (representing the West) beside a white pine (representing Maine). The sentiment conveyed was that "peace should endure as long as these trees should lend their shade to our forests."[47]

Dorr's interest in trees was not restricted to those native to American forests. Shortly after the Peace Tree plantings, the *Journal of the International Garden Club* published a submission from the new park superintendent, an important 1918 Italian-language article by Luigi Parpagliolo on the proposed first national park in Italy. The journal editors turned to Dorr to translate the article in order to show English-speaking readers a model for national park development in other countries. Three years after Dorr's translation appeared, Italy joined the small cohort of countries, including Sweden (1909), Switzerland (1914), and Spain (1918), that had recently created national parks.[48] Situated in the Central Apennines east of Rome, Abruzzo National Park became over time the hub from which radiated a system of parks and protected areas.

In early November 1919, Dorr traveled to Denver and Rocky Mountain National Park to participate for the first time in a National Park Conference. This was the fifth such conference, the location of each successive event shifting in order to expose park superintendents to the regional management challenges faced by their peers. Following the conference, Dorr visited "certain western parks" before returning to Washington, D.C., where he stayed until year's end.[49] The train travel gave him ample opportunity to reflect on what had been achieved—and what had been lost. In the decade following his mother's death in 1901, Richard Hodgson, John S. Kennedy, Waldron Bates, William James, Julia Ward Howe, Thomas Wentworth Higginson, and Henry Pickering Bowditch had all passed on—and since 1911, most notably Henry James, Hugo Münsterberg, and Josiah Royce. Understandably, the superintendent felt a renewed sense of urgency.

As the Roaring Twenties dawned, the overarching goal of federal protection for HCTPR property on Mount Desert Island had been achieved. Dorr had established supportive working relationships with his superiors. Lane, Mather, and Albright recognized the distinctiveness of Maine's national park, and the ability of the Boston Brahmin to stand with Rockefeller and Dr. Eliot. Now, as the automobile transformed American culture, motor and carriage road development within an expanding Lafayette National Park would challenge Dorr with difficulties unforeseen two decades earlier.

CHAPTER FIFTEEN

The Prince of Altruists

Rockefeller and Dorr had different strategies for coping with the final 1915 repeal of the Mount Desert Island automobile ban. One of the most significant controversies on the island was recently characterized in print as a decade (1903 to 1913) of "disobedience, division, and debate."[1] The superintendent accepted the inevitability of the horseless carriage while the philanthropist used his resources to develop roadways on his own property, from which autos could be barred. Carriage roads at the Rockefellers' Forest Hill and Pocantico Hills residences had long provided the family with private respite from the intrusive forces of the Industrial Age.

The 3,000-acre Barr Hill estate on Mount Desert Island enabled Rockefeller to distance himself from distasteful motorcars, re-create the pleasures of another time and place, and exercise his creativity. As his biographer puts it: "Acadia needed roads, and Rockefeller, who shared his father's passion for road-building, was only too anxious to help meet this requirement.... Acadia bears the marks of his own persistent care and effort"—more so than any other park to which he ultimately contributed.[2]

From its inception, the National Park Service adopted a pro-auto policy, trusting that the vehicle "was both good for the country—because it allowed more visitors to enjoy the parks—and good for the park service—because it created broader support for park protection and expansion."[3] The noisy buggy-style contraption affixed to narrow pneumatic wheels seemed ill-suited to the rocky seascape of Mount Desert Island. Following the mass production of vehicles like the Model T Ford, designed for family use, the perception of national parks changed—from retreats for prosperous tourists to destinations for a more representative user group.[4]

Early on, the poor condition of roadways acted as a barrier to widespread visitation. Horace Albright remarked, as he approached Zion National Monument in 1917, "we spent the next uncounted hours bouncing and crashing over some of the worst roads I had ever experienced."[5] The public was ill-prepared for rutted and muddied roadways, severe inclines that ruined gears, and inadequate road maintenance and development. But when a highly publicized twenty-car caravan departed from Denver on August 26, 1920 on the park-to-park highway, those participating hoped to inspire the American people to "See America First." Seventy-six days later—on schedule—the caravan arrived back in Denver having completed the 5,600-mile circuit.

On the East Coast, Dorr and Rockefeller were not alone in appreciating the significance of this automotive achievement for the nation's smallest national park. Dorr gave consideration not only to how new motor roadways might encourage visitation, but also to the separate issue of protecting the privacy of a carriage road system. Bar Harbor selectmen discussed with the park superintendent the feasibility of local bridle paths starting from Hulls Cove and extending across the island, both east and west of Eagle Lake. Intended for horse and pedestrian transit, these projected paths were oriented to intersect the Rockefeller carriage road system.

The 1917 visit by Secretary Lane resulted in his endorsement of two independent systems of roadways. What would be the best strategy for relating the two vehicular systems (trails or paths being the park's third transportation system): one on public land and the other intersecting on private property? The designers of this access network attempted to maintain the separateness of each of the free systems, the central question being: how might hikers, carriage drivers, and motorists bypass one another with minimal contact?

In the years ahead, Dorr and Rockefeller would be challenged to reconcile the democratic ideals implicit in the national park concept with the physically separated roadways, bridges, and gatehouses on the philanthropist's property. Indeed, a comprehensive study of the carriage roads done for the Park Service in the 1980s concluded that "Rockefeller envisioned the carriage road system as a complement to, not a substitute for, Mount Desert's motor road system."[6] In early 1922, Dr. Eliot's grandson, Charles W. Eliot II, published an article that anticipated difficulties for park motor road development. The landscape architect affirmed that "while park roads in the days of carriages were incidental to the broad landscape effects of the park, and were subordinate elements in the design, the requirements of an automobile road are such that whatever may be done, it can not be made subordinate: it dominates the neighborhood."[7] Dorr, for his part, was acutely conscious of the fact that the Atlantic seacoast was best viewed from atop Cadillac Mountain—which was still inaccessible to all but the most energetic hikers. The acquisition of shoreline property and the implied motor road system enabling access to both Cadillac and the eastern shoreline would be one of Dorr's major challenges in the decade ahead.[8]

As well as keeping up with *The New York Times* and other papers, Dorr's winter evenings were spent reading current scholarship on topics as wide-ranging as marine biology, entomology, and geology—and of course the ancient and modern literatures. In his memoirs Dorr states that he "felt most useful here" working on property acquisitions, writing a paper on the park, and arranging for park photographs to be exhibited nationally. In the early days of 1920, Rockefeller received a memorandum from the superintendent that detailed road construction issues: the economic benefits of road modifications, the merits of improved trail access, and the heightened aesthetics that would result from elevated roadways that blended into the surrounding landscape.[9] The island's wealthiest resident was cautioned by Dorr about an important political reality that they faced: specifically, a public perception that carriage transportation was a leisure-class activity that was fundamentally undemocratic.

Implementation of local directives from the superintendent and Mr. Rockefeller were tempered by the third-party bureaucracy in Washington, whose expanding policies could be considered locally as forms of constraint—or enabling tools. Dorr made it clear to his road development partner that he wanted to avoid hostile criticism reaching distant federal authorities that the park was being developed for the pleasure and benefit of wealthy summer residents; or that the Park Service's work was not in harmony with the wild beauty and primeval qualities that first attracted artists in the early days.

Responding to a note from Dr. Eliot in the spring of 1920, Dorr wrote at length about the pursuits that occupied him on the island "...finding much to keep me day after day, until the days grew into weeks and months and Spring is here—Birds are singing now, the squills have opened their bright blue flowers, and rhubarb is pushing its great stalks up in the garden."[10] Although Secretary Lane's approval was in hand, this spirit of renewal prompted Dorr to update his superiors about what had been achieved in the last three years. The picturesque benefits of a carriage road extension into Duck Brook and Witch Hole Pond were aimed at whetting Mr. Rockefeller's appetites. His conversations with Stephen Mather led the superintendent to conclude that a park carriage road system carried out on a scale to make it a public asset was desirable.

This goal was not supported by island village improvement societies, which increasingly expressed concerns about federal planning that ignored their input—and further, that the overall plan should be presented to the public for its approval. Dorr did not at this time engage his critics in the larger issue of how national property was managed. Nor did he offer details to the public about how Park Service policies were authorized. In the first years of Lafayette National Park, Dorr's superiors were not openly encouraging carriage road expansion—but that position would soon change as Rockefeller's land holdings became the largest on the island.[11]

In the late August 1922, Dr. Eliot spoke at a much-publicized gathering of more than 150 Northeast Harbor residents "about the changes in this beautiful island which the establishment of Lafayette National Park may be expected to produce." He stated that he "first saw this Island in 1866 on a short voyage with three younger Harvard men," tracing his discovery of the hill now called Asticou, where Eliot family roots would be established. Mixing autobiographical insights with an account of the origin and development of the Hancock County Trustees of Public Reservations, he sets the stage for remarks by chief park ranger Benjamin Hadley and Arthur E. Demaray, a future National Park Service director who explained why "the most impressive feature of Lafayette National Park [is] the matter of its creation [from lands] given entirely by private owners to the nation."[12]

Two weeks later Eliot journeyed to Bar Harbor where he presided at a tribute to Superintendent Dorr, in appreciation of "the untiring efforts of the gentleman who has devoted years of his life to the development of the National Park." Remarks were offered by A. H. Lynam, letters were read from John A. Peters and other conservation leaders, and Robert Abbe presented Dorr with the names of four hundred island residents who contributed $25,000 for the purchase of parkland.[13] The event was initiated a year earlier by Eliot, Henry L. Eno, Rev. William Lawrence, and Luere B. Deasy, who wanted to secure some relief for Dorr's indebtedness. The donations enabled this committee to purchase from Dorr some of his land holdings, transferring to the park important tracts. As some suspected, Mr. Rockefeller contributed nearly forty percent of the funds.

As Dorr entered into the "quiet stage" of negotiations for western and northern land, he knew that acquisition costs would surely escalate if Rockefeller's involvement were suspected.[14] Dorr's extensive involvement with John D. Rockefeller Jr. in land acquisition has been to the present day historically understated. Rarely was Dorr as explicit as when he noted in a letter to Rockefeller that "the options will be taken in my name, and I will then give you a paper transferring them or the lands' ownership to you, which would not be recorded."[15]

A new local initiative of Mr. Rockefeller began in late January 1922, a project that would keenly occupy his attention for more than three decades—namely, park boundaries and those properties which appeared to have incomplete documentation.. He instructed his attorney to survey these uncertain properties—subject to Dorr's approval—revealing his thoroughness in grasping the pace of park development.[16] He relied on A. H. Lynam to make certain that his carriage road system did not cross public or private property lines, contracting with him for "all of his services, expenses and incidentals in connection with the work that he has done with me and for the Park aside from such work as he is regularly employed by the Park for."[17]

As years turned into decades, neither Dorr nor Rockefeller gave any written indication that their personal and professional relationship with their attorney was anything other than highly satisfactory. The energy and enormous amounts of time that Dorr invested in these endeavors was nowhere reflected in his official monthly reports to his superiors in

Washington. Nonetheless, this effort was appreciatively acknowledged in the land acquisition correspondence from the island's most famous resident. Neither seemed concerned about the risks of their partnership.

Mather's comments in his 1920 annual report about "the first national park to be established within the original United States" lauded the level of visitation, the expanding acreage, and the winter sports that attracted visitors even in the off-season. His immediate subordinate, the detail-oriented Arno Cammerer, thanked Dorr for his first annual superintendent's report. But he also chided him for not conforming to annual report formats, statistical expectations, and timetables that are of "the utmost importance." Dorr's report covered administrative matters, title and deed research, facility issues, visitation, natural history, weather conditions, and future territorial extension. Dorr expressed himself, however, in what can best be described as elevated language, employing expressive literary narrative and allusions that vividly portrayed the island landscape.[18] Over more than two decades, this tension between administrative brevity and narrative expansiveness remained constant.

In his required monthly reports, Dorr repeatedly stressed the distinctive intermingling of natural and cultural elements on Mount Desert Island. He emphasized that—unlike western national parks—Lafayette was created in "a peopled region where human associations replace in a measure the appeal of far-reaching wildness made in other parks. In it, however, one great element of wildness that must endure forever enters in uniquely—that of contact with the ocean and the sight from mountainous heights of its great plain of waters stretching boundlessly away till hidden by the curvature of the earth."[19] Ever mindful of the larger context, Dorr introduced to his superiors the idea that this first seacoast national park could provide a model for the development of an organization-wide marine sciences strategy for the National Park Service.

Even though Dorr repeatedly referenced this unique "seacoast park," the park land at this time offered "no actual contact with the sea."[20] Over the next decade, his land acquisition efforts would be shaped by his conceptual linkage of ocean and landscape. Indeed, a planning document was submitted to Mr. Rockefeller in January 1922; therein he identified that his "first aim has been to give unity to the design, and make the park a single and organic whole." In the plan itself, he refers to the uniqueness of the park because of the "unlimited opportunity for excursion by water through island-sheltered water-ways to yet other points of interest and beauty."[21] Dorr's effort to provide public access to the constant ocean and neighboring landforms is a thematically consistent counterpoint to the development of the park arterial system of paths, motorways, and carriage roads.

Director Mather put out a system-wide request in 1922 for park superintendents to provide suggestions and plans for national park road projects. With Lafayette National Park successfully past its initial formative stage, Dorr had time to conjure mental lists of a multitude of projects that required priority attention. That he might deserve some relief from the pressures of heading an understaffed organization was not a matter of personal resentment. He continued to drive himself ceaselessly—whether in the office studying official documents, in the field studying opportunities for trail, road, and landscape development, in the Somerset Club advocating conservation with fellow members, or in his Oldfarm easy chair drafting correspondence to Mr. Rockefeller and officials in the nation's capital.

In response to Mather's request, Superintendent Dorr wanted to make the case for a five-mile road stretching from Eagle Lake Road, along Eagle Lake and Jordan Pond, to the popular eatery, the Jordan Pond Tea House.[22] When completed it would enable the public and "our rangers to pass readily between the northern and southern sides of our mountain range."[23] Related to this proposal was Mr. Rockefeller's "carefully studied plan for a horse-road system some seven or eight miles in length, encircling at high level the whole broad mass of Jordan, Sargent, and Parkman Mountains," a plan that the Boston Brahmin referred to as "the child of my suggestion."[24] Moreover, the New York philanthropist put forward a *motor* road network separate from the carriageways already in place. Dorr recommended that the Park Service approve Mr. Rockefeller's offer, especially since he was prepared to spend $150,000 to construct the park's first motor road.

Dorr hired Bar Harbor engineer Walters G. Hill to survey a route for a mountain road to the summit of what was known until October of 1918 as Green Mountain, then renamed Cadillac. It was Dorr's responsibility to impress upon Hill the specifics of Mather's policy of modifying the natural landscape. National Park Service historian Richard West Sellars has remarked that under the director "the service manipulated nature in the parks in two fundamental ways—through development and construction to accommodate tourism and by direct interference with flora and fauna."[25] Mather hired engineers, landscape architects, and even biologists from other bureaus to optimize public appreciation of the parks. For island residents with a strict interpretation of the National Park Service's mandate to conserve land *unimpaired,* Mr. Rockefeller's carriage roads and the proposed motor road to the Cadillac summit were conspicuous examples of NPS mismanagement, at least at the local level. Resistance to the possibility of new roadways to the most remote parts of Mount Desert Island was growing.

In 1922, summer resident George Wharton Pepper, a leading member of the Philadelphia bar, represented a group of island summer residents objecting to construction of a carriage road encircling Amphitheater Valley, an especially scenic interior area where streams and pathways converge west of Jordan Pond and Penobscot Mountain. This roadway was the last authorized by Secretary Lane during his meeting with Rockefeller and Dorr in the summer of 1917. Pepper asserted that the island's extensive system of footpaths "was the only intrusion necessary to give access to the wild interior."[26]

Pepper and his allies were opposed to the transformation of private preserves into public parkland; additional road construction as a threat to the wilderness was, perhaps, a target of convenience for resistance to Dorr's development plans. But the net result was that work stoppages on this portion of what is now called the Around Mountain carriage road delayed its completion for more than a decade. In response, Dorr immediately stepped forward and encouraged Rockefeller to redirect his planning toward a "grand northern terminus" for his carriage road system atop Paradise Hill in Hulls Cove, north of downtown Bar Harbor.[27] The complex history of Acadia's road systems included numerous instances of this dynamic involving local resistance and the countervailing strategies of the two collaborators to move forward toward a yet-to-be-defined completed system.

During the first week of June 1922, Stephen Mather and Arno Cammerer arrived in Bar Harbor on an inspection visit that was quite unlike what they had come to expect from visits to other parks. As Dorr's guests at Oldfarm, they were hospitably entertained. The Washington officials quickly discovered, however, that their review of park management was not to be conducted through the window of a moving vehicle. Over several days, Dorr led them by foot over mile after mile of rugged paths, through secluded gorges, and up mountains whose summits could only be attained by strenuous exertion. Dorr was convinced that only first-hand experience would enable the park officials to appreciate his rationale for the proposed trail and road system. He pressed the need for a motor road from the northern end of Eagle Lake to the Jordan Pond House.

Cammerer's inspection report drew a distinction between the rugged appeal of the trail system and the need for accessibility to "features of special interest and beauty…for the older, the less strong and active, or less strenuously inclined, who are the vast majority." While it may appear that less rigorous trails could address the needs of this "vast majority," his remarks are clearly intended as an endorsement of the expanding carriage road system. Furthermore, with accessibility issues in mind, Cammerer stated that it is "the sure conviction that a [summit] road for motorists should lead to the top of at least one of the mountains so that those who cannot climb may get opportunity to receive the inspiration and feel the exaltation of spirit that come with an hour spent on the breeze-swept hills…. In my opinion a road up Cadillac Mountain will not be equaled anywhere in the United States."[28]

Several weeks later, Dorr sent the Cadillac Mountain engineering road survey to Washington accompanied by his justification for a 3.98-mile roadway to the highest summit on the eastern seaboard of the United States. Cammerer's inspection report included unreserved praise for the park administrator: "No one can appreciate, until he has been on the ground and viewed the immense tracts of valuable lands turned over to the Government through his [Dorr's] efforts, and the detailed construction work already done, what a stupendous undertaking it has been. This achievement is quite without parallel elsewhere…. In reviewing these achievements the conclusion is inevitable that no one else than Supt. Dorr could have accomplished what has been done and is being done and will be done…. He has done this modestly and inconspicuously, with whole-hearted endeavor toward one end."[29]

Cammerer had also been updated on the establishment of the Appalachian Mountain Club (AMC) Echo Lake Camp in Southwest Harbor, on land not yet belonging to the government. Dorr clearly understood the inspirational and educational benefit of giving the celebrated outdoors organization formal standing in the park landscape. As the AMC approached its fiftieth anniversary, Dorr set aside thirteen acres of cleared land that he owned opposite the sheer Beech Cliff, which rises six hundred feet on the eastern side of one of the island's most appealing water bodies. Deeded to the AMC in 1934, the camp has been continuously used as a base of exploration and honored as a memorial to the park founder.[30]

In July of 1922, John A. Peters was the guest of honor at an Echo Camp luncheon hosted by the AMC and Lafayette National Park, in recognition of his close association with the park's establishment. Judge Peters acquainted the many who were first visiting the island with the HCTPR's intent in donating land to the federal government, concluding that "I was asked to welcome you to this luncheon as guests. On Reflection I think it is entirely improper. It is your Park—not mine, nor Mr. Dorr's, but yours."[31] Before three cheers echoed throughout the campsite in Dorr's honor, Judge Peters described him as "our own prince of altruists," a particularly memorable description of his friend. In due course, Dorr's critics would home in on the autocratic implications of such "princely" behavior.

Landscape photographer Herbert Wendell Gleason photographed this event. For several years he had been employed as a National Park Service inspector, assigned among other things to take photographs useful to the Park Service for lectures, publications, and exhibits. His responsibilities included photographic site surveys of areas that were candidates for park status. Gleason informed his friend, horticulturist Luther Burbank, that in August 1922 he "was called to undertake some special work for the government down on Mt. Desert Island, and we stayed there three months, not returning home until November."[32] The 1,100 photographs of gardens, residences, and the natural landscape that Gleason produced at that time form the most complete record of island life in the years immediately following the end of the Great War. A lecture advertisement described his many trips taken at Mount Desert Island "awheel, afoot, and afloat" to capture the "lovely lakes and tarns, with songful streams and a wealth of wild flowers."[33]

Earlier, in 1910, the *Boston Transcript* had reported that Gleason combined the qualities of the "indefatigable mountaineer and explorer, the scientific observer, the photographer of rare artistic discrimination and technical skill and a brilliantly entertaining lecturer."[34] Not a member of the picturesque school, Gleason at times photographed human threats to the North American landscape and verbally encouraged his audience to embrace the principles of conservation. His photographs were appreciated as the visual expressions of the Emersonian narrative tradition. Nature was a holy text offering spiritual enlightenment and landscape photography was a form of religious observance.

On the same date as the Echo Lake celebration, eighty-eight-year-old Charles W. Eliot—surrounded at Asticou by two grandsons, two grandsons-in-law, and five granddaughters—drafted a letter to Rockefeller congratulating him on "the good things that you have recently done for this Island and the public." His letter also acknowledged Dorr's success in securing "the gift of a very important piece of land…between Robinson and Dog Mountains and running through from the Sound to Echo Lake…[closing] a bad breech in the holdings for the public on the western side of Somes Sound."[35]

It had been thirteen years since his retirement from Harvard University. Three weeks earlier, Dr. Eliot had written to his former secretary, Jerome D. Greene, that "the kind of biography...I should prefer is a record drawn from my reports and other official documents of the number and quality of the bricks that I built into the walls of Harvard University."[36]

In his role as president of Harvard for four decades, he had come to know a great many illustrious men and women, in numbers that few since his era might claim. And yet in the words of one biographer, Edward H. Cotton, tributes of persons in high places were not worth more than the simple words of Mount Desert Island native Orrin Donnell, who sailed for many years with Dr. Eliot, caring for the boats moored at Dr. Eliot's home. In his words: "Eliot was a man of very high ideals; and he was very strictly honest. His voice—I shall never forget it, it was so strong and clear…. He loved to help young men…. [And] when we were out in the boat and friends and professors were along, he was always talking of Harvard. He was a good cruising companion but interest in the college was never off his mind."[37]

Both Dorr and Rockefeller recognized Dr. Eliot's continuing concentration on Harvard University. Would he be able to sustain interest in park matters in the months and years ahead? The historical record provides no evidence of decision-making without consideration of Dr. Eliot. After working together for nearly a decade, Dorr's appreciation for Mr. Rockefeller is expressed in writing more frequently—and vice versa. Citing his own park work and referring to his own mistakes, Dorr lauded Rockefeller's work as "of the highest order in its thoroughness, its forward vision, and its attention to the details that make or break the beauty of a road or landscape." What Rockefeller had already accomplished in less than a decade "will add to the happiness of generations," said Dorr, clearly meaning to acknowledge that Rockefeller had contributed to his own happiness "in this and in all other ways."[38]

For some time following the 1921 arrival of the Harding administration, there had been predictable anxiety about the chief executive's new interior secretary. Yet Horace Albright called this a "very exciting" period for the Interior Department, for he and his colleagues had been "very much afraid that political considerations might mean our elimination"; with the former Rough Rider Albert B. Fall at the helm, matters looked for a while most promising.[39] Unfortunately, Secretary Fall's effectiveness was short lived. He became the subject of a Senate inquiry regarding his leasing of oil-rich lands in Wyoming in exchange for personal loans. He resigned in March 1923 and was subsequently indicted, convicted, and incarcerated as a key player in the scandal known as Teapot Dome.

Dorr was again in Washington when these unexpected events shook up the Department of the Interior. A former U.S. Postmaster General, Hubert Work, replaced Fall as interior secretary—but not before his predecessor's involvement in the scandal had discredited the Interior Department. Secretary Work "inherited a department beset by infighting and assaulted from the outside because it was considered corrupt and inefficient as well as the enemy of conservation."[40] The physician-turned-cabinet-member acted quickly. He reorganized the department, modified its methods, and educated the public about the need for conservation as a "controlling national policy." The changes must have been viewed favorably, for he was reappointed by President Coolidge after Hoover's death and served for six years in all.

Three months after his appointment, Work learned that Harvard University was awarding an honorary degree to one of his national park superintendents. In June 1923 an honorary Master of Arts was conferred upon George B. Dorr, "a lover of nature who has preserved as a national park the grandest point on our Atlantic Coast."[41] One year later, the University of Maine awarded him an honorary Master of Science. Reflecting the modesty so often attributed to him, Dorr did not mention these honors in his memoirs.

By late summer of 1923 the first 4,300 feet of the Cadillac Summit Road were opened for limited travel. Ever-sensitive to public relations, the superintendent arranged for the road to open early enough for summer residents "to travel over it before returning to their winter homes" as the local paper reported, noting his "thoughtfulness."[42] Of course, road critics may have interpreted this as the superintendent rubbing salt in their wounds.

A close associate of Mr. Dorr spent the summer in Southwest Harbor experiencing the natural diversity of Lafayette National Park. On his return to Washington, Robert Sterling Yard, the executive director of the National Parks Conservation Association (NPCA), wrote the first full assessment of the new park, a timely illustrated critique that was published by the NPCA and circulated throughout Washington during the winter of 1924. *An Analysis of Lafayette National Park* appeared on the fifth anniversary of the park and contained the most thorough account of it available, including detailed descriptions of the natural history, geography, vegetation, and cultural history of Mount Desert Island. Dorr welcomed this analysis written by someone with a strong conservation ethos, editorial savvy, and an organizational commitment to examine the park in all its aspects.

Yard had worked for the U.S. Geological Survey and had contributed to crafting the National Park Service Act. He had also contributed to *The Book of the National Parks,* which was highly praised when it appeared in 1919.[43] Yard's views on wilderness preservation were at times far more strident than those of Dorr. In retrospect, he was "the quintessential purist, damned by some and praised by others for his untiring adherence to the ideals of national parks as the finest example of nature and scenery in the American landscape."[44] Throughout the 1920s, Yard defined and redefined national park standards, going to great length describing "Lafayette's remarkable forest," wherein "the beauty of those woodlands is beyond description," quite an admission for a journalist. Yard described Lafayette National Park as "the national park of the trail walker, scenically extraordinary...it is scientifically unique...[and] complete in itself."[45]

Most national park advocates stressed the utilitarian values of the growing number of federal properties—their recreational, scenic, and restorative value to man. Contrasted with this humanistic justification of conservation, Yard published an extract from one of Dorr's letters that reveals the superintendent's sensitivity to these extrinsic values while advocating as well the intrinsic value of the natural environment. For superintendent Dorr, the park existed in order to preserve an area of beauty and distinction "open and free to all...that all in the future might find in it the pleasure, health and inspiration we have found; to save it from the encroachments of commercialism; and to conserve the wild life, both plant and animal, whose native habitat it was."[46]

In December 1923, Dorr sent to Rockefeller a lengthy summary of land acquisitions (realized and in process), identifying the linkages needed for the evolving system of roads and pathways. His objective was to acquire properties that would result in "unbroken reservations" of land interconnected systematically from north to south, east to west—with suitable points of road access. Dorr was now accustomed to spending mid-winter at the Cosmos Club in Washington, D.C., lobbying for park funding from the congressional appropriations committees.

Following that winter in the nation's capital, he explained to Rockefeller that he had "revisited old haunts and seen them with a new vision," especially the extension of the carriage road system. He traced how the carriage road system might be extended "eastward to encircle Newport [Cadillac] Mountain, as the roads now building do, upon a more extensive scale, the combined masses of Sargent and its associated mountains," a plan that park engineer Hill said would present "no difficulties that cannot readily be over-come."[47] Although this patchwork-quilt method of assembling properties was not fully realized, the intensity of Dorr's commitment to the carriage roads and his effort to shepherd Rockefeller into new territory cannot be doubted.

This revisiting of "old haunts" might have been prompted by the death of "one of the best men who has ever made a Summer home among us."

George Dorr's eulogy of David B. Ogden published in a late October 1923 edition of *The New York Times* surely touched readers, especially those unfamiliar with Ogden family life in Bar Harbor. Inheriting the Cromwell Harbor home built by his father in 1867, the New York attorney was four years older than Dorr and similarly "the circle of his friends was wide, his friendships warm and enduring."[48] Our knowledge of Dorr's 1904 adventures through the eastern Sierras is based almost entirely on letters sent to Ogden immediately after his return from his climb of Mount Whitney.

One wonders whether Dorr's superlative effort to engage the Barr Hill philanthropist in park development could have grown out of some level of awareness that new Rockefeller projects—beginning in 1924—would "compete" with his persistent interest in Mount Desert Island. These included developing the Mesa Verde National Park museum, securing properties in Jackson Hole to eventually create the Grand Teton National Park, funding the establishment of the sugar pine forest approach to Yosemite Valley, and securing a five-million-dollar gift from the Rockefeller Foundation to establish the Great Smoky Mountains National Park. Not to mention Rockefeller's undertaking the most ambitious restoration project in America: Colonial Williamsburg.[49]

While the answer to this question is beyond the scope of this inquiry, on Mount Desert Island park expansion was no longer tolerable to George Pepper, now a United States Senator from Pennsylvania. For more than two years he and his island allies had tried to arouse popular support for preservation of interior wildlands exempt from road intrusion. He threatened to bring the debate over Lafayette National Park road construction into the U.S. Senate. As Yard's publication circulated, it provided a standard against which to measure the reasonableness of the unprecedented assault by those who demanded the cessation of road construction within the park. As the new interior secretary agreed to open hearings in Washington to resolve the issue of road construction in Lafayette National Park, the foreseeable expansion of Mr. Rockefeller's carriage roads and the fate of the park superintendent were at stake.

CHAPTER SIXTEEN

Attack May Come Again

Once Senator Pepper and his allies became aware that road development was progressing in spite of their objections, they abandoned efforts to persuade Dorr and Rockefeller. They instead requested an immediate meeting with Interior Secretary Hubert Work. At that January 1924 meeting, objections were raised against the desecration of wilderness by an increasing number of roads and by environmentally ill-suited bridges that they believed belonged in an urban environment (such as New York's Central Park). Moreover, they expressed concern that carriage roads would eventually become motor roads, spiriting visitors into the hidden recesses of the park. Finally, they claimed that Dorr (and by implication Mr. Rockefeller) had not taken others into their confidence despite many inquiries from their most intimate friends and neighbors. The result was that "a cloud of suspicion has been cast on what [Dorr] really intended to do."[1]

Fortunately, Arno Cammerer documented the meeting. This included a directive to Dorr that the interior secretary wanted "all construction work stopped" until a hearing could be arranged with all the pertinent parties. Furthermore, Dorr was instructed to promptly come to Washington to discuss the matter.[2] Dorr did not comply with this directive, citing its adverse consequences. He explained that it was not possible to wholly interrupt road construction without the stoppage becoming front-page news in local, regional, and national papers. Furthermore, local road construction laborers hired for winter who gave up other work for this assignment—on faith in the continuity of the federal authorization—would be thrown out of work, creating local animosity against the park.

In retrospect, Dorr's behavior seemed to exemplify the tough-mindedness and independence of spirit that his Harvard mentor William James admired so much in Ralph Waldo Emerson and sometimes, for lack of which, faulted other Harvard graduates. For nearly a decade Dorr had done his best to work within the growing bureaucracy of the national park system. Yet to many officials, he was judged as noncompliant. He did not wear the National Park Service uniform, his reports contained scholarly references and allusions that departed conspicuously from the brief informational reports sought by Washington bureaucrats, and the most troublesome matter continued to be his independent management of the park itself. William James would certainly have praised him as being true to the authentic Harvard, for "our undisciplinables are our proudest product."[3]

Interior Department officials were not prepared for this sort of response. Archivist, author, and Bar Harbor summer resident Richard W. Hale Jr. put it well: "Now the National Park Service found on its hands a park that did not obey the rules…for the Lafayette National Park had as its head a 'dollar-a-year' superintendent, who at the flick of a hand could command his friends' wealth, and who was too broad-gauge a scholar to understand government routine." The presence of this "tall, big man, with a striking, down-sweeping moustache…who had a gift for arousing friendship that verged on the remarkable," had become over the last decade a well-recognized public figure, attuned to the political and social context, confident of the appropriateness of his own leadership.[4]

Consequently, Dorr resolved not to let Pepper and his collaborators alter park development. He wisely agreed to travel to Washington as soon as feasible. For the time being he urged Arno Cammerer to make sure that a representative sampling of opinion was solicited prior to the hearing, to avoid the appearance of seeking opinion from a select class. The secretary shifted his stance, permitting construction to continue, although all new construction was delayed until the hearing was over.

A month later Dorr confided to Mr. Rockefeller that though he was able to "forestall" Senator Pepper, this had been an "anxious time" for him over this "fresh attack...upon our work and plans." The superintendent wrote that he had "no question as to the result" of the hearing. Nonetheless, he left a few days later for Washington with a stopover in New York City to meet with Mr. Rockefeller to ensure that we do not "take anything for granted or leave anything undone that may help to present the matter rightly."[5]

One might wonder why Dorr did not enlist his administrative counterparts in the NPS. After all, he had attended a sufficient number of Mather's annual gatherings to develop informal relationships with other park superintendents. Yet the historical record contains little evidence of interchanges between Dorr and his peers. Acadia's superintendent simply avoided the pose of a professional administrator and even managed to ignore—without any reprimand—the requirement that the national park uniform be worn by all Park Service staff. Dorr's substantial personal relationships were his foundation, and there was no shortage of men and women of public standing to speak before Secretary Work on behalf of the park, its roads, and its superintendent.

Since early January, John A. Peters, recently appointed as a United States district court judge, had applied his organizational skills to the issues and personalities involved. HCTPR treasurer George L. Stebbins informed Peters that as a result of his conversation with Rockefeller, Dorr's allies needed to provide the kind of support at the hearing that would "relieve Mr. Dorr" of the task of presenting a fulsome account of the road-building projects. Dorr's friends knew too well his philosophical tendency "to prove too much and talk too long."[6] Peters put this more charitably, saying that Dorr was "so earnest and rather discursive that if allowed free rein, he could take too long and go beyond the important subject [at hand]." Nonetheless, Peters cautioned Stebbins that, in point of fact, Dorr was in charge and "I should not want to do anything to interfere with him."[7]

Peters sent Senator Pepper collegial letters, hopeful that they might correct misunderstandings. After discussing the two motor roads under development, he turned Pepper's attention to the artistic carriage road. Peters viewed this as "absolutely necessary" for administrative purposes (e.g., access for fire control, wildlife management, security, etc.). While agreeing that certain areas required protection against roads, Peters reiterated that Mr. Dorr was authorized to construct and complete the planned road systems, to pursue additional land for the park, and to enlist support for completion of the projects underway.

What Peters actually thought of Senator Pepper's efforts was revealed in a letter he sent to Maine congressman Ira G. Hersey. "I am personally of the opinion that one man from Pennsylvania, even if he is a senator, should not control the destinies of all the people of Maine.... I think that it is an outrage on us, but I cannot say that except to you. You can catch more flies with molasses than with some other things."[8] The next day he received a letter from a Providence attorney claiming that "the interests and wishes of the summer residents who spent hundreds of thousands of dollars to develop Mount Desert and make it beautiful for summer homes should be the first consideration."[9]

When Charles W. Eliot learned of the hearing scheduled for late March, he wrote Secretary Work suggesting that he consider spending a week at Mount Desert Island to see "for yourself under the guidance of Mr. Dorr the extraordinary beauties of the island and its fitness as the site of a National Park." Since Secretary Work and Dorr had not met, Eliot offered an illuminating profile of the superintendent: "I have known him from his boyhood up, and his father and mother before him. He is thoroughly informed about the woods, plant life and animal life on the island of Mount Desert, and he is a man of extraordinary public spirit. He inherited from his father a considerable fortune, which has now all gone into public and semi-public undertakings toward the improvement of Mount Desert Island for the best kind of public enjoyment; so that he is now living on the modest salary he receives from the Government. From the point of view of a public official he has one defect against which precautions can easily be taken. He is liable to talk too long about any business which interests him."[10]

For more than half a century, Charles W. Eliot had abundantly enjoyed the island's beauties as a seasonal resident. But as the hearing neared, his focus on March 20, 1924 was fixed by unprecedented events in Cambridge. Harvard University commemorated his achievements with a ninetieth-birthday celebration. Eliot's former secretary, Jerome D. Greene, was chief marshal of the Sanders Theatre homage to Dr. Eliot as scholar, educator, and citizen. Governor Cox of Massachusetts and William H. Taft, chief justice of the U.S. Supreme Court, paid tribute to his public service as two thousand students outside the theatre gathered, in the words of *The Harvard Crimson* president Carleton MacVeagh, "to give you a fitting reception in their own barbaric way."[11] That newspaper later headlined the event as "Harvard's Greatest Birthday Party," referring to the occasion as the most distinguished event in the history of the university. Curiously, in an interview published four days earlier in *The New York Times,* the unassuming educator had insisted that his philosophy was "wholly derived from others and especially from books."

In his short speech of acknowledgment during the event, Dr. Eliot looked back "upon my life as a boy, sometimes engaged in rough-and-tumble fights which we boys use to have on Boston Common, and I recognize that at a tender age I did display considerable enjoyment of fighting,"[12] adding, "I never stopped any attempts of mine because I encountered opposition." He knew of no better advice for a Harvard graduate than that of former secretary of state, governor of Massachusetts, and renowned orator Edward Everett: "Look forward and not backward—Look out and not in." While Dorr had hoped to be present at the ceremony, preparations for the Washington hearing prevented his participation. This decision was difficult for Dorr to accept, as their friendship had been "one of my most valued and valuable possessions."[13]

Rockefeller also recognized the importance of the Eliot festivities. In language that was exceptional for its depth of feeling and scope, he told Eliot that he was "an example and inspiration to me in many ways. The uniform dignity and courtliness of your bearing, your unfailing courtesy, your splendid self-control, your enormous capacity for work, the pains-taking exactness with which you study the details of every problem upon which you pass judgment, your magnificent breadth of view, your clear insight and your keen vision have long commanded my profound admiration. I have counted it a high privilege to have the more intimate association with you that life on the Maine coast has made possible."[14]

As the hearing date neared, so did related correspondence to Secretary Work increase. One summer resident defended the Dorr-Rockefeller efforts and implied that there was an anti-democratic spirit at the root of those "lovers of nature," who seemed fixated on the scars left by roadways and the fact that public access "interferes with the privacy of their picnics." In a similar spirit, landscape gardener Beatrix Farrand sent an "omelet is not made without breaking eggs" letter to Director Mather. She admitted that road building resulted in temporary defacement, and yet "this should not alarm the most conservative, however, as the scars will be covered in the course of a few years by the planting and arrangements which are carried on simultaneously with the construction."[15]

In responding to Judge Peters, Senator Pepper argued that there were real dangers in developing some areas and leaving others as wilderness, [for] "if we mix them up and try to strike an average everywhere we shall destroy the distinctive character of the island and reduce the whole proposition to a dead level of mediocrity. I should be sorry to have the whole thing degenerate into the Lafayette National Picnic Park with tin cans and egg shells on the side." Pepper's dislike of the superintendent's behavior was apparent when he urged Work to appoint an oversight committee to "to check up on Mr. Dorr's activities... [to] insure against one-man control of a public trust."[16]

Shortly before the formal hearing, the *Bar Harbor Times* published an article under the headline "People of Maine Overwhelmingly in Favor of Lafayette National Park Development," reporting Maine governor Percival Baxter's support. Judge Peters sent Secretary Work a letter affirming that "the value and usefulness of this Park depend upon its accessibility. The mountains have been there a long time but heretofore only a few favored with leisure, lungs and legs have been able to enjoy their beauties."[17]

On March 22, Dr. Eliot sent another letter to Work, which disclosed information of importance to the understanding of Mr. Dorr as a public figure beset with a socially unmentionable disability. Unknown to Dorr, Eliot wrote that he "wants to testify now before the hearing [about] the quality and character of George B. Dorr [since] I know that he will avoid speaking at the meeting if he can properly do so, partly because he dislikes very much to talk even in private about his own qualities and achievements, and partly because he has been from his boyhood afflicted with a stammer which was originally very pronounced and conspicuous, and still is, although he has acquired remarkable control over it. This stammer prevents him from uttering a word for an appreciable length of time."[18]

The evening before the hearing, the Interior Department auditorium was the site of an illustrated lecture by Herbert W. Gleason on Lafayette National Park. The National Park Service sponsored this event, its timing deliberately chosen to provide an opportunity for the public to appreciate the splendors of the park.[19] The photographer had selected images, some colorized by his wife, taken in the three-month Mount Desert Island visit in the fall of 1922 and a later visit in 1923. In this lecture (which he adapted several months later for the New England readers of *The Boston Evening Transcript*), Gleason not only celebrated—in word and image—the natural grandeur of the park, but also reported on the current status of road development within the park. Reaching a more diverse audience than R. S. Yard's analytic article, published six months earlier, the landscape photographer touted Dorr's "keen aesthetic sense" that was writ large in the management of the park. While acknowledging the protest of those opposed to any "gash through the forest" that would result from the proposed roadways, he noted (in contrast) that many island visitors were disappointed when informed that some of the more notable scenic features of the park were not accessible by vehicles—reflecting the expectations of the new generation of motorized travelers.[20]

Even before Secretary Work opened the hearing on March 26, statements by officials from the National Parks Conservation Association, island village improvement societies, businessmen, and other individuals and groups were offered pro forma on both "sides" of the issue. The public record also included oral testimony from key individuals. Neither Dr. Eliot nor Mr. Rockefeller was present. In more than fifty pages of testimony, however, Dorr's comments do not fill an entire page, confirming the effectiveness of the strategy that Eliot and Stebbins had implemented.[21]

Work immediately corrected the misconception that this inquiry was a contest between two parties. Rather, there were three interests: "...those who want to retain the park in a state of nature, those who want to modernize it, and the Department of the Interior, which has to administer it." Arno Cammerer testified that the Park Service stood by the 1922 road and trail development plan, and that it was being carried out "accurately in every detail by the superintendent." Although Senator Pepper testified that no one had acted "more unselfishly for the public interest than Mr. Dorr," the senator clearly believed that "there is no justification" for Rockefeller's "private" carriage roads; these were nothing less than intrusions into a wilderness that must be preserved in its natural state.[22]

Pepper implied that there was a fourth interest at work here as well: the land acquisition policy of the Hancock County Trustees of Public Reservations. In his view, the existing government partnership with a "private" group was suspect. HCTPR treasurer George L. Stebbins explained that—to the contrary—his organization was not a private enclave since it was guided by a public principle and was "eager to follow the directions of people living on Mount Desert Island and the summer people who come here." Furthermore, anticipating the multi-use arguments that would arise in the late twentieth century, Stebbins reminded everyone that having multiple means of accessing the mountains and valleys was important for those who were not sure of foot.

Dorr allowed Senator Pepper's rambling discourse to be his own undoing. Dorr's associates, with their diversity of backgrounds and interests, were a better representation of democracy at its best than Pepper and his followers. Senator Pepper left the hearing well before its close, perhaps aware of the prevailing tone of those offering testimony. It was unclear whether he was present when Maine University president Clarence Little offered "stirring" road development remarks; others present said that Little's remarks "raised large red welts on certain prominent senatorial epidermis."[23]

Several days after the closure of the hearings, Mr. Rockefeller received a summary in which Dorr stressed that "the political situation was plainly a controlling factor on our side." Dorr was uncharacteristically blunt in his comment that "attack may come again; it was the strength we showed, and the political situation, which had prevented [Pepper's success]."[24] Vigilance was necessary to forestall another "attack." Sixteen years later Dorr "vividly" recalled in a letter to Director Cammerer that "had we failed at the conference it would have spelt disaster to the park, into whose history the road accordingly is built, a monument to Mr. Rockefeller's interest and public spirit."[25] However, in 1924, Rockefeller discerned that the hearing had taken its toll on the "worn and weary" Dorr.[26]

Mr. Rockefeller's mind quickly shifted focus when he and his three oldest sons—John 3rd, Nelson, and Laurance—left New York City on June 23, 1924 for a tour of the western parks.[27] Grand Canyon National Park,

Bandelier National Monument, and Mesa Verde National Park were on their itinerary before they headed north to Yellowstone National Park.[28] Superintendent Horace Albright warmly greeted the family on their arrival and guided them to the major sites. He soon learned that this was not the first trip to the oldest national park for the philanthropist; in August 1886 he had visited with his parents and three sisters. After touring Glacier National Park, Rockefeller and his sons returned to Seal Harbor by August 15. At The Eyrie, Mr. Rockefeller wondered how he might further assist Mesa Verde superintendent Jesse Nusbaum in realizing his museum aspirations for that park—and how he could assist Horace Albright in enhancing the beauty of Yellowstone. The long-term effect of this trip was that the National Park Service acquired "an extraordinary new benefactor in the summer of 1924" when Mr. Rockefeller reached beyond Lafayette National Park.[29]

Secretary Work deferred his final decision but allowed all work in progress to continue, a decision that gave Rockefeller and Dorr a free hand. Yet Rockefeller had concerns about "the method of conducting work and control of the expenditure of funds for road building" and to that end a draft letter was sent to Dorr for his consideration as Rockefeller boarded the train for the western parks. Dorr incorporated much of the draft language in his response, including a statement that "any road building that is done in Lafayette National Park must be under my ultimate supervision." Yet he agreed to empower a committee of four to make decisions that would be delayed if they awaited Dorr's review. Under the direction of the committee's chairman, A. H. Lynam, the new arrangement enabled Rockefeller to allocate the required road development funds in response to Lynam's requests. Periodically, Charles Heydt, Rockefeller's personal secretary, would update his employer, securing approval if committee requisitions were warranted.[30]

Resistance, however, did not immediately cease. For more than a year, the Park Service received road construction complaints about unauthorized projects. In each instance the complaint was shown to be groundless since the property in question was outside park boundaries. Secretary Work instructed the Park Service's chief landscape engineer, Daniel R. Hull, to complete a site visit and report his findings. Shortly thereafter, on July 8, 1924, Director Mather again visited Mount Desert Island and spent four days thoroughly analyzing construction activity and meeting with road development opponents.

He was sufficiently impressed by the roadwork quality that he told the Bar Harbor selectmen that, although he had previously thought the construction supervisor for the Going-to-the-Sun Road in Glacier National Park to be "the last word in road construction without landscape marring," he now believed that here in Lafayette National Park "engineer Hill's work reflected the best efforts in road planning."[31] The carriage roads around Rockefeller's Seal Harbor property—and their later extension into the park—had been entrusted to engineer Charles P. Simpson. After he suffered a debilitating illness in 1922, engineering responsibility shifted to his son, Paul D. Simpson. As chief engineer, Simpson spent the next eighteen years completing the system until its administration was turned over to Acadia National Park. Mather then announced his intention to summon National Park Service engineers to Mount Desert so that they might apply the lessons of Lafayette National Park to their own spheres of influence. Such an endorsement must have been heartening to Mr. Dorr.

As Mather was departing, Secretary Work made his first visit to Mount Desert to evaluate park progress and management. *The Story of Acadia National Park,* however, downplays the significance of this inspection tour. Dorr writes that "I found [Secretary Work] had no desire to leave his comfortable car for any horse drawn vehicle; his interests were political and Nature entered into them but little. He left for Washington that afternoon and work continued as before."[32]

In late July, Dorr received Work's official response. In his judgment, the 1922 plan approved by his predecessor "was premature and too ambitious since it contemplated road trail construction in the remote future on lands not actually acquired… [which] led to confusion and discontent."[33] Nonetheless, he formally authorized the connecting link from Jordan Pond to Eagle Lake Road, the carriage road encircling Sargent and Penobscot mountains, and the motor road to the Cadillac Summit. "The hearing did, however, seem to heighten the concern for the motor road's impact on the wilderness quality of the area."[34] Dorr was cautioned by the secretary to exercise great caution in hiding construction scars, a small slap on the wrist in the face of a stunning victory for both Dorr and Rockefeller!

CHAPTER SEVENTEEN

Beginnings and Endings

Now that motor road development could proceed, Mr. Dorr returned his attention to progress in marine research at Salisbury Cove, weighed the implications of a request from the University of Maine for a seasonal biological research site, and responded to the enthusiasm of a friend who was assembling evidence of Mount Desert Island Native American habitation. Exciting as were these research initiatives, they remained subordinate to Dorr's most pressing responsibility: expansion of the boundaries of the 18,000-acre park. He was all the more conscious of this need because of events unfolding in Northeast Harbor, where Dr. Eliot faced the twilight of his life.

The president of the University of Maine, Clarence Cook Little, had been acquainted with Dorr for some time. He spoke in support of Lafayette National Park road development at the 1924 Washington hearings and had awarded Dorr a Master of Science honorary degree. Dr. Little expressed to Dorr his interest in setting up on Mount Desert Island a seasonal biological laboratory for his students. Dorr offered the geneticist the use of his own thirteen-acre property off Schooner Head Road, a mile from the Mount Desert Nurseries.

The University of Maine Biological Station on Mount Desert—as it was then known—first hosted graduate and undergraduate students in the summer of 1924. Some students tracked carrion beetles and collected seaweed while others were drawn to Little's experiments on mice with congenital defects due to inherited cancers.[1] From its inception, Dorr believed that "the Laboratory is destined to grow into one of [Mount Desert's] most interesting and valuable features…and one of its most notable."[2] Little's evening lectures for summer residents aroused interest from automobile entrepreneurs Edsel Ford and Roscoe B. Jackson, a Hudson Motorcar Company entrepreneur.[3] Unpublished documents at the Rockefeller Archive Center demonstrate that Dr. Little's vision for the seasonal laboratory abruptly changed after he became the president of the University of Michigan. He now promoted an enlarged concept of biological research more attuned to the naturalist spirit of Dorr.

After Little departed for Michigan, discussions took place about consolidating the island's two biological laboratories. Rockefeller questioned the need for biological investigation at more than one island location, especially when there was little effort by Little's group to collaborate with the Salisbury Cove laboratory, twenty minutes from downtown Bar Harbor by motorcar. He later wrote that research at the University of Maine Biological Station at Schooner Head "has been seriously hampered and curtailed, if not practically abandoned" whereas the Mount Desert Island Biological Laboratory at Salisbury Cove "has been reorganized…and is now on a sound basis," worthy of his financial support.[4] Perhaps new funding for the MDIBL could revitalize Dr. Little's dormant project.[5]

In late fall 1926, Little sent Roscoe Jackson his requirements for biological work on Mount Desert Island: a central facility, museum, library, and six separate field stations, equipment, and a $1.5-million annual budget.[6] This "preliminary" plan for "the scientific study and conservation of wild life" on Mount Desert was also sent to Rockefeller. This new organization, "The Mount Desert Natural History Society," was described as a field-based scientific endeavor historically associated with the names of Darwin, Lamarck, Agassiz, and Audubon.[7] Little claimed that such field work would "turn practically the whole island into a laboratory," but there is only Little's word that Dorr "heartily approves this whole project." It was unclear whether this field-based model was conceived as a substitute for laboratory research or a supplement to it—and in this state of confusion Dr. Little again reaffirmed the priority of a traditional cancer research laboratory.

At the University of Michigan, its president was described as "brilliant but tactless," and the stormy relationship led to Little's resignation.[8] Surprisingly, he succeeded in convincing Jackson, Ford, and a relative—Detroit department-store magnate Richard Webber—to provide the capital while Dorr offered to donate the land. The new facility would be a memorial to his father, Charles Hazen Dorr.

Roscoe Jackson's sudden death required not only financial adjustments but also rethinking of the name of the institution. Again, Dorr took the initiative, as Dr. Little recognized in his letter to the superintendent: "It seems to be typically unselfish and fine of you to intimate that your previous suggestion concerning the land as a memorial for your father be disregarded if desirable."[9] Accordingly, on May 4, 1929, the Roscoe B. Jackson Memorial Laboratory was incorporated with Dr. Little as president, and Dorr—the superintendent of the newly renamed Acadia National Park—one of several laboratory incorporators. The land transfer for the sum of one dollar was completed July 6, 1929, and in early December, only six weeks after the October 24 stock market crash, the laboratory opened and Little's staff began the process of building a scientific establishment.

Little's cancer researchers developed an inbred strain of laboratory mice used today in scientific research globally. Nearly ninety years later—with twenty-two Nobel Prizes linked to its research—"JAX" is the largest employer in Hancock County. A recent director has described its successful biomedical research into cells, tissues, and organisms as the result of "collaborations between cell biologists, physiologists, biochemists and geneticists with statisticians, physicists, computer scientists, [and] mathematicians."[10] It is most fitting that the JAX campus is now within sight of Dorr Mountain.

With remarkable facility, at this same time Dorr drafted an unpublished essay on the origin, development, management, and place of Acadia within the National Park Service. Written on the tenth anniversary of the 1919 establishment of Lafayette National Park, Dorr situated it within the continuing debate "whether [a park's] true function be conservational, recreational, or educational, or in what degree combined." In the case of Acadia, the "conservation beauty of inspiring quality and the safeguarding of free access to it by the public was the impelling motive, both on the part of those who gave and on that of those in authority who accepted."[11] Was this park of extrinsic or intrinsic value? In clear reference to Charles Eliot's second "Waverly Oaks" essay in *Garden and Forest,* he reaffirmed here that the landscape of Acadia was like a great work of art or a famous ruin. It should be preserved "for the enrichment of the world and its influence on the minds of men." A visit to Acadia's cultural landscape imparted to visitors impressions that would be "a leaven working through the land for nature conservation and the preservation of landscape beauty in all its many types and forms."

This promise of enrichment was embodied in Dorr's friend, Dr. Robert Abbe, who was internationally renowned for his pioneering of surgical innovations. The New York City surgeon's relationship with Pierre and Marie Curie was discussed locally and his well-known island relief map was but the most recent expression of his commitment to the Hancock County Trustees' conservation efforts and the mission of the Bar Harbor Village Improvement Association. Dr. Abbe's health was fragile, the likely consequence of experimentation with a radioactive substance. By 1925 even the governor of Maine was concerned about the "weariness, the fever, and the fret" that the good doctor endured, requiring repeated hospitalization and frequent transfusions.[12] One of the original HCTPR incorporators, Bishop William Lawrence, acknowledged in his memorial essay that Abbe's "work seemed to be finished; his health was failing and invalidism to his life's end was certain."[13]

The chance viewing of a dozen Native American stone implements displayed in Sherman's real estate office window on Bar Harbor's Cottage Street revitalized Dr. Abbe: "When I saw these implements...I was filled with a desire to possess and study them." He purchased the stones and after returning to New York "the idea of utilizing them as a nucleus for a local museum possessed me."[14] Luere Deasy remarked that "hundreds of us cast a glance at [these stones] and passed on." Only the good doctor grasped the significance of these shards and anticipated the educational opportunities implicit in their preservation.

Dorr included a stop at the Abbe residence at Brook End during the summer 1924 visit by Interior Secretary Work, who viewed the archaeological collection while Abbe outlined his museum project. Abbe recalled that Secretary Work "was enthusiastic...and showed me a telegram...conveying a gift of $60,000 from the Laura Spellman Rockefeller Foundation for a similar museum for the Yellowstone Park."[15] Dorr followed up with a letter to Stephen Mather that "my old friend, Dr. Robert Abbe, of New York, has become deeply interested during this past summer, in the establishment of an Indian museum in connection with the Park."[16] If the museum was to become a reality, Dorr knew from his Harvard fund-raising experiences that it would fall on local talent to make it so. Though Dorr's interest in native cultures has been considered by some to be slight, his commitment to realizing the vision of his ailing friend was not.

Following a substantial endowment contribution from Mrs. Walter G. Ladd, Reverend Lawrence sought to expand Abbe's donor cultivation skills, offering him nothing less than a short course in fund-raising, community education, and publicity.[17] Abbe then sent Rockefeller the most recent update of his "Champlain" relief map and a sketch of the proposed museum; in due course Dr. Abbe received a check from Mr. Rockefeller for $15,000 "because of all you have done for the advancement of medical science and for the relief of suffering during a long, highly useful and most unselfish life."[18]

Regional collectors added their own Stone Age treasures to the Abbe holdings, on the condition that the good doctor would guarantee water, fire, and burglar protection in the museum. The Museum of Stone Age Antiquities was incorporated in October 1926. With Dorr as president, Luere B. Deasy as treasurer, and attorney Serenus Rodick as clerk, the museum was the first institution in Maine to support archaeological research. This was not the first expression of Dorr's interest in a museum focused on Acadian regional culture.

Dorr introduced Abbe to Haverford College physics professor and New England historian William Otis Sawtelle, whose Islesford Historical Museum on Little Cranberry Island was being completed. Raised in Bangor, Sawtelle and his family summered on Islesford at the home they built there in 1913. His discovery of local historical documents in a store that he purchased there had sparked an intense level of scholarship and publication, informed by the resources that would soon form the core of the museum. Abbe's familiarity with museum curatorship was enlarged and the overlapping spheres of interest of the two men led to an agreement to share knowledge about artifacts recovered. Dr. Abbe had the advantage of a supportive committee as he planned his museum, whereas Sawtelle felt "very much alone...working as a day laborer unloading brick, wielding pickaxe and shovel, wheeling dirt and keeping busy as the day is long, beginning at daylight and continuing until dusk."[19]

Philadelphia architect Edmund B. Gilchrist, noted for the design of the Islesford Historical Museum as well as a number of local summer residences, received the commission for Abbe's museum, which would be located near Sieur de Monts Spring on land still owned by Dorr's Sieur de Monts Spring Company. Dorr and Gilchrist discussed whether elements of the Georgian Colonial Revival museum on Little Cranberry should be incorporated into this museum as they walked the site and considered design expenses, locally available grades of quarried stone from Dorr's quarry, and shades of roof tiles. They also visited Abbe's Brook End home to view artifacts from the collection. The architect and physician worked out the external and internal design details for the trailside museum, and Abbe was clearly pleased with architectural parallels between the Sieur de Monts Springhouse and the proposed museum building. This affinity was also recognized by landscape architect Beatrix Farrand, who broke ground in November 1926 for the Abby Aldrich Rockefeller Garden at The Eyrie.[20]

Following the land transfer from Dorr to the museum for the sum of $100, he took on the yeoman's responsibilities for erecting the building. Illness and distance prevented Dr. Abbe's active involvement. Despite Dorr's efforts to develop a constructive relationship between the island and the federal government, he chose not to report the use of National Park Service resources for museum purposes. He was confident that his need to account to the NPS would handicap the timely completion of the project. Ann Rockefeller Roberts has verbally commended Dorr for this subterfuge, arguing that if Dorr had waited for museum approval from the Park Service, the establishment of the museum may never have been completed.[21] This too, is perhaps another expression of Dorr's Harvard College unorthodoxy.

As it turns out, Dorr may have misjudged Park Service leadership on museum matters. In a 1927 article in *The New York Times*, Director Mather articulated park policy as "ministering to the minds as well as the bodies and the emotions of the traveling millions." He argued that the rapid progression of the natural sciences in the previous few decades convinced him and his colleagues that the national parks were rich fields for inquiry. Mather also noted that increasing numbers of colleges and universities used one or more of the nineteen national parks as faculty and student laboratories.

Through private initiatives "museums have made their appearances in the parks and monuments... [functioning] as an explanation of phenomena to be seen as they occur in nature on the spot."[22] Furthermore, the University of California–educated director described the park system as "a super-university of the natural sciences, [where] each college [park] presents a personality of its own, specializing on some particular natural endowment." Mather cited anthropological studies at Mesa Verde, geophysical investigations at Yellowstone, and marine studies on the shoreline of Mount Desert Island as research initiatives appropriate for museums.

Dr. Abbe did not live to see his museum completed. News of his death on March 7, 1928 received worldwide coverage. The telegram from Abbe's relatives informing the Bar Harbor community of his death was sent to Oldfarm. A few days later the *Bar Harbor Times* lauded Eliot, Dorr, and Abbe as "a notable trio" responsible for the establishment of Sieur de Monts National Monument and Lafayette National Park.[23] The Bar Harbor Village Improvement Association eulogized Dr. Abbe as "a lover of nature, a man of artistic sensitivity, a scientist, a surgeon, a gentleman of distinguished attainments, and a rarely lovable friend."[24]

Dorr oversaw completion of the museum, which was dedicated on August 14, 1928. A stone tablet in the foyer made it clear that this museum memorialized the life of its founder; it would be another nine years, however, before it formally adopted Abbe's name and became the Abbe Museum. Mr. Dorr encouraged the "Dean of American Archaeology," Dr. Warren K. Moorehead, to engage in fieldwork on behalf of the museum and to prepare a publication on the Native Americans of Mount Desert Island. At a larger scale, scientific knowledge of a culture indigenous to the Atlantic maritime region—called the Red Paint People—was based on his pioneering research in Maine.

Mr. Rockefeller wrote in 1930 that it was part of Dorr's understanding with him to effect the transfer of the Abbe Museum and its endowment to the park, to be owned and operated by the park. That was not accomplished until February 15, 1944, when the Department of the Interior at last secured ownership of the land at Sieur de Monts.[25]

When the Abbe estate was settled in 1928, the only significant gift to someone other than a relative, employee, or organization was a $10,000 bequest to George B. Dorr. Sixteen years later, Dorr reciprocated when his executors directed one-quarter of his estate to the Abbe Museum. His executors knew that Mr. Dorr wished to promote this little museum resting on granite secured from Dorr's quarry—a foundation no less secure than the personal relationship between the two men.

The Abbe Museum Archives contain a most revealing document regarding the friendship between the founder and its first president. Seven years before his death, the physician was honored on his seventieth birthday with hundreds of written expressions of affection by friends and colleagues. Dorr's note to Dr. Abbe used uncharacteristic religious imagery. In his distinctive large script he states that he feels honored to count himself "among your friends. It is a credential that I shall present to St. Peter at the Heavenly Gate; and St. Peter will open wide! But should I get there first I shall not feel that it is all they've cracked it up to be until you come!"[26]

In the summer of 1925 a strenuous agenda faced the seventy-one-year-old superintendent. An increasing numbers of visitors arrived for the tenth summer since the federal government had accepted the first of the Hancock County Trustee properties. Bar Harbor kicked off the season by hosting state executives in a Governor's Day program. The chief executives of many of these United States, their spouses, and the accompanying administrative and public relations support staff were taken on motor tours of the island. This procession "swept triumphantly through an army of cheering people, amid waving flags and brilliant music."

Maine's governor, Ralph O. Brewster, quickly disengaged himself after these events to travel to Millinocket for "a first hand inspection" of the Katahdin territory.[27] Claiming this was a private vacation trip, Brewster and his wife were joined on the July 8 trek to the summit of Katahdin by the state publicity director and six other guests, the eldest being Superintendent Dorr.[28] A decade earlier, Dorr had published an article on the dangers facing this remote forested area despite the benefits of the 1911 federal law, sponsored by Massachusetts senator John Weeks, to protect land against the devastating effects of erosion caused by fire and logging. Dorr's vision for Katahdin was "the establishment under Government protection of such a vast and splendid Bird and Wild Life Breeding Ground and Sanctuary at the heart of the greatest, the wildest, and the most shot-over game land in the East."[29] The 1911 effort to achieve national park status for Katahdin failed, yet by 1920 Maine state senator Percival Baxter called for a Mount Katahdin Centennial Park. That legislation was defeated but in 1923 the State of Maine, now with Baxter as governor, accepted the land to create the ninety-thousand-acre Katahdin Park Game Preserve.[30]

The serial publication *In the Maine Woods* documented the adventure of the group that departed on the proposed Appalachian Trail from Katahdin's Chimney Pond Camp. All but one were amused—if not somewhat concerned—by Dorr's footgear, "a low pair of very light moccasins.... Mr. Dorr, however, smiled a whimsical smile and thought he would be able to keep up. And so the party started, Mr. Dorr in the lead." Three hours later the party reached the Great Basin Slide and pressed toward the summit. "Although he lost a moccasin now and then, [Dorr] led throughout the ascent and was the first on top."[31] In nearly perfect weather, the superb view encompassed more than twenty-five-thousand square miles. Contrary to accepted practice but buoyed by the weather conditions, the governor's party resolved to spend the night on the summit in order to be the first in America to see the sunrise. With the arrival of a storm at midnight, prudence required a speedy descent and "no mishaps were encountered on the trip down outside of Mr. Dorr losing one of his moccasins."[32]

Governor Brewster must have enjoyed Dorr's company on the ascent of 1925, for one month later he and Mrs. Brewster—and several administrative aides—accepted Dorr's invitation to be his houseguests for three days. At "one of the largest receptions ever held in Bar Harbor…Mr. Dorr invited about 700 people to greet Governor Brewster at his home, where for many years distinguished guests have been entertained."[33] Mary Dorr's reputation as an exceptional host was admirably sustained by her son. Oldfarm was again center stage in the social life of the community to an extent that had not been seen in the last thirty years!

During the first week of October 1925, the Eighth National Parks Conference was convened at Mesa Verde National Park. Dorr traveled to and from Mesa Verde by train to participate in his second gathering with other park superintendents, traveling further than any other participant. The two most important topics discussed were expansion of educational initiatives throughout the system and road development partnerships with the Bureau of Public Works. Mather lauded Dorr before his peers regarding the effectiveness of campground utilization in Lafayette National Park ,while Dorr spoke on marine biological research undertaken not at government expense but under the sponsorship of the Wild Gardens of Acadia. He noted especially the horticultural progress made at the Mount Desert Nurseries, where species were being propagated to restore wild plant communities throughout the park.[34] NPS assistant director Arno Cammerer took many engaging photographs showing Dorr and his colleagues situated in the dramatic structural remains of the Native Americans who once inhabited Mesa Verde. One year later, Dorr attended his final superintendent conference held at the Interior Department in Washington, D.C.

Four months after his return from Colorado, Dorr confided to an ailing Rockefeller that at Mesa Verde, "I caught a fresh infection which rapidly developed into an ear attack and abscess, which later broke fortunately—for I was out of reach of surgical aid but was long in healing after I had returned to Boston and put myself under an aurist's care—owing to the constant recurrence of the cold infection which had brought it on.... An anti-vaccine was prepared to treat the condition and I underwent [for] some weeks vaccination treatment, since then I have had no serious attack or development of the old condition." Dorr encouraged Rockefeller to "take my experience into consideration."[35]

As such infirmities befell Rockefeller, he became increasingly concerned about what would befall the park and his carriage road system when Dorr no longer managed Lafayette National Park. He was not alone in thinking along these strategic lines. In August 1926, Arno Cammerer thanked him for the invitation to be his Eyrie houseguest, making clear that "one of the matters that I would like to touch upon while with you, since you mentioned it to me and I therefore know you are interested, is that of an eventual successor to Mr. Dorr."[36] Cammerer suggested several likely candidates. All too soon, Eliot's death would make future management an even more pressing issue.

Charles W. Eliot's interests in Lafayette National Park had "continued unabated" according to Dorr's memoirs.[37] Following the death of Eliot's wife, Grace, in August 1924, the ninety-year-old preservationist immersed himself in long hours of correspondence, relying on family to address his needs. But letters would have to wait for he soon was beset with a disability that prevented him from writing with his right hand. The hand of his son was now actively engaged in drafting new chapters for a second edition of *Mount Desert: A History,* a 1905 publication credited to the late George E. Street. Co-authorship of both editions should be credited to Samuel A. Eliot, for his original contributions are conspicuous.[38] Samuel Eliot approached Dorr and others for new content, provided a continuous historical narrative, and repeatedly reframed his father's principled message that the whole island ought to be treated as if it were a public park.

Sufficiently recovered by June 1925, Dr. Eliot journeyed as "always" to Northeast Harbor. His biographer recounted that "in August he was prostrated by an attack of shingles that lasted more than three months. Never in his life had he had an illness that remotely approached this in degree and duration of suffering."[39] Mr. Rockefeller sorrowfully acknowledged how wretched Eliot must be due to a "malady from which my dear mother suffered frightfully in her later years."[40] Moreover, his eyesight at this time "almost completely failed," an infirmity that Eliot and Dorr shared.[41]

The emphatic wish of Harvard's President Emeritus was that he would be strong enough in 1926 to reach the coast of Maine, to spend his last days at his favorite home, Asticou. That desire was fulfilled and he spent several months in Northeast Harbor with family members, largely confined to his residence. By mid-August he informed his son that he was going to die the following Saturday. Eliot wanted a simple ceremony in the Northeast Harbor Union Church, reflecting that "it would be best for him to die on Saturday because the family, and others who might like to come to Cambridge, would find the Sunday train more comfortable than a week-day train."[42] On Sunday, August 22, he said to an astonished nurse that he saw his parents, and a moment later his head fell to his chest. The end had been painless. He had lived to see the silver anniversary of the incorporation of the Hancock County Trustees of Public Reservations and the tenth anniversary of the formal celebration of the establishment of the Sieur de Monts National Monument, and died on the island where he had spent, with one exception, the last forty-six summers. Twenty-seven years later, in 1953, Judge John A. Peters—clearly a park founder in every sense of the word—would pass away on that same historic date.

Two days later, funeral services were held in the Peabody and Stearns–designed Union Church in Northeast Harbor which Dr. Eliot helped establish nearly forty years earlier. On August 25, the tenth anniversary of the establishment of the National Park Service, Harvard University paid tribute to Dr. Eliot at services in Appleton Chapel.[43] A single bunch of goldenrod and beech tree branches from Asticou covered his coffin. Jerome D. Greene, Eliot's former secretary and now a Harvard Overseer, headed a corps of ushers that guided hundreds to their seats. Following the ceremony, the cortege proceeded to Mount Auburn Cemetery.

On Eliot's birthday seven months later—at a commemorative service attended by 1,500 students, faculty, and alumni—Harvard president A. Lawrence Lowell remarked that "during the first twenty years of [Eliot's] regime, his changes caused the student enrollment to decrease. He appeared to be the underdog. Then, suddenly the country and the world began to realize what he had done. The harvest did not come for twenty-five years, but when it came it was magnificent."[44] A similar conviction was expressed by his son in a letter to Dorr's friend, William C. Endicott Jr., when he rightly isolated "the penetrating and enduring quality of my father's influence."[45]

The HCTPR minutes referred to their first and only president as "unfailing in active interest and wise counsel. The strong influence of his personality, his broad vision and high public spirit will remain always as foundation stones built into the achievement of the Corporation and the history of Mount Desert Island."[46] First Vice-President Dorr chose a different venue, a two-paragraph encomium published in the *Bar Harbor Times*. With simple dignity he stated that it was Eliot's desire "to preserve in openness and freedom to the public the landscape that had so entered into the happiness of his life.... His place in the world will be recorded in the nation's history. His life here is written in the hearts of friends."

Since 1905 Eliot also had served as president of the Massachusetts Trustees of Public Reservations. His fellow trustees remarked that it "may truly be said that the son [landscape architect Charles Eliot] inherited much of his peculiar ability and enthusiasm for Nature and her works from his parent." As in Maine, his presidency there was not that of a figurehead; he attended every meeting except two, over a span of twenty-two years. He was "a remarkable presiding officer—dignified, methodical, precise, alert;

illuminating every subject that came before the meeting."[47] If a future biography of him be written, he preferred that it be drawn from Harvard University annual reports and official documents—and from the number and quality of the bricks that he built into Harvard's walls.

Dr. Eliot fully believed that his joy in work was among his "durable satisfactions," though others interpreted his extraordinary self-control as coldness and austerity. His friend, Harvard Overseer Reverend Paul Revere Frothingham offered this explanation of Eliot's self-control: "But the mastery [of passions] does not mean that such impulses are absent; it means only that they are disciplined and brought into an orderly realm of culture and restraint."[48]

The Eliot tributes persist into the twenty-first century. In a magnificent 2007 address delivered in Northeast Harbor, Harvard University Pusey Minister Peter J. Gomes explained that the Maine landscape "appealed to him, for there is nothing false or artificial about this: it is rugged, natural, and it has a kind of dignity and grandeur that artifice could not improve. That appealed to Eliot's aesthetic…[these] 'durable values of life,' the things that last, that are not creatures of fashion, the things that do not come and go; and out of this aesthetic, out of this feeling for durable values came the principle of preservation."[49] Reverend Gomes concluded that Acadia National Park "is the living memorial to the extraordinary, difficult, inspired, imaginative man, Charles William Eliot."

Would Dorr and Rockefeller be able to carry forward park development without their senior partner? For the last quarter century Dorr and Eliot had provided leadership for the endeavor, with Mr. Rockefeller's contribution limited to the last fifteen years. At the time of Eliot's death, no one on Mount Desert Island was aware of Mr. Rockefeller's interest in "a shabby, down-at-the-heels southern town" in Virginia, as his biographer described it. Yet three months later, the philanthropist had sufficiently researched historic Williamsburg to undertake "the most ambitious restoration project ever undertaken in America."[50] When his commitment became public, those involved with Lafayette National Park's development might wonder whether someone who spent two months every year in Colonial Williamsburg could make up for Eliot's absence—or whether Rockefeller could even sustain his earlier interest.

An exhaustive comparison of the individual contributions of the Acadia Triumvirate is beyond the scope of this biography. While in many ways their personalities were dissimilar (for example, Dorr was passionate and spontaneous, Eliot and Rockefeller both methodical and contained) Eliot's death requires at least reference to dominant character traits—varying in degrees—that they held in common during the critical period from 1913 to 1926.

Keen memory, exceptional respect for intelligence, and an understanding of the importance of clearly defining far-sighted personal goals were shared mental traits. All three applied scientific methods contextually, balanced by the rules of logic and persuasion. Rockefeller's biographer at times described his subject in ways equally applicable to Dr. Eliot and Mr. Dorr: "Tenacity was integral to the man himself—an overriding patience which he showed in all large matters…[which] could easily have developed into arrogance, but of that quality there was not a trace…. There was a kind of formality about him, a tendency toward reticence, which to some who knew him seemed to surround him like a cloud…. Always there was a dignity about him, a quiet detachment, a fleeting appearance of withdrawal...[yet in his letters] no one could express himself with more compelling delicacy and sincerity."[51]

Solitary self-examination and life experience transformed their elitist social inheritances into an appreciation of conservation as a vehicle for promoting democratic values. This "magnificent trinity" shared the ethical conviction that there was permanence; that their intellectually derived concepts of conservation arose from what Dr. Eliot repeatedly described as "durable values."[52] Highly committed to conserving a landscape that was aesthetically unique—and of benefit to Mount Desert Island, New England, and the American citizenry—they showed that a contained, contiguous, and publicly accessible preserve remedied the exclusive property balkanization that was in place prior to their stewardship.

Each possessed a strong antipathy to being told by others what to do, yet their personalities were such that they gave each other "respect, trust, support, and gratitude" for creating and developing landscapes permanently protected by the power of the federal government.[53] At a time when the National Park Service was in its infancy, the private initiatives of the Triumvirate became both a template for national park development via private philanthropy and proof that democracy and conservation were hospitable ideas.

CHAPTER EIGHTEEN

"The Old Order Changeth!"

Mr. Rockefeller's acquisition of Mount Desert Island properties continued. Beginning in 1919 with "his gift to the HCTPR of Beech Hill and the cliff on the western shore of Echo Lake," he was later lauded in 1939 by their historian and son of Dr. Eliot, Rev. Samuel Atkins Eliot, for protecting the island "from unsightly advertising, unnecessary and ugly filling stations, undesirable resorts and from the constant danger of forest fires."[1]

Mr. Dorr also tracked island properties carefully, with an eye to new acquisitions and donations through the Hancock County Trustees to the federal government. Beginning in October 1927, Dorr began a new form of land acquisition. It commenced with the sale to Rockefeller of the first of nearly two hundred properties that would pass between the two during the next decade. The superintendent negotiated with property owners, purchased, and later transferred to the philanthropist real estate that fit their shared vision of the national park; Rockefeller had little need for the HCTPR since the corporation had redefined its mission. The National Park Service left the two to work out such arrangements on their own.[2] Yet now they would develop the park without the wise counsel and political connections of Charles W. Eliot. As Dorr reflected on the long-term implications of the death of Dr. Eliot, he found his life imperiled just a few days before his seventy-fourth birthday.

Dorr was at ease moving around the wintry streets of Boston. On Christmas Eve 1927, as was his holiday custom, he had set out to gather with friends and a few relatives. At 1:30 that afternoon—as he approached Charles Street from the Common—he stepped off the curb and was struck by a moving Willys-Knight sedan. Unconscious and in shock, he was taken to the Phillips House at Massachusetts General Hospital with a five-inch skull laceration and a concussion. He was placed on the "danger list."[3]

Dorr's cousin Louisa Endicott and her husband, William—the two relatives in greater Boston with which he had the strongest attachment—visited Dorr and urged him to convalesce at their nearby Marlborough Street residence. Five days later, on his birthday, Dorr was also visited at the hospital by his Harvard College class secretary, who later published an account of "his miraculous escape from more serious injuries."[4] On his release, Dorr took advantage of the Endicotts' hospitality, recovering his strength in their good company for nearly two months until he left for Washington on park business.[5] For several years thereafter, Dorr spent his birthday and the Christmas holidays with the Endicott family.

In early April of 1928, conversation on Mount Desert Island was concerned with the possibility that President Coolidge might be spending his summer in Bar Harbor. Maine's Governor Brewster, who had climbed Katahdin with Dorr three years earlier, contacted the White House in the hope that the Vermont-born chief executive might favor a summer vacation in his own New England. Oldfarm was suggested as the site for the summer 1928 White House.

An editorial in the *Bar Harbor Times* supported this proposal and provided a glimpse into the condition of Dorr's residence nearly a half century after its completion. The very name *Oldfarm* "suggests the mellow atmosphere of an earlier New England, a New England that built spacious, rambling houses and furnished them with the best that its ships brought home across the seven seas. Oldfarm is such a house and is so furnished. Its balconies and many windows command the most inspiring views of mountains and sea. Its grounds and spacious and broad lawns and lovely gardens would assure the president of being always protected from the gaze of the merely curious.... [None of the Bar Harbor estates] appeals to us as being so strikingly suited to use as the summer home of a New England President of the United States as does Oldfarm." All three floors were fitted with tasteful family furnishings relocated from Dorr's former Commonwealth Avenue home.[6] Sadly, the invitation was not accepted; Coolidge opted for the five-thousand-acre estate of oil baron H. C. Pierce, on an island in Wisconsin's Brule River.

Media promotion of the park and its chief administrator was also fostered by Samuel A. Eliot, who included a chapter he authored on Lafayette National Park in his revision of George E. Street's 1905 classic, *Mount Desert: A History*.[7] Therein Dorr's leadership and the importance of R. S. Yard's 1924 analysis of the park were generously described. Samuel A. Eliot's son adopted a quite different attitude toward park development. In 1926, Dr. Eliot's grandson, the National Capitol Park and Planning Commission landscape architect Charles W. Eliot II, was asked by the Bar Harbor Village Improvement Association to lead a committee to research island development and prepare a report.

Some summer members of the BHVIA believed that park management was not adhering to the plan that they believed they had helped to shape. Eliot's committee began with the conviction that the future health of the whole island was bound up in the future of the park. That park policies consequently required greater local scrutiny—if not authorization—was seen by the BHVIA as derivative of this interrelationship. The draft report implied that park development was uncharted by park superintendent Dorr. In finalizing their report, committee members advanced numerous arguments against road development, stressing the negative environmental impact of such expansion. As the key authority, Eliot identified the topographic areas that were significant for their wilderness character and scenic, scientific, and historic features. These were recommended for inclusion in the park. Of course, the historical evidence is that Dorr and Rockefeller had collaborated in explicit plans for park development since 1921. And as Ann Rockefeller Roberts reaffirms, those plans "had the very real approval of the National Park Service."[8]

Yet the 1928 BHVIA publication, *The Future of Mount Desert*, showed no awareness that Mr. Dorr, NPS assistant director Arno Cammerer, or NPS chief landscape architect Thomas C. Vint had crafted another planning document the preceding September.[9] At the national level, Vint and Daniel R. Hull had initiated a rustic design style for national park development "that responded to the practical necessity for modernizing facilities, while remaining firmly footed in the theory and practice of American landscape park design."[10] Vint pioneered "master planning" procedures that standardized the planning approach for every park, devising sensitive approaches to road construction within the context of landscape scenery. Charles W. Eliot II spent two days conferring with Cammerer and Vint. The thirty-six-page "Memorandum on a Development Plan for Lafayette National Park" addressed the BHVIA concerns, concluding that the Park Service should "continue in every way possible with park policies and laws to cooperate with representatives of adjacent communities in the betterment of scenic conditions of the islands." Reference to "park policies and laws" meant that the Park Service would aim at consistency across the system by applying formal landscape principles that would be adapted to the constraints of local topography.

Nonetheless, Rockefeller judged *The Future of Mount Desert* as a deliberate initiative to gain control of park development and island wilderness areas. In his view their strategy was to disrupt his road construction and realign park development leadership following the elder Eliot's death. "To undertake to get out of these diverse ownership interests of this island an agreement on a common plan for the development of the Island seems to me utterly impossible."[11] The attractively published report was described by its chairman as setting "forth the Ideal but has been restrained in making definite suggestions," entrusting to island "leaders and groups" the conservation and enhancement of the "Glories of Mt. Desert."

Eliot's report did not arouse public support and "apparently just faded away."[12] The many island-wide recommendations contained therein were generally not supported by Rockefeller or the Park Service. Despite this response, over the next six decades Charles W. Eliot II scrutinized the development of Acadia National Park with a degree of persistence and abiding concern that rivaled the historic conservation efforts of his grandfather. He fiercely argued for the importance of acquiring additional properties that established "whole natural units" and not imposing artificial boundaries on future development.

Dorr moved gradually away from park administrative matters. During the working season, he reported that he "spends the greater part of every day in the field personally supervising work in progress."[13] In September 1929 the fruits of the field work of one researcher, Edwin Raisz, appeared in the *Annals of the New York Academy of Sciences.* This engineer and Hungarian immigrant had just completed graduate studies at Columbia University with a dissertation on "*The Scenery of Mt. Desert Island: Its Origin and Development.*" Therein he acknowledged that this research was "made possible by the courtesy of Mr. George B. Dorr, creator and superintendent of Lafayette National Park, who covered the author's field expenses and at all times rendered the most generous aid."[14] Two years later, Raisz joined the faculty of the Institute of Geographical Exploration at Harvard University where over the next two decades he produced thousands of landform maps, redefining what the printed map can represent.

When not in the field, Dorr turned to the classical texts and the literary traditions that had inspired him during his Harvard undergraduate years and subsequent travels. One piece of evidence to this effect is found in a brief letter from Henry van Dyke, a summer resident of Seal Harbor. A clergyman, professor of English literature at Princeton, diplomat, and a widely published author who wrote essays in the tradition of Thoreau, Burroughs, and Muir, van Dyke informed Dorr that he had followed up on "our pleasant conversation" at dinner earlier in the week. The issue was "our old friend Virgil in the *Divine Comedy.*"[15] These few sentences about van Dyke's rereading of Dante—coupled with a flurry of requests to the Globe Book store—signal Dorr's re-immersion in the literature of ancient Greece.

This redirection away from park administrative matters came to the attention of his superiors in Washington. In late September 1928, Mr. Dorr hosted Arno Cammerer and Michigan congressman Louis C. Cramton. According to Cammerer in a report to Rockefeller, Cramton—the chairman of the powerful House Appropriations Committee—"was told [by Dorr] of various offers of land at various points outside the island proper, such as Schoodic Head."[16]

These "various offers" had first come to light at a dinner in late September 1922 at the Jordan Pond House. Mrs. Louise Hartshorne Moore Leeds, wife of New York industrialist Warner Mifflin Leeds and the widow of Gouldsboro financier John Godfrey Moore, held a one-third interest in property situated on an impressive peninsula across Frenchman Bay from Bar Harbor. Moore's success in telegraph, railroad, and banking enterprises had provided sufficient capital for development of Grindstone Neck into a most prosperous community. After purchasing Schoodic Point, Moore built a nine-mile carriage road to the point and to the summit of Schoodic Head. When he passed away in 1899, his widow and their two daughters inherited the property.

Twenty years after marrying Mr. Leeds, she encountered Dorr at a social event at the Jordan Pond House. Dorr reported in *The Story of Acadia National Park* that "I chanced to sit next [to] a neighbor of mine on the Bar Harbor shore, Mrs. Warner M. Leeds ... [who] asked if I would not like to have her interest, a third, in [the] Schoodic Peninsula." Dorr visited the 2,000-acre Schoodic Peninsula the next day and learned that such a transaction was dependent on convincing her two daughters—who held equal shares—to follow suit. The donation fell through when Mrs. Leeds died shortly thereafter. Nonetheless, Dorr retained his belief that there were other strategies to secure this "rock-built projection of the mainland into the Atlantic Ocean."

At that time, Charles W. Eliot had not been indifferent to this opportunity to add several thousand acres to the park. In his younger days he had repeatedly climbed Schoodic Head. He was convinced that this peninsula should be added to the park and "the Head itself should be preserved in all its own beauty of geologic structure and forest decoration for the enjoyment of future generations." It was not until 1927, however, following the death of Mrs. Leeds, that Dorr convinced her daughters to donate their portion of the peninsula to the HCTPR, adding to the earlier gift of Mrs. Leeds's own share. The completion of this transaction would momentously extend the activities of the trustees to the mainland.

But to accept such offers, the Lafayette National Park Act, which limited park acquisitions to Mount Desert Island, would have to be amended. Although Cramton did not interact with Rockefeller at this time, Cammerer reported in a later letter to him that the congressman "was inspired by the work you had done...on those roads which he conceded were in workmanship far beyond results that could be accomplished by us in our road work in other parks."[17] Cramton informed Dorr that he would support a bill expanding the domain of the park beyond the island. As the bill worked its way through the congressional process, the scope of the park boundaries was extended to include the headlands and islands off the coast of Mount Desert Island, in part to prevent unsightly views from the park.[18]

Afterwards, Cammerer sent Rockefeller an update on his discussions with Cramton, recommending that an associate superintendent position should be funded to "take all administrative burdens off the shoulders of Superintendent Dorr," who would thereafter have as "his sole duty the acquisition of lands for the enlargement of the park." With the support of Arno Cammerer, a special provision was inserted in the pending legislation exempting Dorr from civil service age limitations.[19]

Cammerer then discussed the plan with Dorr, "who was much pleased, and thoroughly in sympathy with the plans."[20] Cammerer informed Rockefeller that Dorr "immediately agreed to an arrangement whereby [his] services could be made available indefinitely, without fear of retirement, until his most important work in connection with the extension of park areas could be concluded, or at least as far as his physical condition would at any time permit...[and] I felt that this would be a real solution of some of our vexing local problems, without hurting Mr. Dorr's feelings or standing, and Mr. Dorr appeared relieved when I told him of this plan."[21]

Eight days before Dorr's seventy-fifth birthday, the recently appointed interior secretary, Roy Owen West, informed Congress that he strongly recommended the passage of the Acadia National Park Act (H.R. 5088). In this renaming of the park, Director Mather recognized the historic lineage of the Native American term *acadie*, stressing in his annual report that this geographic term was in use "before recorded explorations of the area by either the French or English."[22]

The legislation renaming Lafayette and the new mainland property as Acadia National Park was signed by President Coolidge on January 19, 1929. No longer was the park an island enclave. It encompassed 11,000 acres, which Dorr would enlarge to 27,870 acres by the time of his death—or more than five times the size of the original monument in 1916. Tom Butler, author of a recent work on wildlands philanthropy, put it well: "This ideal name would stick, conveying both the contemporary understanding of 'Acadia' as the North Atlantic coast region settled by the French, and its historical derivation from Arcadia, the 'rustic paradise' of Greek mythology."[23]

Dorr never mentioned the narrowing of his responsibilities in *The Story of Acadia National Park,* leaving readers with the impression that his administrative duties remained unaltered. NPS officials focused on the importance of completing the major road projects currently underway. After nearly fifteen years of the Dorr administration, his strengths in researching, negotiating, and developing the landscape remained undiminished. Approaching the years of the Great Depression, John D. Rockefeller Jr. and Park Service officials took great pains to ensure that Dorr was consulted on all important matters. But would Dorr honor the new limitations? For him there was a choice; for Stephen Mather that turned out not to be the case.

In Washington, there was once again a new Interior Department Secretary. Roy O. West was replaced by Stanford University President Ray Lyman Wilbur following the election of President Hoover. On election eve 1928, Stephen T. Mather suffered a stroke that left his vocal apparatus and entire right side paralyzed. It took him a month to realize that his professional life was over. As his biographer expressed it: "The national parks were now out of his hands forever."[24]

To no one's surprise, Mather expressed his preference for Albright as his successor—and Albright was quickly appointed director of the National Park Service. Congressman Cramton lauded Mather's achievements before the House of Representatives, concluding that "as he builded [sic] so wisely, his work will stand. There will never come an end to the good that he has done. Can any man desire a more wonderful career?"[25] Despite some progress in managing his disability—and profitable interactions with his colleagues throughout 1929—on January 22, 1930 Mather suffered a second stroke and died in Brookline, Massachusetts. George B. Dorr and Assistant Superintendent Benjamin Hadley attended the funeral services for the man who had grown the number of national parks from fourteen to twenty-one and the national monuments from eighteen to thirty-three. Theodore Roosevelt would have shouted "Bully!"

Mather had always wanted plaques and memorials kept out of the parks, yet with the arrival of the Roosevelt administration support for recognition of Mather's achievements came from the office of Mrs.

Roosevelt as well as the new secretary of the interior, Harold L. Ickes. A memorial bronze plaque recognizing Mather by British sculptor Bryant Baker was installed in all parks and monuments. Over the last eight decades countless visitors have paused and reflected on the words placed beside Mather's bas-relief profile on the thirty-by-thirty-five-inch plaque atop the summit of Cadillac Mountain: "He laid the foundation of the National Park Service, defining and establishing the policies under which its areas shall be developed and conserved unimpaired for future generations. There will never come an end to the good that he has done."

Part of Rockefeller's original plan, approved by Secretary Lane in 1917, was the Amphitheater carriage road—which remained unconstructed. According to Dorr, if Rockefeller could secure lands connecting the Cadillac Summit road with the new road along the oceanfront, the philanthropist would carry the expense of building "the missing link in his horse-road system, and, purchasing the necessary lands, [construct] a motor road along the shore from the Sand Beach to Hunter's Brook." Accordingly, Rockefeller submitted plans to Washington for a loop motor road connecting Cadillac Mountain with the ocean and extending Ocean Drive.

Later that summer, Rockefeller accepted an invitation to speak at the Pot and Kettle Club, a Bar Harbor association of influential summer residents. He agreed to this venue to clarify his role in executing the road development plan that had been posted for weeks in the park office. His audience was unaware that the philanthropist was—to a limited extent—previewing an announcement that would headline the local paper two weeks later: "Rockefeller Offers to Build a $4,000,000 Motor Road for Park." The *Bar Harbor Times* referred to this fourteen-mile-long scenic motor road, connecting Cadillac Mountain with Frenchman Bay, as "Ocean Drive."[26]

The Interior Department accepted Rockefeller's proposal despite his insistence that the Otter Cliffs Naval Station be relocated. Yet this could only be accomplished if the U.S. Navy–owned radio-receiving station at Otter Cliffs was removed *and* the Town of Bar Harbor ceded land on Ocean Drive to the Park Service. The military had supported at the outset of World War I the communication innovations of Alessandro Fabbri, a yachtsman and Bar Harbor summer resident, who had built the elaborate wireless station. Town officials were agreeable since they found merit in the creation of a loop road that would follow the coastline, provide motorized access for tourists to scenic vistas, and realize Mr. Dorr's vision of a seacoast national park.[27]

The military, however, raised stern objections. As the time limit set by Rockefeller for accepting his offer drew near, no resolution appeared likely. *The Story of Acadia National Park* recounts the fascinating challenges that Dorr overcame in bringing an end to the impasse, culminating in the Navy Department accepting his arguments that the newly acquired Schoodic Peninsula property, across Frenchman Bay, was an excellent location for the facility.[28] Big Moose Island at the tip of the Schoodic Peninsula was selected; in exchange the Park Service received the Otter Cliffs land to continue the Park Loop Road. After the radio station was dismantled, Congress authorized the transfer of the Naval Station from Otter Cliffs to Schoodic Point in February of 1935.[29] After three years of inactivity on the costly extension of Ocean Drive, this solution enabled Rockefeller to move forward with his original proposal.[30]

There were two side stories to the Park Loop Road that were playing out at this time. For more than a decade, Dorr had not realized his plans for the Sieur de Monts Spring, which he still owned and wanted to develop as a botanical exhibit. Dorr was aware that Rockefeller wanted to secure the spring, and felt the philanthropist was "bent on having it" rather than actually needing it. When Rockefeller heard that Dorr refused to sell, he reportedly said that he would sooner abandon the massive road-building plan than not secure both the Springhouse and Great Meadow. According to Dorr, Mr. Rockefeller was informed that the park superintendent wanted the roadwork to continue and would give up the spring. His only condition was that the property must be donated to the government when Mr. Rockefeller's purposes for it were served.[31]

The second issue prompted Rockefeller to contract with the Olmsted Brothers, the premier landscape architectural firm with whom Charles Eliot had been associated four decades earlier. A dispute needed to be settled between Dorr and Rockefeller about the route connecting the Kebo Mountain section of the Loop Road with Ocean Drive and the location of the entrance road to Sieur de Monts Spring.[32] Dorr and Rockefeller differed about the park entrance road, the track of a motor road around The Tarn watershed, and the line of access to the Loop Road.

Immediately south of Sieur de Monts Spring lies a glaciated valley, situated between Dry (now Dorr) and Champlain mountains. Along the western flank of Champlain there was a town road connecting Bar Harbor and Otter Creek, and within the gorge was a wetland known as Little Meadow. Shortly before the establishment of the national monument, large granite stepping stones had been placed at the northern end of the meadow, impeding water flow. This impoundment deepened the water level to create the pond soon known as *The Tarn,* which "improved the reflective capacity of The Tarn to mirror the surrounding mountains," and encouraged aquatic vegetation.[33] As the Park Loop Road issue loomed large, Dorr believed that the picturesque beauty of the area was at risk.

Town residents did not take a stand on either side of this very public issue. They were concerned that Rockefeller might abandon motor road projects, reducing his work force amid rising concerns about the deepening of the Great Depression. The Town of Bar Harbor voted to donate the requested portion of Ocean Drive to the federal government so that Rockefeller could build the oceanfront motor road, pending a decision on the exchange of Schoodic Peninsula land for the U.S. Navy station at Otter Cliffs. This concession unified Rockefeller and Dorr in their desire to redirect the roadway away from The Tarn and toward Ocean Drive.

More often than not, when matters of disagreement occurred the external authority was Frederick Law Olmsted Jr., "whose unique combination of talent, preparation, and family legacy provided the cornerstone for a career" that more than a decade earlier had included drafting the Organic Act of the National Park Service, which to this day defines the Park Service's core purposes.[34] Olmsted's facility for reconciling conflicting views was well known. Olmsted favored Dorr's route, which ran the road north of the Sieur de Monts Spring area and along the east side of The Tarn (west of Champlain Mountain), not Rockefeller's more intrusive route at the foot of Dry Mountain and along the west side of The Tarn. After resistance from both parties, in the end Olmsted's exhaustive study of alternate routes and the logic behind each resulted in a shared vision.[35] The recreational use of The Tarn to fish, to skate, and to ice-boat in the winter and the site of a shoreline connector trail to other park paths had been preserved.

Ultimately, Mr. Rockefeller conceded the larger issue that made such a specific solution necessary. In a fulsome letter at that time to pioneering landscape architect Henry V. Hubbard, Rockefeller acknowledged that "Mr. Dorr's projects and my projects, all in the interest of the park, are very intimately inter-related and inter-dependent. Neither of us can develop our ideas most fully or most satisfactorily without the complete cooperation of the other."[36]

The Hancock County Trustees of Public Reservations moved away from the vision of Charles W. Eliot in 1929. On August 20 they opened The Black House on the outskirts of Ellsworth as a public museum. George Nixon Black Jr. had bequeathed to the HCTPR the historic house and original furnishings of Colonel John Black, who had built the house in 1827 on his 180-acre estate. This promotion of a cultural facility signaled a departure of the trustees from their land trust mission of nearly three decades—fourteen of which as a land trust partner to the federal government. Some must have wondered if there was merit in Rockefeller's suggestion that the trustees should disband now that their mission had been realized. Instead, without any formal declaration, they shifted from land conservation for public recreation to the preservation and stewardship of a museum committed to Downeast education and research.[37] Nine days later the group's minutes reported that it conveyed "to the United States all lands owned by the Corporation [the Hancock Country Trustees] on Mount Desert Island."

The distance between the HCTPR and park management had increased throughout the late 1920s. To carry out a growing array of park management activities, staff growth was mandated. In early spring of 1930, Mr. Dorr "personally recruited" Ardra Tarbell to serve as clerk and administrative officer.[38] In the early years, Ms. Tarbell (who served for almost forty years) was responsible for the orderly maintenance of a massive number of land data records, title abstracts, deeds, and maps that were constantly required by attorneys and park staff.[39]

A quarter-century after Mr. Dorr's death, Ms. Tarbell orally recorded her lasting impressions of the park founder. "He looks very well. This is something I think will never fade…for he had very distinguished look…And when he was happy, of course, his mustache would curl up, you know….

When he was down in spirits, it sort of drooped." He carried a cane, "just for something to carry, I guess, and balance...he was very happy to see somebody enjoying the estate...[telling me] to keep on. Go anywhere I wanted to." The superintendent was "a very popular guest among the wealthy summer residents...entertained by all of them...he went to teas and luncheons and dinners almost every day, the weeks around, all summer long."

Ms. Tarbell described him as the soul of courtesy and thoughtfulness, a great scholar with a command of "many languages that he spoke and read fluently." Moreover, she learned from Dorr's secretary, Grace Oakes, with whom she lived in an Oldfarm estate cottage, that Dorr always read the Classics in their language of origin until sleep overtook him. Indeed, what the biographer of Charles Sprague Sargent said of that great Harvard botanist would aptly apply to his cousin, George B. Dorr: "[He] advanced into old age with majesty...he moved through his days with the deliberate, assured pace that had served him all his adult years, toward death, which neither attracted nor frightened him."[40]

Other staff additions were put in place by Thomas Vint, who dispatched members of his growing team of landscape architects to the parks. Many of these had only recently become available, having been displaced by the Depression from their customary employment. Dorr described this constructive initiative as "the first practical contact this park has had with the Landscape Division of the National Park Service."[41] As work on the Cadillac Summit Road neared completion, newly hired NPS landscape architect Charles E. Peterson arrived to assist Dorr in creating an updated road and trail development plan. Widely considered today as a pioneer in historic preservation, the young man at first was viewed somewhat less highly by the park superintendent.

Subterfuge wasn't a term that normally applied to Dorr's methods, yet the arrival of Peterson resulted in its amusing application. Ardra Tarbell recalled that Dorr "didn't want anybody messing around with the trail system." He devised a diversion whereby Peterson was taken around and introduced by Dorr to every young woman he could think of, all in the name of hospitality. These females were impressed and "started calling to entertain [Peterson], to go swimming and one thing or another, golfing and tennis, and they kept him so busy, we know he never saw a trail and he was here a couple of months."[42] But Peterson had the last laugh, for he judged the Summit Road work as unsatisfactory. As he later recounted, "I told [Bureau of Public Roads engineer Leo Grossman] it was the worse [sic] piece of landscape damage ever inflicted on a national park."[43] The landscape disfigurement, guardrail issues, and inadequate summit parking were among his laundry list of project failures that could have been avoided —thought Vint—if a Park Service landscape architect had been on site.

Beyond the aesthetics of scenery lay a more vexing issue. Since the establishment of the Yosemite Valley sanctuary in 1864, scenic preservation was the imperative that justified conservation decision-making. Over the last half century, questions had been raised—and preferences argued—in Bar Harbor and elsewhere about whether the scenic landscape was as important as the "parks total natural system, including not just the biological and scenic superstars, but also the vast array of less dramatic species such as grasses and soil fungi."[44]

To interpret landscape as mere scenery "gives precedence to appearance at the expense of habitability and risks trivializing landscape as decoration."[45] Dorr's pioneering promotion of scientific inquiry anticipated a new understanding of parks as interrelated ecological complexes; deeper contexts existed beneath surface appearances. Dorr did not express this philosophical distinction in the environmental language that has evolved over the last half century, but his awareness of this issue was suggested in "Acadia, the Seacoast Park," and elsewhere in his writings.[46]

Even though Dorr was frequently visited by Interior Department administrators, the visit in late spring of 1930 by Horace Albright and Arno Cammerer imbued Dorr with new standing. Despite his fifteen years in leadership positions within the NPS, Albright had never been in Acadia National Park or the state of Maine. Dorr met them in Bangor in early June and drove them to Mount Desert Island. They traveled the new road built east of Eagle Lake and Jordan Pond, visited Seal Harbor and Mr. Rockefeller, and saw the Otter Cliffs radio station. The following day they covered Rockefeller's carriage roads, and explored Somes Sound in a motorboat. Guided by Frederick Law Olmsted Jr., they saw new roadways near Great Meadow and The Tarn. Finally, they climbed to the Beehive summit to get a comprehensive view of road route possibilities. Much impressed, Albright related to Rockefeller that he also approved Dorr's program for "road construction that is deemed necessary on the Schoodic Peninsula."[47]

A month later, the first trip by automobile to the summit of Cadillac Mountain was completed. National Park Service officials and federal and state engineers motored to the summit with the superintendent on a road that would not be formally opened until 1932. Although Dorr was enthused about this achievement, Cadillac Mountain was not his favorite of the island's chain of summits. After all, he had hiked to the summits of Mount Whitney, Mount Mitchell, and Katahdin. By comparison, the unrivaled height of the high point on Mount Desert Island was similar in stature to Snowdon in Wales, which Dorr had climbed as a young man. In Dorr's unpublished essay on "Champlain Mountain and the New Park Road," he stated his preference for Champlain as "the most interesting mountain in the entire Mount Desert chain." His enthusiasm for Champlain's eastern flank, a "magnificent cliff, rising almost a sheer eight hundred feet; then after passing through a stretch of open woodland and across a second meadowland…the mountain terminating above in a splendid headland known as The Beehive and the mountain heights of Gorham, with wonderful surf-cut cliffs and caves showing how the coast has risen in the last and recent glacial invasion."[48]

Even as the summit motor road was nearing completion, opponents to Rockefeller's road project continued to write letters to the editor of the *Bar Harbor Times* reiterating complaints voiced over the past decade: "road construction plans have been secretive"; "roads desecrate the scenery"; and in the words of Trustee Edward S. Dana, "the judgment of the summer residents should carry great weight for we have made the Island what it is to-day."[49] The public nationwide was ill prepared for the late January 1931 announcement that appeared in *The New York Times:* "J. D. Rockefeller Jr. Drops Park Project." He asked the director of the National Park Service to release him from the four-million-dollar road construction commitment that the government had accepted the prior September. The philanthropist stated that he did not want to be the cause of ongoing criticism and had "no desire to be put in the position of forcing upon even a small minority of the people who frequent Mount Desert Island something that they do not want."

An outpouring of public support for the road project resulted.[50] A large and enthusiastic gathering of local businessmen met immediately—with Dorr as their guest—to unanimously approve the road-building program, prior to his departure for Washington to consult with NPS officials. Official and private conversations about the reversibility of Rockefeller's announcement were actively pursued. Many residents reaffirmed earlier convictions that the roads would be a boon to tourism, that construction would promote employment for year-round residents, and that the methods employed by Dorr and Rockefeller "should and will stand as a lasting tribute to their memory for the present and future generations [for] their methods have been proved to improve and beautify."[51]

Mr. Rockefeller "calmly withstood the controversy and remained steadfast in his views of how Ocean Drive should be built. As he said to Cammerer, 'I am simply not interested except on the terms of my original offer.... People are interested in blocking something which they think I have my heart set on doing. If they know I am indifferent, then the proposal begins to be considered on its merits; and when, as in this case, the merits are found to be very considerable, like all other blessings they brighten as they take their flight.'"[52] Having planned the project carefully, Rockefeller would ultimately stay the course despite the obstacles put in his path.

In early February, Maine legislators, Superintendent Dorr, and Secretary Wilbur met in Washington to discuss a strategy for overcoming the stalemate. Matters took a turn for the worse when the House Appropriations Committee disapproved a funding request to remove the Otter Cliffs radio station. Dorr stressed the dramatic increase in park visitation and the increases anticipated even as the Depression deepened.[53] Dorr's forecast was born out by the headline that later appeared in the *Bar Harbor Times* in October: "Park Attendance Believed to Have Topped Yellowstone." Only with the coming of the new Roosevelt administration was Dorr able to convince a reluctant director of the Bureau of the Budget of the validity of the next project, the formidable Schoodic road plan, securing the requisite funding at a time of budgetary cuts.

As the 1931 visitation season wound down, Dorr was visited by Conrad L. Wirth, an NPS land-planning official recently hired by Albright. Dorr identified with Wirth, knowing that his father was a horticulturist and park planner who had fostered in his son similar passions.[54] For nearly a week, the superintendent acquainted "Connie" Wirth with the challenges faced by the park. He received useful input from the man who would implement forthcoming Civilian Conservation Corps programs and then rise in the ranks to become NPS director in the 1950s.

No year in the early history of the Acadia National Park rivaled 1932 for the frequency of visitation by National Park Service officials—and the public expression of appreciation for its superintendent. Director Albright arrived in late May for wide-ranging management discussions that included review of the preparations for the dedication of the Cadillac Summit Road and discussions with Mr. Rockefeller. The director was sufficiently impressed to remark that it "was one of the most interesting days of my national park career."[55]

A month later, Interior Secretary Ray Lyman Wilbur and his wife were Dorr's guests at Oldfarm. Following a thorough tour of park property, Wilbur surprised more than a few during his visit by announcing his intention to develop the most ambitious of Department of Interior projects: "an inter-park highway. Starting here we can go through to the other great parks of the East…[which] should measure up to the Western system which we hear so much about."[56] Following Wilbur's return to Washington, Rockefeller heard from him that "your roads are admirable, your bridges beautiful, and your plans complete." The philanthropist made clear that the achievement was not his alone, stating that Wilbur's positive reactions "must gratify Superintendent Dorr, who is entitled to the credit therefore."[57]

Clearly pleased at the extent of official interest, Dorr's official monthly report acknowledged that "The old order changeth! No longer is Acadia an isolated number of the national park system, having no contact with it except by correspondence, or an occasional visit from officials from Washington and the field services."[58]

CHAPTER NINETEEN

Cadillac Summit Road Dedication

As strange as it must seem, the only interview of George Bucknam Dorr ever published appeared in *Maine Highways* in 1932. This brief article by journalist B. Morton Havey rings with the interviewer's exasperation: "On the day I interviewed Mr. Dorr warning was given by friends that he would talk for hours on the subject of Acadia National Park—but that I had better watch out if any attempt was made to lead him onto the subject of George Bucknam Dorr." This charming article revealed the difficulty faced by any biographer trying to counter Dorr's playful strategies to avoid personal disclosure.[1] Stymied by the Boston Brahmin's ability to "courteously, but efficiently, avoid my direct questioning," the interviewer departed with only "the many intimate facts regarding his life and public career which pass from mouth to mouth…[for Mr. Dorr] does not feel it necessary or expedient to associate his own personality with Acadia National Park."

That others would "associate" his personality with the park was again demonstrated by events that unfolded one month later, at the July dedication of the Cadillac Summit Road. The Havey interview of Mr. Dorr was prompted by the conviction that the summit road would become Maine's greatest attraction, a scenic road to the highest point on the Atlantic coast between Labrador and Brazil. Secretary Wilbur and his wife had departed just three weeks earlier, after an inspection trip that clearly was intended to ensure that all preparations were in place for this highly publicized dedication. The unacknowledged contributions of day laborers, heavy equipment operators, stone masons, engineers, architects, and construction foremen were sidelined when Bangor's daily newspaper declared that "this wonderful scenic highway has come into being as a monument to the foresight and hard work of one man—George B. Dorr, superintendent of Acadia National Park."[2]

Contrary to the hopes of those who planned the events, weekend rain and fog enveloped the hundreds who traveled to the summit to dedicate the mountain road. The official party on July 23, 1932 included the secretary of the Navy (and great-great-grandson of the second president of the United States), Charles Francis Adams III, representing the Hoover administration, and Joseph W. Dixon, a Progressive Montana governor and former Bull Mooser who was currently first assistant secretary of the Department of the Interior.[3] Thirty-seven naval officers from vessels moored in Frenchman Bay, the governors of Maine and Rhode Island, as well as multiple United States senators and representatives were also present. The participation of hundreds of other prominent individuals from island towns and beyond displaced any thought that this was exclusively a Bar Harbor festivity. Surrounded by the press corps and filmmakers, Superintendent Dorr was greeted by spirited march music as he cut a narrow silver ribbon at the entrance to the 3.86-mile mountain road.[4] Surrounding him was "his whole Park 'family' as he calls it." John D. Rockefeller Jr. was not present due to a very severe case of shingles, which incapacitated him for much of the summer. John D. Rockefeller 3rd stood beside Dorr to represent his ailing father, without whom perhaps none of Acadia's roads would have been constructed.[5]

The master of ceremonies, Judge Luere Deasy, decided that the torrential downpour necessitated the program's relocation to the Malvern Hotel in downtown Bar Harbor. Charles Francis Adams III spoke to those present about an incident fifteen years earlier, when he had stood with Mr. Dorr on Schooner Head and heard his friend expand at length on what the park should become. John E. Nelson, who had succeeded John A. Peters in the U.S. House of Representatives, likened Dorr to Stephen Mather—declaring that what Mather had been to the National Park Service, so was Dorr to Acadia National Park. If that were not praise enough, assistant secretary Dixon suggested that no time should be lost in erecting a bronze plaque to Mr. Dorr, while others suggested naming a mountain after him. Two weeks earlier on July 4, the Stephen Tyng Mather Memorial Plaque had been installed—on Mather's birthday, in fact—at the summit loop trailhead adjacent to the Cadillac Mountain parking lot.[6] Finally, Judge Deasy asked for a moment of silence in tribute to Charles W. Eliot. After the Malvern luncheon for five hundred invited guests, an afternoon tea and a dinner-dance for two hundred at the Bar Harbor Club completed what must have been a tiring day for the superintendent.

Historian Max Farrand, husband of landscape gardener Beatrix Farrand, sent letters of appreciation for the summit road to Rockefeller and Dorr.[7] In his response, the ailing Rockefeller provided the Yale intellectual an unequivocal statement of praise, affirming that without Mr. Dorr "permanent preservation of the beauties of this island for the use of all the people would never have come to pass."

Close Dorr family friend William C. Endicott Jr. knew best what the completion of the Cadillac Summit Road meant to Dorr, and in congratulating him put his achievement and personality in a larger historical context. After apologizing for missing the celebration, Endicott wrote: "You…must have found it a very moving occasion for you have been a great public servant who in spite of opposition has accomplished great things and who has always been dignified and patient in the face of many trials. How proud your father and mother would have been to see the climax of your work completed, for the drive must always be one of the famous drives of the world. Much love from us both…. [And] when the end comes you must make plans to be buried upon the island in the midst of the nature which your thoughts and vision has rendered immortal. It means a great deal for you all to be buried on the island; nothing to be buried at Mt. Auburn."[8]

Local businessmen had discussed the opportunities for commercial enterprises atop Cadillac Mountain, an obvious notion given the precedent established decades earlier when hotels and a cog railway had drawn visitors to the summit. They reasoned that visitation need not involve deprivation. Since the opening of Yellowstone National Park sixty years earlier, private entrepreneurs had argued that the public could be provided with essential services at no cost to conservation.

Since the beginning of the National Park Service, Stephen Mather and his successors had opened the gates to segments of the hospitality industry. Motivated by the profit incentive, "Park concessioners regularly sought to increase their customer base, frequently cajoling park officials to approve new facilities or activities designed to entice more visitors."[9] Yet as Mather's biographer framed the issue: "[the Park Service] did not insist upon [concessions] or even necessarily advocate it. If private operators came in, how closely should they be watched? Should profits be regulated…[or should they have the] freedom to soak the citizens on the citizens' own recreation grounds?"[10]

For nearly two decades, concessioners had been kept off Mount Desert Island park land because visitors had easy access to the nearby island communities with their bountiful resort services. Even closer was the hospitality available at the Jordan Pond Tea House (purchased by Mr. Rockefeller in 1924, then leased back to the McIntire family, who operated it until 1945). To consolidate private enterprise initiatives, the Acadia Corporation was formed in 1933. Mr. Dorr served ex-officio along with the five corporation members, who disclaimed profit as a motivation for involvement. According to Acadia Corporation spokesperson Judge John A. Peters, the "high-class enterprise" was established by Hancock County residents "to cover the situation in a way acceptable to the park people and others interested in proper development of that section. We don't want the concessions handled in any cheap, indifferent or objectionable way."[11]

Yet from its inception, Acadia Corporation investors were ill-prepared to support the costs of quality. The teahouse design by Grosvenor Atterbury (who had designed the two carriage road gate lodges at Brown Mountain and Jordan Pond) was considered too expensive to execute, so a facility was constructed atop the Cadillac summit for one-fifth the cost. Dorr's straightforward intent here as well as at concession outlets at Sieur de Monts Spring and Thunder Hole was to provide visitors with opportunity for a pleasant meal, a view inconsistent with the policy of Cammerer, who ruled out "any service within the park that could better or equally be met at the nearly small towns."[12] In these early years the "high-class enterprise" envisioned by Acadia Corporation member Peters was not realized. Nonetheless, in 1939 Cammerer told Mr. Rockefeller—a corporation investor—that in each of the last five years the corporation had returned a profit—and that net gains were reinvested rather than dividends being issued. The associate director cautioned that "close supervision and control" was necessary to prevent the "erection of buildings and the installation of services…in areas which we desired to keep sacred and free from intrusion."[13]

Cammerer had more pressing concerns than the so-called "hot dog stand" atop Cadillac. He sent a confidential memo to Director Albright raising questions about Dorr's administrative competence. Acknowledging that the finances of the park were "in far better shape than they ever have been…[and] we need to have no fear that Mr. Dorr will get into trouble going counter to accounting practice, because of the fact that [Assistant Superintendent] Lynam is in control of the accounts."[14]

Placed in charge of park administrative matters by Cammerer in 1928, Harry Lynam was nearly two decades younger than the superintendent. But he periodically experienced pain from angina pectoris, and Cammerer realized that Mr. Dorr might outlive his second-in-command. Nonetheless, he recommended that should Dorr "relinquish that position by death, or otherwise" then Lynam should be appointed superintendent for a period not to exceed six months. Ever sensitive to political issues, Cammerer mentioned Lynam's special relationship with Rockefeller and left no doubt that Lynam had "a better knowledge of the park's administration requirements than Mr. Dorr, or anyone else up there."

Having entered federal service in 1904 as bookkeeper in the Treasury Department, Cammerer had been a "by-the-book" bureaucrat, exceptionally committed to documenting every detail. This was a luxury that the action-centered Mr. Dorr could not afford. The extent of Cammerer's obsession was revealed in his May 1939 letter of resignation on the advice of his physicians. He noted with pride that "from 1933 to 1938 I took 13 days ½ hour of annual leave, 14 days of sick leave, but put in 5,327 and one-quarter hours or 222 days overtime, exclusive of overtime in the field."[15]

Lynam and Mr. Rockefeller shared some degree of Cammerer's frustration. Identifying properties owned by the Wild Gardens of Acadia as distinguished from Dorr's personal holdings remained a vexing problem when transfers to the federal government were being considered. From his desk in The Eyrie, Rockefeller wrote to Lynam that "both you and I know that Mr. Dorr really in the bottom of his heart wants to do the thing that will make the lands which he has taken such pleasure in acquiring and which he has so enjoyed owning most useful to the public in the years to come.... I feel you and I will only be showing the genuineness of our friendship for Mr. Dorr in seeking in any way we wisely can to help him reach a satisfactory solution." Three weeks later, Lynam informed Rockefeller that Dorr "did not take kindly to the suggestion." The matter was put aside for the time being. Six months later the philanthropist again urged Lynam to "help Mr. Dorr so arrange his affairs that what he really desires to have done with his property after he passes on will be done. His lack of experience in matters of this kind may result in his not knowing how best to accomplish that end."[16]

Dorr's mind was preoccupied with more immediate matters. He wanted to rebuild the trail beside Rockefeller's Ocean Drive roadway, upgrade the Bear Brook and Sieur de Monts Spring areas, and extend park facilities and trails to newly acquired lands on the western side of the island. While private "auto-camps" were increasing on the perimeter of parkland, NPS landscape architect Charles Peterson drafted in 1932 the first plan for a campground within the park, responding to The Employment Stabilization Act of 1931 requiring every federal bureau to develop "plans for construction projects for a relief workforce in the event that the economic depression should continue."[17]

As the nation neared the third anniversary of the 1929 stock market crash, the newly elected administration of Franklin D. Roosevelt faced a country paralyzed by a collapsed economy. In the months before FDR's March 1933 inauguration, four thousand banks failed. One in four employable men and women were without jobs. In the first hundred days of Roosevelt's New Deal, profound changes resonated throughout the country. Under the leadership of Interior Secretary Ickes, the National Park Service would reap benefits that remain unrivaled to this day.[18]

Ickes considered himself a conservationist cut from the same cloth as Teddy Roosevelt and Gifford Pinchot, and was determined to rebuild and expand the authority of the Interior Department. What was needed was the identification and acquisition of new parkland, infrastructure development, the elevation of landscaping and design values, and a phenomenal expansion of the labor force. Despite Albright's identification with the Hoover administration, Ickes wanted Albright to remain as NPS director. Confidentially, he requested that Albright serve as his unofficial assistant in the rebuilding of nearly every facet of the Interior Department administration, shifting the mission of the department to conservation—if not in name then at least in function.[19] Albright also represented the Interior Department on the New Deal Council that Roosevelt created to put unemployed young men to work in national forests and parks. Consequently, Albright had less time for the national parks, and many routine tasks defaulted to Arno Cammerer. Nearly three decades later, Horace Albright would characterize Secretary Ickes as the "greatest conservation Secretary."[20]

Winter 1933 signaled Dorr's return to Washington, this time to lobby for the transfer of the Otter Cliffs radio station to the Schoodic Peninsula. With the excitement of new policies to address the economic calamity, Roosevelt's New Deal principle, "Action, and action now!" was not ignored by Dorr. From the opaque announcement of a relief program in his March 4 inaugural address to a headline in the *Chicago Tribune* seven days later that the Interior Department would be a participant, it was clear to the politically savvy Dorr that opportunity had presented itself to address park infrastructure issues. The president and his aides developed unemployment relief measures that moved through the emergency legislative process with phenomenal speed. Following congressional approvals on March 31, the Emergency Conservation Works Act was placed on the desk of President Roosevelt, who signed Executive Order 6101 on April 5, enabling the first enrollee to be processed two days later.

In his memoirs Dorr recalls that he stayed in Washington "until the opening of spring…[and] I took up the C.C.C. camps and the acquisition of sub-marginal and kindred lands…with those in charge… asking for two C.C.C. camps in the eastern and western sections of the Park."[21] Of the New Deal programs, three would have the most lasting effect on Acadia: (1) The Emergency Conservation Works Project, later renamed the Civilian Conservation Corps (CCC); (2) The Civil Works Administration (CWA); and (3) The Emergency Relief Act (ERA). These New Deal programs "catapulted the park service into a national recreational planning and state park development agency."[22]

For Horace Albright, "one of the most momentous experiences of my Park Service career" began on April 9, when he was invited to travel with the Roosevelt party back to the nation's capital from the Hoover Camp on the Rapidan River. Seated in the touring car jump seat with the president, he used this opportunity to explain "how wasteful and inefficient it was to have several different organizations handling parks, and why the Interior Department and the National Park Service should have control over them all." A transfer of authority over national military and historic parks would give the Park Service holdings in every part of the country. Albright's organizational plan was opposed by Congress, but the president found it "sensible" and took the proposal to yet another level. His June 10, 1933 Executive Order 6166 consolidated within the Park Service all War Department battlefields, parks, monuments and cemeteries, fifteen national monuments from the Forest Service, and all District of Columbia parks and public buildings.[23] On the heels of this achievement, Albright informed Secretary Ickes of his decision to leave public service in early August, enabling his successor to start anew with an enlarged National Park Service.

In late May 1933, Dorr welcomed Harold Ickes and Horace Albright to Maine. Their early-morning flight from Boston coupled with fair weather enabled the park inspectors to observe Deer Isle, Southwest Harbor, The Eyrie, the Schoodic Peninsula, and road development along Otter Cliffs, The Beehive, and Champlain Mountain before landing in Bangor to the enthusiastic welcome of the park superintendent.[24] Not only was he interested in the logistics of his CCC request, rumors circulated about the new secretary, a passionate man who labeled himself "America's No. 1 Curmudgeon." Albright's biographer described Ickes "as an administrator who often got what he wanted by calculated intimidation and vituperation." In the days ahead, would Dorr be perceptive enough to discern "Ickes's tenderheartedness and the fact that his legendary curmudgeonly personality was essentially contrived"?[25]

After journeying from Bangor to Bar Harbor with his guests, Dorr hosted lunch at Oldfarm with Frederick Law Olmsted Jr. and others before departing for a motor trip up Cadillac Mountain.[26] Olmsted pointed out to the secretary the major features of the summit and the landforms to be observed before the party departed for Seal Harbor, where they enjoyed the view from The Eyrie's front porch, though Mr. Rockefeller was in Williamsburg at this time. This overnight visit would not have been complete without visits to Sieur de Monts Spring, the former Charles Homans residence, and the Amphitheater carriage road. Albright later reported to Rockefeller that "it was wonderful to get the Secretary so early in his administration to get such a very comprehensive view of Acadia's problems, and to get fully in his mind the scope of the road program."

The public was informed that the Park Service had been charged with oversight of six hundred CCC camps staffed by 120,000 social relief enrollees and six thousand supervisors. The two camps quickly approved for Acadia meant that for nearly a decade Acadia National Park would have a steady supply of human resources that it had not known before—or since! Within weeks of Dorr's return from Washington, he had a youthful (though inexperienced) labor force to achieve goals that he had thought beyond the scope of his years—and beyond all expectations of the federal government.[27]

This was but one program in the "first one hundred days" of federal action impacting Mount Desert Island. The McFarland Camp above Eagle Lake was occupied by an advance detail in late May 1933. The main body of the camp arrived shortly thereafter. By September, tents had been taken down and the new barracks occupied.[28] A second camp on Long Pond near Southwest Harbor was in service by June. A third camp, on the mainland in Ellsworth, focused on road approaches to the island and the Schoodic Peninsula.

Acadia's chief ranger, Benjamin Hadley, was officially appointed assistant superintendent on June 9, 1933, a new position despite nearly a decade of references to A. H. Lynam as assistant superintendent. Both Dorr and Lynam greeted the appointment with pleasure. Hadley's promotion provided organizational continuity in the event that the seventy-nine-year-old superintendent was unable to fulfill his responsibilities.

A workforce of six hundred single men between the ages of eighteen and twenty-five was now available throughout the year. During their six-month enrollment, they were paid $30 a month, $25 of which automatically went to their families. Some island residents expressed anxiety about the unprecedented impact of so many young men on the four island townships, but in the long run, misbehavior concerns proved to be unfounded.

In all, more than a thousand men worked on more than thirty different projects that were designed to train enrollees in new skills for future employment. Their supervisors were expected to adhere to high NPS standards for workmanship and complete each documented project on time. To these ends, they developed, improved, and restored trails, overhauled park signage, applied design features to park roads, landscaped road and trail byways, expanded and beautified public areas, constructed new visitor facilities, implemented drainage and erosion control, and attended to a host of forest management issues from insect threats to fire hazards.[29]

Since Maine's national park was of a more manageable size than the large western parks, Acadia was closely scrutinized to determine whether the CCC-infused park could continue to balance the twin directives of the 1916 Organic Act: to preserve lands in their natural state and make these scenic properties accessible to the public for recreation. Resident landscape architects prepared detailed project drawings conforming to National Park Service standards but delayed action until approval was secured from Thomas Vint.[30]

With so many modifications of the landscape—intended and unintended—concerns arose about whether the CCC crews were applying the desired landscape aesthetic.[31] Assuming that these landscape values could be articulated, could they then be enforced to the point of uniformity in application? This was the challenge that National Park Service management faced in the years ahead when Arno Cammerer became NPS director. Horace Albright had been courted repeatedly by the U.S. Potash Company, and after Hoover's defeat he was sorely tempted to resign his government position. To ensure that his departure did not negatively impact on the Park Service, "in June 1933, with the park service safely established in the affections of the new secretary, Albright was convinced that he could publicly announce his intention to resign."[32] As to whether these dramatic intentions were conveyed to his Oldfarm host a month earlier, the historical record is silent.

In spite of his resignation, Albright's role in the evolution of the National Park Service did not end. In the decades ahead, the tireless second director of the Park Service worked behind the scenes as a parks and conservation consultant, promoting the NPS agenda and resolving challenges in particular parks. Acadia National Park had no small place in those efforts. On the day Albright completed his tenure as director, he wrote to Rockefeller expressing his gratitude "for all the interest you have taken in national park affairs during my administration.... The privilege of enjoying your friendship and your confidence, and the inspiration of your character and ideals have meant more to me personally than I can ever express."[33] Two months later, Rockefeller wrote to him that "it is you who have been chiefly responsible for the development of the national parks, there are hundreds and thousands, yes, millions of people whose lives have been made happier, richer, better because you, their unknown friend, have opened to them nature's treasure store of beauty."[34]

When Arno Cammerer was promoted to the directorship in August, he became the third chief administrator in the first seventeen years of the service. His immediate junior was Arthur E. Demaray, who had two decades of government service rising from draftsman with the U.S. Geological Survey to an administrative post with the Park Service in 1917. He possessed extensive knowledge of all phases of the service. Demaray's expertise in fiscal and budgetary matters inspired confidence from House and Senate committees who authorized the millions of dollars that he then directed to national park road construction. In the absence of Mather and Albright, where would these two seasoned Park Service officials take the NPS in fulfilling their obligations to the irascible Interior Department secretary's efforts to support the New Deal?

Dorr returned from Washington later in August and as part of his daily routine made his way to nearby Dorr Point. A few days later Oldfarm staff noticed that Dorr had failed to return from the point when expected. He was found lying unconscious on a ledge, the tide just a few inches away, having suffered a severe heart attack. Warned by physicians that he might have but six months to live, Dorr set himself to a recovery routine that included running up stairs—insisting that the heart muscle can only be strengthened by hard exercise.

As the weeks passed and he neared his eightieth birthday, Dorr slowly recovered. He told his cousin Thomas Wren Ward Jr. that he was distracting himself with "work once more on the old Ward letters and [I] hope to make good progress with them." Through research, he resolved family history inconsistencies that had not been addressed in *The Ward Family Papers,* published by Tom's father at the turn of the century. Dorr admitted that the story the family letters told was "scattered and fragmentary, giving glimpses only here and there."[35]

Dorr was a self-referential person, strongly inclined to transfer what he studied to his own life. Surely he knew that others felt discomfort that he relied so heavily on his memory. He resisted the sensible arguments of Dr. Eliot, Harry Lynam, and Rockefeller that he document his private holdings and personal history. Yet he continued to churn out accurate official reports, essays, memoirs, and correspondence—all based on his phenomenal memory. Dorr well knew that his own personal history was likewise "scattered and fragmentary," but that was not an issue that much troubled him. However, he now began to admit this limitation and ask for help when needed.

How could he not be mindful of his mortality when he considered that in the fourteen years since the national park was established, his friendships with Franklin K. Lane, Charles Pickering Bowditch, William James, Alfred Mayer, David Ogden, Josiah Royce, Charles W. Eliot, Charles Sprague Sargent, Guy Lowell, and Robert Abbe had all come to an end? The passing of those who had been dear to him prompted Dorr to post a letter in September to Mount Auburn Cemetery requesting information on the Dorr family lot and the status of perpetual care for the gravesite. His many questions regarding who had established the existing level of care, when such arrangements had been made, and whether additional payments were necessary to "secure its maintenance in its intended good condition," suggest that he may have neglected the family gravesite.[36]

Since his graduation from Harvard sixty years earlier, Dorr had provided his class secretary with only the briefest information about his activities. In a surprising turnabout, he modestly offered roughly six hundred words on the genesis of what he regarded as his lasting achievement. "My life these half dozen years offers little outstanding of which a tale might be told. One lives more interiorly and less actively as the years go by. But the story of the Acadia National Park…I will gladly tell. It sprang from a desire I shared with President Eliot, a friend and neighbor on these shores, to make safe from disfigurement, and free access to the public of the future, a great coastal landscape wherein for a term our own homes were set."[37] This self-characterization—that the man pales by comparison with the monument—reinforces the *Maine Highways* Dorr interview published earlier.

Was Dorr claiming too much in sharing with Eliot a "desire" to open the island to public access and spare it disfigurement? Surely Dr. Eliot was the project's initiator; it was he who first brought together in Seal Harbor in August 1901 those incorporators who became the Hancock County Trustees. Moreover, as its president, Eliot was a key figure in framing the organizational mission that guided the trustees. However, in executing that mission, Dorr was the prime agent or executive officer of an expanding desire (i.e., vision) to realize the mission under changing circumstances. In this context, the shared credit that Dorr claims is fair.

Eight years after the death of Harvard's President Emeritus, Dorr's classmates and other Harvard alumni learned—through Dorr's report—of Eliot's role in establishing the national park in Maine. Granted, it was unlikely that there were large numbers of readers of that entry. But Dorr had well documented for his alma mater another dimension to the deceased president—his conservation achievement in Downeast Maine. Despite his commendable efforts, to this day many Mount Desert Island residents know little about Harvard's President Eliot; likewise, "few Harvard people know much about the Mount Desert Eliot" according to the late Reverend Peter J. Gomes.[38] In a 2007 talk in Northeast Harbor, Gomes eloquently encouraged studious attention to "The Preservation Legacy of Charles William Eliot" in both locations, for the founders need to be remembered "not for their sakes but for our sakes, and not for the sake of the past but for the sake of the future."

In the years since Eliot's death, public confidence in the future had been sorely shaken. The economic hardships of the Depression threatened the foundations of American democracy. In July 1934, island community leaders seized the opportunity to showcase the enduring beauty of Mount Desert Island to five hundred members of the Garden Club of America. Even for a resort community noted for its grandeur, horticultural entertainment on this scale was unprecedented. The Garden Club of Mt. Desert planned itineraries for the ninety-three clubs that convened at the Building of the Arts. The program began with a visit to the Mount Desert Nurseries followed by fifteen garden tours. Renowned landscape architect Beatrix Farrand's Reef Point estate was open, but for many the highlight was a Seal Harbor garden that had resulted from a creative collaboration spanning two decades. The Abby Aldrich Rockefeller Garden at The Eyrie was the outcome of Mrs. Rockefeller, the client, educating Farrand in East Asian aesthetics—a little-known and underappreciated fact.[39]

Shortly after the late-summer departure of the garden enthusiasts, Dorr was visited by Horace Albright, in his new role as a consultant to the National Park Service. This was again to Dorr's advantage because a few days later Secretary Ickes arrived and spent a week with Albright focusing upon the prospects of an auto road between the end of the road Rockefeller built near Eagle Lake and Sieur de Monts Spring. At this time neither Dorr nor Rockefeller would exert much influence on the two prominent Washington visitors. The philanthropist was absent from his Seal Harbor summer residence for the first time in twenty-five years, and Dorr was incapacitated by a severe leg wound that—in the pre-antibiotic era—posed a substantial threat to the elderly gentleman. The gravity of the situation was not lost on Dorr, who began to draft plans for his personal property. Albright informed Mr. Rockefeller that "Mr. Dorr is not in very good health. He has decided to make very definite plans for disposing of his property and for carrying on his work after he is gone. He has asked me to serve on a committee which he is organizing to handle his affairs."[40] But for the time being, Albright well represented the interests of both.

On October 2, 1934 Dorr received a first-day cover of the seven-cent Acadia postage stamp that received notice in *The New York Times*.[41] Despite his satisfaction at this recognition, Dorr was not unaware that his incapacities multiplied. Nine months after his Acadia visit, Albright received a grim private communication from Dorr's secretary: "Mr. Dorr walked to the Spring and back, Sunday, while he was alone. The wound of last year which is in his leg will not heal. His system fights it, of course, or he would have gangrene. But he looks well, eats well. Mr. Dorr cannot see, Mr. Albright. That much is certain. He cannot distinguish people in the room, but with a strong light and glass he still can read."[42]

Both Dorr and Rockefeller had been concerned about the health of Harry Lynam, whose heart disease had been evaluated—at Rockefeller's insistence—at The Hospital of the Rockefeller Institute for Medical Research.[43] Lynam then contracted shingles, prompting an empathetic response from Rockefeller, who had recently suffered through the same painful affliction.[44] The two friends met at Rockefeller Center in early December, before Lynam departed for Pasadena, where he intended to winter with his wife and daughter. The announcement of Lynam's death two weeks later was disheartening for Mr. Rockefeller—and a severe blow to Dorr.[45] Both were more than Lynam's clients. Each had relied on his expertise, advice, and friendship. From 1910 to 1924 he had been secretary of the Hancock County Trustees; he was a conservation advocate whose legal expertise and social connections made him essential to the successful conveyance of property titles to the federal government. Without his legal skill and support for the objectives of the Hancock County Trustees, it is quite likely that Sieur de Monts National Monument would not have been established.[46]

On the heels of Lynam's death, Horace Albright informed Rockefeller that Dorr's eighty-first birthday was imminent. He suggested that a few of Dorr's friends send him some words of greeting and good cheer. Dorr was "not well and may not see another birthday.... [His] Christmas has been a sad one on account of Mr. Lynam's death. He will feel very keenly the loss of his old friend and associate."[47] Director Cammerer's birthday greeting ignored Dorr's administrative role and focused instead on his rich life, full of loyal and devoted friends. Felicitations from Secretary Ickes referred to Acadia National Park as a "monument to your public spirit and farsightedness for without those efforts the park doubtless would not have come into being."[48]

In Boston the temperature reached seventeen degrees below zero on December 29, 1934. It was colder still in Bar Harbor as Dorr had Rockefeller's latest letter read to him, "...isolated in the dead of winter in your cozy library on Mount Desert island.... Mrs. Rockefeller and I count our friendship with you as one of the happiest of the many delightful things that have come into our lives as a result of our having made Mount Desert island our summer residence. It was you who brought about the establishment of Acadia National Park. Without you the thing could never have been done, nor can I think of any other person with sufficient patience, kindliness and tact to have accomplished so difficult an undertaking.... [Our] contact with you during these many years...has been a constant pleasure and happiness to us."[49] The repeated references to Mrs. Rockefeller were not gratuitous. In 1917, Eliot wrote to the philanthropist: "Your best advisor, is, of course, Mrs. Rockefeller."[50] While we have considerable details on Abby's role in the restoration of Colonial Williamsburg, a full account of how she influenced the development of Acadia awaits scrutiny.

The historical records do not provide a clinical diagnosis for the visual impairment that had repeatedly beset Dorr since his college days at Harvard. Glaucoma had cost his mother the sight in one eye during the last decade of her life, however, so Dorr decided to follow the advice of his Boston ophthalmologists and undergo surgery, which was completed with some success.[51]

Dorr's spirits were lifted when he learned that Rockefeller had sent Secretary Ickes a letter containing a magnificent offer: To deed to the government for inclusion in Acadia National Park all of the remaining lands that he had acquired for construction of his roadway network, with the exception of Seal Harbor lands associated with The Eyrie. This donation would make possible "a Park motor road from the sea on the South at Seal Harbor to Frenchman Bay on the north at Bar Harbor." This letter summarized the acreage and cost of land previously donated; the offer would add 3,835 acres to the 2,700 already gifted—representing a personal expenditure of four million dollars.[52]

This news buoyed Dorr, who had witnessed Rockefeller's investments over the last decade at Colonial Williamsburg, Great Smoky Mountains National Park, Shenandoah National Park, not to mention investments in the western parks. Yet Rockefeller's interest in Acadia had not waned—and in some respects his vision had expanded. Many years later, the conservationist and president of the New York Zoological Society, Henry Fairfield Osborn Jr., wisely described Rockefeller with words that apply as well to Dorr, saying, "Vision alone was not enough. Wealth alone was insufficient. Concept of the plan as a whole, arduous attention to detail and even passion for perfection, feeling for color and beauty, respect for working associates, talent for administration, patience and, lastly, tolerance of criticism and even of misunderstanding of purpose—all these qualities were brought into play, for all were essential to the fulfillment of the vision."[53]

Despite the additional pressure on the Interior Department in managing the growing number of park properties, Harold Ickes and Horace Albright journeyed to Acadia in late May 1935 as they had ten months earlier, surveying by air the island coastline and the Schoodic Peninsula. Congress had recently authorized an exchange of Schoodic Peninsula land between the Park Service and the U.S. Navy. Over the last two years artesian wells had been drilled, roads constructed, and Rockefeller "signaled his pleasure in this newly accessible Schoodic District of the Park by funding and overseeing an elegant new brick-and-beam 'Acadian lodge,' hoping to set a park-like tone for the new Navy radio signal base that opened in February 1935."[54]

Dorr invited Olmsted to lunch before the four drove to the top of Cadillac for Olmsted's explanation of the scope of the carriage and automobile road systems. Following a visit to Schoodic with Mrs. Rockefeller, her husband sent a note of "heartiest congratulations" to Dorr on his success there. Five days later, the Rockefellers walked the new Ocean Drive trail from north to south, and were "charmed with the system" thus far completed.

The superintendent invited Rockefeller to meet with him on the Oldfarm porch on August 29. The philanthropist asked about Dorr's health, for he surely was aware of his heart attack in 1933, his persistently infected leg wound, and his recent glaucoma surgery. Rockefeller was direct, asking Dorr whether his executors would cooperate in fulfilling the plans of the multimillionaire. Dorr laughed and wryly asked whether Rockefeller thought Dorr's death was imminent. The philanthropist seriously responded that it was his practice to close up his affairs every night, whereupon Dorr humorously inquired whether Rockefeller did not really think that once a week would be sufficient. Failing to see the off-color humor of this exchange, Rockefeller was unresponsive. Surely after nearly two decades of collaboration with Dorr, he was by now aware of his liberality, especially when it contrasted so starkly with Rockefeller's daily due diligence.[55] For several hours the two talked of land acquisition issues, Rockefeller "looking around to make sure that no one was within hearing," as Dorr looked appreciatively off to Bald Porcupine Island and sipped his favorite beverage, Ballantine East India Pale Ale—which he had long imbibed at the Somerset Club in days gone by.

CHAPTER TWENTY

The Mather Era Closes

For decades Dorr bathed in an ocean pool over a flat stretch of rock at the base of Dorr Point, several hundred yards from his Oldfarm bedroom. This steep little peninsula jutted from the Oldfarm estate into Frenchman Bay. Using granite blocks from his quarry, Dorr had walled in a fifty-foot bathing pool, leaving spaces where water could flow in and out. A swim before breakfast in this sheltered cove invigorated him—not just when the weather was temperate, but year-round![1]

His daily activities involved a quarter-mile walk to Storm Beach Cottage—his year-round residence now, in the mid-1930s; Oldfarm was often leased when not serving as a residence for special guests. After a hearty breakfast, household staff would read to him selections from *The New York Times*. Then there were letters to be dictated to his secretary or into his much-used Dictaphone, books to be ordered from Boston's famous Old Corner Bookstore, and scholarly articles to be secured from their authors.

The afternoon would involve tasks in his ANP office and usually a drive through the park, inspecting the progress of various projects. Never had there been so much activity in Acadia. The full force of the Civilian Conservation Corps was working to remove brush and deadfall, plant trees to remedy road-building disfigurements, correct erosion problems, and construct and improve hiking trails. The workers were "sons of Maine farmers, woodsmen, mill workers, and quarrymen," who took pride in their work.[2] Whether Dorr felt up to social engagements or hiking his beloved trails depended on the acuity of his vision and his physical strength. Attention to the Mount Desert Nurseries was a daily pleasure.

As the fall of 1936 waned, the superintendent approved a park site for a "large central museum" where the results of scientific studies within the park would be gathered, processed, and exhibited. For more than a decade the National Park Service had encouraged alliances with scientists—and provided allocations—to document distinctive features of each park. The Abbe Museum was nearing the end of its first decade, while the Islesford Museum collections stretched the capacity of William Otis Sawtelle's facility. Park naturalist Maurice Sullivan and field curator Ralph Lewis worked diligently to attract scientists to the park.[3] While Dorr provided administrative oversight in these areas, in the evening hours he read, annotated, and edited the extensive Ward and Dorr family papers or composed drafts of his memoirs. Only when the daylight fell was Dorr most comfortable with matters that were familiar, personal, and full of "historical associations."

To look at Oldfarm in the distance from Storm Beach Cottage must have at times been emotionally disconcerting. The habits associated with Oldfarm's rooms, furnishings, and creature comforts would still exert their pull: the gilded Chippendale mirror where he checked his tie across from the Governor Winthrop–style secretary in the lower front hall, the comfort of the high-backed Sheraton drawing room chair, the bronze thirty-inch-high figure of Beethoven in the den, the Egyptian fireplace screen in the dining room, and the walnut rocking chairs in the Sea Room where he spent many reflective hours as his gaze pulled him toward Frenchman Bay.[4]

The preservation of the Oldfarm estate—the most cherished of his physical possessions—was now his dominant concern. He worked on drafts for federal officials, stressing the history of the property and the extent of the original purchase in 1868: "The original Oldfarm grant acquired by my father extended back from the Compass Harbor shore and the Storm Beach point for a measured mile, ending on the precipitous slope of Champlain Mountain…with Bear Brook and Beaver Dam Pool at its base."[5] Many parcels that made up this highly desirable shoreline had been gifted to the government or sold in order to secure other parcels that unified the park landscapes. As he located the documentation needed to justify the federal government acceptance of Oldfarm, Dorr turned his attention to the larger story of the park. He prepared for publication a first-hand account of the origin and development of Acadia National Park, the only record of the individuals, institutions, events, and natural phenomena that factored into the Acadia National Park story. For five years Dorr redrafted this manuscript; on specific details he queried attorney Richard W. Hale Sr. about the Black family's connections with the Hancock County Trustees of Public Reservations.[6]

Two letters written in the summer of 1936 give further evidence of his concentration of effort. In response to an invitation to renew his membership in the Trustees of Public Reservations in Massachusetts, Dorr responded with simple directness: "For many years now [I've] regarded myself as no longer an active or contributing member, [for] my work in Maine, of which state I long ago became a citizen, demanding all that I can give to wild life and landscape conservation."[7] One month later, Dorr informed a friend, Dr. William Jay Schiefellin, that over the last two or three years he had "drawn out…of all activities not connected with my National Park work," focusing instead on editing "oldtime papers" that he hoped to have published.[8]

The first drafts of Dorr's history of Acadia National Park had been started years earlier as short, unconnected essays on its evolution. He now recited to his secretary the interconnecting historical details as well as new content. The memoirs were then typed, read to their author, and revised through innumerable drafts. In 1939, Dorr asked the National Park Service's editor-in-chief, Isabelle F. Story, to assess his typescript account of the growth and development of Acadia National Park from 1901 through 1919. With typical thoroughness, he responded to her critique with a six-page letter addressing (point by point) her editorial concerns, thanking her for her "suggestions and comment on [my story], which is just what I want."[9]

For the first fifteen years of its existence, Lafayette National Park had enjoyed a certain standing as the only national park east of the Mississippi River. Dorr milked the exclusivity of the park as a political asset, well aware that his superiors were actively pursuing opportunities to expand the number of parks in the eastern United States. Director Mather responded positively to initiatives in Tennessee, Virginia, and North Carolina to create national parks in the Smoky and Blue Ridge mountains. Though they were quickly federally authorized, it would take more than a decade until sufficient funds were raised to dedicate the Great Smoky Mountains National Park in 1934 and Shenandoah National Park the following year. Dorr welcomed these additions, for they were the culmination of general arguments that he had publicly articulated two decades earlier for conserving the unique natural environments of the eastern United States. But how would Dorr react to an effort to establish another national park in Maine?

Appalachian Trail Conference president Myron Avery, an admiralty lawyer employed by the U.S. Maritime Commission, advocated a national park centered in the Katahdin area. This was not a novel idea, for Maine Congressman Frank Guernsey had introduced legislation in 1911 for a Katahdin forest reserve and national park—and Dorr had written a supportive letter to the *Boston Herald*. This wilderness was a prized objective of Percival Baxter, Dorr's friend who had spent the last twenty years trying to secure the Maine Legislature's approval for a Katahdin state park bill. Great Northern Paper Company owned the land and resisted Baxter's pressure while he was governor, from 1920 to 1925. Immediately after being succeeded by Ralph Brewster, Baxter acquired six thousand acres from Great Northern at his own expense—which he donated in 1930 to the State of Maine. Myron Avery repeatedly expressed concern about the inadequate facilities and services provided by the state, convinced that a strong organization was needed to provide visitor lodging and food services. But Baxter favored a wilderness enclave, and his unresponsiveness prompted Avery to launch a political campaign to establish a Katahdin national park.[10]

Brewster, now a U.S. congressman, agreed in the spring of 1937 to sponsor the bill in Washington, but in June 1938 Congress adjourned without taking action on it. The force of the legislation had been undercut by the hostility between Baxter and Brewster. The long-term "forever wild" plans of Baxter eventually resulted in his donation of 202,000 acres to the State of Maine. Brewster, with his opposing view, recommended the commercialization of Maine's proposed national park by introducing "great hotels" within the region.

Mainers reacted negatively to the image of influential travelers in luxury accommodations akin to those Stephen Mather had developed the previous decade at Yosemite National Park's grand Ahwahnee Hotel. An unsympathetic Baxter reminded Mainers that his donated parkland must follow the principles established in the Adirondacks forty years earlier: the land must be kept forever wild. Those who were fearful of over-development voiced their disapproval, and Congress adjourned in June 1938 without acting on the Brewster bill.[11] Dorr sat on the sidelines and watched Avery's plans unravel. Acadia's superintendent would not live to see Baxter's acquisitions culminate in the creation of America's third-largest state park—the largest ever donated by one man.

September 1936 brought news to Oldfarm that lifted Dorr's spirits. Harvard was celebrating its tercentenary. Dorr did not attend, although he later read that Franklin Delano Roosevelt had been seated in a red velvet chair to the right of Harvard president James Bryant Conant while a fellow island resident, Samuel Eliot Morison, delivered one of the many celebratory orations.[12] Dorr's cousin, Thomas Wren Ward Jr., was an honored guest. Dorr later wrote to Tom that the two of them "are the last of our generation in our Grandfather Ward's family." The Boston Brahmin said that he regretted not being able to attend, but that "my sight went back on me some four years since and I go nowhere now where people congregate, but my mind is as active still and interested as ever. With others to read to me, my days are full."[13]

Three months later, in December 1936, he was moved to travel by news that William Crowninshield Endicott Jr. had suffered a sudden heart attack and died. With great sorrow, Dorr caught the train to Boston where he comforted Endicott's widow, his second cousin Marie Louise (Thoron) Endicott. She and Dorr journeyed together to Salem for the funeral. His relationship with the Endicotts had flourished after 1898, when Louise (granddaughter of Samuel Gray and Anna Barker Ward) and her family relocated from New York City to 163 Marlborough Street, Boston. The furnishings, incremental improvements, and cultural remnants of the Endicott home provide a context for the Boston hospitality that Mary and George Dorr cultivated, especially important as a benchmark since only remnants of Oldfarm survive.[14] During summers the Endicotts often stayed at Oldfarm, especially when Trustee Endicott's official voice as president of the Abbe Museum was needed.

In 1912, Endicott and Dorr had become members of the Trustees of Public Reservations in Massachusetts but played no active role for the next two decades. Endicott was best known for a decade of service as president of the Massachusetts Historical Society. His influence on cultural preservation was also reflected in his presidency of the Essex Institute, vice-presidency of the Peabody Museum, and an incorporator of the Society for the Preservation of New England Antiquities. Endicott's biographer identified the importance to Endicott of stewardship, since "relatives and friends of older generations possessed something which would soon be lost in the changing world."[15]

Dorr's May 1933 visit with the Endicotts to the former Ward and Dorr properties in Canton, Massachusetts, sparked his essay, "Country Home in Canton," which is notable here because Dorr wrote it as a personal homage to William C. Endicott Jr.[16] Dorr's established reputation for consistency in the retelling of experiences is here coupled with emotional underpinnings that make the unpublished essay among his most worthwhile writings. The plan of his grandmother's home is described and lavish attention given to the estate gardens, especially the bounty derived from the orchards that his grandfather had planted. Canton provided, in Dorr's own words, his first "great education" in how to "love the country and the wilderness about us without the need of company." Coming full circle after a very social existence as Acadia's steward, Dorr's final years increasingly resonated with longing for the solitariness of his youthful summers in Canton.

None of Dorr's friends possessed as strong a sense of the scope and depth of "historic associations," his deeply felt catch phrase. Conveying nothing of the detached antiquarian, Endicott persuaded men and women of his generation and the next to turn over their ancestors' surviving family papers, portraits, and heirlooms for study and preservation. His attentiveness to the cultural dimension of history was a phenomenal counterpoint to Dorr's commitment to the natural landscape in which that culture was expressed.

Endicott was among the last of that generation that had witnessed the Civil War. He was part of a generation that had embraced a Progressive philosophy and that achieved unprecedented success in developing and conserving landscape, as well as the cultural bounty held in public museums and libraries. Dorr and others had helped the public understand that even small enclaves of wildness had value not only for their own sake but also because they shaped and informed nearby communities to their advantage. While many residents of Mount Desert Island would only discern the economic benefits of the park, a larger number took the long view and appreciated the value of conserved wildness—even though acknowledging that many remote spots were too easily accessed by Rockefeller's carriage roads.

Dorr's sight occasionally improved to the point where he could read again, and he focused his energies during these periods on ancient Greek literature. With a dictionary at hand, he was unwilling "to read [it] in translation or with the aid of others which hampers always one's full appreciation of the original, which, save in matters of artistry, one does get, I think, in its full spirit, when one works things out for oneself, gaining gradually, I read the whole *Odyssey* through and read it thoroughly."[17] (In his characteristic wordy manner, with cautiously introduced qualifiers as sentences unfolded in his mind, his memoirs could be a challenging read.) He then read the *Iliad* and the plays of Aeschylus, benefiting from recent secondary literature on the Classics.[18]

Rollo Walter Brown's published description of the declining years of George Herbert Palmer, Dorr's first philosophy professor at Harvard, resonates with what we know about Dorr's final decade: "When he could no longer read he had the nurse read to him. 'Let's have some more of *The Odyssey*,' and he would tell her just where in his translation. 'Read that.' He listened, his face alight, his great shaggy brows standing high. 'That's good! That's good! Read that again!' Who had anything to propose that was better than keeping in the presence of the great?"[19]

As the Great Depression persisted, park visitation, staffing, and budgets increased—in part because of CCC improvements that inspired visitation system-wide. Before the onset of World War II, the CCC "would build more than 97,000 miles of fire roads in national forests, combat soil erosion on 84 million acres of farmland, and plant three billion trees—[and] during that time, some $218 million would be pumped into projects solely with the national parks—including trails and buildings that remain to this day."[20] At the outset of the second Roosevelt administration in 1937, more than a half million visitors—including an international audience—were able to enjoy the automobile-accessible scenery along Kebo Mountain, Otter Creek, and the Cadillac Summit.[21] Dorr was also acquiring and developing properties on the western half of the island, working with Rockefeller to develop camping venues and roadside access to Ship Harbor's rocky shoreline.

The resort community culture had fundamentally changed now that many of the children of the wealthy no longer returned to Bar Harbor to summer on the estates of their parents and grandparents. Of course, this generational disinterest in property conservation is what Charles W. Eliot had predicted forty years earlier. According to Benjamin Hadley, the park attracted "a different class of people—a well-to-do middle class which can afford to take two or three weeks or even a month's vacation in the summer.... They patronize our restaurants and they buy plenty of oil and gas." In the aggregate they are described as "far better spenders than millionaires and furnish sounder substance for the growth of any community."[22]

Dorr's continuing engagement was evident in his arrangements for a congressional delegation that visited the island and its coastline in June 1937. Congressman Brewster was joined by seven other members of the House Naval Affairs Committee and Senator Theodore Francis Green of Rhode Island to inspect Mount Desert Island as a possible site for a naval airbase. In the end, this initiative was not pursued. Nonetheless, Oldfarm was the weekend residence for the delegation, a formidable undertaking for the superintendent and his household staff. He arranged a boat trip along the coast, a visit to Jackson Laboratory, seaplane flights over the island, and introductions and social gatherings at many island locations.[23] This gathering is the last surviving image of the Dorr estate as a center of hospitality. Oldfarm would never again be the site for company of this standing.

Interior Secretary Harold Ickes returned to Mount Desert Island immediately after Dorr learned of the death of his Berkshire friend, Edith Wharton.[24] More than three decades earlier Dorr's visits to Wharton's Lenox residence, The Mount, had been a source of pleasure for both these horticultural enthusiasts. Wharton had been absent from America for nearly three decades, her literary career supporting her life in the French countryside—and she returned to America only for honors at Yale and for the 1913 wedding of her niece, Beatrix, to historian Max Farrand. She died in her Pavillon Colombes villa on August 12, 1937 and was buried at the American cemetery at Versailles.

Secretary Ickes planned to spend two weeks in seclusion at the unoccupied Homans' House at Great Head, where he intended to work on his autobiography.[25] On the twenty-first anniversary of the establishment of the National Park Service, Ickes' diary entry refers to Dorr as "eighty-four years old and when I called on him Wednesday [August 25] afternoon at his home, I found him to have little use of his eyes. During the last couple of years he has been operated on for glaucoma and he also has the beginning of a cataract. I must say that he is gallant about it all."[26]

The Secretary noted that when he had visited two years earlier in 1935, Dorr was rereading Greek classics in the original but now depended on others to read to him. Nonetheless, Ickes entered into the privacy of his diary his own "sin of envy whenever I am in Mr. Dorr's house. He has such beautiful things in the way of furniture and dishes and ceramics, especially dishes, that my mouth literally waters," a curious application of a phrase frequently employed by Edith Wharton. Ickes removed any inference that Dorr had been in active pursuit of luxury, pointing out that most of the furnishings were a family legacy. Dorr responded wistfully that he did not know what was to be the fate of these "real treasures." Implicitly, Ickes regarded the vigorous Dorr as the authentic "treasure" for "he is of Harvard and he was a close friend of the late President Eliot, Dr. Oliver Wendell Holmes, and others with a distinct intellectual and social background...a man of real culture...[with] no impairment of his intellectual vigor."

Before Ickes returned to Washington on September 10, he toured the island with Rockefeller, paying particular attention to carriage road development and other road projects underway. On no fewer than three occasions, Ickes was Rockefeller's dinner guest. At The Eyrie, Ickes admired the furnishings and marveled at the "the enormous amount of money that must have been spent" on the gardens—an impression of current affluence that Ickes nowhere associates with Oldfarm. Shortly after his departure, Dorr learned of the death of friend and landscape photographer Herbert Wendell Gleason—which made the winter months of 1938 no easier to bear. The CCC continued their labors while land acquisition and road development plans were coordinated between Washington, Bar Harbor, and wherever Rockefeller happened to be in his travels.

At Rockefeller's request, former Park Service director Albright again visited Oldfarm in late June 1938 to assess Dorr's property holdings, their relationship to the completion of Rockefeller's roadways, and the health of the superintendent. In his highly detailed eight-page report, Albright identified two stalled land issues. One involved the heavy expense of Dorr mortgaging his properties following investment losses suffered during the Great Depression. The other issue was Dorr's insistence—as he had expressed it six months earlier in a letter to the director—that the government must assure him that Oldfarm and the nurseries "would be permanently secure in its wild beauty and kept open for the public...[since this] has been the purpose inspiring me in all the work that I have done throughout for the Park's creation and extension."[27] This concern for the fate of Dorr's most cherished physical possession would dominate his thinking in the years ahead.

Albright's report to the National Park Service—copied to Mr. Rockefeller—provided exceptional insight into matters about which Dorr was understandably silent. Albright "...found Superintendent George B. Dorr in poor health. He is almost totally blind. It is a mystery how he manages to get around his house, and up and down stairs as well as he does. He is growing thinner. He has angina pectoris, and the presence of this coronary trouble was confirmed recently by a Boston heart specialist. It is causing him some serious discomfort and at night rather serious sweating, which breaks up his sleep. His associates believe him to be in a rather serious state, and I think he himself regards his own condition as quite hopeless. Two or three times he told me that he would not be here long, and might go at any moment. Another time he humorously referred to having his valise packed."[28]

In a discussion at Storm Beach Cottage that ran well into the early hours of the following morning, Dorr's property holdings and their respective mortgages were identified. Albright recommended—surely with Rockefeller's own objectives in mind—which holdings should be liquidated and at what cost. Curiously, Albright remarked that he thought Dorr's affairs overall were "in good shape" despite $46,000 in mortgages with income limited to his annual federal salary of $3,000. His inheritance by this time was totally gone. To be sure, he had recently received $100,000 from the sale of the Great Meadows to Mr. Rockefeller, yet Albright thought that "it is probably true that he used some of that money to buy other lands for the park...[making] further sacrifices out of his own funds to facilitate land acquisition [for the park] in the western part of the Island."

While no mention was made of a last will and testament, "it seems clear that Mr. Dorr has made arrangements for the disposition of everything he has upon his death, and [if the mortgages are liquidated] everything goes to the public." The George B. Dorr Foundation was established—with HCTPR attorney Serenus Rodick and assistant superintendent Ben Hadley at the helm—to "administer Oldfarm, the homes, antiques, books, fine glassware, and other heirlooms, which Mr. Dorr has. The income, if any, was intended to cover expenses associated with publishing a history of the park, and other essays and papers that he has prepared." After several hours reviewing Dorr's "voluminous" manuscripts, Albright characterized them as "well prepared' and "very interesting." Dorr made provisions for the management of the Mount Desert Nurseries, but Albright recognized that these lands and others would likely have to be sold to liquidate Dorr's indebtedness. Albright asked whether Rockefeller—who was being copied on this matter—might want to consider taking control of the situation by buying the mortgages. "The great danger in delay is, of course, that Mr. Dorr may not live until the end of the summer."[29]

Rockefeller's self-described "cold blooded" response was that "the Dorr houses, their contents, the surrounding lands and the nurseries...should be sold, the monies derived therefrom after paying the debts of the estate to be used...for the development and upkeep of the Wild Gardens of Acadia."[30] In Rockefeller's view, those houses only had value "in proportion to their intrinsic merit," not because Dorr once owned this land and not because "everyone who knows Mr. Dorr loves him." Many landscape historians have since disagreed with Rockefeller's assertion that the stature of a property owner does not confer preservation value on said property.

In a confidential memo to Serenus Rodick in late November, Rockefeller quoted a letter he received from Horace Albright. Dorr had written to Albright to express his agreement with the Dorr land gift plan that Albright had brokered in June. Dorr confides that the "long-continued depression has placed me in a position of commitment to the bank which does not leave me free to do what otherwise I would wish." The superintendent clearly wished "to get all the immediate problems that I can work out while I am here to cooperate."[31] In due course, Dorr transferred property directly to the government (or through Rockefeller) when the latter paid a portion of Dorr's "indebtedness amounting to ten thousand five hundred dollars."[32] After years of effort, Rockefeller's philanthropy made possible "the continuation of the Sieur de Monts Spring Road to the Schooner Head Road, without crossing over any land other than that of the Government." By the end of 1938 there remained only the one property, owned by a Chicago financier, standing in the way of completion of the motor road circuit known today as the Park Loop Road. No progress had been made, however, on the preservation of Oldfarm by the end of 1938.

Immediately following his eighty-fifth birthday, Dorr informed Serenus Rodick that "in case anything should happen to me unexpectedly, by night or day, I have made plans, carefully thought out, for my last resting place at the long journey's end." Three park staff, including Ben Hadley, worked on the site for the scattering of his ashes.[33] Dorr also exchanged several letters with Mount Auburn Cemetery regarding gravesite plantings for the Dorr family plot, road and rail transportation for his body, cremation, and the options for the containment of his remains and their transport to Maine.[34]

Yet another indication of Dorr's attentiveness to the inevitable was his forthrightness in sharing with others his own uncertainties about his abilities. In a letter to his attorney David O. Rodick (older brother of Serenus Rodick) regarding concession practices of the Acadia Corporation, he admitted that his command of detail was no longer immediate and spontaneous, but increasingly dependent on association and context. "Experience has taught me not to trust too confidently in my own recollection of things said and done, whether they be remote or near. So much, too, depends upon what I would call the context, the way things come up and all that has bearing upon what is said and done."[35]

Dorr was by now the most senior of park superintendents—in both age and years of park management—and so each of the Interior Department secretaries and NPS directors informally consulted with him on vexing issues. The historical documentation shows no inclination on Dorr's part to meddle in the affairs of other park managers or to direct his energies to the development of all-encompassing NPS policies. Such singularity of purpose protected him from most disparaging remarks of park colleagues and superiors. Clearly, this was not his motive. Rather, his singular interest was the preservation of Acadia's land and seascapes.

Similarly, no fully developed conservation philosophy—in the boldest sense of the word—was evident in Dorr's extant writings. Scattered throughout his official, personal, and published writing, however, are expressions of recurring principles derived from long experience. In the first quarter of the twentieth century, conservation pioneers at Acadia and other national parks and public sanctuaries selected, tested, and integrated conservation standards that frequently lacked the conceptual rigor now taken for granted. Much later, conservation institutions would be developed along with their legal apparatus, operational policies, and stabilized vocabularies. Dorr was one of the few pioneers who gave expression to key conservation principles—interpreted anew with each generation—of the modern environmental movement. More importantly, over four decades he applied these key concepts organizationally to create, develop, and prepare Acadia National Park for the challenges of the last half of the twentieth century.

These ten central conservation concepts are either quoted directly from Dorr's writings, or from composites or contemporary expressions of insights scattered across Dorr's body of work:

Civic Engagement—"I sought to carry the local community, the County and the State along with me in the Park's development so that all might feel that it was for their interest no less than that of the general public that it should be made."[36]

Indivisible Landscapes—The artificial separation of nature and culture is a handicap to conservation initiatives. A natural landscape is historically indivisible from a cultural landscape. Linguistically we may define them as distinct, but their intermingling is an inescapable fact.[37] The integration of natural and cultural initiatives on Mount Desert Island was described by Robert S. Yard as the "perfect model" for national park development in the eastern United States.

Complementariness—"The natural condition of the parks must be disturbed as little as possible consistent with necessary development in the public interest," and conversely, it is "the cultural value invested in natural places through their physical development as parks that best assures the preservation of those places in a relatively natural state."[39]

Self-Determination—A strong belief in the capacity of the individual to envision new possibilities, initiate change, and provide leadership directed at preserving landscapes with distinctive attributes. This is one "characteristic that seems to distinguish New England's approach from those of other regions."[40]

Ideal Landscapes—National parks are all-too-human efforts—in a geographically defined place—to realize an ideal landscape. As Dorr expressed it: "[Federal protection provides] a sanctuary and protecting home for the whole region's plant and animal life, and for the birds that ask its hospitality upon their long migrations. Make it this and naturalists will seek it from the whole world over, and from it other men will learn similarly to cherish wild life in other places."[41]

Temporality—The richness or distinctiveness of a conserved landscape resides in human sensitivity to its past, present, and future—and *not* to its utility from a single temporal point of reference. In Dorr's essay on "Man and Nature" he emphasized that: "In nothing is conservation needed more than in saving all that is economically possible of the pleasantness and freedom of Nature in regions accessible, even by travel, to the vast, town-dwelling populations of the future; in preserving the features of scientific interest or landscape beauty that widen men's horizon or quicken their imagination.... The essential important thing is to save now...for its expansion later."[42]

Promoting Significance—Also in "Man and Nature," Dorr focused on what is worthwhile, what is of value. Conservation is "concerned with the inner life of men. With Nature in its beauty and freedom shut out from so many lives in these industrial and city-dwelling times...[it is] a matter of supreme importance to preserve in their openness, in their unspoiled beauty, and the interest of their wild life, their native trees and plants, their birds and animals, the places where the wealth and human significance of these things are greatest."[43]

Selectivity—"I have always been from the first scrupulous not to include land within the National Park bounds that we could not develop so as more than to justify in the public interest our removing it from taxation or residential development."[44]

Aesthetic Coherence—Conservation inevitably transforms the architecture of an area of natural beauty when an aesthetic is applied that protects scenery and improves access, interfering with their pre-existing character as little as possible. As in art conservation, one follows the design maxim to never do anything that cannot be undone. Dorr insisted that the paramount aim of aesthetic conservation should be "to give unity to the design, and make the Park a single and organic whole."[45]

Democratized Beauty—"The main thing is to open [conserved areas] as widely as may be to the people while yet keeping it as a source of re-creation and save it from vulgarization. To make it something that will uplift and inspire its visitors, while giving them new health and vigor...to develop all the possibilities that it offers for study along many fields for the giving out of ideas to a great audience," Dorr wrote with perhaps less-than-ideal clarity.[46] Moreover, Mount Desert historian Judith S. Goldstein concludes, "the beauty of Mount Desert—the power of its landscape—emerged as an attraction and economic force in its own right...[when] a succession of artists, writers, merchants, hotel owners, developers and rusticators thrust the landscape to front stage."[47] And Dorr would have the last word, that "the conservation of beauty of inspiring quality and the safeguarding of free access to the public—was the impelling motive, both on the part of those who gave [to create the Park] and of those who in authority accepted."[48]

Once again, Cammerer spent several days in mid-April of 1939 at Oldfarm discussing park issues with Dorr. In the weeks ahead, however, Acadia would be among the least of Director Cammerer's concerns. On May 1 he suffered a severe coronary thrombosis, which Horace Albright attributed in part to the severe strain owing to his official responsibilities.[49] The months ahead were difficult for Cammerer, and this visit to Oldfarm was his last.

In accepting Dorr's gift of a 150-year-old, eight-foot-high Sheridan clock for the newly married Nelson Rockefeller, Nelson's father wrote that Dorr should be satisfied "to reflect upon the immense contribution you have made to the permanent development of this Island and to its protection and preservation for the enjoyment of all the people! You have done a wonderful piece of work. No one knows better than I do how important it is and how unselfishly you have given of your time, your thought, your strength, and your means to the accomplishment of the desired ends. I rejoice in what you have done and am proud to have been your silent partner in some phases of the work."[50]

As the decade closed, John D. Rockefeller Jr. continued the pace of his land donations to the government, which he had spoken about to Dorr several months earlier.[51] One parcel made it feasible to construct a new approach to the park motor road system: the Hulls Cove entrance, used by most visitors to this day. Director Cammerer asked Dorr to present the proposal to the Bar Harbor selectmen at the town's 1940 annual meeting in March, since the plan included a transfer of authority over Eagle Lake Road to the National Park Service—a highly sensitive proposal.[52]

While Rockefeller and park officials discussed the language of the Bar Harbor warrant article, Interior Department officials worried about whether they could secure congressional approval for the development and maintenance costs associated with Rockefeller's proposed gifts. After all, America's involvement in the war in Europe seemed inevitable. Following the invasion of Poland by Germany, the Commonwealths declared war. In the United States, federal funds were redirected to preparations for this global threat.

As spring approached, Bar Harbor received news of the death in Portland of Luere B. Deasy. His importance to Acadia National Park's development is not best reflected in his service as treasurer of the Lafayette National Park Museum of Stone Age Antiquities, nor his later presidency of the Abbe Museum. As one of the original incorporators of the HCTPR, he became its president on the death of Charles W. Eliot in 1926 and served in that office until the end of his life. Their minutes rightly stressed Deasy's role as "a pioneer in the movement for the preservation of [Mount Desert Island's] unique beauty, and the conservation of its shores and mountains for the enjoyment of the whole people."[53] Deasy the first law firm in Eden, and for nearly six decades his partners and clients weighed his decisions. The legal and moral authority of his judgments were compelling. To his great-great-grandson, William Horner, who has deeply researched his ancestor's involvement in park development, Deasy "sensed that the Park could become a world heritage [site], and affirmed that this commons had been conserved from the degradation of division and development for profit by private hands."[54]

Several months after the death of Judge Deasy, Dorr received news of the passing of yet another friend, a relative that he had known his entire life. In mid-July *The New York Times* announced the death in Boston of

Dorr's first cousin, banker Thomas Wren Ward Jr.[55] It was Tom who had resided with Ralph Waldo Emerson's family, had prepared for Harvard at the Sanborn School in Concord, had traveled with Agassiz to explore the Brazilian jungle, and had become a lifelong "chum" of William James.[56]

The year after his death, the prestigious *New England Quarterly* published a troubling back story of how Tom's successful banking career had been secured at a previously untold price. Ward's secretary, Margaret Snyder, wrote that "the Paleolithic canyons of Wall Street…[had] worn Ward's faith to impotence with their sterile confines."[57] In his youth, Ward had had an "obsessive desire" to settle in the West, to build bridges and roads there—a plan that his father opposed due to the young man's frail health. As a "consolation prize" Ward was sent off on the Agassiz adventure before entering a banking career.[58] Convinced that "all our best men went West" and that there "a man could stand up full height beneath a challenging sky," Ward never crossed the great river separating the eastern United States from the frontier. Whether his cousin George was aware of Ward's alleged sense of personal failure is not known. For Dorr, that river had long been crossed.

These very recent deaths—of Edith Wharton, Judge Deasy, Herbert W. Gleason, William Endicott Jr., and now Tom Ward—increased Dorr's sense of urgency to put to paper the many personal experiences that he had carried thus far only in his memory. Scores of topics were identified and listed. Some received expanded essays but most were never formally explicated. Among the undeveloped topics were accounts of canoeing in New England waters, rowing and sailing, Newport in the early days, Palm Sunday and Easter in Rome, old Etruscan cities, and the geological history of Campagna, Italy.[59]

One topic, however, that was brought to fruition referenced "the beginning of Mount Desert social life," a benchmark event that occurred several years before the Civil War. In an article Dorr wrote for the widely read publication of the Appalachian Mountain Club, he alluded to the diary of New York attorney Charles Tracy, who had traveled to Mount Desert Island in 1855 for a month-long visit.[60] Two dozen Tracy family members had been joined by the celebrated Hudson River School artist, Frederic Church. In 1932, Tracy's daughter donated the original diary to the library named after her husband, J. Pierpont Morgan. The copy that had been in Dorr's possession and served as the basis for his essay would remain untouched in the archives of the Jesup Memorial Library. A half century would pass before a wider audience grasped the significance of this visit, which had launched the island's Gilded Age hotel era and the residential development of Bar Harbor.

Nearly a half century after the Tracy visit, the allies of Charles W. Eliot provided a framework to conserve what Tracy's family and guests had found so endearing about Mount Desert Island. Nearly forty years later the HCTPR published *An Historical Sketch and a Record of the Holdings of the Trustees,* authored by C. W. Eliot's son, Samuel Atkins Eliot. In booklet form, it not only included a clear narrative and property list but a map that allowed the public to grasp for the first time the extent of the philanthropy that had brought into being the national park. It also contained a quote that signaled to the country yet again their importance to the nation; for the historian of the Great Smoky Mountains National Park wrote to HCTPR secretary Serenus Rodick in 1933 this tribute:

"'[The Trustees] started something,' which has already gone from the coast of Maine to the Shenandoah Valley; over the Great Smokies; as far west as California, and is now calling for a dominion of two thousand square miles in my home state—the so-called Land of Flowers. For my part, I can recall no such triumphant march of an idea (whether good or bad) in the history of this country since the Armistice."

During the summer of 1940, President Franklin Roosevelt received from Dorr a brief letter of support for his handling of the "difficult and complicated problems of our time during these last seven years." On the heels of the passing of Tom Ward, Dorr sent Roosevelt another letter containing an exceptional proposal that preoccupied him for the next eighteen months. Dorr offered his family home and its furnishings as a gift to the United States. Following the extensive donation of natural landscapes to the federal government, the Oldfarm philanthropist now offered a cultural landscape. His initial offer was that Oldfarm would serve as "a summer home for the National Executive."[61]

This carefully crafted offer raised questions about Dorr's expectations. Did Dorr seek counsel from friends and attorney David Rodick before making the offer? Did he weigh the timing of the offer, expecting that the president would be more or less inclined to accept the offer with a presidential election—for his unprecedented third term—a mere three months distant? Did he see himself administering the park and managing the Mount Desert Nurseries from Storm Beach Cottage?[62]

The foremost issue not alluded to in Dorr's proposal was the attachment that Roosevelt felt for Hyde Park and Warm Springs, Georgia. For more than two decades Mr. Roosevelt had visited the spa community, hopeful that the warm mineral waters would relieve—if not improve—his paralysis. The spacious thirty-six-room mansion at Hyde Park had family associations that were surely known to Dorr. Twelve years earlier, he had offered Oldfarm as a summer residence to President Coolidge. Now the property was being offered as an outright gift to the federal government for use by the chief executive.

Three weeks later, President Roosevelt wrote and declined the offer. He knew of "no provision of law…which would authorize me to accept it for the purpose you mention." The president pointed out that Dorr's property could be "accepted by the Secretary of the Interior as part of Acadia National Park…with the understanding that it be made available for use by the President and his principal executive officers."[63] To think that Dorr was unaware of this option after nearly a quarter-century of leadership within the National Park Service seems implausible. The entire scenario may have been a ruse to provide Dorr with leverage in realizing his larger goals.

With the president weighing in on the merits of the offer, Dorr improved his chances of convincing the National Park Service to accept his land, renouncing any claim on property contiguous with Storm Beach Cottage and securing the park office at its Main Street location. This strategy was based on a condition that the government would reimburse the superintendent for personal expenses involved in establishing and maintaining it. Dorr had reasons for concern, for he knew of important National Park Service transitions taking place that summer. The June 19 resignation of Arno Cammerer created system-wide uncertainty about future Park Service leadership.[64] Also, there was the usual pre-election apprehension about continuity within the Interior Department after the November election.

Dorr asked Horace Albright to review once again "the details of the matter with me so that the original purpose of the gift be carried out as fully as well as conditions may permit."[65] Under the new proposal, while Dorr lived he would retain ownership of Storm Beach Cottage and adjacent structures and land, as a place of work and study, reserving the right to dispose of the land in his will as he wished. Dorr knew that Albright was right—after nearly a quarter-century the Mather Era was over. Lest there be any doubt, in late April of 1941, Dorr and Rockefeller received news of Arno Cammerer's death at fifty-seven years of age. His obituary rightly credited him with "the most extensive improvements to national park areas in the history of the service."[66]

The new director, Newton B. Drury, faced many challenges, not the least being to chart a new course at a time when the CCC was being disbanded and the nation being readied for war. Following Albright's resignation in 1933, Drury had been offered the director position but declined. In the intervening years, his conservationist activity had brought him wide notice. Over two decades he had led the Save-the-Redwoods League, an organization that conserved the ancient forests along the Northern California–Oregon coast from encroachment.

Drury anticipated resistance in his new position, since unlike his predecessors he lacked NPS credentials. No doubt the new director had heard of the grand old man of the system. What priority would he assign to one of the smallest national parks? How would he respond to Dorr's efforts to educate him about the distinctive problems faced by a landscape quite different from the Drury's familiar environment? Would there be an affinity based on the commonality of their coastal environments? Would Dorr now be able to convince the new NPS director that the non-commercial values embedded in the Oldfarm landscape could be—and should be—preserved by the National Park Service?

CHAPTER TWENTY-ONE

A Full and Useful Life

As the United States ramped up for war, in the spring of 1941 the Army Corps of Engineers made preparations to occupy a site on the Cadillac Mountain summit. It hoped to monitor the locations of hostile submarines that ventured into coastal Maine waters. By the end of the year, the summit road was closed to the public and remained so for the duration of the war. Throughout the year, Superintendent Dorr skirmished with the federal government over his proposed donation of the 96 acres of Oldfarm and adjacent properties. Often housebound, Dorr conceded that "one of the regrets I have from a partial blindness that has come upon me these last few years is that it prevents me from keeping up the winter visits I use to make for so long to Washington and the loss of contact it has brought with friends."[1]

His official documents, correspondence, memoirs, and publications repeatedly characterized Oldfarm as the wellspring, the inspiration, and the model for Acadia National Park. It was the cultural and natural landscape "from which the Park has sprung." Sixty years after its construction, its acceptance by the government would be public recognition for the continuing value of Dorr's momentous efforts. For "what I am now offering represents the crown and completion of this work I undertook so long ago for our Public Reservations here and the development of Acadia National Park."[2]

Assistant Superintendent Hadley saw Dorr's motivation for federal ownership of Oldfarm in emotional terms: "His sentimental attachment to his summer home which had grown with the years since his father purchased the property…would be perpetuated; the property would ultimately serve a particular purpose for the park by furnishing in Storm Beach Cottage…a park superintendent's residence, and that Oldfarm House would become a guest house for government officials, particularly the president and cabinet members."[3] Hadley did not fully grasp Dorr's position on this matter, attributing to "sentiment" an attachment that Dorr was convinced was based on cumulative historical developments, rationally grounded.

Dorr could have delayed the matter by simply bequeathing Oldfarm through his estate planning documents. Such behavior, however, was inconsistent with the action-centered and progressive strategies Dorr had practiced in establishing the park. Given his age, Dorr's urgency to complete negotiations with the federal government was understandable. Before this donation was finally settled, scores of proposals, revisions, property appraisals, tax records, evaluations, congressional authorizations, maps, amendments, and statements of reservation on the part of Dorr and the National Park Service would be exchanged. The protracted bureaucratic haggling about acceptance of yet another donation from the Brahmin philanthropist taxed his patience but not his persistent resolution.

While the monetary value of the Oldfarm holdings was acknowledged by the NPS, the correspondence about its value as a park holding was dominated by the assessment that the site was unremarkable—when measured against the enchantments of Cadillac Mountain, Jordan Pond, or The Beehive. But should a landscape like Oldfarm be measured against such "enchantments"? Could Oldfarm and The Beehive be incommensurable, possessing no common quality? These deeper questions about cultural and natural landscapes remained unresolved at the time.

In addition to the question of the value of the property, there was no NPS precedent for accepting the private residence of a superintendent. This administrative reaction must have surprised Dorr, who clearly was politically savvy but not a political person. Information about his party affiliation and voting record have resisted discovery. He formed alliances with friends and acquaintances regardless of party affiliation. And so it is ironic that Washington would use Dorr's ownership of Oldfarm as a reason for not accepting his offer. Historically, this was the same counter-argument used by politicians in the nation's capitol in 1915, when Dorr had come forward with the offer to the federal government of the Hancock County Trustees' *privately owned* lands. Within a year, Wilson had overruled this objection and created Sieur de Monts National Monument. Two decades later the old gent at Oldfarm must have wondered: have the bureaucrats learned nothing?

As the Civilian Conservation Corps' presence in Acadia National Park was withdrawn, Ben Hadley once again focused on day-to-day operations, sparing Mr. Dorr these tasks.[4] En route to Washington to participate in the Superintendent's Conference, Hadley stopped in New York for a meeting that Dorr had arranged with John D. Rockefeller Jr. to explain the proposed Oldfarm donation. Rockefeller did not endorse Dorr's arguments for including his estate in the park, writing later to Dorr that "our association together in Acadia Park matters will always be one of the happy features of my life. Nor shall I as a summer resident of Mount Desert Island ever cease to be grateful to you for having brought about the permanent preservation of the beauties of that incomparable island."[5]

Horace Albright also understood Dorr's priorities, heroically representing Dorr's interests to the new director, Newton Drury.[6] Dorr knew that the endorsement of Mather's right-hand man would go far "in getting what I offer recognized on its true basis," describing Albright as among his "most intimate" of friends. The Park Service consultant shifted Drury's attention away from Dorr's residence to Park Service control of a small complex of buildings at the corner of Main Street and Park Road in Bar Harbor, a half-mile north of Oldfarm. In 1919, at his own expense, Dorr had built these to serve as park headquarters and had paid to maintain them ever since. The government paid him $1,500 annually in rental fees. The superintendent now proposed that they be purchased for $17,500—later reminding the Park Service that it had incurred no expense for Dorr's lodging for the last two decades.

With remarkable candor he confessed that this solution was necessary because of his lack of attentiveness to the management of his many scattered parcels of land. "I found myself indebted to [the Bank] to the amount of twenty-five thousand dollars, secured…upon my various properties here, including Oldfarm." Government acceptance of his offer would clear off Dorr's indebtedness. As to Oldfarm, he was "asking nothing in return but its right use."[7] Drury's assistant director, Arthur E. Demaray, believed that once this indebtedness was cleared, then additional tracts of land would be donated to the federal government within Dorr's lifetime or through his executors.[8] Director Drury assured Dorr that although there were "many obstacles to overcome in these trying times," the Oldfarm proposal had received a sympathetic hearing by the House Appropriations Committee.

Dorr might no longer be able to travel, but that did not silence him. In a lengthy letter typed by his highly valued secretary, Phyllis Sylvia, Dorr updated Edward T. Taylor, chairman of the House Appropriations Committee, on Demaray's visit. He candidly lay bare that he had "neglected" his personal affairs, and left them "in others' hands who failed to read in season the changes that had come over properties that for so many years had been deemed secure and sound." Dorr says that it was too late to salvage "but a fraction of what had given me such freedom in the past."[9] The resulting indebtedness needed to be balanced before clear title could be conveyed to the federal government.

Newspapers in Portland and Bangor carried lengthy Associated Press reports credited to the National Park Service in Washington affirming that Taylor's committee had recommended the appropriation of $37,500 to enable Dorr to donate his estate to the federal government. The estate was appraised by unnamed parties at $150,000 not including the library, valued at $25,000.[10]

Dorr discussed this issue and the park office matter later that spring when the NPS director arrived at Oldfarm on a "trip just especially to see you." Following the visit, Newton Drury informed Rockefeller that his "trip to Acadia was a hurried one, but I wanted to meet Mr. Dorr and observe conditions on the ground in at least a cursory fashion." Drury and Dorr knew that the consent of two Senate committees and the full Senate were still needed following the House vote approving the Oldfarm appropriation. Mr. Demaray testified that an important consideration was that the park superintendent had given lands worth $100,000 to the federal government over the last two decades.[11]

Dorr decided that the time was right to acquaint islanders with one facet of the Oldfarm donation. Well aware that many national park entrances had no proximity to established centers of culture, he drafted a lengthy letter that appeared on May 3, 1941 in the *Bar Harbor Times,* which explained to the community that his offer to the government was based on his desire to permanently secure the park office in its present location. Within a half mile of the Bar Harbor village green, it would continue to be "the central distributing station of the Park."[12]

But as summer arrived negotiations took an alarming downward turn. In testimony before Congress the Park Service's legal counsel erroneously included Storm Beach Cottage as one of the Oldfarm estate structures. Dorr could not understand the source of such an obvious error, since it would leave him without shelter. After further inquiry he discovered that when the Park Service's assistant chief counsel, Donald E. Lee, visited the park, David Rodick and Ben Hadley had suggested Storm Beach Cottage "to give the Government yet fuller measure in return for its acceptance of my offer."

Arno Cammerer pointed out to Dorr that the property values provided by the real estate agent selected by the Park Service were much lower than those the superintendent had provided—and so corrections were needed.[13] In a thirteen-page letter, Dorr provided evidence of Lee's incomplete attention to a host of relevant matters—stopping short of accusing the attorney of rudeness. Dorr emphatically insisted that "no one had been given the slightest authority" to offer Storm Beach Cottage. "The Park has no need for it, no use of it to make, and, stripped of my personal belongings, it is but a simple farm house, of slight value."[14] The Boston Brahmin made clear to Washington officials that after his parents' deaths the much smaller residence was made over "as a pied-à-terre to come and leave my personal belongings in when I was away travelling and Oldfarm was rented." Dorr had helped to build Storm Beach Cottage with his own hands sixty years earlier. He roots his attachment in a literary allusion: "As Touchstone the Clown says of Audrey in Shakespeare as he presents her to his master as his newly-wedded wife: 'Truly, a poor thing, Sir, but mine own.'"[15]

In his memoirs, Dorr again reflected on the "historic associations" that led to his conservation career and on that occasion late in life saw it as a psychological adjustment following the death of his parents. For Storm

Beach Cottage "is where I have lived and worked these many years since I was left alone and took up my work of landscape gardening and wild life conservation and the Park's creation." The inclusion of the phrase "left alone" may be of little or no consequence. The repeated parental references throughout his memoirs, however, leave a distinct impression that their deaths led to the most formidable rite of passage in his life. Recall that immediately following his mother's death, in 1901, he had repeatedly asked for Julia Ward Howe's assistance in dealing with his loss. Her final directive to him to embrace his new circumstances had provided the redirection that crystallized his conservation career: "Dear George, I love to go over the past with you, but you must not dwell on it too much. The future is before you; you must think of it."[16]

Dorr further explained to Demaray that he hoped that a simple building to house his books on landscaping, gardening, and classical literature could be constructed and maintained near the Oldfarm propagation nursery. He also wished to discuss with his superiors the disposition of his professional papers, administrative records, and memoirs. He suggested the establishment of Acadia Press, "an association to receive and edit such papers as I may leave."[17] Dorr's concerns about his intellectual property would prove to be well founded.

Two weeks after Drury's return to Washington, Dorr posted a highly detailed three-and-a-half-page letter requesting that the Park Service complete a number of Oldfarm projects he had intended to finish. These included an addition to the library adjacent to Storm Beach Cottage, installation of a pergola on the site of the original farmhouse, a chimney for the residence of his housekeeper and her family, the prohibition of motorcars on the property, a new building at the Main Street entrance to Oldfarm, and so on. We can assume that Dorr knew these expectations would irritate the Park Service and perhaps force a resolution of this much-belabored process. Dorr may have been moved to resolve all these matters when Demaray cautioned in late September 1941 that "prospects of obtaining funds to do more that the essential maintenance work required to keep the park operating are extremely remote during these troubled days when all available funds are needed for defense purposes."[18] On November 7, 1941, Dorr and the Department of the Interior reached an agreement.

It was Dorr's good fortune that the legal and political process was in place, since one month later the United States declared war on Japan. The legislative bill expanding the park to include the National Park Service office site, Oldfarm, and select properties was authorized before the close of the congressional session. Within a week of his eighty-eighth birthday, Dorr received "final word from Washington my gift had been accepted."[19] The last piece of his physical legacy had found security within the laws of the land.

A Park Service press release announced Dorr's transfer to the federal government of "several tracts of exceedingly valuable lands" appraised at $90,455 and purchased for $37,500 (prior to the payment of an outstanding mortgage of $20,200 and taxes and fees). A *Boston Herald* editorial referred to the Oldfarm landscape as "Dorr's Park." Newton Drury called the final result a "fitting tribute to your generosity and service."[20]

One community asset to which Dorr was much attached was the Building of the Arts. As president of its Founders Committee, this performing arts facility had presented internationally renowned artists to fashionable island residents since its opening in 1907. During the Depression years it had fallen on hard times and taxes went unpaid. Dorr issued a call to stockholders "to reestablish the use of the building and to preserve it." The economic level of the community and changing tastes contributed to declining interest. At Dorr's urging, in June 1941, Rockefeller purchased the deed at a sheriff's sale, a questionable investment of $300. He challenged community leaders to quickly consider innovative uses of the property, especially its utility as a museum.[21] Dorr argued that incorporating the building into the park would enrich the landscape—through the historical associations of the facility and new opportunities for public service—if Rockefeller donated it to a receptive Interior Department.

The Boston Brahmin's "eloquent plea for the preservation of the Building of the Arts" was ineffective. Park naturalist Maurice Sullivan informed Dorr that the facility was structurally unsuitable for a museum and furthermore it "is outside the national park boundaries, off the park circuit or any main line of travel, and cannot easily be found."[22] By late May 1942, Drury reported to Rockefeller that "our museum experts do not believe its location is satisfactory…or that remodeling would result in a practical museum layout." Moreover, the "prospects of obtaining funds to do more than the essential maintenance work required to keep the park operating are extremely remote during these troubled days when all available funds are needed for defense purposes."[23] A recent article puts it more starkly: by the summer of 1942 "the resort was a virtual ghost town, with many cottages shuttered that season." Serenus Rodick received a proposal to turn "the property into a dance hall, extending the building on the north side and selling beer, soft drinks," and other novelties.[24] Since Bar Harbor showed little interest in saving the structure, when a third party offered a modest sum for the Building of the Arts, Rockefeller accepted. Dorr had saved Oldfarm but had lost the Building of the Arts! Yet again, Dorr and Hadley were not on the same page.[25]

Director Drury continued to be impressed by the donations of land by John D. Rockefeller Jr. Since 1935, they had "practically doubled the park area and, with the park loop road recently taking form, we find that Acadia actually provides a new park for the visitor and will be a different park to those who have known the island for many years."[26] In identifying Acadia as "a new park," Drury fused Rockefeller's interests with Dorr's earlier accomplishments, thereby uniting the two philanthropies.

After the public became aware of the extent of his recent gifts to the federal government in Maine, Dorr received a most uplifting letter from Mesa Verde National Park's superintendent, Jesse Nusbaum. As an archaeologist, Nusbaum's impressive credentials had led Stephen Mather to select him as superintendent of Mesa Verde, the first national park established (in 1906) for its natural *and* cultural value. As the first national park archaeologist, Nusbaum's persistent enforcement of the Antiquities Act made him a very effective—if uncommon—park administrator. His predecessors had bowed to local political pressures and tolerated concessionaire abuses, overgrazing, and the looting of artifacts. As a result of Mather's professionalization of park management, Nusbaum received support to remedy abuses, which he discussed with Dorr and their peers when he hosted the 1925 Superintendents Conference.[27]

Nusbaum wrote in January 1942 to thank Dorr for "your diligence and devotion to the cause, your courage in the face of expressed opposition of long entrenched wealthy residents, and your gifts of property beyond your ability to give." Nusbaum claimed no credit for originality, informing Dorr that more than a decade earlier it had been Rockefeller who offered such flattering remarks about the Acadia superintendent. Implicitly, he acknowledged in Dorr a kindred, unorthodox spirit, since both of them tolerated no more than a veneer of bureaucratic conformity.[28]

Both Dorr and Nusbaum complained repeatedly about "useless" reports. Earlier when the NPS director informed Nusbaum that other superintendents complied with their monthly reports, the latter had exploded: "I admit I have been negligent in the matter—I would rather be doing the work—helping with it, no matter how strenuous, than writing reports to Washington telling how much 'I' was accomplishing."[29] But in his letter to Dorr, he closed with a memorable personal remark, characterizing Dorr as nothing less than "the patriarch of our Service." With Cammerer's recent death still on his mind, Dorr knew that this accolade rightly belonged to Mr. Mather alone.[30]

Dorr now turned his attention to the personal items in his estate, consisting of articles of furniture, papers and writings, silver and china. He transferred the powers to oversee these items from the Dorr Foundation to his estate trustees because of "the uncertainties of life," and the "loss, through increased infirmity, of the power to take such action myself." These powers would henceforth reside with a group of friends in whom he had "complete trust and confidence": Mrs. Richard W. Hale, her son Richard W. Hale Jr., and his secretary, Mrs. Phyllis S. Sylvia.[31]

Executor John A. Peters recommended that a literary executor be appointed and that Richard W. Hale be approached to serve as his estate attorney of record—a somewhat risky choice since the senior partner in the prestigious Boston firm of Hale and Dorr was ninety-one years of age. Peters cautioned Hale that the superintendent was "quite helpless on account of his blindness, and when he gets a matter on his mind it becomes magnified and he feels that he must act at once." Hale agreed and suggested his son as professionally well suited to be Dorr's literary executor.[32]

By June 1, 1942 Dorr's will was revised once again. Moreover, Peters and Hale increased their oversight of Dorr's well-being. Corrective measures were taken after the superintendent fell in the Oldfarm bathroom and lodged against the door, unable to right himself. Shortly thereafter, in August of 1943, the death of Richard W. Hale resulted in Peters taking on the senior Hale's role and the drafting of Dorr's last will, which was finalized August 13, 1943.

Dorr's monograph, *Acadia National Park*, was published and distributed to NPS officials in 1942. This brief work began with President Eliot's invitation to Dorr and others to establish a land trust in 1901 and concluded eighteen years—and seventy-eight pages—later with the establishment of the park. On his forty-seven years of life prior to the establishment of the Hancock County Trustees in 1901, Dorr offered nothing biographical.[33] He then directed his attention to describing the growth and development of Acadia National Park over the previous two decades, drafting content in typescript that remained incomplete at the time of his death. This work was finalized and published posthumously by his estate trustees, even though there was no specific directive to that effect in Dorr's will.[34]

It is curious that despite Dorr's progressive efforts to expand the seacoast of Acadia National Park, he made no mention in his memoirs of the significant donation of several tracts of land on Isle au Haut, an island of less than twelve square miles, southwest of Mount Desert Island. A preliminary report undertaken by Ben Hadley in the spring of 1943 documented that 2,700 acres of that island had been offered as an extension to Acadia National Park. The descendants of the famous maritime mathematician, Nathaniel Bowditch the Navigator, made the offer. The family friendship that began between Dorr's maternal grandfather and the elder Bowditch had continued through several generations, as the Bowditch family increased their property holdings on Isle au Haut to become the dominant social force. And yet as Charles W. Eliot had forecast in general terms fifty years earlier, "the heirs of the Bowditch's [sic] no longer have interest in the greater party of the holding, and wish to be relieved of the burden of ownership and taxation."[35] The large donation significantly increased the size of the park and offered "bold, seaward looking cliffs… more exposed and remote than any now in park ownership." Ben Hadley's negotiation of the gift contained the historical reminder that the acquisition of Isle au Haut "is in line with a plan proposed by Superintendent Dorr many years ago, and [its] fulfillment will create an ocean-connected island national park unique in the federal park system."[36]

On New Year's Eve, 1943, Dorr's final documented correspondence with Mr. Rockefeller consisted of a brief note thanking him for his congratulations upon Dorr's ninetieth birthday, "a milestone not to be passed lightly." The park superintendent recognized that the war kept Rockefeller's attention directed elsewhere, yet "when at last its passing shall permit your coming I shall warmly welcome your return." His worsening condition raised doubt that he would see the Rockefellers again.[37]

Dorr continued to reside at Storm Beach Cottage with his housekeeper, Grace Oakes, who kept Rockefeller informed. Her employer was eating and sleeping well, though he was frail and moved about the estate in his darkened universe only with assistance from household staff.[38] By late spring, Dorr's friends were increasingly concerned about his health. Recently appointed Acting Superintendent Hadley informed Horace Albright that Dorr was "spending his days at Oldfarm reviewing the past in his mind's eye... [most] interested in following his trains of thought to source materials in the encyclopedia, of which he has several, having the material read to him. I spend several hours a week with him talking over matters of interest, past, present, and so far as possible, future."[39]

In late June, Dorr was visited by his Seal Harbor friend of more than four decades, fellow HCTPR trustee George L. Stebbins. Dorr greatly respected the island resident for his trail-building initiatives on behalf of the Seal Harbor Village Improvement Society and his donation, with others, of 3,600 acres encompassing the western slope of Cadillac Mountain, Pemetic Mountain, and the southern Bubble. Behind such actions was Stebbins's conviction that "the most important development in the history of the Island" was the establishment of the Hancock County Trustees.[40]

Following the death on May 4 of Dorr's close friend and neighbor, attorney and diplomat Dave H. Morris, Stebbins was elevated to the presidency of the HCTPR.[41] As the last prominent local public figure to see Dorr prior to his death, Stebbins reported to Rockefeller that "I called on George Dorr the other day and the now old man was pathetic. He is a very helpless blind man and said [to me] 'I cannot read so I just sit here and think.'"[42] A month later he passed along news from Ben Hadley that "the afternoons and evenings were very hard on the old man because of his total blindness and lack of diversion...it would help him a great deal if he could have a proper person to read to him for a few hours."[43]

Another blow had come in late June with the death of housekeeper Grace Oakes, who "brought to her work a wide knowledge of people and affairs which she had gained in newspaper work," preparing park news releases until her failing health forced retirement in late 1943.[44] Dorr communicated to Director Drury that her successor needed to be "someone familiar with the past and able to pick up the threads that are in my mind, not an outsider to whom all would need to be explained." He asked his superior whether he could "run down, if only for a few days, and look over the [historical] material I have gathered?"[45] In that letter, Dorr impressed upon Drury the importance he attached to the assembled archival documents as an important educational resource for "future students of our history long after I and all our present generation have passed upon their way." Finally, he stated that Ben Hadley, "who has become my alter ego now that I can no longer see," shared Dorr's desire that Drury pay a visit. Because of wartime travel restrictions and other Park Service priorities, Drury's visit was delayed.

Meanwhile, Judge Peters, Stebbins, and Hadley met in early July and discussed Dorr's need for a "proper person to read to him for a few hours... some one of intelligence with a calm disposition and infinite patience because Mr. Dorr's interest is to stop the reader and have the reader look up various questions."[46] Their concerns did not result in timely action. The superintendent of Acadia National Park died on a warm, dry Saturday morning, August 5, 1944 in Storm Beach Cottage. A handwritten letter from Ben Hadley to his immediate superior, Arthur Demaray, described Dorr's final minutes as "peaceful, [for awakening] at his usual time and while on his way to the bathroom his heart failed. He slumped to the floor and the end came at once. Just as he would have had it could he have placed the order."[47] Documents in the Mount Auburn Cemetery Historical Collection attribute his death to myocarditis arteriosclerosis.

The following day Hadley explained to the NPS director that in the end Dorr had "maintained his usual tranquil spirits and never did he utter a word of complaint about his loss of sight and gradually diminishing physical strength. On the contrary, he seemed to derive a great deal of comfort through mental review of the past, his early associations, his work in creating the park, and his many allied interests. Whenever he spoke of the approaching end it was with the knowledge and satisfaction of having lived a full and useful life."[48]

Two days later, Bar Harbor businesses closed for an hour during Dorr's funeral at St. Saviour's Episcopal Church. Whether the Rockefellers were at the funeral service cannot be determined from the church archives, though several relatives received from the Rockefellers a cross of red roses and white sweet peas for Dorr's "happy and well earned release."[49] Immediately afterward, Dorr's body was transported by rail to Cambridge for cremation at Mount Auburn Cemetery, the final resting place of his parents, his brother, and other Ward and Dorr relatives.[50]

No great outpouring of grief followed Dorr's death. Most of his contemporaries had predeceased him, while others recognized that his life had been long and filled with personal achievement and the satisfactions of public philanthropy. Regional newspapers emphasized that New England had lost a valuable citizen, whose landscape stewardship had uniquely benefited the nation.[51] The *Boston Herald* characterized him "as a scientist…a far-seeing man" who realized his dream.[52] The Appalachian Mountain Club published an obituary in *Appalachia*, recognizing him as a "friend of conservation who has devoted a lifetime to preserving the beauties of Mount Desert for the enjoyment of posterity."

With no fanfare, his ashes were returned by train from Cambridge to Bar Harbor, where Ben Hadley reported to Horace Albright that his remains were "scattered on the Oldfarm land which he loved so dearly at a spot which he personally selected."[53] As the years passed, the location of Dorr's final resting place became a source of local conjecture. One fictional anecdote described a conversation between two upper-crust ladies sipping afternoon tea in downtown Bar Harbor. They supposedly witnessed Dorr's ashes scattered from a passing airplane; as some of the ashes floated down into their teacups, one of them exclaimed, "Oh dear, it's Mr. Dorr."[54] In Hadley's monthly report to the Interior Department, he stated that "the ashes were scattered in a woodland glade on the Oldfarm property."[55] Seven years later, he privately reported to Director Drury that "his ashes [were] scattered near Beaver Dam Pool at the northwestern foot of Champlain Mountain."[56] This was a favorite spot for Mary Dorr, where her son—as Chairman of the BHVIA Bicycle Path Committee—had in 1895 built a bicycle path around the pond.

Privately, Hadley insisted that "there can be no regret in his passing, rather we should feel a relief that he was spared a lingering illness or physical incapacity which would have made him utterly helpless." The acting superintendent penned several brief summaries of Dorr's life, each offering highly reliable information that was unavailable elsewhere. He was convinced that Dorr's cultural background—though for so many years it had not appeared to give Dorr meaningful purpose—"was probably the greatest factor in influencing him in later life to engage in Park work. The second factor undoubtedly was his mother's enthusiastic love for gardening." As Dorr's successor, Hadley recognized that Dorr's social position was "one of the chief practical factors" that led to his "magnificent career."[57]

In the most touching homage to Dorr's infusion of scholarship into administrative reporting, Hadley's September 1944 *NPS Monthly Report* abandoned bureaucratic mendacity by introducing what may be the most unconventional obituary in the National Park Service archives. He found inspiration in the otherwise gloomy final chapter of the *Book of Ecclesiastes*: "Or Ever the Silver Cord be Loosed. On the morning of August 5, the immortal spirit of George Bucknam Dorr returned unto God who gave it. So was closed the earthly pilgrimage of a really great man, the creator of Acadia National Park, its first, and at his death, its only Superintendent. He labored intensely to bring the park into being, he nurtured it tenderly once it became real, he saw it increase in stature, and he left it a monument to his work of nearly a lifetime."

So began Hadley's lengthy tribute to his mentor.[58] Despite Mr. Rockefeller's reservations about his qualifications, Hadley had courageously mimicked Dorr's literary flourishes at risk to his own career. Subsequent interviews and internal discussions throughout the fall, however, supported his December 15, 1944 appointment.[59] Senior park administrators wrote to Hadley of their sense of personal loss, though Director Drury echoed the "grand old man" homage of Jesse Nusbaum when he wrote that "if it were not for men like George B. Dorr, there would be no national parks."[60]

But the complaints about Dorr's administrative reticence were not silenced—nor lost on Ben Hadley. One month after Dorr's death, a memorandum from the National Park Service Regional Director officially documented his concern about Dorr's unorthodoxy: "Acadia worked a little too independently of the rest of the Service and failed to keep us informed or keep us in touch with what was going on and what they were thinking."[61]

On September 2, Beatrix Farrand wrote to Newton Drury that "Mr. Dorr spoke to me once or twice about certain arrangements he thought possible in case a memorial to him was discussed." Still residing at Reef Point, the landscape designer was pleased when Drury immediately responded stating that a "fitting memorial for Mr. Dorr" was desirable and that he would pursue it when he returned from his travels.[62] Beatrix Farrand initiated the process taken up by Dorr's executors that eventually resulted in a granite memorial—at the base of a mountain that would also bear his name.

Two weeks later, the family of Harold Ickes visited the park once again, lodging at the Homans House amid the Oldfarm furnishings that Dorr had relocated there. On his return to Washington in mid-September, Secretary Ickes discussed with Arthur Demaray the possibility of changing the name of Flying Squadron, the severe mountain jutting between Cadillac and Champlain mountains, to Dorr Mountain. Hadley argued that to keep his name alive, a physical feature of the park should bear it, for "he was a man of rugged stature, of rock-like integrity, and of eminent scholarly attainments and culture." Nothing could be more fitting than to perpetuate his name in one of the park's granite mountains "which so well characterizes the attributes of the man."[63] The Interior Department's United States Board on Geographic Names approved the proposal on June 15, 1945.[64]

The motivations for using the name of the superintendent for a prominent landscape feature of the park might have been all to the good. But would it have received his approval? The idea had been proposed more than two decades earlier when Dorr was engaged in what became the mountain renaming controversy. Those who knew him best recognized this reticence; he believed it was the park that was paramount, not its "father," superintendent, and best-known advocate. Hadley understood this. It was not a specific mountain but the park itself that was "a monument to his memory." Hadley's report predicted that "at best, two generations hence, Dorr's labor will become legend, and his name forgotten or but casually recalled." It is this author's hope that this biography will be security against the realization of that prediction.

Few have had the depth of experience to assess adequately the achievement of Acadia National Park's founders. One knowledgeable exception has been conservationist W. Kent Olson, former president of Friends of Acadia: "If the Yankees who conserved Acadia had waited for Congress to create the selfsame park, it never would have happened. The principal founders were John D. Rockefeller Jr. (chief lead donor and financial backer), Harvard College President Charles W. Eliot (philosopher king of the park idea), and the tireless George B. Dorr (benefactor turned park superintendent). These are not men who dallied.... I marvel at how visionary the park's founders were. Assembling Acadia was an immense act of gift giving, brilliant conservation politics, and foresight, informed by a powerful reverence for place in a time when 'awesome' had a meaning. The park was a land-planning accomplishment of nationwide significance perfectly timed within Maine."[65]

CHAPTER TWENTY-TWO

Epilogue

To decide how to best apply the authority George B. Dorr had granted to his estate trustees, executors John Peters and Phyllis Sylvia deliberated with the three trustees: Bowdoin College President Kenneth Sills and seasonal residents Mary Newbold Hale and her son, Richard W. Hale Jr., a Harvard-educated historian (at this time he was researching his 1949 history of Bar Harbor, a community project that attorney David O. Rodick commissioned to celebrate Eden's sesquicentennial).[1] The Hales had been held in Dorr's high regard in the closing years of his life.

Four days after Dorr's death, acting park superintendent Ben Hadley inventoried the extensive Oldfarm estate. In due course the china, silverware, furnishings, art, books, and miscellaneous personal possessions were appraised at less than $25,000.[2] Living simply within his means, Acadia's founder had retained family possessions but not added to them. As negotiated several years earlier, these possessions became federal property, and while a few would be added to the collections in the park archives, the bulk would be sold to offset Dorr's debts.

The eight-room, two-bath, one-and-a-half-story Storm Beach Cottage that had often been Dorr's residence was the staging area for the appraisal and disposition of his property. Three adjacent outbuildings included a twenty-by-forty-foot structure that Dorr called the Park Library, even though it included hundreds of books that did not relate to Acadia or to the National Park Service. Since a bibliographic inventory was not taken, historians are unable to fully decipher Dorr's reading behavior. Eventually, his scholarly library was auctioned off to the highest bidders.

As fall gave way to winter, Dorr's executors realized that finalizing the August 13, 1943 "Will of George B. Dorr" would be protracted.[3] That document directed that a few household possessions go to the family of executor Phyllis Sylvia—for the last twelve years, his confidential secretary. Estate versus park ownership was at times unclear. A small safe was found in the Oldfarm cellar that contained family letters, correspondence with prominent literary and political figures, and genealogical records. Three years would pass before Judge Peters could finally distribute Dorr's very limited assets, arrange the donation of family papers and artifacts to historical and literary societies, finalize the income from the sale of dozens of properties, and design and dedicate a lasting memorial.[4]

Dorr had been an ardent proprietor of the Boston Athenaeum, the distinguished membership-based library, for fifty years. The share that he held had belonged to his father for the preceding forty-nine years and had been issued in 1822 to Samuel Dorr, an Athenaeum trustee and donor. A revered portrait of Samuel Dorr painted by George P. A. Healy was gifted by George Dorr's executors to the Athenaeum.[5] Two months before the death of President Roosevelt, an article was published in *Athenaeum Items* on "Healy and the Dorrs," wherein library staff recalled "the George Dorr in whose memory" the portrait is displayed. With obvious allusion to his botanical reputation, the librarians emphasize that "the ivy of memory is a long-lived and hardy plant. It flourishes in many works of art bequeathed from time to time to the Athenaeum and is set off throughout our building by the beauties of color constantly renewed in the flowers that speak alike for a memory and for a living devotion to the Library."[6]

Resolution of Dorr's land holdings first required title searches, appraisals, and the determination of which parcels might be of interest to the park or other parties. Mr. Rockefeller urged the executors to donate all holdings to the federal government.[7] Judge Peters, however, speaking for the executors, decided to sell the properties to anyone willing to ultimately gift the land to the federal government. The Judge reminded Rockefeller that Dorr could have donated this property to the park prior to his death if that had been his intent.

Consequently, "we would come nearer to carrying out Dorr's will by selling this land than by giving it to the Park."[8] In the end, the philanthropist sent Judge Peters a check for $6,000 for the purchase of the Dorr properties, which he subsequently gave to the federal government.[9]

Historic corroboration of the documentation in the Judge John A. Peters archive was uncovered in 2011 when the legal archive of Bar Harbor attorney and conservator Douglas B. Chapman was made available to this author and physician William Horner, a descendant of Luere B. Deasy. The Chapman firm was the successor of the law firm of Luere Deasy, A. H. Lynam, and brothers David and Serenus Rodick. From 1884 to 1948 they had championed the interests of their clients and community. For sixty years Dorr was their client, his personal and conservation interests exceptionally well served; in addition, for nearly a half century this firm was entrusted with the legal affairs of John D. Rockefeller Jr. pertaining to Mount Desert Island.

It quickly became clear that Dorr's estate plan was flawed. His expectations greatly exceeded his resources. The executors were directed by the will to consider ways to develop and improve the estate through scientific, educational, and aesthetic innovation. Dorr encouraged them to devise ways to further botanical, marine, and ornithological research; to engage student study of landscaping, forestry, and gardening; and to publish studies, illustrations, and descriptions about native wildlife inhabiting Acadia's seascape and landscape. His executors recognized that it would be "impossible" to carry out such ambitious projects.

The erection of a memorial to Dorr's achievement, however, was feasible. Beatrix Farrand's suggestion was reframed by attorney J. Archibald Murray two months after Dorr's death. He suggested to fellow members of the HCTPR that a tablet be placed in Dorr's memory on the summit of Cadillac Mountain.[10] At the 1945 HCTPR annual meeting, Judge Peters proposed that a committee be appointed to consider this issue—one that he agreed to chair. The site first considered was a jutting crag on the eastern face of Flying Squadron Mountain, where more than thirty years earlier George B. Dorr had routinely found scenic splendor and the necessary solitude to plan the establishment of a national park.[11] Several months earlier, the National Park Service had recommended that Flying Squadron Mountain be renamed Dorr Mountain, a change approved by the U.S. Board on Geographic Names on June 15, 1945.[12]

In pursuit of adequate language for the memorial stone within Acadia National Park, Peters recalled being impressed by the 1936 memorial to banker James Jackson Storrow, after whom Boston's two-mile crosstown expressway, Storrow Memorial Drive, was named. Peters favored the language because it commemorated Storrow's conservation efforts in pressuring the legislature to approve the construction of the Charles River Dam, which led to the Boston Embankment (now the Esplanade) with its promenade of grass and walkways.[13]

Adapted by Peters, the proposed inscription was reviewed by Dorr's estate trustees as well as Rockefeller, Hadley, George L. Stebbins, and Horace M. Albright. An English professor at Bowdoin College was contacted to make sure of the grammatical correctness of the language.[14] Hadley consulted Bar Harbor landscape designer Robert W. Patterson who in 1937 had "designed a similar tablet to the memory of Alessandro Fabbri" on the Park Loop Road at Otter Cliffs.[15] Peters was convinced that "Mr. Dorr's modesty was such that I think that we should avoid any fulsome expressions, and I have tried to stick to nothing but the truth."[16] Consensus was achieved regarding tablet language and Peters's thoughts now turned toward the selection of the artist to fabricate the memorial—whether it be of slate or bronze—and where to locate it.

The site on "a relatively smooth cliff face with a generally eastern exposure…a bold granite outthrust" on the side of Dorr Mountain was reconsidered.[17] Hadley could now access the Cadillac summit, where an Army outpost established during the war years had prohibited public access. Park staff removed a large slab of granite from the top of Cadillac to hold the memorial plaque. Hadley favored its placement "where it will not be under more than occasional scrutiny."[18] Ultimately the selected site was shifted from the mountain path to a more accessible area adjacent to the Sieur de Monts Spring and the Abbe Museum, both so important to Dorr. The architect selected for the memorial, R. Clipston Sturgis, had designed residences, libraries, schools, railroad stations, and public buildings throughout New England. Just a few years younger than Dorr, he was a former president of the American Institute of Architects and like Dorr, was a member of the Tavern Club and the Union Boat Club. Sturgis agreed to design the tablet for his old Harvard chum for no charge.

The dedication of the George Bucknam Dorr Memorial took place on August 29, 1947. Roughly fifty guests attended the ceremony officiated by Hancock Count Trustees of Public Reservations President Stebbins, the only surviving member of the original HCTPR executive committee. Dressed in blue blazer and white slacks, John A. Peters, now retired from the bench, stated the obvious reason for this gathering: that the memorial serve as a permanent record, erected "to advise posterity of the name of their benefactor and the boundaries of his life."[19] Mr. Rockefeller was not present—the HCTPR trustees had failed to invite him.

Prior to the memorial's unveiling by park rangers, Peters reminded guests of the lumberman's impact on the island and the 1913 attempt in Augusta to revoke the HCTPR charter, "where [Dorr] descended upon the Maine Legislature like an aroused lion in defense of its cub. I was at Augusta at the time...and witnessed the battle, which turned out to be one-sided... [for Dorr was] resourceful, indefatigable and irresistible. A modest scholarly gentleman, a philosopher, a scientist, a man dealing in ideas...[he was] a shrewd, hard-boiled, effective master-lobbyist...[who] knew the strings that control men's actions and how to pull them."[20] No other characterization of Mr. Dorr contains such a detailed description of his attributes!

The carefully approved language that Peters wrote for the memorial stone has been read by millions over the intervening decades:

In Memory of
GEORGE BUCKNAM DORR
1853–1944

Gentleman Scholar
Lover of nature

Father of this
NATIONAL PARK

Steadfast in his zeal
To make the beauties
of this Island
available to all

Six weeks later, on October 17, 1947, a refuse area located three miles from the northwest boundary of the park caught fire. Initially controlled by the Bar Harbor fire department, drought conditions and gale force winds fanned the embers so rapidly that it engulfed the entire eastern part of Mount Desert Island. Before the inferno was brought under control on November 6, scores of historic homes were destroyed. The Mount Desert Nurseries were gone. Oldfarm was not. Ninety thousand mice inbred over two hundred generations at the Jackson Laboratory were killed when fire engulfed the facility.[21] Moreover, nearly nine thousand acres of Acadia National Park were blackened, including the forests along Ocean Drive, the original Beehive and Bowl properties donated in 1908 by Eliza Homans, and the Sieur de Monts area containing the Dorr Memorial.[22] Rockefeller's controversial carriage roads were crucial for firefighters as some had foreseen. Without the access that they provided to fire hot spots, "Seal Harbor and Northeast Harbor would have burned."[23]

Judge Peters quickly informed Mr. Rockefeller that the intense fire had cracked and splintered the stone and tablet of the Dorr memorial. Peters laid partial responsibility at the doorstep of Superintendent Hadley, who had sought to protect the memorial by encasing it in a heavy wood covering, which "brought the fire...right home to the stone and the tablet."[24] A duplicate replaced the original within the year. Rockefeller echoed the earlier language in Hadley's obituary for Dorr, when the philanthropist wrote that "like the boulder on which the tablet was erected, which neither fire nor frost will affect throughout the ages, stands the record written on the Island itself of Mr. Dorr's great life work."[25]

Resolution of the Dorr estate had been delayed by the bereavement of Serenus Rodick following the death of his brother and partner, David, in November 1946.[26] Within a year, however, the protracted clearance of land titles for the Dorr estate was completed—despite the passing of Serenus, as well. Both brothers had lived to fifty-three years of age. Other attorneys in the firm would carry forward the traditions of Bar Harbor's earliest legal firm. Unfortunately, credit for park development is often erroneously assigned exclusively to those "from away." National and local archives provide overwhelming evidence that the professionalism and conservation ethos of native Mainers—including Peters, Deasy, Lynam, the Rodick brothers, and Douglas B. Chapman—was nothing less than essential to the development of Acadia National Park.

At this point, the only remaining task for the Dorr executors was the distribution of the estate income. Lacking sufficient resources to establish the cultural and scientific objectives stipulated in Dorr's will, they decided that one-half would be directed to the Jesup Memorial Library, one-quarter to the Abbe Museum, and the remaining quarter to the Hancock County Trustees of Public Reservations. The George B. Dorr estate account amounted to $27,085. After modest trustee commissions were subtracted, the $25,731 was proportionately distributed three days before Thanksgiving in 1947.[27]

Estate executor Phyllis Sylvia arranged for the publication in 1948 of an expanded version of Dorr's 1942 published memoir, *Acadia National Park*. The new content covered events between 1907 and 1933 relating to motor and carriage road construction on Mount Desert Island and the Schoodic Peninsula. Retitled *The Story of Acadia National Park*, it has never gone out of print, though more than one estate trustee thought that the new content "was not of sufficient public interest to authorize publication." She claimed that "Dorr was insistent upon the publication of this part of the history." According to Ben Hadley, Dorr had relied exclusively on memory in composing the entire manuscript. He understood that his legacy was not only the park itself but Oldfarm as well, and the narrative told of how the home of his parents gave rise to the conservation of island landscape.[28]

Trustee Mary N. Hale removed from Oldfarm all written documents she deemed to be of historic interest. These memoirs consisted of research notes, published writings, correspondence, essays, experimental horticultural results, and park development draft documents. Despite Hale's insistence that the vast collection of so-called "Dorr Papers" were "the property of Mr. Dorr's Trustees," in her absence from Oldfarm, distant relatives, friends, and park staff roamed through the estate with their own purposes in mind.[29]

Mrs. Hale turned her attention to documents that antedated the establishment of the Hancock County Trustees. Dorr's paternal ancestors over six generations originated when the seventeenth-century Englishman Edward Dorr set foot on these shores. The biographical profiles written by

Charles and George B. Dorr were deposited with the New England Historic Genealogical Society. Similarly, Ward and Gray family correspondence was welcomed by the Salem Maritime National Historic Site since Dorr's maternal ancestors were "important during the brilliant era of Salem shipping."[30] The Massachusetts Historical Society received the bulk of the Ward Family Papers, while the Boston Athenaeum received more than fifty letters from prominent early 19th-century Bostonians. Houghton Library at Harvard University acknowledged receipt of a dozen letters received by Mary and Charles Dorr from James Russell Lowell, Henry Wadsworth Longfellow, and *Harper's Monthly* essayist George W. Curtis.[31]

Some park administrative records were relocated to the park office while the Jesup Memorial Library, which Dorr had helped establish forty years earlier, accepted his memoirs. The library's board of directors responded positively to Mrs. Hale's offer to plan a memorial exhibit for Mr. Dorr.[32] The success of this exhibit of Dorr artifacts inspired an expanded permanent exhibit of Bar Harbor historical artifacts. By 1997 these growing collections—including the *Dorr Papers*—were relocated to the Bar Harbor Historical Society Museum, nearby.

Ben Hadley's involvement with preservation issues arose only when his superiors asked for an accounting. Hadley recounted his take of Dorr's idiosyncrasies: "He maintained no office and had no clerical assistance. Such correspondence as he conducted he did in longhand or had done by a public stenographer. Not being any hand to keep things in an orderly fashion, he probably soon lost track of any copies which he might have retained," a claim at odds with the findings of this author. Hadley's characterizations of Dorr's behavior did not convince his superiors.[33]

Others who interacted with Dorr well recognized that his administrative documentation over three decades was extensive. The historic record provides abundant evidence that Dorr kept letters, memoranda, probate records, maps, surveys, personnel records, scientific reports, and a wide array of official documents that he referenced repeatedly. His distinctive handwriting finds abundant expression in the National Archives, the Rockefeller Archive Center, and the files of his attorneys. Dorr not only preserved family correspondence but the documentation necessary for successful administration.

To what extent Dorr's personal and public records were discarded as the residence was emptied cannot be accurately determined. Care was exercised by the estate executors, though there is ambiguity about whether they or the Park Service controlled the paper trail left at Oldfarm. There is evidence, however, of vehicles leaving Oldfarm en route to the town refuse site. Former Northeast Harbor Library director Robert Pyle recounts that the town police chief in the years immediately following World War II, Maitland Murphy, reported retrieving papers signed on White House stationery by Calvin Coolidge that had blown out of a vehicle exiting Oldfarm.[34] Bar Harbor historian Raymond Strout reported that near the Jackson Laboratory he retrieved documents from Oldfarm that had been lifted by the wind out of trucks headed to the town dump. The man who sought to conserve nature for the public good had his own intellectual legacy inadequately served.

Certainly, Dorr would have been deeply touched by the thoughtful intentions of his trustees to realize his objectives. On the other hand, Park Service planning for Oldfarm was taking a turn that would have greatly disturbed him, especially since he had persisted in the most methodical manner to secure the Interior Department's written commitment that his property would be "rightly cared for once it is in the Government's hands."[35] As Hadley and other NPS officials prioritized responses to the fire of 1947, Oldfarm inventories and appraisals were shuffled from one desk to another.

In September of 1948, two NPS specialists unfamiliar with the park and its history—engineer J. H. Denniston and architect Aloysious Higgens—evaluated the Oldfarm structures and estimated the expense involved to rehabilitate and maintain them.[36] They detailed site options, including an administrative headquarters for the park, a park museum, or a concession furnishing lodging and meals to park visitors. Another option was the one accepted because it held the promise of generating revenue for the government: to raze some or all of the buildings on the Oldfarm estate.

Their NPS field report on the site recommended that the main residence be gutted. Upwards of $3,000 could be salvaged from household contents that remained after shelving, doors, and other utilitarian items were removed for park purposes. NPS Director Newton Drury informed Hadley that "on October 8 [1948] we obtained at long last approval for the razing of Old Farm."[37] The Interior Department authority behind

Drury's directive has not been uncovered. In the fall of 1950 the Dorr family residence was sold for eighty-seven dollars. The new owner wished to secure revenue from its physical elements, which were carted off after demolition. Little more than the foundation remained.

Maine's state historian, Earle G. Shettleworth Jr., emphasized during an interview with this author that many have not learned about the interdependence of conservation and preservation. At Acadia National Park during the postwar era, the National Park Service sought to conserve the land unimpeded by historic structures. Unfortunately, "they razed this last evidence of the earliest cottage culture which was so deeply tied to the evolution of the park. They had not learned that conservation does not require removal of man's footprint—to the contrary, historical truth requires its inclusion."[38] In effect, the Park Service authorized the destruction of the oldest designed historic structure in Acadia National Park.

Superintendent Hadley had been succeeded in 1953 by Frank R. Givens, reassigned from Joshua Tree National Monument. Fifteen months later, Phyllis Sylvia visited Oldfarm and wrote to Mr. Rockefeller that she was "much depressed after seeing the grounds in utter ruin." She recalled that Dorr's greatest wish had been that Oldfarm might be kept as a place of refuge and of study for those interested in the flora and fauna of Mount Desert Island, concluding with a challenge to all future park employees: "If one who gave his all to make Acadia National Park possible is so soon forgotten, there would seem to me to be no incentive for others to try to carry on the work which he started."[39]

Shortly thereafter, Mr. and Mrs. Rockefeller visited the property and found that only a portion of the Oldfarm residence's first-floor walls remained. Roadways were blocked by fallen trees; wreckage was everywhere. Rockefeller wrote to the new NPS director, landscape architect Conrad L. Wirth, offering to supplement "any funds which the National Park Service had planned or expected to devote…to help in the early and adequate putting to order of the property."[40] Mr. Rockefeller's earlier views of the legacy value of the site had increased significantly.

Five months later, in a lengthy letter to the philanthropist on the role of interpretation in the national parks, Wirth encouraged "self-use by the visitors," affirming that Oldfarm "fits into this plan very well, and I know that you are especially interested in what can be done there." He promised to direct Superintendent Givens to clean up Oldfarm and improve the road and parking area. He further proposed (1) to place a floor on the Oldfarm foundation as "a platform for the same views that Mr. Dorr and his guests had from the home"; (2) to place a nearby "wayside exhibit" to tell the story of park development and Dorr's place in that process; and (3) to cover the whole Oldfarm foundation with a low, broad roof beneath which two exhibit rooms would be constructed to frame a view to the sea.[41]

Director Wirth carefully incorporated into his letter elements from an "Interpretive Plan for Acadia National Park" completed several days earlier by Howard R. Stagner, a highly regarded NPS naturalist. His later publications on preservation brought him into the director's inner circle at a time when Wirth's "Mission 66" NPS initiative prioritized development of the parks for recreational tourism.[42] On Mount Desert Island, Wirth supported the central thesis of Stagner's plan: Oldfarm was "the logical place to interpret the story of the preservation of Acadia National Park.... In contrast to the western parks, [Acadia] was saved for America through personal labors and sacrifice even before the matter of its establishment came before Congress. Furthermore, the pattern set by that movement... influenced the preservation movement far beyond the limits of Acadia. The Dorr site, with its many associations with the early history of Acadia and Bar Harbor, epitomizes this story."[43]

Mr. Rockefeller responded in May 1955 with a check for $5,000 to stimulate the process and defray some of the projected $22,400 expense. From Colonial Williamsburg he wrote that he was pleased with Wirth's plan and enclosed the funds "to make sure that the necessary cleanup work was done," satisfied that "Mr. Dorr's place will shortly become a valuable addition to Acadia park and, at the same time, a worthy tribute to him as father of the Park."[44] Unfortunately, no documents have been uncovered regarding the implementation of this plan or the utilization of Mr. Rockefeller's funds for other purposes.

In the intervening seven decades, the Oldfarm property has been "naturalized." The severe Maine coastal weather, abuse, and neglect have taken their toll. Flowerbeds have been entirely suffocated by bramble, erosion has reshaped land contours, shrubbery has died due to the absence of light, historic roadways and paths have been obliterated or redirected by the impact of daily visitors. No scientific studies of the property's flora and fauna have been completed as part of a restoration plan. Of this once-artfully crafted habitat, only Storm Beach Cottage—now a residence for park staff—is actively maintained.

Nowhere in the Denniston-Higgens report was there an awareness that Oldfarm was a designed historic landscape. Drawing inspiration from the English picturesque movement, Bar Harbor families—such as the Dorrs—laid out elaborate villas set in landscaped high ground overlooking Frenchman Bay. "The picturesque emphasis on irregularity, variety, and roughness was especially suitable to the broken terrain, rock outcrops, streams, and fine stands of trees found along the Maine coast."[45] Of the prominent architects who designed these cottages, academically trained architect Henry Richards spatially oriented the structures to reflect the owners' sensitivities to optimizing the natural features of the existing landscape. But in the years since, the Park Service has acquired sufficient expertise to appreciate—as did prescient naturalist Howard R. Stagner—how this neglected cultural landscape could have a level of integrity restored.[46]

What ought to be the future of Oldfarm? To minimally recapture the era of the first quarter-century of the National Park Service, when the superintendent entertained distinguished citizens and public officials? To reconstruct the rusticator ambiance of the last two decades of the nineteenth century? To demonstrate how natural and cultural forces shaped the development of the park? To partially realize the lofty property goals in Dorr's will? Since Oldfarm is the park property closest to downtown Bar Harbor, could it not be interlaced with wayside exhibits and restored gardens that would draw visitors and acquaint them with the deep horticultural roots of this national park?

The Park Service has responded in recent years with the installation of an Oldfarm wayside exhibit and ranger-guided tours focused on the "Missing Mansion." Today's park managers have inherited a much-degraded landscape at Oldfarm, but they also have accumulated decades of organizational experience in caring for—and educating the public about—the broad variety of cultural and natural resources held within the national park system. A first priority in the second century of Acadia should be finding a "right use" for the Oldfarm site. This will ensure that island residents and park visitors are further educated about Acadia's remarkable history—and the many fine people and cultural movements so closely tied to this park through the unparalleled efforts of George B. Dorr.

Much earlier, Charles W. Eliot had written about the generational impact of great wealth. John D. Rockefeller Jr. showed, at sites across America, how inherited wealth could be turned to conservation purposes. In 2015 his last surviving son, David, celebrated his hundredth birthday with a gift of a thousand acres adjacent to Little Long Pond in Seal Harbor; in transferring ownership to the local Land and Garden Preserve, he emphasized the "lasting interest and importance [of his donation] to a broader part of the community," refocusing his philanthropy to benefit island villages.

Yet for the scholarly George B. Dorr, perhaps the best understanding of his legacy is reached by examining his later years via a distinctive principle articulated by the classical author Appius Claudius Caecus, a fourth-century BCE Roman statesman highly regarded for the wisdom of his counsel on public affairs. One of his memorable moral maxims provides the most accurate description of what Dorr would struggle to achieve: *faber est suae quisque fortunae.* That is, everyone is the architect of his own fortune.

Dorr's fortune was not his family inheritance, despite its utility in purchasing hundreds of land parcels on Mount Desert Island. He rigorously applied his financial assets, time, social acumen, and organizational and persuasive skills to design and protect landscapes and seascapes worthy of public interest. Long before his death, those who knew him best recognized that this designed, public, federally protected park was his fortune. We who live on into the second century of Acadia National Park are challenged in many ways unanticipated by Acadia's founders. As the stewards of this fortune—citizens, park advocates, and civil servants—it remains to be seen whether we can carry forward the ideals of this phenomenal conservationist.

Acknowledgments

The seeds of this biography track back to visits beginning three decades ago, when my wife, Elizabeth, and I relocated to New England and were drawn to the Acadia National Park that she had enjoyed in her youth. She accompanied me on research trips; at times I was Watson to her Holmes. When cancer threatened her in 2010, the first draft of the manuscript was put aside. Gentle nudging from friends prompted my return to the book, which is dedicated in her memory.

Of the many hands and minds that have contributed to this book, librarians must first be lauded. Randi Ashton-Pritting and Kim Farrington at the University of Hartford, Barbara Hickok at Southern New Hampshire University, and Colgate University librarian Joanne Schneider facilitated access to resources.

Massachusetts provided the rich loam for this biography. With the exception of the *Ward-Perkins Family Papers* at the University of California, Santa Barbara, the primary Dorr and Ward family manuscripts are located in greater Boston at the Massachusetts Historical Society, the New England Historic Genealogical Society, and Harvard University. While all exceeded my expectations, special thanks must be given to Harvard archivist Barbara Meloni, who contributed mightily to my understanding of the academic culture that nourished Dr. Eliot, Charles Eliot, and Dorr. Archivist Meg Winslow opened the collections of Mount Auburn Cemetery to reveal more than a century of Dorr and Ward family funeral arrangements, contextualized through dialogue with its president at that time, preservationist William C. Clendaniel. Berkshire historian Cornelia Gilder's engaging publications were supplemented with her personal tour of the Ward and Dorr family estates at what became Tanglewood Music Center. The G. Stanley Hall papers at the Robert H. Goddard Library at Clark University document Dorr's interest in psychical research, ably explained to me by Mott Lind.

Innumerable trips were necessary to access archival documents and other resources. The Library of Congress, the National Park Service History Collection at Harpers Ferry Center, and the National Archives and Records Administration provided key public documents. NPS historian Richard Quin deciphered Record Group 79 at the NARA facility in College Park, Maryland. The U.S. Board on Geographic Names provided scores of documents regarding George B. Dorr's renaming of mountains.

Michele Hiltzik Beckerman, Thomas Rosenbaum, and Dr. Darwin Stapleton of the Rockefeller Archive Center in Tarrytown, New York, explained the complexities of their card classification system. While I sifted through documents in the RAC reading room, my wife was entertained in the mansion dining room by staff tales about the Rockefeller legacy. Michele's tireless interest in the Rockefeller legacy at Seal Harbor bolstered the biographical narrative.

The former superintendent of Acadia National Park, Sheridan Steele, opened doors to the William Otis Sawtelle Collections and Research Center. Curators Brooke Childry, John McDade, and the ebullient Marie Yarborough responded with enthusiasm to my interest in the neglected history of the park founder. Acadia's Chief of Resource Management, Rebecca Cole-Will, sustained my interests in the most current park cultural landscape reports, kept me centered on publication, and evaluated the manuscript.

Nearby, Abbe Museum collections and interpretation director Julia Gray deepened my understanding of the relationship between the park founders and the Wabanaki. Nancy Howland and Ruth Eveland at the Jesup Memorial Library kept their microfilm reader functioning against all odds. The friendship of the late Franklin H. Epstein, M.D. showed me much more than what was revealed in his centennial history of the Mount Desert Island Biological Laboratory. Northeast Harbor Library director Bob Pyle enthusiastically traced the impact of the Eliot family on his community. Maine State Historian Earle Shettleworth Jr. illumined Acadian culture. Bowdoin College librarians Judy Montgomery and Caroline Moseley graciously answered my questions about rarely consulted nineteenth-century journals and the Bowdoin presidency of Kenneth Sills, one of the Dorr estate executors.

Mount Desert Island Historical Society president William Horner monumentally influenced the thoroughness of this biography when he persuaded Bar Harbor attorney Douglas A. Chapman to open his rich historical archive—derived from the clients of Deasy, Lynam, Rodick, and Rodick. Woodlawn Museum's director, Joshua Torrance, shared the museum archive of the Hancock County Trustees of Public Reservations and convinced the Hale & Hamlin law firm in Ellsworth to permit our access to the Judge John A. Peters archive.

Among the dozens of interviews undertaken, those with Ann Rockefeller Roberts and Wildwood Stables director Ed Winterberg situated the carriage roads within a larger framework. My final thoughts on Dorr's horticulture pursuits were influenced by Beatrix Farrand scholar Judith Tankard, Anne Kozak's insights into the Wild Gardens of Acadia, and Betsy Hewlett's historical research into the Mount Desert Nurseries. Historian Judith S. Goldstein challenged me to reconsider the nuances of the personal relationship within the Triumvirate. Genealogist Alice M. Long eased ancestry complexities.

Special thanks go to Simon Howard, descendant of Rosalind and George Howard, the ninth Earl of Carlisle. Castle Howard archivist Christopher Ridgway and curator Anna Louise Mason located dozens of letters demonstrating the Howard family's ties with Americans like the Dorrs.

The Friends of Acadia communications director, Aimee Beal Church, not only supervised this publication but rolled up her sleeves and invested in it the highest level of editorial scrutiny and stamina. The fullness of her historical knowledge of the park is staggering; her questions and impeccable logic forced me to repeatedly peel away the layers in my reasoning. FOA president David MacDonald and his staff deserve special mention for their encouragement of this partnership as well as their efforts to contextualize this publication within 2016 programming for the Acadia Centennial.

A number of my letters and articles, many of which found their way in whole or in part into this book, were published in the *Mount Desert Islander, Chebacco Magazine, Friends of Acadia Journal, The Beatrix Farrand Society News,* the *Woodlawn Museum Newsletter,* and *The Mount Press.* Deft critiques of the entire manuscript were generously provided by Kevin Coakley-Welch, Jack Russell, Donald Lenahan, William C. Clendaniel, and Maureen Fournier (who graciously wrote the Foreword). Invaluable professional assistance was provided by editor and indexer Wendy Catalano of Stoneham, Massachusetts, proofreader Jane Crosen of Penobscot, Maine, and graphic designer Karen Zimmermann of Bar Harbor, Maine.

I am grateful to loved ones that were strongly supportive of this creative process: my sister-in-law Linda S. Bard, Ralph and Penny Holibaugh, William Hannaford Jr., Morris and Barbara Powazek, Georgeanne Diehl, Barbara Lisafeld, Judith A. Miller, Anne and Lance Funderburk, William Nelson, and Shelly Perron. Without the financial advice and sage counsel of Jay Gershman, the project would surely have floundered. Yet it was the penultimate Sage, my University at Buffalo dissertation director, the late John Peter Anton, who kept me centered throughout my life—as did my wife—on the humanistic aspirations that proved to be at the heart of the conservation effort on Mount Desert Island.

Errors, omissions, and other shortcomings that remain in this work are entirely my own.

Ronald H. Epp
Cornwall, Pennsylvania
October 2015

Endnotes

INTRODUCTION

[1] Late nineteenth-century tourist guides vividly portray the natural attractions of the landscape. See the works of Benjamin DeCosta, especially his *Scenes in the Isle of Mount Desert, Coast of Maine* (New York: [n.p.], 1868) and Clara Barnes Martin, *Mount Desert, on the Coast of* Maine. 6 ed. (Portland, Maine: Loring, Short & Harmon, 1885).

[2] Bunny McBride and Harald Prins, *Indians in Eden* (Camden, ME: Down East Books, 2009) and their *Asticou's Island Domain*, Vol. 1 (Boston: National Park Service, 2007).

[3] G. B. Dorr, "Our Seacoast National Park," *Appalachia* 15 (1920): 174–81.

[4] G. B. Dorr, "Conservation Plans for Mount Desert," undated typescript. *Dorr Papers*. B.2.f.1. Bar Harbor: Bar Harbor Historical Society.

[5] G. L. Stebbins, "Random Notes on the Early History and Development as a Summer Resort of Mount Desert Island and Particularly Seal Harbor." Typescript. William Otis Sawtelle Collections and Research Center. Acadia National Park. B.7.f.8. References herein to the Sawtelle Research Center (SRC) are to a now-dated organizational system. In 2012 the Northeast Museum Services Center completed a new finding aid, reorganizing park resource management records (1854–2012).

[6] Van Wyck Brooks, *The Flowering of New England: 1815–1865* (New York: E. P. Dutton & Co., 1936), 7.

[7] Philip Shabecoff, *A Fierce Green Fire: The American Conservation Movement* (New York: Hill & Wang, 1993), 46.

[8] C. W. Eliot. "The Forgotten Millions," *The Century Magazine* 40, #4 (August 1890): 556-65; *John Gilley, Maine Farmer and Fisherman* (Boston: American Unitarian Association, 1904).

[9] See historian Richard W. Judd, *Common Land, Common People: The Origins of Conservation in Northern New England* (Cambridge: Harvard University Press, 1997).

[10] See *Twentieth-Century New England Land Conservation: A Heritage of Civic Engagement*. Ed. Charles H. W. Foster (Cambridge: Harvard University Press, 2009).

[11] A contemporary of Dorr, U.S. Congressman William Kent (1864–1928), and his wife donated the redwood forested land in California that became Muir Woods National Monument in 1908. Strictly speaking, this was a private donation and not a gift from a public land trust. See Tom Butler. *Wildlands Philanthropy: The Great American Tradition* (San Rafael, CA: Earth Ware Editions, 2008), 2–9.

[12] See Ann Rockefeller Roberts, *Mr. Rockefeller's Roads: The Untold Story of Acadia's Carriage Roads and their Creator* (Camden: Downeast, 1990), Ch. 2.

[13] Joseph L. Sax, "Buying Scenery: Land Acquisitions for the National Park Service," *Duke Law Journal* (September, 1980): 710.

[14] Indeed, Dorr's service was so highly valued that he was legislatively exempt from the provisions of mandatory retirement.

[15] H. V. Hubbard, "Landscape Development based on Conservation," *Landscape Architecture* (April 1939): 105; ten years earlier, Rockefeller wrote to Hubbard that Dorr "is a man of great personal magnetism, extraordinary culture, splendid background, and my warm personal friend." September 18, 1929. Rockefeller Archive Center. Office of Messrs. Rockefeller. Record Group 2. Series 1. Homes. B.110.f.1097. Hereafter abbreviated as RAC III.2.I. B.110.f.1097.

[16] See R. W. Sellars, *Preserving Nature in the National Parks: A History* (New Haven: Yale University Press, 1997; a change in NPS policy was signaled in Horace. M. Albright's article "Research in the National Parks," *Scientific Monthly* 36, #6 (1933): 483–501.

[17] Ann W. Spirn, *The Language of Landscape* (New Haven: Yale University Press, 1998), 99.

[18] Van Wyck Brooks, *New England: Indian Summer*. 487.

[19] *Dorr Papers*. B.1.f.14.

Chapter One: FIRST IMPRESSIONS

[1] See Sam Bass Warner Jr., *Streetcar Suburbs: The Process of Growth in Boston, 1870–1900*. 2nd ed (Cambridge: Harvard University Press, 1978).

[2] Pamela J. Belanger, *Inventing Acadia: Artists and Tourists at Mount Desert* (Rockport, ME: Farnsworth Art Museum, 1999). See also John Wilmerding, *The Artist's Mount Desert: American painters on the Maine Coast* (Princeton: Princeton University Press, 1991).

[3] S. E. Morison, *The Story of Mount Desert Island* (Boston: Little, Brown & Co., 1960), 9.

[4] See John K. Howat, *Frederic Church* (New Haven: Yale University Press, 2005). On the fourth trip of Frederic Edwin Church to Mount Desert Island in the company of the Tracy family, see *The Tracy Logbook 1855*. Ed. Anne Mazlish. (Bar Harbor: Acadia Publishing Co. 1997).

[5] Clara Barnes Martin, *Mount Desert on the Coast of Maine*. 6th ed. (Portland: Loring, Short & Harmon, 1885) and Benjamin De Costa, *Scenes from the Isle of Mount Desert, Coast of Maine* (New York, 1868), *The Handbook of Mount Desert, Coast of Maine* (Boston: A. Williams, 1871).

[6] *Dorr Papers*. B.1.f.13. Bar Harbor Historical Society. See also "Charles Hazen Dorr," Version 2. *Dorr Collection*. New England Historic Genealogical Society.

[7] *Dorr Papers.* B.2.f.3; B.2.f.6.

[8] *Dorr Papers* B.2.f.16; B.1.f.14. Charles Dorr purchased this property with a partner; Dorr's father later purchased that share and acquired additional holdings. The naming of the property varies: Oldfarm is preferred to Old Farm.

[9] Dorr to President Franklin D. Roosevelt. August 1, 1940. *Dorr Papers.* B.1.f.13.

[10] The late University of California librarian Donald Fitch carefully analyzed the massive *Ward-Perkins Family Papers.* See his masterful "Ward-Perkins Papers," *Soundings: Collections of the University of California at Santa Barbara Library* 16 (1985): 18–77.

[11] See Harriet Manning Whitcomb, *Annals and Reminiscences of Jamaica Plain* (Cambridge: Riverside Press, 1897), 50–51; the standard study of Parkman is by Mason Wade, *Francis Parkman* (New York: Viking, 1942); and for interesting context for Bussey Woods, see S. B. Sutton, *Charles Sprague Sargent and the Arnold Arboretum* (Cambridge: Harvard University Press, 1970).

[12] See Julia Ward Howe, "Social Boston Past and Present," *Harper's Bazaar* XLIII, #2 (February 1909): 108. With roots in the early Christian Church, Unitarianism denominationally emphasizes the unity of God, rejecting the identification of Jesus Christ with God.

[13] O. W. Holmes, *The Autocrat at the Breakfast Table* (New York: Heritage Press, 1955).

[14] Cleveland Amory, *The Proper Bostonians* (New York: E. P. Dutton, 1947), Ch. 1.

[15] *Thomas Wren Ward Papers.* Massachusetts Historical Society. See also *The Samuel Gray Ward and Anna Barker Ward Papers.* Series I. Harvard University; and H. Ellery and Charles P. Bowditch. *The Pickering Genealogy* (Cambridge: University Press, 1897), Vol. 2: 337–339.

[16] See Walter Muir Whitehead, "Remarks on the Canton trade and the manner of transacting business," *Essex Institute Historical Collections* 73, #4 (1937): 303–310. See also Foster Rhea Dulles, *The Old China Trade* (Boston: Houghton Mifflin Co., 1930).

[17] On the Gray family, see Edward Gray, *William Gray of Salem, Merchant* (Boston: Houghton Mifflin Co., 1914) and *William Gray of Lynn, Massachusetts and Some of his Descendants* (Salem: Essex Institute, 1916). The Gray family of Lynn, Massachusetts, dates from 1706 and includes respected nineteenth-century merchants, civic representatives, financiers, and academics.

[18] Architect Charles Bulfinch (1763–1844) designed the Massachusetts State House immediately before designing all of the connected private homes on adjacent Park Street. For a detailed account of several generations of celebrated residents on Park Street, see Robert Means, *Old Park Street and its Vicinity* (Boston: Houghton Mifflin Co., 1922).

[19] Roy A. Foulke, *The Sinews of American* Commerce (New York: Dun & Bradstreet, Inc., 1941), 329–330. On Barings, there is no rival to R. W. Hidy's *The House of Baring in American Trade and Finance* (Cambridge: Harvard University Press, 1949). The most lucid assessment of the Ward family involvement in American diplomacy is Jay Sexton's *Debtor Diplomacy: France and American Foreign Relations in the Civil War Era 1837–1873* (Oxford: Clarendon Press, 2005), 12–14, 20–53.

[20] Ronald Story, "Harvard and the Boston Brahmins: A Study in Institutional and Class Development, 1800–1865," *Journal of Social History* 8, #3 (1975): 102. See also

Josiah Quincy, *The History of Harvard University* (Cambridge: John Owen, 1840), Vol. 2: 364, 385.

[21] See Robert A. McCaughey, "The Usable Past: A Study of the Harvard rebellion of 1834," *William and Mary Law Review* 11, #3 (1970): 595. In 1838, Ward offered his letter of resignation as Harvard College Treasurer, which was refused by President Josiah Quincy because of his need for Ward's skills in the project to erect Gore Hall. See *Records of the Treasurer of Harvard University. 1830–1842* (Harvard University Archives). As he relinquished this position, he allied himself with a dozen others in raising funds—for the first time—to fill gaps in the library collection. See Kenneth E. Carpenter, *The First 350 Years of the Harvard University Library* (Cambridge: Harvard University Press, 1986), 80–81.

[22] Ralph Waldo Emerson, *The Journals and Miscellaneous Notebooks of Ralph Waldo Emerson. Volume VII. 1838–1842.* Eds. A. W. Plumstead and Harrison Hayford (Cambridge: Harvard University Press, 1969), 404. See Eleanor M. Tilton, "The True Romance of Anna Hazard Barker & Samuel Gray Ward," *Studies in the American Renaissance, 1987,* 53–72; and Carl F. Strauch, "Hatred's Swift Repulsions: Emerson, Margaret Fuller, and Others," *Studies in Romanticism* VII, #2 (1968): 63–103.

[23] See Charles M. Lamb, "The Summer Colony at Lenox," *Munsey Magazine* 17 (1897): 674–680. The definitive studies of Samuel Gray Ward are by David Baldwin: *Puritan Aristocrat in the Age of Emerson: A Study of Samuel Gray Ward* (University of Pennsylvania dissertation, 1961), and "The Emerson-Ward Friendship: Ideals and Realities," *Studies in the American Renaissance 1984.* Ed. Joel Myerson, 299–324.

[24] Pittsfield Massachusetts Probate Records. B.139, 299. The most authoritative documentation of Highlawn is the brilliant study of Cornelia Brooke Gilder, *Hawthorne's Lenox: The Tanglewood Circle* (Charleston: The History Press, 2008), 59–62.

[25] *Star Papers; Experiences of Art and Nature* (New York: J. C. Derby, 1855), 267–268.

[26] Gilder, *Hawthorne's Lenox*, 114, n. 10 quoting the *Gleaner and Advocate.* September 15, 1874.

[27] David B. Baldwin, *Puritan Aristocrat in the Age of Emerson: A Study of Samuel Gray Ward,* passim.

[28] Edward Waldo Emerson, "Samuel Gray Ward," *The Early Years of the Saturday Club: 1855–1870* (Boston: Houghton Mifflin Co., 1918), 110–117. In this first of a three-volume series, E. W. Emerson's essay on Ward reveals his central role in the club's formation. See Amy Lowell's review of the aforementioned publication, *The New York Times,* May 23, 1919, 80. At this time Sam was unaware that his nephew, George B. Dorr, would later mirror the self-impression of his uncle—who saw himself as a student and literary man rather than as a continuation of the seven generations of Ward merchants that preceded him.

[29] Henry James, *Notes of a Son and Brother* (New York: Charles Scribner's Sons, 1914), 130. See the *Bowditch Family Christmas Collection* at the Massachusetts Historical Society for an account of this family tradition begun in 1836.

[30] Thomas Wren Ward purchased this property March 27, 1850, which was later reacquired by his widow from Charles and Mary Dorr in February 1864. (Norfolk County Registry of Deeds. Dedham, MA. B.193, p. 153; B.329, p. 271) It is unclear whether the residence was a marriage gift or whether the Dorr family at some point purchased the property from Ward or his estate.

[31] *The Thomas Wren Ward Papers.* B.13.f.5.

[32] The Bar Harbor Historical Society Museum contains transcriptions, published writings, drafts, correspondence, essays, and other personal memorabilia of the founder of Acadia National Park. A 2004 guide to *The George Bucknam Dorr Papers,* prepared by this author, facilitates use of this unprocessed memorabilia. See B.2.f.2.

[33] Anna Barker Hazard Ward. January 3, 1854. *Ward-Perkins Family Papers.* B.4.f.14. University of California, Santa Barbara.

[34] "Charles Hazen Dorr," *Dorr Collection.* New England Historic Genealogical Society.

[35] Fitch. *Ward-Perkins Family Papers,* 19.

Chapter Two: DR. ELIOT SAILS INTO FRENCHMAN BAY

[1] Henry James, *Charles W. Eliot: President of Harvard University 1869–1909* (Boston: Houghton Mifflin Co., 1930), I, 319–321.

[2] James, *Charles W. Eliot,* I, 321.

[3] In the seventeenth century the extended Eliot family had six Harvard graduates, nine in the next century, and eventually fourteen in the nineteenth century.

[4] James, *Charles W. Eliot,* I, 14.

[5] March 24, 1934. *Ward-Perkins Papers.* B.5.f.20. University of California, Santa Barbara. Library; Charles P. Bowditch to William C. Endicott Jr., January 18, 1921. *Endicott Family Papers.* B.24.f.27. Massachusetts Historical Society.

[6] *Thomas Wren Ward Papers.* B.1.f.25. *Endicott Family Papers.* B.34.f.27. Massachusetts Historical Society. Boston, MA.

[7] Thomas Wren Ward to John Ward, July 18, 1854. *Thomas Wren Ward Papers.* B.2.f.26. Samuel G. Ward's life deserves a fuller and more timely examination beyond the remarkable dissertation of David B. Baldwin, *Puritan Aristocrat in the Age of Emerson: A Study of Samuel Gray Ward (*University of Pennsylvania, 1961). This study of Dorr's uncle raises questions about how Sam and his peers were able to shake off Puritan religious zeal and belief in the inherent corruption of the world of commerce.

[8] The Ward-Dorr property today is a multipurpose conservation area known as Pequitside Farm. As late as 1870 the Dorr portion of the property was also occupied by a coachman, family nurse, and three domestics. (*1870 Census Records.* Canton, MA, 45 [226].) See Canton Historical Society's Pequitside maps for 1875 and 1895, *www.canton.org/maps/* and the Chris Brindley essay, "Pequitside Farm," on the Canton Historical Society web site. Following a 1933 visit with his closest relatives, Louise and William C. Endicott Jr., Dorr once again walked the Canton property. He recalled those halcyon days in a ten-page essay rich in detail, especially the physical character of his grandparents' country home and the surrounding environment. The "Country Home at Canton" essay contains more contextual detail and emotional fabric than other musings on family residences. The Massachusetts Historical Society collection of *Endicott Family Papers.* B.35.f.29 included this unattributed essay; in 2007 I provided stylistic evidence of Dorr's authorship.

[9] Dorr's early interest in biological phenomena—and later promotion of biological inquiry on Mount Desert Island—may have been connected to his mother's uncle, F. C. Gray, who resided two doors away from the Thomas Wren Ward family residence at 3 Park Street. Gray's last will and testament designated Harvard College as beneficiary of $50,000 to establish and maintain a museum of comparative zoology.

See Marjorie B. Cohen, *Francis Calley Gray and Art Collecting for America* (Cambridge: Harvard University Press, 1986), 4–5.

[10] Robert Grant, "The North Shore of Massachusetts," *Scribner's Magazine* 16, #1 (1894) offers the best firsthand account of why the shore at Cape Ann proved so appealing to "men of comfortable means."

[11] *Dorr Papers.* B.1.f.14. Bar Harbor Historical Society. Frances Anne Kemble (1809–1893) was a celebrated British actress and author who lived in Lenox beginning in the 1830s in a residence called The Perch. See Cornelia Brooke Gilder, *Hawthorne's Lenox: the Tanglewood Circle* (Charleston, SC: The History Press, 2008), 49–54.

[12] March 5, 1933. Rockefeller Archive Center. III.2.I. B.83.f.827.

[13] G. B. Dorr, "Children of the Hon. Samuel Dorr," *Dorr Collection.* New England Historic and Genealogical Society. Boston, MA.

[14] Maud Howe Elliott, *Three Generations* (Boston: Little, Brown & Co., 1911), 24.

[15] G. B. Dorr, "Charles Hazen Dorr," Version 1, 101. *Dorr Collection.*

[16] Mary Ward Gray Dorr to Lucy Ward Lawrence, December 24, 1854. *Thomas Wren Ward Papers.* B.7.f.12.

[17] See Ronald Story, "Class and Culture in Boston: The Athenaeum, 1807–1860," *American Quarterly* 27, #2 (1975): 178–199.

[18] *Dorr Papers.* B.1.f.13.

[19] *Thomas Wren Ward Papers.* B.8.f.4; *Ward-Perkins Papers.* B.3.f.37. See also the Mount Auburn Cemetery Historical Collections, #235. For background, see Barbara Rotundo, "The Rural Cemetery Movement," *Essex Institute Historical Collection* 109 (1973): 231–240, and also her "Mount Auburn Cemetery: A Proper Boston Institution," *Harvard Library Bulletin* 22 (1974): 268–279.

[20] The extensive array of titles purchased by Harvard College with the Thomas Wren Ward bequest can be recovered with an Internet search on *Google Scholar.* Ward was treasurer of the Boston Athenaeum (1828–36), while Samuel Dorr was a trustee (1826–27); George B. Dorr's Athenaeum membership derived from the latter relationship through Charles H. Dorr.

[21] *Samuel Gray Ward and Anna Barker Ward Papers.* III. 1386. Harvard University.

[22] Ronald Story, *The Forging of an Aristocracy. Harvard and the Boston Upper Class, 1800–1870* (Middletown, CT: Wesleyan University Press, 1980), 48–49.

[23] James, *Charles W. Eliot,* I, 3.

[24] Grindall Reynolds, "Memoir of Joseph Lasinby Brown," *Memoirs of the Social Circle in Concord, Second Series (from 1795–1840).* (Cambridge: Riverside Press, 1888), 1–14.

[25] The Dorr Collection contains fulsome family biographical essays by Charles Hazen Dorr and his son, George. See Charles Hazen Dorr, "Hon. Samuel Dorr," Dorr Collection, NEHGS.

[26] March 22, 1924. *Charles W. Eliot Papers.* B.95. Harvard University Archives.

[27] Charles W. Eliot to Hubert Work. March 22, 1924. *Charles W. Eliot Papers.* B.95. Harvard University Archives. Dorr's parents may have turned to the now classic publication *Stammering and Stuttering: Their Nature and Treatment* (New York: Hafner Publishing, 1967 reproduction of the 1861 edition). Regarding sensory limitations, Dorr's cousin, Thomas Wren Ward Jr., became deaf as a result of a childhood illness. See Ralph Waldo Emerson, *The Letters of Ralph Waldo Emerson,* Eds. Ralph L. Rusk and Eleanor M. Tilton (New York: Columbia University Press, 1995), Vol. 8, 551, n.17; Vol. 5, 142, 176.

Chapter Three: THE MOST IMPRESSIONABLE YEARS

[1] The land for the public garden had been leased in 1837 to Horace Gray Sr., father of the better-known U.S. Supreme Court Justice, Justice Horace Gray. See Edward Gray. *William Gray of Lynn, Massachusetts and Some of his Descendants* (Salem: Essex Institute, 1916), 16–17.

[2] Bainbridge Bunting, *Houses of Boston's Back Bay* (Cambridge: Harvard University Press, 1967), 1–3. See also Nancy S. Seasholes, *Gaining Ground: A History of Landmaking in Boston* (Cambridge: MIT Press, 2003).

[3] David B. Baldwin, *Puritan Aristocrat in the Age of Emerson: A Study of Samuel Gray Ward* (University of Pennsylvania dissertation, 1961), 239–240. George Cabot Ward partnered with his brother Sam in New York, continuing the Barings business until George's death in 1887. Thus, "for sixty years all the American business of the London firm" had been in the hands of two generations of the Ward family. H. Ellery and Charles Pickering Bowditch, *The Pickering Genealogy* (Cambridge: University Press, 1897), Vol. 2, 839.

[4] Bunting, *Houses of Boston's Back Bay,* Appendix A; figure 47 offers a glimpse of #18 in a rare photograph. See also Roger G. Reed, *Building Victorian Boston: The Architecture of Gridley J. F. Bryant* (Amherst: University of Massachusetts Press, 2007).

[5] *Jack Hall or the School Days of an American Boy* (Boston: Jordan Marsh & Co., 1888), 52*;* see also Henry Adams, *The Education of Henry Adams (*New York: Modern Library, 1983), Ch. 2 and 3.

[6] Henry Cabot Lodge, *Early Memories* (New York: Charles Scribner's Sons, 1913), 89; see also James Lovett, *Old Boston Boys and the Games They Played* (Boston: Little, Brown, & Co., 1908), 17.

[7] *Dorr Papers.* B.1.f.14. Bar Harbor Historical Society.

[8] *Thomas Wren Ward Papers.* B.3.f.26–27. Massachusetts Historical Society. See also Deborah P. Clifford, *Mine Eyes Have Seen the Glory* (Boston: Atlantic Monthly, 1978), 40–45 and Louise Hall Tharp, *Three Saints and a Sinner* (Boston: Little, Brown & Co., 1934), 72–75, 258.

[9] See Maud Howe Elliott, *Three Generations* (Boston: Little, Brown, & Co., 1923) and *This Was My Newport* (Cambridge: Mythology Corp., 1944); see also *Memories Grave and Gay* (New York: Harper & Brothers, 1918) by her sister, Florence Howe Hall.

[10] See Mark A. De Wolfe Howe, *The Boston Common: Scenes from Four Centuries* (Boston: Houghton Mifflin Co., 1921), 52, 58–59.

[11] Van Wyck Brooks convincingly examines the postwar years' scattering of the younger generation in *New England Indian Summer* (New York: E. P. Dutton & Co., 1940), 184–203.

[12] William's brother, Henry James, remarked that this "companionship was of a family connected with ours through an intermarriage, Gus Barker, as Mrs. S. G. Ward's nephew, being Tom's first cousin as well as ours." Henry James, *Notes of a Son and Brother* (New York: Charles Scribner's Sons, 1914), 130. On the Thayer expedition, *Brazil Through the Eyes of William James. Letters. Diaries, and Drawings, 1865–1866.* Ed. Maria Helena P. T. Machado. Trans. John M. Monteiro. (Cambridge: Harvard University Press, 2006).

[13] *Dorr Papers.* B.1.f.14.

[14] Ronald Story, "Harvard Students, the Boston Elite, and the New England

Preparatory System, 1800–1876," *History of Education Quarterly* 15, #3 (1975), 288.

[15] William Lawrence, *Roger Wolcott* (Boston: Houghton, Mifflin & Co., 1902), 21.

[16] *Dorr Papers.* B.1.f.13. See also "Charles Hazen Dorr," Version 2. Dorr Collection. New England Historic and Genealogical Society.

[17] Robert Grant, *Fourscore: An Autobiography* (Boston: Houghton Mifflin & Co., 1934), 33.

[18] *Dorr Papers.* B.1.f.13.

[19] Laura Richards and Maud H. Elliott, *Julia Ward Howe: 1819–1910* (Boston: Houghton Mifflin & Co., 1916), I, 214, 238. See also *Letters of Henry Wadsworth Longfellow.* Ed. Andrew Hilen (Cambridge: Harvard University Press, 1966), IV. 476.

[20] Mark A. DeWolfe Howe, *Memories of a Hostess: A Chronicle of Eminent Friendships* (Boston: Atlantic Monthly, 1922), 35.

[21] Cleveland Amory, *The Proper Bostonians* (New York: E. P. Dutton, 1947), 107, 129.

[22] Edward F. Payne, *Dickens Days in Boston (*Boston: Houghton Mifflin Co., 1927), 206.

[23] December 27, 1867. Dickens to Georgiana Hogarth. *The Letters of Charles Dickens.* Ed. G. Storey (Oxford: Clarendon Press, 1999), XII, 518.

[24] Payne, *Dickens Days in Boston*, 206, and M. A. DeWolfe Howe, *Memories of a Hostess*, 149–150.

[25] Samuel Eliot Morison, *Three Centuries of Harvard, 1636–1936* (Cambridge: Harvard University Press, 1936), 323.

[26] *The Development of Harvard University Since the Inauguration of President Eliot 1869–1929.* Ed. Samuel Eliot Morison (Cambridge: Harvard University Press, 1930), xixl–lxxviii. See also Morison's "The Harvard Presidency," *New England Quarterly* 31, #4 (1958): 435–436. On Eliot's impact on faculty, see R. A. McCaughey, "The Transformation of Academic American Life: Harvard University 1821–1892," *Perspectives in American History* VIII (1974): 239–332.

[27] *The Letters of Ralph Waldo Emerson*, Ed. Eleanor Tilton (New York: Columbia University Press, 1995), VII, 84.

[28] Ralph Waldo Emerson, *Essays and Lectures* (New York: Penguin Putnam Inc., 1983), 73–92.

[29] See Ronald A. Bosco and Joel Myerson, *Ralph Waldo Emerson: A Bicentennial Exhibition at Houghton Library of the Harvard College Library* (Cambridge: Harvard College Library, 2003), 76.

[30] *John Langdon Sibley's Private Journal, 1846–1882.* June 30, 1870 entry. *Hul.harvard.edu/lib/archives/refshelf/Sibley.htm.*

[31] *Admission Book, 1860–1873.* 63–64. Harvard University Archives. See also *Harvard College. First Report of the Class of 1874 Secretary.* Harvard University Archives.

[32] *Harvard Class Book of 1874.* Dorr entry. Harvard University Archives. See the *Quinquennial Catalogue of Officers and Graduates of Harvard University 1636–1905* (Cambridge: Harvard University Press, 1905) for Dorr and Ward entries.

[33] See Edward S. Martin, "Undergraduate Life at Harvard," *Scribner's Magazine XXI, #5* (1897): 534. On Cambridge itself prior to Eliot's tenure, see Charles Eliot Norton, "Reminiscences of Old Cambridge," *Cambridge Historical Society Publications* I (1905–1906): 11–23.

[34] Robert Grant, "Harvard College in the Seventies," *Scribner's Magazine* 21, #5 (1897): 564.

[35] Harley P. Holden, "Student Records: The Harvard Experience," *The American Archivist* 39, #4 (1976): 461–467.

[36] *Scales of Merit*. 1848–1874. Harvard University Archives. See also Faculty of Arts & Sciences. *Absence Records*. 1870–1874 as well as *Absences from Recitations*. 1870–74. Harvard University Archives.

[37] *Dorr Papers*. B.1.f.2. Dorr stated in his memoirs that his experiences in this region awakened within him the desire to become a landscape painter, a feeling that "stayed with me for years." Little did Dorr know that his father's friend, James Russell Lowell, wrote in August 1871 to his daughter Mabel, of similar emotions as he climbed Green (Cadillac) and Newport (Champlain) mountains. *New Letters of James Russell Lowell*. Ed. M. A. DeWolfe Howe (New York: Harper & Brothers, 1932), 156–157.

[38] Henry James, *Notes of a Son and Brother*, 108.

[39] Amory, *The Proper Bostonians*, Ch. 13. See also *The First Catalogue of the Hasty Pudding Institute of 1770* (Cambridge: Hasty Pudding Club, 1926).

[40] Moses King, *Harvard and its Surroundings*. (Cambridge: Moses King Publishers, 1882), 57. See also *Education, Books and Mortar: Harvard Buildings and their Contribution to the Advancement of Learning* (Cambridge: Harvard University Press, 1949), 72. Considerable insight can be found in the comprehensive academic documentation provided by Dorr's friend, Francis Randall Appleton, *The Appleton Papers*. B4.f.5. The Trustees of Reservations. Archives and Research Center. Sharon, MA.

[41] Charles Eliot Norton, "Francis James Child," *Proceedings of the American Academy of Arts and Sciences* 32, #17 (1897): 333–339. For recent interpretations see Robin Varnum, "Harvard's Francis James Child: the Year of the Rose," *Harvard Library Bulletin* 36 (1988): 291–319; and on his key friendship see, M. A. DeWolfe Howe, "The Scholar-Friends," *Harvard Library Bulletin* 5, #2 & #3 (1951).

[42] O. B. Bunce, "On the Coast of Maine," *Picturesque America*. Ed. William Cullen Bryant (New York: D. Appleton & Co., 1872), Vol. 1, 4–5; see also Sue Rainey, *Creating 'Picturesque America,' Monument to the Natural and Cultural Landscape* (Nashville: Vanderbilt University Press, 1994), 87.

[43] Barry Mackintosh, "The National Park Service: A Brief History," 1999. *www.nps.gov/parkhistory/hisnps/NPSHistory/briefhistory.htm.*

[44] The untitled poem was sent by Lowell to Charles Dorr on March 13, 1869. The original is in the Houghton Library, Harvard University. See also Martin B. Duberman, "Twenty-Seven Poems by James Russell Lowell," *American Literature* 35, #3 (1963): 322–332.

[45] The use of "Esquire" in reference to George Dorr coupled with his brother's legal apprenticeship may have led Judith S. Goldstein to infer that George Dorr "intended to practice law with his brother." Judith S. Goldstein, *Tragedies and Triumphs* (Somesville, ME: Port in a Storm Bookstore, 1992), 11. This term, however, commonly referred to a gentleman. Lacking evidence of legal education, it is unfortunate that her claim was erroneously restated by Dayton Duncan & Ken Burns, *The National Parks: America's Best Idea* (New York: Alfred A. Knopf, 2009).

[46] R. H. Conwell, *History of the Great Fire in Boston: November 9 and 10, 1872*. (Boston: B. B. Russell, 1873), Ch. 4.

[47] Maud Howe Elliott, *Three Generations*. 107–108; see *Dr. Holmes's Boston*. Ed. Caroline Ticknor (Boston: Houghton Mifflin Co., 1915), 69–83.

[48] For historical background on ophthalmological medicine in this era for the symptoms that Dorr described, see R. C. Laughlin, "Glaucoma: a Historical Essay," *Bulletin of the Institute of the History of Medicine* 2, #5 (1934): 141–163; Alvin A. Hubbell, *The Development of Ophthalmology in America 1800–1870* (Chicago: W. T. Kenner & Co., 1908).

[49] Elbridge Gerry Kimball's *Scrapbook of Harvard Undergraduate Life, 1873–1877* in the Harvard University Archives contains an unrivaled portrait of Harvard College student culture.

[50] See George Herbert Palmer, *The Autobiography of a Philosopher* (New York: Greenwood Press reprint, 1968). See also *George Herbert Palmer 1842–1933: Memorial Essays* (Cambridge: Harvard University Press, 1935), 50.

[51] *Dorr Papers.* B.1.f.2.

[52] *Sibley's Private Journal.* June 19, 1874. See the Harvard student publication, *The Magenta* (III. #10. June 19, 1874) for essays on Class Day, 1874. Also Clifford K. Shipton, "John Langdon Sibley, Librarian," *Harvard Library Bulletin* 9, #2 (1955): 236–261.

[53] *Sibley's Private Journal,* June 23, 1874. See also *The Boston Evening Transcript.* June 23–25, 1874.

[54] Walter M. Whitehill, *Boston and the Civil War* (Boston: Boston Athenaeum, 1963), 12. *Harvard Class Book of 1874,* 229. This is a sentence from the earliest surviving handwritten Dorr document.

[55] Benjamin L. Hadley to Robert W. Shankland. March 30, 1949. Acadia National Park. Sawtelle Collections and Research Center (hereafter ANP. SRC.). B.2.f.1.

Chapter Four: THE LONG JOURNEY TO MOUNT DESERT ISLAND

[1] *Dorr Papers.* B.2.f.3. Bar Harbor Historical Society.

[2] According to Cleveland Amory, "Grandfather on the Brain" is a Boston phenomenon dating from the days when the grandfather merchant was the key figure of Boston society and "was entitled to almost godlike respect." *The Proper Bostonians* (New York: E. P. Dutton, 1947), Ch. 3.

[3] *Dorr Papers.* B.1.f.2.

[4] *Dorr Papers.* B.2.f.3.

[5] T. Roosevelt. *The Works of Theodore Roosevelt.* Ed. Hermann Hagedorn (New York: Scribner, 1926), XIII, 563, 565. This syndrome has been recognized by contemporary scholars, one of whom points to Henry Adams as the "paradigm of the Harvard graduate who, because of his aristocratic ideals and vocational incompetence, was relegated to an inactive, ineffectual role in post–Civil War America." Joan D. Hedrick, "Harvard Indifference," *New England Quarterly* 49, #3 (1976): 358.

[6] A family acquaintance, Richard Henry Dana, documented that Mary Dorr upheld her society role in England, reporting that he had "dined with Mrs. Dorr, of Boston, 'very informally' as by invitation. See *Hospitable England During the Seventies* (Boston: Houghton Mifflin, 1921), 241.

[7] On November 2 his father bought a separate 300-square-foot family plot near the Ward lot on Walnut Avenue purchased by George's maternal grandfather. William's remains were re-interred from lot #1151 to lot #4474. Mount Auburn Cemetery Historical Collections, #235, 4474. Cambridge, MA and the *Dorr Papers.* B.1.f.13.

[8] George Howard succeeded his uncle as Earl of Carlisle in 1889. Robin Gibson, "Forthcoming Exhibitions: 'George Howard and his Circle' at Carlisle," *The Burlington Magazine* 110, #789 (1968).

[9] As the result of a 2010 research query from the author, curators at Castle Howard (located in the eastern United Kingdom, fifteen miles north of York) discovered in their archives forty-eight letters spanning the years 1876 to 1906, exchanged between George and Mary Dorr and four Howard family members. These letters have been transcribed and annotated by the author and Howard Castle archivist Anna Louise Mason.

[10] Dorothy Howard Eden, *Rosalind Howard, Countess of Carlisle* (London: Hogarth, 1959), 132.

[11] Castle Howard is familiar to many as the luxurious setting for the televised adaptation of Evelyn Waugh's 1945 novel, *Brideshead Revisited.* See also John Dixon Hunt, *Gardens and the Picturesque* (Cambridge: MIT Press, 1992), 19–48, and Venetia Murray, *Castle Howard* (New York: Viking, 1994).

[12] See G. B. Dorr, "Automatic Writing," *Dorr Papers.* B.1.f.13. This practice later prompted William James to call for experimental inquiry into the phenomenon, providing readers with his extensive notes. *The Proceedings of the American Society for Psychical Research* 1 (1889): 548–564. Dorr's position was that automatic writing was "hard to accept and difficult to discredit."

[13] Mary Dorr to Rosalind Howard, November 10 and 16, 1877. *Dorr Family Correspondence.* J24/7. Castle Howard Archives. See also William H. Hunt, *Pre-Raphaelitism and the Pre-Raphaelite Brotherhood* (London: Macmillan & Co., 1905).

[14] In November 1889, the Howards' eldest daughter, Mary, married Oxford professor Gilbert Murray. In his unfinished autobiography, Murray recollected his first social encounter (1884) with his future mother-in-law, Rosalind Howard. See *Gilbert Murray: An Unfinished Autobiography*. Jean Smith and Arnold Toynbee, eds. (London: George Allen & Unwin, 1960), 87, 100. Similarly, in *Castle Howard,* Murray quotes Rosalind's daughter as describing her mother as having "an eye like Mars, to threaten and command" (New York: Viking, 1994, 189). Current Howard Castle curator Christopher Ridgeway states that even by modern standards Rosalind was a very strong woman.

[15] Duncan Wilson's biography of Murray contends that George Bernard Shaw modeled the bossy fictional character in *Major Barbara* (Lady Britomart) on Rosalind Howard, the aunt of British philosopher Bertrand Russell. *Gilbert Murray 1866–1957* (Oxford: Clarendon Press, 1987), 109–11. The fullest Howard family study is by Virginia Surtees, *The Artist and the Autocrat* (London: Michael Russell, 1988); Charles Robert offers a more pointed portrayal of Rosalind in *The Radical Countess* (Carlisle: Steel Brothers, 1962).

[16] Mary Dorr to Rosalind Howard, October 10, 1877, August 14, 1878, May 26, 1890. *Dorr Family Correspondence*. J24/7.

[17] This estate transfer occurred after Susan Elizabeth Dorr's death in 1889. See also R. S. Jackson and Cornelia Gilder, *Houses of the Berkshires 1870–1930* (New York: Acanthus, 2006), n. 32. For a thorough discussion of the Dorr family residence in Lenox, see Cornelia Brooke Gilder. *Hawthorne's Lenox: The Tanglewood Circle* (Charleston: The History Press, 2008), 59–62.

[18] Mary's correspondence with Rosalind Howard for 1877 and 1878 refers to seven occasions of previously unknown physical interaction (shared accommodations, visits,

etc.) between Julia Ward Howe, her daughter Maud, and Mrs. Dorr.

[19] Olivia R. Agresti's *Giovanni Costa: His Life, Work and Times* (London: Gay and Bird, 1904) refers to Mary Dorr's patronage of Costa (227); similarly, her pursuit of the Burne-Jones watercolor titled "Hope" is discussed by W. G. Constable's "'Hope' by Edward Burne-Jones" in the *Bulletin of the [Boston] Museum of Fine Arts* 39 (1941), 12–14. Both artists received acclaim in the early years of the Grosvenor Gallery: see "The Grosvenor Gallery," *The Nation,* #673 (May 23, 1878): 338–339.

[20] *Dorr Papers.* B.1.f.1

[21] *Dorr Papers.* B.1.f.1.

[22] Nothing in Dorr's memoirs suggests that he and Linda Wadsworth took part in a romantic or amorous relationship; yet this sole report of his infatuation and its mythological echoes has fueled speculative interpretations. Typical is Sargent F. Collier's claim that Dorr "failed in the single romance of his life." *The Triumph of George B. Dorr: Father of Acadia National Park* (Bar Harbor: S. F. Collier, 1964), 13.

[23] Mary Dorr to Rosalind Howard, October 10, 1877. *Dorr Family Correspondence.* J24/7.

[24] George Dorr to Rosalind Howard, November 7, 1877. *Dorr Family Correspondence.* J24/7.

[25] Dorr to Arno Cammerer, May 1939. ANP. SRC. B. 4.f.11.

[26] *Dorr Papers.* B.2.f.3.

[27] Mary Dorr to Rosalind Howard, August 14, 1878. *Dorr Family Correspondence.* J24/7.

[28] Mary Dorr to Rosalind Howard, March 29, 1879. *Dorr Family Correspondence.* J24/7.

[29] See Samuel Eliot Morison's celebrated essay on "rusticators" in his *Story of Mount Desert Island* (Boston: Little, Brown & Co., 1960), Ch. 8.

[30] Because of Mary Dorr's early engagement to the brother of Julia Ward—the mother of the wife of Henry Richards—the Richards family regarded Mary Dorr as a member of their extended family. One stylistic rendering by A. C. Oakey that the Dorrs considered was published in *Building a Home* (New York: D. Appleton & Co., 1881), 57–67; Oakey added a half-page of notes about the "House on Mount Desert, ME," in *American Architect and Building News* 2, #1 (1877). Tom St. Germain's *Acadia Hiking Guide* (Bar Harbor: Parkman, 2000), 10th ed., misidentifies the Oakey drawing of C. F.[sic] Dorr's home as Oldfarm, when Henry Richards is the architect of record.

[31] An Oldfarm inventory is available at the Sawtelle Research Center. B.3.f.10.

[32] Tudor Richards, the late grandson of Henry Richards, interview with the author, December 12, 2005. The earliest map of what would become Oldfarm was discovered by the author in 2011. The August 15, 1877 map of the Charles Hazen Dorr property is by architect—and family friend—E. W. Bowditch. Douglas Chapman Archive. Map Room. A. H. Lynam File. Bar Harbor, ME.

[33] *Ninety Years On, 1848–1940* (Augusta: Kennebec Journal Press, 1940), 315.

[34] Samuel A. Eliot, "The Romance of Mount Desert," *New England Magazine* 20, #6 (1899): 697.

[35] One additional trip to Europe was undertaken according to a one-page travel list: "1882—Trip to Central Italy & Sicily." *The Dorr Collection.* New England Historic Genealogical Society. Boston.

[36] Mary Dorr to Rosalind Howard, May 26, 1890. *Dorr Family Papers.* J24/7. Castle Howard Archives.

[37] Edward L. Rand and John H. Redfield, *Flora of Mount Desert Island, Maine*

(Cambridge: John Wilson and Son, 1894).

[38] Henry W. Foote II, "A Desert Place Apart: A Sermon in Memory of Samuel Atkins Eliot (1862–1950), A Leader of this Union Church," *Bar Harbor Times,* July 12, 1956. Foote was a clergyman at Harvard Divinity School, a hymnologist of renown, and a cousin of Samuel Atkins Eliot II.

[39] Henry James, *Charles W. Eliot: President of Harvard University, 1869–1909* (Boston: Houghton Mifflin Co, 1930), V.1, 344.

[40] Charles W. Eliot II, "Eliots and Asticou Foreside, Northeast Harbor: Notes." Access to this document resulted from an interview with landscape architect Patrick Chassé, Mount Desert, ME. October 2004.

[41] John M. Bryan, *Maine Cottages: Fred L. Savage and the Architecture of Mount Desert* (New York: Princeton Architectural Press, 2005), 39. There was only one year, 1887, when the family journeyed to Europe and did not vacation in Northeast Harbor.

[42] Charles Eliot, *Charles Eliot Landscape Architect.* (Amherst: University of Massachusetts, 1999), 26. The Mount Desert Island Historical Society Archives and the Gray Herbarium Library at Harvard University contain Champlain Society logbooks and annual reports.

[43] The online *Maine Memory Network* includes the Champlain Club Camp and Log [Books], including photographs and transcriptions. *www.mainememory.net.* On Rand's three forms of protection for the scenery of Mount Desert, see the *First Annual Report of the Champlain Society, 1880.* 56–58. *Papers of Edward Lothrup Rand.* B. AK 5.5–. Archives. Gray Herbarium Library. Harvard University Libraries.

Chapter Five: RESTLESS INDECISION

[1] The United States Census documents four Oldfarm inhabitants: Charles, Mary, George, and a 35-year-old servant and housekeeper, Mary O'Brien. Two curious entries concern the occupation of father and son. Charles is listed as a farmer, though "gentleman farmer" better reflects his role on the estate. Six years after graduating from Harvard, George is listed as a student.

[2] B. Hadley to Newton Drury, September 9, 1944. National Archives and Records Administration. RG79.CCF 1933–049/ Acadia/B.794.

[3] A. M. Tozzer, "Charles Pickering Bowditch," *American Anthropologist* 23 (1921): 353–357.

[4] "Philosophy," *Dorr Papers.* B.1.f.14. Bar Harbor Historical Society.

[5] Cornelia to Charles Bowditch, August 19, 1888. *Charles P. Bowditch Family Papers.* B.8.f.4. Massachusetts Historical Society.

[6] Henry Lane Eno, "The Birds of Old Farm: an Intimate Study of a Bird Sanctuary," *Sieur de Monts Publications* 21 (1919); compare with Eno's "The Seacoast National Park in Maine," *Sieur de Monts Publications* 3 (1916).

[7] The definitive source is Bruce Kuklick's *The Rise of American Philosophy, Cambridge, Massachusetts 1860–1930* (New Haven: Yale University Press, 1977).

[8] W. James to H. James, July 11, 1887, and August 24, 1888. *Correspondence of William James.* III. Eds. Ignas K. Skrupskelis and Elizabeth M. Beadsley. (Charlottesville: University of Virginia Press, 1994).

[9] *Dorr Papers.* B.2.f.3.

[10] R. W. B. Lewis, *Edith Wharton: A Biography* (New York: Harper & Row, 1975), 79,

compare with 49. On "Trix," the most reliable source is Judith B. Tankard, *Beatrix Farrand: Private Gardens, Public Landscapes* (New York: Monacelli Press, 2009), esp. 9–24.

[11] Beatrix Farrand, *The Bulletins of Reef Point Gardens* (Bar Harbor: Island Foundation, 1997), xiv.

[12] See Michael Holleran, *Boston's 'Changeful Times': Origins of Preservation & Planning in America* (Baltimore: Johns Hopkins University Press, 1998), Chapters 1–2.

[13] Mary Jane Wilson, "Benjamin Bussey, Woodland Hill, and the Creation of the Arnold Arboretum," *Arnoldia* 64, #1 (2006): 2–9.

[14] Richard B. Woodward, "Carving Green out of Urban Gray," *The New York Times*, January 5, 1997. H38.

[15] Quoted by Witold Rybczynski, *A Clearing in the Distance: Frederick Law Olmsted and America in the 19th Century* (New York: Simon & Schuster, 1999), 354.

[16] In 2007 I discovered in the attic of The Great House at the Crane Estate, Ipswich, MA (owned by The Trustees of Reservations), the 152-page Charles Eliot scrapbook misfiled with the *Papers of Charles W. Eliot II.* Its existence was known at that time to only one family member, Lawrence Eliot of Ipswich, the son of Charles W. Eliot II, whom I interviewed July 12, 2007. The scrapbook contains the invitations, minutes, and news clippings for the last two decades of the nineteenth century. It is conserved by The Trustees; it is held in their Archives and Research Center, Sharon, MA.

[17] Peter Dow Bachelder's *Steam to the Summit: The Green Mountain Railway* (Ellsworth: Breakwater Press, 2005) is the well-researched standard text on the role of the cog railway as an effort to capitalize on the island tourist business.

[18] See Bill Horner, M.D., "Luere B. Deasy, A Maine Man," *Chebacco* XI (2010): 6–31.

[19] Bar Harbor Village Improvements Association. *Minutes.* September 20, 1888. By 1891, the Charter of the BHVIA referred more expansively to "public improvements" extended to "other parts of Mount Desert Island," even as village improvement societies were being established in other island villages. For a broader view, George E. Waring, "Village Improvement Societies," *Scribner's Monthly* 14 (May 1877): 97–106; B. G. Northrop, "The Work of Village Improvement Societies," *The Forum* (March 1895): 95–105.

[20] Stephen J. Hornsby, "The Gilded Age and the Making of Bar Harbor," *Geographical Review* 83 (1981): 17–32.

[21] In 1893 Dorr formed the BHVIA Bicycle Path Committee to further his interest in pleasure-cycling routes from Bar Harbor to scenic locations. For the fullest account of BHVIA path development, see Margaret Coffin Brown, *Pathmakers: Cultural Landscape Report for the Historic Hiking Trail System of Mount Desert Island* (Boston: National Park Service and Olmsted Center for Landscape Preservation, 2006), 42–57.

[22] Cleveland Amory, *The Last Resorts* (New York: Harper & Brothers, 1953), 283; J. Royce to Mary Dorr, September 21, 1892. *The Papers of Josiah Royce.* HUG 1755.12. f1. This classification scheme was modified in 2009; all references are to the pre-2009 arrangement. Harvard University Archives.

[23] John Glendenning, *The Life and Thought of Josiah Royce.* Rev. ed. (Nashville: Vanderbilt University Press, 1999), 144.

[24] "Philosophy," *Dorr Papers.* B.1.f.14.

[25] Royce to George Dorr, May 2, 1891. *The Papers of Josiah Royce.* HUG 1755.12.f1.

[26] J. Royce, *The Spirit of Modern Philosophy: An Essay in the Form of Lectures*

(Boston: Houghton Mifflin, 1892). To my knowledge, this is the first English-language work by a male American philosopher dedicated to a woman to whom the author was not related.

[27] J. E. Creighton, *Philosophical Review* 1 (1892).

[28] R. Grant, *Fourscore: An Autobiography* (Boston: Houghton Mifflin Co., 1934), 281.

[29] Grant, 281–282.

[30] Robert L. Moore, *In Search of White Crows* (New York: Oxford University Press, 1977), 143–148; Gay W. Allen, *William James: A Biography (New York: Viking Press, 1967),* 282–283. The American Society for Psychical Research published his initial study of Mrs. Piper, a work read by Society members Mary and George Dorr. See also William James, *Memories and Studies* (New York: Longmans, Green, & Co., 1912), 173–206.

[31] M. A. DeWolfe Howe, *Barrett Wendell and his Letters (*Boston: Atlantic Monthly, 1924), 310.

[32] *Dorr Papers.* B.1.f.13.

[33] Henry James, *The Bostonians* (New York: Random House,1956), xvi.

[34] See E. H. Wilson's encomium in the *Harvard Graduates' Magazine* 35 (1927): 605–615.

[35] *Graduate School of Arts and Sciences. Admission Books.1886–1911.* B.1. Harvard University Archives.

[36] *Student Records of the Graduate Department: 1887–1892.* 117; *Yearly Returns. 1889–90; Library Charging Records. 1887–1889.* Harvard University Archives.

[37] Richard S. Jackson and Cornelia Brooks Gilder, *Houses of the Berkshires 1870–1930* (New York: Acanthus Press, 2006), 48.

[38] January 27, 1889. G. Dorr to Louise Endicott. *Endicott Family Papers.* B.29.f.4. Massachusetts Historical Society.

[39] For a full description of the Lenox wedding and the guests, see *The Philadelphia Inquirer* 121, issue 83, October 4, 1889.

[40] Walter Muir Whitehill, *William Crowninshield Endicott* (Salem: Peabody Museum, 1938).

[41] Oliver Wendell Holmes, *The Poetical Works: Poems from Over the Teacups* (Boston: Houghton Mifflin, 1892). The title, in French, translates as "The House of Gold."

Chapter Six: BETWEEN BOSTON AND MOUNT DESERT ISLAND

[1] "The Waverly Oaks," *Garden and Forest 3* (February 19, 1890): 85–86.

[2] "The Coast of Maine," *Garden and Forest* 3 (February 19, 1890): 86–87. Eliot traveled to Germany in 1885–86 and discovered at the estate of Prince Ludwig Heinrich Hermann von Pückler a model for reforming landscape architecture in America. See the ten articles in "Pückler and America." Ed. Sonja Duempelmann. *Bulletin of the German Historical Institute.* Supp. #4 (2007).

[3] "Waverly Oaks," *Garden and Forest* 3 (March 5, 1890): 117–118. These articles are gathered in President Charles W. Eliot's 1902 homage to his son, *Charles Eliot: Landscape Architect.* (Amherst: University of Massachusetts Press/Library of American Landscape History, 1999).

[4] *Charles Eliot: Landscape Architect.* Preface by Robin Karson: v; for a revealing assessment of Eliot's life, see Keith N. Morgan's Introduction and Norman T. Newton's

Design on the Land: The Development of Landscape Architecture (Cambridge: Harvard University Press, 1971), Ch. 22.

[5] "The Forgotten Millions: A Study of the Common American Mode of Life," *The Century Magazine,* 40 (1890): 556–564; nine years later Eliot published a detailed profile of one of those forgotten millions, *John Gilley, Maine Farmer and Fisherman* (Boston: Houghton Mifflin, 1899). On a more personal level, he stated "Were it not for the summers at Mount Desert, I would hardly have more time for life reflection and real living than an operator in a cotton mill." Edward Cotton, *The Life of Charles W. Eliot* (Boston: Small, Maynard & Co., 1926), 372.

[6] Richard W. Judd, "Reshaping Maine's Landscape: Rural Culture, Tourism, and Conservation, 1890–1929," *Journal of Forest History* 32, #4 (1988): 183. See also Judd's "Grass-Roots Conservation in Eastern Coastal Maine: Monopoly and the Moral Economy of Weir Fishing, 1893–1911," *Environmental Review* 12, #2 (1988): 80–103.

[7] Judd, "Reshaping Maine's Landscape," 184. See also Judd's *Common Lands, Common People: The Origins of Conservation in Northern New England* (Cambridge: Harvard University Press, 1997).

[8] Mary Dorr to Rosalind Howard, May 26, 1890. *Dorr Family Correspondence.* J24/7. Castle Howard Archives. York, UK.

[9] George B. Dorr, *Harvard Class Reports. 1894. Harvard Class of 1872.* Harvard University Archives.

[10] Edmund Swinglehurst, *Cook's Tours: The Story of Popular Travel* (Poole: Blandford Press, 1982), 97; W. Fraser Rae, *The Business of Travel* (London: Thomas Cook and Son, 1891), 244–245.

[11] Peirs Brendon, *Thomas Cook: 150 Years of Popular Tourism* (London: Secker & Warburg, 1991), Ch. 7, 12.

[12] Janne Ahtola, "Thomas Cook & Son and the Egyptian Season." *https://kansalliskirjasto.finna.fi/Record/arto.512541*

[13] Mary Dorr to Samuel G. Ward, undated letter missing the first page. *Thomas Wren Ward Papers.* B.3.f.28. Massachusetts Historical Society. Boston.

[14] The landscapes and seascapes—"beautiful beyond words"—that Mary painted en route have not survived.

[15] T. W. Higginson, *Old Cambridge* (New York: Macmillan Co., 1899), 147–196. For a fuller account, see Mary C. Crawford. "The Higginson Family," *Famous Families of Massachusetts* (Boston: Little, Brown, & Co., 1930), I, 254–279.

[16] M.G. Ward to S. G. Ward, June 28, 1892. *Ward-Perkins Papers.* University of California, Santa Barbara.

[17] J. Royce to W. James, October 17, 1892. *The Papers of Josiah Royce.* HUG 1755.12.f.1. Harvard University Archives. Royce's extensive correspondence with Mary G. Dorr spanned the years 1889–1899.

[18] "Philosophy," *Dorr Papers.* B.1.f.14. Bar Harbor Historical Society.

[19] November 19, 1938. *Dorr Papers.* B1.f.14. See the Mount Auburn Cemetery Historical Collections, #4474, for additional details on the burial. Mary Ward and family nurse Elizabeth Hind were also interred on this plot; in 1945 a gravestone for George Bucknam Dorr was placed there following his cremation.

[20] "Mary Ward Dorr," *Yellow House Papers. The Laura E. Richards Collection.* Gardiner Library Association and Maine Historical Society. RG. 9B.f.11.

[21] "Charles Hazen Dorr," Ver. 2. *Dorr Collection.* New England Historic and Genealogical Society.

[22] Massachusetts Judicial Court Archives. *Probate Record Book.* Vol. 799, 8–13.

[23] For background on Robert Grant, see William Phillips, "Robert Grant, 1852–1940," *The Saturday Club: A Century Completed 1920–1956.* Eds. E. W. Forbes and John H. Finley Jr. (Boston: Houghton Mifflin Co., 1958), 73–80.

[24] January 5, 2006. Elizabeth Bouvier email to Ronald Epp. Ms. Bouvier is head archivist for the Massachusetts Supreme Court; see also Massachusetts Supreme Judicial Court Archives. Docket #92160. April 12, 1900. Using an inflation calculator, the Charles Dorr estate in 2015 would be worth more than a half million dollars.

[25] Mary Dorr to Rosalind Howard, February 12, 1893. *Dorr Family Correspondence.* J24/7. Castle Howard Archives.

[26] Reid Badger, *The Great American Fair.* (Chicago: Nelson Hall, 1999), 21; for a photographic history of the fair, see Norman Bolotin and Christine Laing, *The World's Columbian Exposition* (Urbana: University of Illinois Press, 2002). See also Erik Larson, *The Devil in the White City* (New York: Crown Publishers, 2003).

[27] John E. Haar and Peter E. Johnson, *The Rockefeller Century* (New York: Charles Scribner's Sons 1988), 32–33.

[28] Ibid., 33.

[29] I am indebted to the Beatrix Farrand Society at Garland Farm (Bar Harbor) for assistance. Archivist Martha Harmon and landscape historian Judith B. Tankard provided photocopies from Farrand's "The Book of Gardening, 1893–1895," *The Beatrix Jones Farrand Collection, 1866–1959.* Environmental Design Archives, University of California, Berkeley. Tankard's *Beatrix Farrand: Private Gardens, Public Landscapes* (New York: Monacelli Press, 2009) provides an impressive number of new insights into the personal and professional life of her subject.

[30] *Harvard Class of 1874. Report of 1894.* Harvard University Archives.

[31] This view was suggested by Eugene Taylor, lecturer in psychiatry, Harvard Medical School. My interview with him took place at the Harvard Faculty Club. August 22, 2007; see also Taylor's "William James and Depth Psychology," *The Varieties of Religious Experience: Centenary Essays.* Ed. Michel Ferrari (Charlottesville: Imprint Academic, 2002), 11–36.

[32] *Reports of the Visiting Committees of the Board of Overseers of Harvard College. Academical Series II.* Harvard University Archives; visiting committee reports also appear occasionally in the *Harvard Graduates' Magazine.*

Chapter Seven: LANDSCAPE AS OUR COMMON HERITAGE

[1] Van Wyck Brooks, *New England, Indian Summer, 1865–1915* (New York: Dutton & Co., 1944), 409.

[2] G. B. Dorr, "Man and Nature," *Sieur de Monts Publications* 7 (1916).

[3] Dorr reflects here the spirit of Henry David Thoreau. See John Hanson Mitchell, *Walking Towards Concord* (Reading, MA: Addison-Wesley Publishing Co., 1995), 4.

[4] Margie Coffin Brown and Christian Barter, "Acadia Style: Using Historic Precedents to Rehabilitate Hiking Trails," *APT Bulletin: Journal of Preservation Technology* 35, #2–3 (2004): 81–82. See also Brown's *Pathmakers: Cultural Landscape Report for the Historic Hiking Trail System of Mount Desert Island,*

I. (Brookline, MA: National Park Service and Olmsted Center for Landscape Preservation, 2006)

[5] The most thorough biographical information on these path pioneers will be found in *Trails of History: the Story of Mount Desert Island's Paths from Norumbega to Acadia* (Bar Harbor, ME: Parkman Publications, 1993) by Tom St. Germain and Jay Saunders. Village-by-village contextual information is most thoroughly reported by Brown, *Pathmakers,* I, 42–97. The Chapman Archive in Bar Harbor contains the most substantial collection of historic maps developed by Dorr, frequently developed collaboratively with John D. Rockefeller Jr.

[6] G. B. Dorr, "Garden Approaches to the National Monument," *Sieur de Monts Publications* XVII (1916). See also Ronald H. Epp, "George Dorr's Vision for Garden Approaches to Acadia National Park," *Chebacco: The Magazine of The Mount Desert Island Historical Society* VI (2004): 55–63.

[7] Clara Martin, *Mount Desert on the Coast of Maine,* 6th ed. (Portland, ME: Loring, Short & Harmon, 1885), 47; see also botanist M. L. Fernald's description of the consequences of forest removal in "An Acadian Plant Sanctuary," *Sieur de Monts Publications* V (1916).

[8] William Howarth, *Thoreau: A Literary Guide to the Mountains of New England* (Boston: Beacon Press, 2001), 4.

[9] Thomas W. Higginson, "Footpaths," *The Atlantic Monthly* 26, #157 (1870): 513–521.

[10] Higginson, "Footpaths," 521.

[11] St. Germain and Saunders, *Trails of History*, 9–11; Margaret Coffin Brown, *Pathmakers.* 58 ff. One of the fullest contemporary studies of our relationships with a particular place is *The Experience of Place* by Tony Hiss (New York: Alfred A. Knopf, 1990).

[12] Steve Perrin's *Acadia: The Soul of a National Park* (Bar Harbor: Earthling Press, 1998) provides the best reading of the trail experiences akin to what Dorr encountered a century earlier.

[13] Michael Holleran, *Boston's 'Changeful Times': Origins of Preservation and Planning in America* (Baltimore: Johns Hopkins University Press, 1998), Ch. 5.

[14] September 26, 1894. *The Correspondence of William James.* William James, Ignas K. Skrupskelis, E. M. Berkeley, Henry James. (Charlottesville: University of Virginia Press, 1992), VII, 548.

[15] *William James: Selected Unpublished Correspondence 1885–1910.* Ed. F. J. D. Scott. (Columbus: Ohio State University Press, 1986), 123. The James family frequently spent summers taking "mountain tramps" in the White Mountains.

[16] July 14, 1895. *Ward-Perkins Papers.* B. 6 and 7. University of California, Santa Barbara; see also Donald Fitch, "The Ward-Perkins Papers," *Soundings* 16 (1985): 52–60.

[17] G. W. Helfrich and Gladys O'Neil, *Lost Bar Harbor* (Camden, ME: DownEast Books, 1982).

[18] John M. Bryan, *Maine Cottages: Fred L. Savage and the Architecture of Mount Desert* (New York: Princeton Architectural Press, 2005); for deep historical context, see Jaylene Roths, "Fred Savage, the Cottage Builder," *The History Journal: Mount Desert Island Historical Society* 2 (1999): 39–56.

[19] Cleveland Amory, *The Last Resorts* (New York: Harper & Brothers, 1953), 272.

[20] *To Be Young Was Very Heaven* (Boston: Houghton Mifflin Co., 1967), 108.

[21] *Bar Harbor Village Improvement Association Minutes.* July 1895. Bar Harbor Historical Society.

[22] G. B. Dorr, "The Harden Farm Road in its Course around the Meadow," undated typescript. ANP. SRC. B.3.f.6. Regarding the origins of the national park concept, Dorr recounts in a March 4, 1936 draft memorandum for the Bar Harbor Town Meeting that the Great Meadow project was undertaken "years before there was any thought of the national park." Instead, the interest was in path development and preservation. Douglas Chapman Archive. File 555. Bar Harbor.

[23] Amory, *The Last Resorts*, 322.

[24] ANP. SRC. B.1.f.16; I am grateful to Maine rail historian Paul Moccia for referencing official rail and navigation guides that Dorr would have consulted in 1895. Email March 16, 2008.

[25] Henry David Thoreau, *The Maine Woods.* Ed. J. J. Moldenhauer. (Princeton: Princeton University Press, 1972).

[26] G. B. Dorr. October 15, 1895 [Moosehead Lake]. ANP. SRC. B.1.f.16, 3.

[27] Samuel G. Ward, *Ward Family Papers* (New York: Riverside Press, 1900), 117.

[28] January 13, 1895. *The Correspondence of William James.* III, 11.

[29] G. B. Dorr, "The Mount Desert Nurseries." ANP. SRC. B.3.f.9.

[30] "Employment for Many," *Bangor Daily Whig and Courier*, December 11, 1899. A notice of incorporation appeared earlier in *The National Nurseryman* 6–7 (1898–1899), 65, reporting that G. B. Dorr was president of the nursery and Mary Gray Dorr was its treasurer.

[31] October 23, 1898. *Papers of Josiah Royce.* HUG 1755.12.f.1. Harvard University Archives.

[32] *Report of the Visiting Committees of the Board of Overseers.* Academical Series II, 1874–1909. Harvard University Archives.

[33] Bliss Perry, *And Gladly Teach: Reminiscences* (Boston: Houghton Mifflin, 1929), 223; H. Münsterberg, "Philosophy at Harvard," *Harvard Graduates' Magazine* 9 (1901): 474–483. For background, see Bruce Kuklick, *The Rise of American Philosophy: Cambridge, Massachusetts, 1860–1930* (New Haven: Yale University Press, 1977), 127–401.

[34] Gordon Abbott Jr., *Saving Special Places: A Centennial History of The Trustees of Reservations: Pioneer of the Land Trust Movement* (Ipswich, MA: Ipswich Press, 1993), 21–25. See also Norman Newton, *Design on the Lands: The Development of Landscape Architecture* (Cambridge, MA: Harvard University Press, 1971), 318–336; and Judith B. Tankard, "Charles Eliot: Education of a landscape Architect," unpublished manuscript, 1987. Loeb Library, Harvard University.

[35] Henry James, *Charles W. Eliot: President of Harvard University, 1869–1909* (Boston: Houghton, Mifflin Co., 1930), II, 91–92.

[36] "Sieur de Monts National Monument: Addresses upon its Opening." *Sieur de Monts Publications* II (1916): 13–14; see the trustee statement on Eliot's death in the *Records of the Standing Committee of The Trustees of Public Reservations.* #42. March 26, 1897. Trustees of Reservations. Archives and Research Center. Sharon, MA.

[37] Charles W. Eliot, *Charles Eliot: Landscape Architect.* (Amherst: University of Massachusetts Press and Library of American Landscape History 1999). See especially Keith N. Morgan's Introduction.

Chapter Eight: FIN DE SIÈCLE

[1] Samuel Eliot Morison. *One Boy's Boston: 1887–1901* (Boston: Houghton Mifflin, 1962), 79–80.

[2] Richard Overy, "Heralds of Modernity: Cars and Planes from Invention to Necessity," *Fin de Siècle and its Legacy*. Eds. Mikulas Teich and Roy Porter (Cambridge: University Press, 1990), 54–79.

[3] Richard W. Judd, "Reshaping Maine's Landscape: Rural Culture, Tourism, and Conservation, 1890–1929," *Journal of Forest History* 32, #4 (1988): 180–190.

[4] Judd, "Reshaping Maine's Landscape," note 23.

[5] Samuel Gray Ward, *Ward Family Papers* (New York: Merrymount Press, 1900), Preface, 70.

[6] September 23, November 19, and December 3 1893. *Thomas Wren Ward Papers*. B.3.f.28. Massachusetts Historical Society. Boston.

[7] David Baldwin, *Puritan Aristocrat in the Age of Emerson: A Study of Samuel Gray Ward* (Philadelphia: University of Pennsylvania dissertation, 1961), 296.

[8] S. G. Ward. *Ward Family Papers*. This study made use of the Charles Eliot Norton copy at Harvard University.

[9] Emerson—who had idealized friendship in his famous 1841 essay—revealed in his letters to Ward why he valued "the blessings" of *imperfect* friendships. Charles Eliot Norton, *Letters from Ralph Waldo Emerson to a Friend* (Boston: Houghton, Mifflin & Co., 1899); see Sara Norton and M. A. DeWolfe Howe, *The Letters of Charles Eliot Norton* (Boston: Houghton, Mifflin & Co., 1932).

[10] November 4, 1900. *Thomas Wren Ward Papers*. B.3 f.28. Massachusetts Historical Society. See also Mount Auburn Cemetery Historical Collections, #235. Cambridge.

[11] Together, the two family histories cover the period 1762 to 1899, providing twentieth-century Ward descendants with a history of the challenges faced by four generations.

[12] Philip Ziegler. *The Sixth Great Power: A History of One of the Greatest Banking Families, the House of Barings, 1762*–1929 (New York: Alfred A. Knopf, 1988). Without equal is the scholarship of Ralph W. Hidy, especially *The House of Barings in American Trade and Finance: English Merchant Bankers at Work, 1763–1861* (Cambridge: Harvard University Press, 1949).

[13] *Ward Family Papers*. 69.

[14] See the *Dorr Collection*, New England Historic Genealogical Society. Boston. Therein is the largest repository of George Bucknam Dorr family memorabilia.

[15] *Dorr Papers*. B.2.f.3. Bar Harbor Historical Society. Bar Harbor. See also January 18, 1943 typescript by G. B. Dorr on the House of Barings and his Uncle Sam's role in the destruction of "the full commercial history of the period." See also *Thomas Wren Ward Papers*. B.8.f.4.

[16] *Thomas Wren Ward Papers*. B. 9–13.

[17] M. A. DeWolfe Howe, *John Jay Chapman and his Letters* (Boston: Houghton Mifflin Co., 1937), 195–196.

[18] Richard Jackson and Cornelia Brooke Gilder, *Houses of the Berkshires 1870–1930* (New York: Acanthus Press, 2006), 203–210; Cornelia Brooke Gilder, *Hawthorne's Lenox: The Tanglewood Circle* (Charlotte: The History Press, 2008), 59–63.

[19] Edith quoted in Millicent Bell's Edith Wharton and Henry James (New York: Braziller, 1965), 78. See Ronald H. Epp, "Wild Gardens and Pathways at The Mount: George B. Dorr and the Mount Desert Influence," *Edith Wharton and the American Garden* (Lenox: The Mount Press, 2009), 81.

[20] December 21, 1901. *Biltmore Guest Book.* Biltmore Company Archives. Asheville, NC.

[21] John M. Bryan, *Biltmore Estate: The Most Distinguished Private Place* (New York: Rizzoli, 1994). Ch. 1.

[22] *Letters of Sarah Wyman Whitman* (Cambridge: Riverside Press, 1907); on Wyman's character, see Richard C. Cabot's obituary address in *Sarah Whitman* (Boston: Marymount Press, 1904).

[23] *1901 Diary.* Louisa Endicott. *Endicott Family Papers.* B.30.f.7. Massachusetts Historical Society.

[24] Mount Auburn Cemetery Historical Collections, #4474.

[25] *The Yellow House Papers. The Laura E. Richards Collection.* Gardiner Library Association and Maine Historical Society. RG.9. B.f.11. No one is more knowledgeable about the Richards Collection than its former curator, Danny D. Smith, who described the sketch as a "...caricature [for] there is no depth of analysis. These completely unguarded comments are merely a summation of the ill will most of the members of Boston's elite social circles must have recounted among themselves." Smith letter to R. H. Epp, July 26, 2005.

[26] Regarding Mary's marriage and the impact on her sons, Laura Richards reports an incident when her father, the architect Henry Richards, was overseeing Oldfarm construction. To "the long suffering and patient Charles Dorr, Mrs. Dorr had given directions about setting out certain plants...then gone off and left directions with her husband.... [On her return she] attacked Charles fiercely.... Finally, after rating him soundly, she said, 'I thought you had some sense!' 'I had,' replied Charles Dorr, 'before I married you.'" *The Yellow House Papers.* RG.9. B.f.11.

[27] October 23–25, 1901. Julia Ward Howe. "Journal." *The Yellow House Papers.*

[28] Ibid.

[29] November 5, 1901. *The Letters of Charles Eliot Norton,* Vol. 2, 315.

[30] Record 118768, *Probate Record Book.* Vol. 799, 8–13. Massachusetts Supreme Judicial Court Archives. Boston. See also the abstract filed May 28, 1902. Hancock County Registry of Deeds. f.377–167. If her son predeceased her, the trustees administered charitable trusts, recognizing Mary's wish that trust income be used as a "helpful influence in the life of the city of Boston, aiding where the need shall seem greatest and the opportunity best."

[31] A penciled "1901 Inventory & Valuation" for G. B. Dorr's holdings offers insight into Dorr's wealth. It appears from this list of twenty-nine holdings, that Dorr had assets of $68,380. An *undated* Mount Desert Nurseries inventory lists assets on the 12.5-acre property at $33,985. Applying an inflation calculator reveals that these two assets would amount to nearly $3,000,000 by 2015. The Douglas B. Chapman Archive. Map Room. A. H. Lynam file. Bar Harbor, ME.

[32] December 16 and 17, 1901, Julia Ward Howe. "Journal." *The Yellow House Papers.*

[33] Donald Fitch, "The Ward-Perkins Papers," *Soundings* 16 (1985): 19

Chapter Nine: THE BIRTH OF THE TRUSTEES

[1] *An Historical Sketch and a Record of the Holdings of the Hancock County Trustees of Public Reservations* (Bar Harbor: 1939).

[2] Robin Karson's preface to Charles W. Eliot's *Charles Eliot: Landscape Architect* (Amherst: University of Massachusetts Press, 1999), v.

[3] Judith S. Goldstein's *Tragedies and Triumphs* (Somesville, ME: Port in a Storm Bookstore, 1992) superbly develops this theme, which is expanded in her *Majestic Mount Desert* (Somesville: Somes Pond Press, 1996) and *Majestic Mount Desert II: Collected Essays* (Somesville: Somes Pond Center, 2014).

[4] I am indebted to Mount Desert Island surgeon William Horner for the interview he granted me on June 25, 2009 about Luere Deasy, his great-grandfather. Additional details in "Luere B. Deasy: A Maine Man," *Chebacco* XI (2010): 6–31.

[5] HCTPR file. Douglas B. Chapman Archive. Bar Harbor, ME

[6] Horace Albright, *Reminiscences of Horace M. Albright* (New York: Columbia University Oral Research Office, 1960), 99. The definitive work on Theodore Roosevelt's conservation efforts is Douglas Brinkley's *The Wilderness Warrior: Theodore Roosevelt and the Crusade for America* (New York: HarperCollins, 2009).

[7] C. W. Eliot to L. B. Deasy, November 28, 1902. The State Incorporation was approved by the HCTPR on March 28, 1903. HCTPR file. Douglas B. Chapman Archive.

[8] G. R. Stebbins, "Random Notes on the Early History and Development as a Summer Resort of Mount Desert and Particularly Seal Harbor." Typescript. 1938. Anne Funderburk Collection. Seal Harbor, ME.

[9] Sargent F. Collier, *The Triumph of George B. Dorr* (Bar Harbor: S. F. Collier, 1964), 14.

[10] Charles W. Eliot, *The Right Development of Mount Desert* (privately printed, 1904).

[11] William H. Wilson, *The City Beautiful Movement* (Baltimore: Johns Hopkins University Press, 1989), 10.

[12] Eliot, *Right Development,* 12.

[13] Charles W. Eliot, "The Need of Conserving the Beauty and Freedom of Nature in Modern Life," *The National Geographic Magazine* 26 (1914): 67.

[14] Bill Horner, "From Horses to Horsepower: Mount Desert Island's Ten-Year War for the Automobile," *Chebacco* XIV (2013): 86–106. Also Richard A. Savage. "The Bar Harbor Auto War," *Down East* (August 1975): 66 ff.

[15] This reform movement was reflected first in the 1893 Columbian Exposition. The city should not be the paramount symbol of economic development and industrialization; instead, legislative statutes should be reconfigured so that urban landscapes inspire and bring to fruition civic virtue and the opportunity (paraphrasing Frederick Law Olmsted) to see, hear, smell, and feel nothing of the bustle and jar of the streets. See "The City Beautiful Movement," *http://xroads.virginia.edu/~cap/citybeautiful/city.html*

[16] Bainbridge Bunting, *Harvard: An Architectural History* (Cambridge: Harvard University Press, 1985), 179. See also George Santayana's illuminating "The Harvard Yard," *Persons and Places: the Background of My Life* (New York: Charles Scribner's Sons, 1944): 186–202.

[17] *Harvard University 1960: An Inventory for Planning* (Cambridge: President and Fellows of Harvard College, 1960), 4–4–B. See Dorr to Eliot, November 18 and

December 27, 1902. *Records of the President of Harvard University. Charles W. Eliot.* B.36. Harvard University Archives. See also Karl Haglund, *Inventing the Charles River* (Cambridge: MIT Press, 2003), 194–205.

[18] *Edward Waldo Forbes, Yankee Visionary* (Cambridge: Fogg Art Museum, 1971), 48–81. The Forbes memoir and commentary is available online. Charles U. Lowe, "The Forbes Story of the Harvard Riverside Associates," *http://lowell.unix.fas.harvard.edu/house/Forbes/new_forbes.shtml*

[19] A list of Dorr's alumni associates was published in the *Cambridge Tribune*, v. 29 (February 2, 1907): 1.

[20] Appleton to George F. Peabody, June 5, 1914. *Appleton Papers.* The Trustees of Reservations, Archives and Research Center. B.6.f.19. These *Papers* contain richly detailed records of Appleton's Harvard College years (1871–75), which mirror the academic environment of George Dorr who was one year ahead of Mr. Appleton. Additional information is included regarding his alumni leadership in raising alumni funds (B.5.f.10; B.6.f.18,19,40; B.7.f.6).

[21] "To Bring Harvard Yard to Charles," *The New York Times* (September 6, 1903), 28; the definitive study of this process is Sharon Cooney's *The Harvard Riverside Associates: Land Acquisition South of the Harvard Yard, 1903–1918.* Harvard University Archives.

[22] Dorr to Eliot, May 10, 12, and 16; June 15; and October 28, 1907. *Records of the President of Harvard University, Charles W. Eliot.* B.83.

[23] H. Münsterberg to G. B. Dorr, April 28, 1901. *Subscription Records: Subscription for Emerson Hall, 1901–1905.* Harvard University Archives.

[24] O. W. Holmes to G. B. Dorr. April 6, 1902. *Subscription Records.*

[25] Margaret Münsterberg, *Hugo Münsterberg: His Life and* Work (New York: D. Appleton & Co., 1922), Ch. 7.

[26] January 15, 1902. *Annual Reports of the President and the Treasurer of Harvard College.* Harvard University Archives. See also *The Memoirs of Members of the Social Circle in Concord.* Third Series (Cambridge: Riverside Press, 1907).

[27] Sanborn to Dorr, February 13, 1902. *Correspondence to William Torrey Harris.* Vault A35. Unit 1.f.12, Concord Free Public Library Special Collections.

[28] Dorr to Sanborn, February 18, 1902. *F. B. Sanborn Collection.* B1.f.2. Howard Gottlieb Archival Research Center, Boston University.

[29] R. S. Yard to H. C. Bryant, June 24, 1931. National Park Service. *Harper's Ferry Center Library Collection.* RG19. 1936–1950. K1810. Harper's Ferry, WV.

[30] July 1, 1902. Gray Herbarium Archives. Harvard University; see also R. A. Daly. "Biographical Memoir of William Morris Davis (1850–1934)," *National Academy of Sciences Biographical Memoirs* 23 (1944): 263–295. Davis' impressive earth science research is represented by more than five hundred book and serial publications.

[31] Roberts to Dorr, January 2, 1903. ANP. SRC. Box I.f.3; this letter is the only known evidence that Dorr completed his planned camping trip "by way of Oregon and Washington…[to spend] a few weeks camping out there or among the Canadian Rockies."

[32] Quoted by Jonathan N. Romine. *Eugene Lusk Roberts: an Architect of Physical Education in the American West: 1910–1950* (Provo: Doctoral Dissertation, Brigham Young University, 1984), 63; the *Eugene Lusk Roberts Papers, 1912–1972* in the Brigham

Young University Archives are also useful. See also Jared Farmer, *On Zion's Mount* (Cambridge: Harvard University Press, 2005), 180–189.

[33] *Sieur de Monts Publication*, #14.

[34] *The History of the Harvard Travellers Club 1902–1933* (Cambridge: S. Marcus Press, 1933). *100 Years: 750 Meetings. Harvard Travellers Club. May 27, 2003.* Pamphlet.

[35] Dorr to Eliot, November 18, 1902. *Records of the President of Harvard University. Charles W. Eliot.* B.36.

[36] David Hagedorn. "The Biltmore inspires a gilded Thanksgiving," *The Washington Post.* November 21, 2014.

[37] Wharton to Dorr, December 28, 1902. *Edith Wharton Collection.* B.24.f. 753. Beinecke Rare Book and Manuscript Library. Yale University. Dorr signed the Biltmore guest book, November 27, 1902. Biltmore Company Special Collections, Asheville, NC.

[38] Richard C. Cabot to C. W. Eliot. March 9, 1903. *Records of the President of Harvard University, Charles W. Eliot.* B.31.

[39] F. G. Peabody. *Reminiscences of Present-Day Saints (*Boston: Houghton Mifflin, 1927), 148–149.

[40] Grace C. Long. "The Ethics of Francis Greenwood Peabody: A Century of Christian Ethics," *Journal of Religious Ethics* 18 (1990): 57.

[41] See B. J. Bernstein, "Francis Greenwood Peabody: Conservative Social Reformer," *New England Quarterly* 36 (1963): 323.

[42] Peabody. *Reminiscences,* 146–148; and F. G. Peabody, "Alfred Tredway White," *Harvard Graduates' Magazine* 29 (1921): 577–583.

[43] Lawrence T. Nichols, "The Establishment of Sociology at Harvard," *Science at Harvard University: Historical Perspectives.* Eds. Clark A. Elliott and Margaret W. Rossiter (Cranbury, NJ: Associated University Presses, 1992), 201–205.

[44] Peabody, *Reminiscences,* 137, 148.

[45] *Boston Transcript.* April 27, 1903. Dorr to Eliot, April 14, 1903. *Records of the President of Harvard University. Charles W. Eliot.* B.36.

[46] *Subscription Records for Emerson Hall, 1901–1905.* Harvard University Archives.

[47] Dorr to Eliot, May 15, 1903. *Records of the President.* B.36.

[48] ANP. SRC. B.I.f.3 contains a detailed trip expense statement, the only evidence to corroborate Dorr's letter to Eliot. Other than the Bowditch family papers in the Massachusetts Historical Society, for H. P. Bowditch see Manfred Bowditch, "Henry Pickering Bowditch: An Intimate Portrait," *www.asp.org/publications/tphys/legacy/1958/issue4/7.pdf*, by his son; on his brother, see "Charles Pickering Bowditch," *American Anthropologist* 23, #3 (1941): 353 ff.

[49] George Cooke, "The Emerson Centennial," *New England Magazine* 28, #3 (1903): 255–26.

[50] See the "Robbins Collection of Herbert Wendell Gleason Photographic Negatives of Images of Concord, Mass. 1899–1937." Special Collections. Concord Free Public Library. Concord, MA. See also online primary resources available from The Walden Woods Project and the perceptive insights of Finis Dunaway in "Gleason's Transparent Eyeball," *Natural Visions: The Power of Images in American Environmental Reform* (Chicago: University of Chicago Press, 2005), 14.

[51] Evidence for this probability can be found in the exhibit catalog and membership list, Boston Camera Club. Archives of American Art, Smithsonian Institution, Washington, DC.

[52] Wharton to Dorr, September 3, 1904. Edith Wharton Collection. B24, f.753.

[53] Ronald H. Epp, "Wild Gardens and Pathways at the Mount: George B. Dorr and the Mount Desert Island Influence," *Edith Wharton and the American Garden* (Lenox: The Mount Press, 2009), 75–87

[54] Dorr's November 7, 1904 forty-page typescript letter to his Bar Harbor neighbor and friend, David B. Ogden, provides the best rendering of the several extant versions. A fourteen-page preamble titled "A Trip through the California Sierras" relates the westward journey prior to the Ogden narrative. ANP. SRC. B.2.f.9.

[55] Josiah Royce to President Benjamin Wheeler. July 31, 1904. *Papers of Josiah Royce.* Harvard University Archives. See Ann Lage, "The Peaks and the Professors: University Names in the High Sierras," *Chronicle of the University of California.* #3 (2000): 91–98.

[56] G. B. Dorr, "A Trip through the California Sierra," Version 1. Email communication with Ramond DeLea Jr. March 29, 2010.

[57] Dorr to Isabella Story, October 6, 1939. National Archives and Records Administration. RG 79. NPS. Central Classified Files. 1933–1949. Acadia-General. B.797.

[58] Dorr to Ogden, "A Trip through the California Sierras," 8.

[59] Shortly after Dorr's departure, William Mulholland (1855–1935) began purchasing Owens Valley ranches, not for local irrigation as the farmers believed. Instead, his highly controversial objective was to secure water rights for a 233-mile gravity-fed Los Angeles Aqueduct to satisfy the growing water needs of Los Angeles County. See Wikipedia. "California Water Wars." *https://en.wikipedia.org/wiki/California_Water_Wars*

[60] For context, see two Sequoia Natural History Association publications: Lary M. Dilsaver and William C. Tweed, *Challenge of the Big Trees* (San Francisco: 1990) and Howard R. Stagner, *The Giants of Sequoia and Kings Canyon* (Three Rivers, CA: Sequoia Natural History Association, 1958).

[61] Dorr to Ogden, "A Trip through the California Sierras," 24.

[62] Steven J. Holmes. Foreword to Linnie Marsh Wolfe. *Son of Wilderness: The Life of John Muir* (Madison: University of Wisconsin Press, 2003), xv.

Chapter Ten: GATHERINGS

[1] John M. Bryan, *Maine Cottages: Fred L. Savage and the Architecture of Mount Desert.* (New York: Princeton Architectural Press, 2005). Appendix.

[2] Mount Desert Island garden historian Betsy Hewlett responded (May 9, 2015) by email to my query about William Miller. As a former Oldfarm gardener, Dorr's nursery manager could be relied upon "to source plant material in Europe as well as new markets that were opening in Asia at this time."

[3] "Mount Desert Nurseries," June 26, 1912.

[4] Edith Wharton to Sally Norton, June 15, 1905. *Edith Wharton Collection.* S.II.f.899. Beinecke Rare Book and Manuscript Library. Yale University. New Haven.

[5] Arthur Cushman McGiffert Jr., *Pilot of a Liberal Faith: Samuel Atkins Eliot 1860–1950* (Boston: Beacon, 1976), 202.

[6] Francis H. Eliot, "Patriarchal Picnics," *Atlantic Monthly* (July 1953): 55–56; see also Henry James Jr., *Charles William Eliot: President of Harvard University, 1869–1909*

(Boston: Houghton Mifflin, 1930), II, 175.

[7] Francis H. Eliot, 57–58.

[8] Charles W. Eliot, *The Durable Satisfactions of Life* (New York: Thomas Y. Crowell & Co., 1910), 128–130.

[9] Francis Greenwood Peabody, "Alfred T. White," *Reminiscences of Present-Day Saints* (Boston: Houghton Mifflin Co., 1927): 153.

[10] Charles W. Eliot, *The Durable Satisfactions.* 131.

[11] Dorr to Eliot, August 14, 1905. *Records of the President of Harvard University. Charles W. Eliot.* B.83. Harvard University Archives.

[12] Dorr to Eliot, February 5, 1906. *Records of the President.* B.83.

[13] Dorr to Eliot, June 25 and August 6, 1906. *Records of the President*. B.83. Copies of deed transfer, December 8, 1906. Unboxed clippings. Map Room. Douglas B. Chapman Archive. Bar Harbor, ME.

[14] Hancock County, Maine, *Registry of Deeds.* Vol. 432, p. 456; Vol. 435, p. 357.

[15] Münsterberg to Dorr, December 6, 1905. *Subscription Records. Subscription for Emerson Hall. 1901–1905.* Harvard University Archives. Dorr contributed $1,000 in addition to his "generous energy." Münsterberg's wife described Emerson Hall's architectural design as "simple, adequate, without superfluous ornamentation, and harmonious with Robinson Hall opposite." Margaret Münsterberg, *Hugo Münsterberg* (New York: Appleton & Co., 1922), Ch. 9.

[16] "Emerson Hall Opened," *Boston Evening Transcript,* December 27, 1905; *The Harvard Crimson,* January 3, 1906.

[17] Mark A. DeWolfe Howe, *John Jay Chapman and his Letters.* (Boston: Houghton Mifflin, 1937), 202.

[18] James to Münsterberg and C. W. Eliot, December 27, 1905. *The Correspondence of William James.* Eds. Ignas K. Skrupskelis and Elizabeth M. Berkeley (Charlottesville: University of Virginia, 2004). Vol. 11, 128–129.

[19] *William James: Selected Correspondence 1881–1910,* Ed. F. J. D. Scott. (Columbus: Ohio State University Press, 1986), 388–390.

[20] *Harvard Graduates' Magazine* 14 (1905–06): 571.

[21] "Emerson and Scholars," *Harvard Graduates' Magazine* 14 (1905–06): 383 f.; the December issue included a photograph of Emerson Hall opposite Eliot's essay on the durable satisfactions of life, a not accidental juxtaposition of content.

[22] Mark A. DeWolfe Howe, *John Jay Chapman,* 22.

[23] Nelson W. Aldrich Jr., *Old Money: the Mythology of America's Upper Class* (New York: Alfred A. Knopf, 1988), 50–51.

[24] *A Brief History of the Somerset Club of Boston 1851–1913* (Boston: Somerset Club, 1913) and *The Somerset Club 1851–1951* (Boston: Somerset Club, 1951).

[25] Dorr's Commonwealth Avenue residence was maintained year-round by a staff that included a parlor maid, cook, and housekeeper. 1910 *United States Census Records,* Suffolk County, Massachusetts.

[26] M. A. DeWolfe Howe, *A Partial (and not Impartial) Semi-Centennial History of the Tavern Club 1884–1934* (Boston: Tavern Club, 1934), 145.

[27] Wilcomb E. Washburn, *A Centennial History 1878–1978: The Cosmos Club of Washington* (Washington, DC: Cosmos Club, 1978); Dorr also resided briefly at the University Club—both in Washington and New York City—and the Engineer's

Club in Boston.

[28] Eliot to Dorr, May 15, 1905. *Subscriptions for Emerson Hall.*

[29] *Robbins-Mills Collection.* III, f.2. Special Collections. Concord Free Public Library. Concord, MA.

[30] Eugene Taylor, "William James on Psychopathology," *Harvard Library Bulletin* 30 (1982): 472.

[31] Alice James to Dorr, April 1906. *Letters from Other James Family Members,* Harvard University. Alice reassured Dorr that she and the recent widow of physician and psychical researcher Richard Hodgson have "boundless confidence" that Dorr will look out for her son's interests, a reference to decisions made following Hodgson's death. Since Hodgson left no will, Dorr and Harry (at Dorr's insistence) were legally appointed executors of Hodgson's personal estate.

[32] See Ch.15 of R. W. B. Lewis, *The Jameses: A Family Narrative (*New York: Farrar, Straus and Giroux, 1991).

[33] G. B. Dorr, *Dorr Papers.* B.1.f.13. Bar Harbor Historical Society.

[34] On Dorr's inquiries, see James H. Hyslop, "A Review of Recent English Proceedings," *Journal of the American Society for Psychical Research* V (1911): 141–170.

[35] James to Dorr, February 8, 1905. *The Correspondence of William James.* Vol. 10. 633; James to J. G. Paddington, February 13, 1907, Vol. 11, 320.

[36] *Essays on Psychical Research* (Cambridge: Harvard University Press, 1986). See the Murphy and Ballou edition for Dorr's role in the Rockland Harbor (Maine) "Owl's Head" sittings with Miss Margaret Bancroft.

[37] See Krister D. Knapp, *To the Summerland: William James, Psychical Research and Modernity* (Boston: Boston College dissertation, 2003). The classic family study is by R. W. B. Lewis, *The Jameses.*

[38] James to Dorr, March 10 and 24, 1909. *Correspondence of William James.* Vol.12. 173, 188.

[39] Hall to Dorr, April 16, May 28, 1909. *G. Stanley Hall Papers.* B27.f.9.

[40] Linda Simon, *Genuine Reality: A Life of William James* (New York: Harcourt Brace & Co., 1998), 287.

[41] In January 1908 she received nearly ten million dollars in the final settlement of her husband's estate. *Bar Harbor Record.* July 28, 1909; see also *The New York Times,* May 28, 1899, MS2.

[42] G. B. Dorr, *The Jesup Memorial Library* (Bar Harbor: privately printed, 1911), 5.

[43] The Mount Desert Transit Company was incorporated January 1, 1907, and the incorporators included Mr. Dorr, Mr. Kennedy, and Albert H. Lynam. The objective was a forty-mile rail line from Ellsworth through Trenton to Eden.

[44] J. M. Bryan, *Maine Cottages: Fred L. Savage and the Architecture of Mount Desert* (New York: Princeton Architectural Press, 2005), 287–294, Savage was also supervising architect of the Jesup Library, *Bar Harbor Times,* July 6, 1910.

[45] G. B. Dorr, *A New Building for Music at Bar Harbor* (Bar Harbor: privately printed, 1906). ANP. SRC. B.3.f.9. In the same file, see Dorr's September 16, 1907 first annual report to the newly renamed Bar Harbor Association of Arts. In 2011, the Bar Harbor Historical Society Museum recovered from Ogden family descendants an important six-page letter by Dorr to David Morris, detailing the construction process.

[46] Dorr to Eliot, September 6, 1906. *Records of the President of Harvard University.*

Charles W. Eliot. B.83. The Oldfarm guest book lists many more guests than in previous years, a likely response to the venues offered at The Building of the Arts.

[47] Owen Johnson, "The Building of Arts at Bar Harbor," *The Century Magazine* 56 (Sept. 1908): 678.

[48] Wharton to Dorr, July 24, 1906. *Edith Wharton Collection.* S.II. B.24.f.753.

[49] Wharton's January 1906 letter refers to her hope for more "good talks on horticulture, free-will, and predestination." See Ronald H. Epp, "Wild Gardens and Pathways at The Mount," *Edith Wharton and the American Garden* (Lenox: The Mount Press, 2009): 75–87.

[50] George Howard to George Dorr, October 29, 1906; Dorothy Howard to George Dorr, October 30, 1906; George Howard to George Dorr, November 8, 1906. *Dorr Family Correspondence.* J24/7. Castle Howard Archives. Arriving in Washington, D.C., Dorr's introductions enabled George and Dorothy Howard to be entertained by the Associate Justice of the U.S. Supreme Court, Oliver Wendell Holmes, and other distinguished acquaintances. The personal papers of Dorothy Howard are in the archives of Girton College, the University of Cambridge, where she received her B.A. in 1905.

[51] Julia Ward Howe, January 31, 1908. "Journal." *The Yellow House Papers. The Laura E. Richards Collection.* Gardiner Library Association and Maine Historical Society. RG. 18.

[52] Conjecture about Dorr's sexuality persists. See the late Sturgis Haskin, "Hiding our Heroes," *Chelsea Station Magazine,* May 28, 2014.

Chapter Eleven: TRUSTEE FIRST STEPS

[1] Char Miller, *Gifford Pinchot and the Making of Modern Environmentalism* (Washington, D.C.: Island Press, 2001), 138.

[2] Dayton Duncan, *The National Parks: America's Best Idea, An Illustrated History* (New York: Alfred A. Knopf, 2009), Ch.1–2; see also the companion film of the same title by Ken Burns.

[3] See Douglas Brinkley, *The Wilderness Warrior: Theodore Roosevelt and the Crusade for America* (New York: HarperCollins, 2009), Chapter 13, for a lucid explanation of Pinchot's utilitarian philosophy.

[4] Anne Whiston Spirn, "Constructing Nature: The Legacy of Frederick Law Olmsted," *Common Ground: Toward Reinventing Nature.* Ed. William Cronin (New York: W. W. Norton, 1995), 101.

[5] R. Waldbauer and Sherry Hutt, "The Antiquities Act at Its Centennial," *CRM Journal* 3, # 1 (Winter 2006), 36–48.

[6] On the centennial of the Antiquities Act, I presented this history in an address at the ninetieth anniversary celebration of the establishment of the Sieur de Monts National Monument. Sieur de Monts Spring. Acadia National Park. August 22, 1906.

[7] Hal Rothman, *America's National Monuments: the Politics of Preservation* (Lawrence: University Press of Kansas, 1989), xv. See also *The Antiquities Act: A Century of American Archaeology, Historic Preservation, and Nature Conservation.* Eds. David Harmon, F. P. McManamon, and D. T. Pitcaithley (Tucson: University of Arizona Press, 2006).

[8] John C. Miles, *Guardians of the Parks* (Washington, DC: Taylor & Francis, 1995), 12.

[9] *Addresses and Proceedings of the First National Conservation Congress.* 1909, 75, *http://memory.loc.gov*); see also Char Miller, *Gifford Pinchot.*

[10] Theodore Roosevelt, *A Book Lovers Holiday's in the Open* (New York: Charles Scribner's Sons, 1916), Ch. 10.

[11] Char Miller. *Gifford Pinchot.* Ch. 9.

[12] Char Miller, *Gifford Pinchot*, 226–227.

[13] *American Civic Association's Movement for a Bureau of National Parks* (Washington, D.C.: American Civic Association, 1911), 15.

[14] Horace M. Albright, "Great American Conservationists," *Conservators of Hope: The Horace M. Albright Conservation Lectures* (Moscow, ID: University of Idaho Press, 1988), 26; see also *Pioneers of American Landscape Design*. Eds. Charles Birnbaum and Robin Karson. (New York: McGraw–Hill, 2000), 249–251.

[15] G. B. Dorr, *Acadia National Park* (Bangor: Burr Printing, 1942), 6–7. According to C. W. Eliot, Dorr was bedridden in May from "a recent surgical operation…[and] not in condition to do business." HCTPR file. # 2063. Douglas B. Chapman Archive. Bar Harbor. This incident conflicts with the timing of the news since *Acadia National Park* dates the incident in September.

[16] G. B. Dorr. "Some Thoughts Concerning Acadia National Park, Planning for the Future." December 10, 1940 typescript. ANP. SRC. B.2.f.2.

[17] Homans to Eliot, May 7, 1908. *Records of the President of Harvard University. Charles W. Eliot.* B.83. Harvard University Archives.

[18] Margaret Coffin Brown, *Pathmakers: Cultural Landscape Report for the Historic Hiking Trail System of Mount Desert Island* (Brookline: National Park Service and Olmsted Center for Landscape Preservation, 2006), 64–69. See also Donald Lenahan, *The Memorials of Acadia National Park* (Bar Harbor: D.P. Lenahan, 2010).

[19] C. W. Eliot to L. B. Deasy, August 15, 1908. Douglas B. Chapman Archive. #2068. The firm of Fenton, Chapman, Wheatley & Kane, P.A. succeeded attorneys L. B. Deasy & A. H. Lynam (et. al), who represented the HCTPR, Mr. Dorr, and Mr. John D. Rockefeller Jr.

[20] Quoted in John Wilmerding's *The Artist's Mount Desert: American Painters on the Maine Coast* (Princeton: Princeton University Press, 1994), 38.

[21] Pamela J. Belanger, *Inventing Acadia: Artists and Tourists at Mount Desert* (Rockport, ME: Farnsworth Art Museum, 1999), 126; see Belanger for the 1850 Frederic E. Church pencil sketch of *Sand Beach and the Beehive from Great Head,* fig. 30.

[22] G. B. Dorr, *Acadia National Park,* 7.

[23] Dorr to Eliot, September 28 and 29, 1908. *Records of the President.* B.83. Peter Dow Bachelder's *Steam to the Summit* (Ellsworth, ME: Breakwater Press, 2005) is the definitive work on the railway. See also "Cadillac Mountain Road" in the monumental study by Richard Quin and Neil Maher, *Acadia National Park Motor Roads* (Washington, DC: Historic American Engineering Record, 1994), 1–7. Dorr's stock holdings in the Green Mountain Carriage Road Company between 1908 and 1917 remain an unexplained anomaly. Chapman Archive. JDR Jr. Papers. B.143.R9.

[24] G. B. Dorr, *Acadia National Park.* 7. Dorr's investment in the short-lived Green Mountain Carriage Road Company was also underwritten by John S. Kennedy. Chapman Archive. JDR Jr., Papers. B.143.R21.

[25] G. B. Dorr, *Acadia National Park*, 8.

[26] Dorr's March 22, 1941 letter to House Appropriations Committee Chairman, Edward T. Taylor. ANP. SRC. B.4.f.1.

[27] September 13, 1909. Hancock County Trustees of Public Reservations Archives.

Woodlawn Museum, Ellsworth, ME; trustee title to five acres atop Bar Hill on Sea Cliff Drive was also secured at this time.

[28] Samuel Eliot Morison, *Three Centuries of Harvard, 1636–1936* (Cambridge: Harvard University Press, 1936), 396.

[29] September 16 and 28, October 2, 1908. *Records of the President.* B.83. See also Donald P. Lenahan, *The Memorials,* 30–31.

[30] George B. Dorr, "The Sieur de Monts National Monument, *Sieur de Monts Publications* IX (1916). Additional detail is found in Dorr's essay on "The House of De Monts or Mons" and his handwritten research notes among the *George B. Dorr Papers* at the Bar Harbor Historical Society. B.2.f. 12. David Hackett Fischer emphasizes (see note 31) that Pierre Dugua had various forms of his place name: De Mons, de Monts, De Montz, or his favorite, Montz. The explorer's naming liberality also applied to his family name, contributing to historical misinterpretation.

[31] David Hackett Fischer, *Champlain's Dream* (Toronto: Random House, 2008), 153. On the development of the spring site, see the *Bar Harbor Times,* September 18, 1915. Regarding springwater trademark and patent documents, see Chapman Archive. JDR Jr. Papers. B.143.D8.

[32] The complete series is available in the Archives, Northeast Harbor Library. Northeast Harbor, ME.

[33] G. B. Dorr, *Acadia National Park,*13. See also William S. Tod, Esq. to G. B. Dorr, March 1, 1910 on the legal strategy for securing Kennedy estate payment to Dorr. Chapman Archive. JDR Jr. Papers. B.143.R21.

[34] Hancock County Trustees of Public Reservations. *Minutes.* September 13, 1909; the fullest documentation on this topic is in the Chapman Archive, HCTPR. #2063.

[35] Peter Morrison, *History of the Bar Harbor Water Company, 1873–2004, and Cultural Resource Assessment of Water Company Facilities, Acadia National Park, Bar Harbor, Maine (*Bar Harbor: National Park Service, 2005), 78.

[36] G. B. Dorr, *Acadia National Park,* 16.

[37] G. B. Dorr, *Acadia National Park,* 17. See the Dorr memorandum on eminent domain, January 18, 1911, Chapman Archive. HCTPR file. # 2063; and Fred C. Lynam May 2, 1913 memorandum to Bar Harbor Water Company executive committee chairman, W. H. L. Lee. JDR Jr. Papers. B.143.D4.

[38] See the personal insights of Dorr estate trustee Richard W. Hale Jr. in his *Story of Bar Harbor* (New York: Ives Washburn, 1949), 195.

[39] G. B. Dorr, *Acadia National Park,* 17.

[40] Dorr to Eliot, February 24, 1915. *The Papers of Charles William Eliot.* B.95; in 1912, Upper Hadlock Pond was also protected, thus establishing public watersheds for Bar Harbor, Seal Harbor, and Northeast Harbor.

[41] Anne Funderburk, "George Stebbins was Key to Creation of Acadia," *Mount Desert Islander.* August 25, 2005.

[42] George L. Stebbins, "Random Notes on the Early History and Development as a Summer Resort of Mount Desert Island and Particularly Seal Harbor." Typescript. This 1941 document was obtained from his granddaughter, Anne Funderburk, who was first interviewed July 11, 2003. The Maine Historic Preservation Commission in Augusta holds significant collections of Mount Desert Island history, including a G. L. Stebbins photo album of ninety-five black-and-white images of Seal Harbor.

Chapter Twelve: MR. DORR GOES TO WASHINGTON

[1] G. B. Dorr, *Hardy Plant Descriptions* (Cambridge: Riverside Press, 1913).

[2] MHS Medals. ANP. SRC. #53558–53562; on the MDN visit see the *Transactions of the Massachusetts Horticultural Society 1914–1915.* Pgs. 229–230.

[3] A. E. Thatcher. Oral History. ANP. SRC.

[4] G. B. Dorr, *Acadia National Park* (Bangor: Burr Printing, 1942), 20.

[5] *Annual Report of the Trustees of Public Reservations.* Vols. 1–6 passim. 1891–1897. The Trustees of Reservations. Archives and Research Center. Sharon, MA.

[6] Dorr to Eliot, May 26, 1914. *The Papers of Charles William Eliot.* B.95. Harvard University Archives. See "First Public Announcement of the Plan to Form a National Park Upon Mt. Desert Island," published in the Eighteenth Annual report of the American Scenic and Historic Preservation Society (New York: 1913), a three-page Society announcement. Acadia National Park Library. Vertical File.

[7] G. B. Dorr, E. Howe, and M. L. Fernald, "The Unique Island of Mount Desert," *National Geographic Magazine* 26 (July, 1914): 74–89.

[8] Reed C. Rollins, "Fernald as a Botanist," *Rhodora* 53, #626 (1951): 57.

[9] Charles W. Eliot, "The Need for Conserving the Beauty and Freedom of Nature in Modern Life," *National Geographic Magazine* 26 (July, 1914): 67–73.

[10] Char Miller. *Gifford Pinchot and the Making of Modern Environmentalism* (Washington, DC: Island Press, 2001), 273. See also G. Pinchot, *Breaking New Ground* (Washington, DC: Island Press, 1998).

[11] See Caroline M. Hickman, "Building for Science: Carnegie Institution of Washington's Geophysical Laboratory," *Washington History* 13, #1 (2001): 32–51.

[12] *Dorr Papers.* B.2.f.2. Bar Harbor Historical Society.

[13] Horace M. Albright and M. A. Schenck. *Creating the National Park Service: The Missing Years* (Norman: University of Oklahoma Press, 1999), 269. The 1914 meeting sparked a deep relationship spanning three decades.

[14] D. C. Swain, "The Passage of the National Park Service Act of 1916," *Wisconsin Magazine of History* (Autumn 1966), 6.

[15] Robert Shankland, *Steve Mather of the National Parks* (New York: Alfred A. Knopf, 1951), 56.

[16] Horace M. Albright and M. A. Schenck. *Creating the National Park Service,* 30–38.

[17] "Hetch Hetchy," The Sierra Club. *www.sierraclub.org/ca/hetchhetchy/*

[18] See Keith W. Olson, *Biography of a Progressive: Franklin K. Lane, 1864–1921* (Westport, CT: Greenwood Press, 1979).

[19] Robert W. Righter, *The Battle over Hetch Hetchy: America's Most Controversial Dam and the Birth of Modern Environmentalism* (New York: Oxford University Press, 2005), 118.

[20] "Conservation: Hetch Hetchy Valley." *Records of the President.* Box 92.

[21] See Keith W. Olson, *The Biography of a Progressive*, passim.

[22] Robert Shankland, *Steve Mather of the National Parks,* 58.

[23] Horace M. Albright, *Birth of the National Park Service: The Founding Years, 1913–33* (Salt Lake City: Howe Brothers, 1985), 86.

[24] Dorr maintains that Dr. Theodore S. Palmer, a zoologist in charge of game preservation with the Agriculture Department's Biological Survey, suggested the national monument idea. *Acadia National Park* (Bangor, ME: Burr, 1942), 27; see W. L.

McAtee, "In Memoriam: Theodore Sherman Palmer," *The Auk* 73 (1956): 367–377.

[25] Hal Rothman, "Second-Class Sites: National Monuments and the Growth of the National Park System." *Environmental Review* 10, #1 (1986): 44-56. See also Francis P. McManamon, "The Antiquities Act and how Theodore Roosevelt shaped it." *The George Wright Forum* 31, #3 (2014): 324–344.

[26] Hal Rothman. "Second-Class Sites," 49. For historical background, see *The Antiquities Act: A Century of American Archaeology, Historic Preservation, and Nature Conservation.* Eds. David Harmon, F. P. McManamon, and Dwight T. Pitcaithley (Tucson: University of Arizona Press, 2006).

[27] On the evolving spirit of conservation philanthropy, see the impressive narrative of Tom Butler, *Wildlands Philanthropy: The Great American Tradition* (San Rafael: Earth Aware, 2008), 2–9.

[28] *Boston Herald* letter republished in the *Bar Harbor Record,* January 29, 1913. See also F. E. Guernsey, "Mount Katahdin as a National Park," *Proceedings of the Bangor Historical Society, 1916;* and Neil Rodhe, *The Interrupted Forest* (Gardiner, ME: Tilbury House, 2001), 304–305.

[29] David Rockefeller, *Memoirs* (New York: Random House, 2002), 30–32. Over the ensuing years he expanded the number of rooms in The Eyrie to 107, adding additional acreage and extensive gardens.

[30] "A Brief History of Forest Hill." *www.fhho.org/history.asp.*

[31] See Tom Pyle, *Pocantico: Fifty Years on the Rockefeller Domain* (New York: Duell, Sloan and Pearce, 1964).

[32] Margaret Coffin Brown, *Pathmakers: Cultural Landscape report for the Historic Hiking Trail System of Mount Desert Island*(Boston: National Park Service and Olmsted Center for Landscape Preservation, 2006), I, 99.

[33] Ann Rockefeller Roberts, interview. August 26, 2003. Southwest Harbor, Maine.

[34] Ann Rockefeller Roberts, *Mr. Rockefeller's Roads: The Story Behind Acadia's Carriage Roads.* 2nd ed. (Camden, ME: Down East Books, 2012), 71.

[35] Somesville historian Judith S. Goldstein understandably uses "The Triumvirate" as a descriptor in her *Tragedies and Triumphs: Charles W. Eliot, George B. Dorr, John D. Rockefeller Jr., the founding of Acadia National Park* (Somesville, ME: Port in a Storm Bookstore, 1992) and *Majestic Mount Desert* (Mount Desert, ME: Somes Pond Press, 1996).

[36] More to the point, as Dorr's confidant and executor of Dorr's last will and testament, Peters's hundreds of pages of documentation on the man he called "the prince of altruists" provide us with a new reading of conservation history.

[37] Dorr to Peters, January 22, 23, and February 13, 1915. *Hon. John A. Peters Papers. Dorr Estate Correspondence.* Hale & Hamlin, LLC. Ellsworth, ME. Housed in the attic of the oldest building in Ellsworth, these papers have not been inventoried.

[38] Dorr to Eliot, April 15, 1915. *The Papers of Charles William Eliot.* B.95. Harvard University Archives; A. H. Lynam later fulfilled many of the legal requirements for both Dorr and Rockefeller after Deasy's 1918 appointment as Associate Justice of the Maine Supreme Judicial Court.

[39] R. W. Hale Jr. *The Story of Bar Harbor* (New York: Ives Washburn, 1949), 197–198.

[40] Eliot to Rockefeller, February 25, 1915. Rockefeller Archive Center. III.2.I. B.59.f. 441. Hereafter the RAC abbreviation will be utilized. This is one of the most revealing letters exchanged between the two men, and with its many references to Mr. Dorr it

shows that they accepted common principles.

[41] Dorr to Eliot, February 24, 1915. *Records of the President,* B. 95, "Lafayette National Park" folder.

[42] One indication of the extent of Dorr's leadership in HCTPR land acquisition is that, of 129 trustee properties acquired between 1901 and 1939, 53 properties (from small parcels to tracts of more than 1,000 acres) were executed by Dorr during a brief eight-year period between 1908 and 1915. See the most important trustee document: Samuel A. Eliot, *The Hancock County Trustees of Public Reservations: a Historical Sketch and a Record of Holdings of the Trustees.* (Bar Harbor: 1939), 15–31.

[43] Eliot to Rockefeller, February 25, 1915. RAC. III.2.I. B.59.f.441.

[44] Eliot to Dorr, February 25 and March 4, 1925. *The Papers of Charles William Eliot.* B.95.

[45] Dorr to Eliot, March 1, 1915. *The Papers of Charles William Eliot.* B.95.

[46] David Rockefeller and J. W. Ernest, "John D. Rockefeller Jr. and Acadia National Park," 1969. RAC. III.2.I. B.83.f.821.

Chapter Thirteen: MONUMENTAL ACHIEVEMENT

[1] Even Stephen T. Mather and his assistant Horace M. Albright were listed in personnel records at three-quarters time. (Horace M. Albright, *The Birth of the National Park Service: The Founding Years, 1913–33* (Salt Lake City: Howe Brothers, 1985), Ch. 3.

[2] As selectman, Dorr attended the Otter Cliffs Naval Radio Station Commissioning Ceremony, which took place August 28, 1917, as a response to the United States entry into war with Germany. ANP. SRC. B.19.f.13.

[3] Dorr to Eliot, April 7, 1915. *The Papers of Charles William Eliot.* B.95. Harvard University Archives; see also *Bar Harbor Times,* April 10, 1915.

[4] Historian Richard Hale Jr. claims that Dorr was too frequently absent to be an effective selectman. R. W. Hale Jr., *The Story of Bar Harbor* (New York: Ives Washburn, 1949), 214–215.

[5] *Bar Harbor Times,* April 15, 1916; see also *Town of Eden Minutes: Annual Report of the Municipal Officers,* 1915–1918. Beginning in 1911, ten deeds were transferred from Dorr's ownership to the Town of Eden in order to increase the Kebo Valley golf links acreage. Douglas B. Chapman Archive. Box 555. Bar Harbor, ME.

[6] Judith S. Goldstein, *Crossing Lines: Histories of Jews and Gentiles in Three Communities* (New York: William Morrow, 1992), 185.

[7] Dorr to Eliot, April 7, 1915. *The Papers of Charles William Eliot.* B.95.

[8] "Purposes of the Wild Gardens of Acadia." Douglas B. Chapman Archive. John D. Rockefeller Jr. Papers. B.147.WG8. Though unsigned, the document reflects other sigfned and dated WGA charter documentation in files WG1-7.

[9] RAC. III.2.I.B.85 f.840.

[10] G. B. Dorr, "An Acadian Plant Sanctuary," *Sieur de Monts Publications* V (1916).

[11] *Commissions du Roy et de Monsaigneur l'Admiral au sieur de Monte, pour l'habitation 'es terres de Lacadie Canada, & autres endroits en la Nouvelle France.* 1915.

[12] Jeffrey Killion, *Sieur de Monts Spring, Acadia National Park: Cultural Landscape Inventory* (Brookline, MA: National Park Service and Olmsted Center for Landscape Preservation, 2009), 50–52.

[13] Stephen J. Hornsby et al. *Cultural Land Use Survey of Acadia National Park* (Bar Harbor: National Park Service, 1999), 129.

[14] "DeMonts and Acadia," *Tercentenary of DeMonts' Settlement at St. Croix Island. June 25, 1904.* (Portland, ME: Maine Historical Society, 1905), 10-35. see also G. B. Dorr, "The Sieur de Monts National Monument, *Sieur de Monts Publications* IX (1917); "The Sieur de Monts National Monument as a Huguenot Memorial," *Sieur de Monts Publications* XXIII (1919).

[15] See *The Bar Harbor Times.* June 16, 1917. Between 10,000 and 50,000 copies of each title were published by the Government Printing Office or by the Wild Gardens of Acadia (at Dorr's expense). Four of these publications are no longer extant; a surprising loss in the face of such a large print run.

[16] H. M. Albright and M. Albright Schneck, *The Mather Mountain Party of 1915* (Three Rivers, CA: Sequoia Natural History Association, 1990), 24; see *Reminiscences of Horace Albright* (New York: Columbia University Oral Research Office, 1960), 34 ff. and D. C. Swain, "The Passage of the National Park Service Act of 1916," *Wisconsin Magazine of History (*Autumn 1966): 4–16.

[17] Linda Flint McClelland, *Building the National Parks: Historic Landscape Design and Construction* (Baltimore: Johns Hopkins University Press, 1998), 124. Primary resource located in the NPS History Collection. Harpers Ferry Center. RG37. S.II. Container 31.

[18] D. Swain, "The Passage of the National Park Service Act of 1916," 15–17. Mather's companions were Albright; Congressmen John Riker and William Kent; American Civic Association officers J. Horace McFarland, Richard B. Watrous, and Henry A. Barker; Assistant Attorney General Huston Thompson; Herbert Quick of the *Saturday Evening Post*; Gilbert Grosvenor, editor of *The National Geographic*; and Emerson Hough, a leading reforestation proponent.

[19] R. Shankland, *Steve Mather of the National Parks* (New York: Alfred Knopf, 1951), 101.

[20] Robin W. Winks, "The National Park Service Act of 1916: 'A Contradictory Mandate'?" *Denver University Law Review* 74, #3 (1997): 575–623.

[21] Horace M. Albright and Marian A. Schneck, *Creating the National Park Service: the Missing Years* (Norman: University of Oklahoma Press, 1999),110.

[22] "National Touring Week," *The New York Times*, July 30, 1916.

[23] Horace Albright reports that while Mrs. Mather lived in Chicago, her husband resided at the Cosmos Club. "He hated being alone. He rarely was. He loved entertaining friends and did so with a lavish hand." *Creating the National Park Service,* 175.

[24] These NPS proposals are available online through the Library of Congress as part of the American Memory Project: "The Evolution of the Conservation Movement, 1850–1920." *http://www.loc.gov/teachers/classroommaterials/connections/conservation/*

[25] Eliot to Bullard, September 9, 1915. *Dorr Papers.* B.1.f.5. Bar Harbor Historical Society.

[26] Dorr to Eliot, April 1916. *The Papers of Charles William Eliot.* B.95.

[27] Gerald Williams, National Monuments and the Forest Service. (Washington, DC: National Park Service, 2003).

[28] Dorr to Eliot, July 1,1916. *The Papers of Charles William Eliot.* B.95.

[29] Albright, *Creating the National Park Service,* 128–129.

[30] D. C. Swain, "The Passage of the National Park Service Act of 1916," 4; see also *America's National Park System: The Critical Documents.* Ed. Lary M. Dilsaver (Landham, MD: Rowman & Littlefield, 1994). See also "Celebrating the National Park Service Centennial: 1916–2016," an online historical bibliography. *http://npshistory.com/agency_history.htm*

[31] Dorr to Lane, July 12, 1916. National Archives and Records Administration (NARA). RG79. Central Classified Files. Acadia. Misc. Rpts.

[32] Hal Rothman, *America's National Monuments: The Politics of Preservation* (Lawrence: University Press of Kansas, 1989), 105.

[33] Hal Rothman, *America's National Monuments,* 106.

[34] "Sieur de Monts National Monument: Addresses Upon Its Opening," *Sieur de Monts Publications,* II. I am much indebted to Mount Desert Island historian Jack Russell for extracting the significance of Deasy's use of repeated references to the new "park." Physician Bill Horner, Deasy's great-grandson, published "Deasy: A Maine Man," *Chebacco* XI (2010): 6–31.

[35] "Petition of the Mount Desert Transit Company," *Railroad Commissioners of the State of Maine: Forty-Ninth Annual Report* (Augusta: Kennebec Journal, 1907). 112–114.

[36] See Nancy Cervetti, *S. Weir Mitchell, 1829–1914: Philadelphia's Literary Physician* (University Park: Pennsylvania State University Press, 2012).

[37] See G. B. Dorr, "The Marine Biological Laboratory at Salisbury," *A Laboratory by the Sea: The Mount Desert Island Biological Laboratory 1898–1998.* Ed. Franklin H. Epstein, M.D. (Rhinebeck, NY: River Press, 1998), 11–14.

[38] See Mary Frances Williams, "The Harpswell Laboratory, 1898–1920: A Marine Biological Station," (South Harpswell, ME: 1985), 99–100. Typescript copy secured from the late MDIBL director (1985–1995), Franklin H. Epstein, M.D.

[39] Dorr to Rockefeller. March 20, 1921. RAC. III.2.I.B.0.f.1103. A three-page pamphlet had been circulated on a "Proposed Biological Laboratory on Mt. Desert Island to be Established in Memory of Dr. S. Weir Mitchell." Chapman Archive. Map Room. A. H. Lynam file.

[40] See *The Mount Desert Biological Laboratory: Weir Mitchell Station. Twenty-Ninth Season.* 1927. The preface details the 1922–23 acquisition of the McCagg and Ogden land tracts.

[41] W. Berger, "The Pioneer Days, 1898–1951," *A Laboratory by the Sea,* 27.

[42] See the March 1948 MDIBL Project Memorandum for David Rockefeller, RAC III.2.I.B.79.f.801.

[43] Dorr to Eliot, September 8, 1916. *The Papers of Charles William Eliot.* B.95; see also Eliot to Rockefeller, June 3, 1916. RAC. III.2.I.B.59.f.441.

[44] Margaret C. Brown, *Pathmakers: Cultural Landscape Report for the Historic Hiking Trail System of Mount Desert Island* (Brookline, MA: National Park Service and Olmsted Center for Landscape Preservation, 2006), 67–74. See also Donald P. Lenahan, *The Memorials of Acadia National Park* (Bar Harbor: D. P. Lenahan, 2010). Newly granted access to the John D. Rockefeller Jr. Papers in the Chapman Archive provides the scholarly community for the first time with Dorr's plan for the Jesup Memorial Path. Dorr to Thomas DeWitt Cuyler. March 1, 1916 and September 15, 1916. B.143.D52.

[45] Dorr to Lincoln Cromwell, February 19, 1917. *Records of the President.* B.95.

[46] Dorr to Albright, October 29, 1916. NARA. RG79.CCF.1907–39. Acadia. Misc.

Rpts. Three days later Dorr submitted the first "Sieur de Monts National Monument Annual Report." NARA. RG79.CCF.1907–39. Acadia. Misc. Rpts. Annual.

[47] R. Shankland, *Steve Mather of the National Parks*, 95–99.

Chapter Fourteen: THE FIRST EASTERN NATIONAL PARK

[1] *J.I. G. C.* I, #1 (August 1917): 507 ff. Later reprinted as *Sieur de Monts Publications* XXII (1919).

[2] Beatrix Farrand, "The National Park on Mount Desert Island," *Scribner's* 61 (April 1917): 494.

[3] *The Proceedings of the National Parks Conference, Washington, D.C.* (Washington, DC: GPO, 1917), 220–223. The park vs. monument distinction arose in Dorr's disagreement with landscape architect James S. Pray over Mount Desert Island's worthiness for national park status. Dorr to Eliot, July 31 and August 2, 1917. *The Papers of Charles William Eliot.* B.95. Harvard University Archives.

[4] R. Shankland, *Steve Mather of the National Parks* (New York: Alfred Knopf, 1951), 109–110. See also Horace M. Albright, *The Birth of the National Park Service: the Founding Years, 1913–33* (Salt Lake City, UT: Howe Brothers, 1985), 51–53.

[5] Horace M. Albright and Marian Albright Schenck, *Creating the National Park Service: The Missing Years* (Norman: University of Oklahoma Press, 1999), 299, 308–309; see also *Reminiscences of Horace M. Albright* (New York: Columbia University Oral Research Office, 1960), 40.

[6] Dorr to Eliot, September 28, 1919. *The Papers of Charles William Eliot.* B.95. On Southwest Harbor park planning, see March 7, 1917 letter from John D. Rockefeller Jr. to George Dorr and a September 28, 1919 letter from Dorr to Charles W. Eliot. Douglas B. Chapman Archive. Bar Harbor. JDR Jr. Papers. B.143.D13.

[7] Dorr to Eliot, September 25, 1919. *The Papers of Charles William Eliot.* B.95.

[8] Dorr to Eliot, February 7, 1918. *The Papers of Charles William Eliot.* B.95; Dorr to Albright, September 22, 1917. National Archives and Records Administration. RG79. CCF.1907–39.B.1. Appropriations. f.1.

[9] Ann Rockefeller Roberts, *Mr. Rockefeller's Roads: the Story Behind Acadia's Carriage Roads.* 2nd ed. (Camden, ME: Down East, 2012), 96–99.

[10] Lane to Eno. September 2, 1917. *The Letters of Franklin K. Lane: Personal and Political.* Eds. A. W. Lane and L. H. Wall (Boston: Houghton Mifflin Co., 1922), 257.

[11] Lane to Dorr, September 2, 1917. *The Letters of Franklin K. Lane*, 257–258.

[12] Dorr to Eliot, April 10 and May 2, 1918. *Records of the President.* B.95.

[13] Peters to Dorr, July 6, 1918. *Hon. John A. Peters Papers. Dorr Estate Correspondence.* Hale & Hamlin LLC. Ellsworth, ME. On July 13, the *Bar Harbor Times* gave front-page attention to the Senate's passage earlier that week of the national park legislation.

[14] Eliot to Dorr, March 11, 1918. *The Papers of Charles William Eliot.* B.95.

[15] Eliot to Rockefeller, September 3, 1919. RAC. III.2.I.B.59.f.441.

[16] H. M. Albright and M. A. Schenck. *Creating the National Park Service*, 269.

[17] "Mount Desert National Park." House of Representatives. Subcommittee of the Committee on the Public Lands. May 30, 1918. *Catalog.hathitrust.org/Record/009600606*

[18] April 10, 1918. ANP. SRC. B2.f.12.

[19] Albright, *The Birth of the National Park Service*, 69.

[20] Albright and Schenck, *Creating the National Park Service*, 271; see also his *Birth of the National Park Service*, 69ff.

[21] Eliot to Melcher, October 3, 1918. *Records of the President*. B.95.

[22] October 28, 1918. Chapman Archive. JDR Jr. Papers. B.147.D59.

[23] Chapman Archive. Map Room. A. H. Lynam file.

[24] Eliot to Dorr, September 27, 1918. *The Papers of Charles William Eliot*. B.95.

[25] "Lafayette National Park," Department of the Interior: Office of the Secretary. September 27, 1919. Chapman Archive. Map Room. A. H. Lynam file.

[26] Albright, *Creating the National Park Service*, 270–271; see also R. H. Epp, "From Monument to Park: Voices of the Advocates," *Friends of Acadia Journal 7, 3* (Winter 2002), 8–9.

[27] Dorr to Peters, April 3, 5, and 18, 1919. *Hon. John A. Peters Papers*. Hale & Hamlin, LLC. Ellsworth, ME.

[28] A. Scott Berg. *Wilson* (New York: G.P. Putnam's Sons, 2013). 20.

[29] Ibid.

[30] Albright, *The Birth of the National Park Service*, 85f. The director offers several pages of illuminating comments on Dorr's strategic moves.

[31] Over the next eight decades Acadia National Park was promoted as the first national park east of the Mississippi. Some have argued that this claim is historically inaccurate. In 1875 on the shores of the Great Lakes, the U.S. Congress established Mackinac National Park just three years after Yellowstone National Park. In 1894 the War Department abandoned protection of the site, and the following year the property was gifted to Michigan with the stipulation that it be maintained as a state park. "Thus, Mackinac National Park became a footnote in most histories of the U.S. national park system." (Kathy S. Mason, *Natural Museums: U.S. National Parks, 1872–1916*. (East Lansing: Michigan State University Press, 2004), 40.

[32] William S. Bridgman, "Lafayette National Park," *Munsey's Magazine* LXVII (1919): 438–448. *The New York Times* also took note, referring to the new park as "an inevitable turning point for [auto] tours in New England." Quoted in *Auto Era* 19 (December 1919): 18.

[33] Richard Quin, "Acadia National Park Roads and Bridges Spanning Jordan Stream on Gardiner-Mitchell Hill-Jordan Stream Road." Historic American Building Survey/Historic American Engineering Record ME-31. 1994. The Library of Congress holds the whole of this definitive HABS/HAER study by Neil Maher and Richard Quin.

[34] Ann Rockefeller Roberts. *Mr. Rockefeller's Roads*, 153–162.

[35] Donald C. Swain, *Wilderness Defender: Horace M. Albright and Conservation* (Chicago: University of Chicago Press, 1970), Ch. 5; Albright & Schenck, *Creating the National Park Service*, 328–333; see also R. Shankland, *Steve Mather of the National Parks*, 166.

[36] United States Board on Geographic Names Archives, Interior Department. Washington, DC. Documents provided by USBGN Executive Secretary Roger L. Payne, February 6, 2003, especially the letter of April 9, 1919.

[37] Dorr to Lincoln Cromwell, February 19, 1917; Dorr to Eliot, May 7, 1919; Eliot to Dorr, May 9, 1919. *The Papers of Charles William Eliot*. B.95.

[38] G. B. Dorr to Frank Bond, April 9, 1919. USBGN.

[39] The unforeseen social effects of Dorr's nomenclature revisionism are fully

developed in my "Superintendent Dorr and the Mountain Naming Controversy," *Chebacco* XV (2014): 84–94.

[40] *Town Records of Eden*. V. 11.

[41] Dorr to Mather, March 3, 1920. NARA. RG79.CCF.1907–39. Acadia. B.3.f.4.

[42] Benjamin Hadley résumé and cover letter by G. B. Dorr. November 10, 1919. Chapman Archive. Map Room. A. H. Lynam file.

[43] F. C. Lynam to Peters, March 24, 1920. *Hon. John A. Peters Papers*. Dorr Correspondence.

[44] September 26, 1919. NARA. RG79.CCF. 1907–39. Acadia. B.3.f.4; see also A. H. Lynam. Trustee Meeting Announcement. April 18, 1918.

[45] Eliot to Dorr, September 8, 1918. *The Papers of Charles William Eliot*. B.95.

[46] Eliot to Dorr, July 24, 1919. *The Papers of Charles William Eliot*. B.95.

[47] *Bar Harbor Times*, July 30, 1919.

[48] "The National Park of the Abruzzi," *Journal of the International Garden Club* III, #3 (Sept. 1919): 421–430. For background, see *Ninety Years of the Abruzzo National Park, 1922–2012*. Ed. Luigi Piccioni (Cambridge: Cambridge Scholars Publishing, 2012) as well as Piccioni's "Nature Preservation and Protection in Nineteenth-and Twentieth-Century Italy, 1880–1950," *Nature and History in Modern Italy*. Eds. M. Armiero and Marcus Hall (Athens, OH: Swallow Press, 2010): 251–267.

[49] Dorr to JDR Jr., December 9, 1919. RAC. III.2.I.B.86.f.848.

Chapter Fifteen: THE PRINCE OF ALTRUISTS

[1] William Horner, "From Horses to Horsepower: Mount Desert Island's Ten-Year-War for the Automobile," *Chebacco* XIV (2013): 86–106.

[2] Raymond B. Fosdick, *John D. Rockefeller, Jr.: a Portrait* (New York: Harper & Brothers, 1956), 304–305.

[3] *America's National Park Roads and Parkways: Drawings from the Historic American Engineering Record*. Eds. Timothy Davis, T.O. Croteau, and C.H. Marston (Baltimore: Johns Hopkins University Press, 2004), 4.

[4] John C. Miles, *Wilderness in National Parks: Playground or Preserve* (Seattle: University of Washington Press, 2009), 33–37.

[5] Lee Whiteley and Jane Whiteley, *The Playground Trail: The National Park-to-Park Highway* (Boulder: Johnson Printing, 2003), 20.

[6] G. B. Dorr to John D. Rockefeller Jr., January 12, 1921 and March 20, 1921. Douglas B. Chapman Archive. Bar Harbor. JDR Jr. Papers. B.148.D1.

[7] Charles W. Eliot II, "The Influence of the Automobile on the Design of Park Roads," *Landscape Architecture* 13, #1 (1922): 29.

[8] See Neil Maher, "Acadia National Park Motor Roads," *Historic American Building Survey/Historic American Engineering Record* ME-11, 1997. The Library of Congress.

[9] Dorr to Rockefeller, January 2, 1920; see also July 22, 1920. RAC. III.2.I.B.85.f.839.

[10] Dorr to Charles W. Eliot, January 2, 1920; see also April 14, 1920. *The Papers of Charles William Eliot*. B.95. Harvard University Archives.

[11] See William D. Rieley and Roxanne S. Brouse, *Historic Resource Study for the Carriage Road System: Acadia National Park, Mount Desert Island, Maine* (Charlottesville, VA: Rieley & Associates, 1989).

[12] "N.E.H. People Hear of National Parks," *Bar Harbor Times* (August 23, 1922), "Dr. Eliot on History of Mt. Desert Island," *Bar Harbor Times* (August 30, 1922).

[13] The Chapman Archive (JDR Jr. Papers. B.148.f.27) provides correspondence and financial records for this tribute. See Rockefeller's letters of August 30 and September 15. 1919 to Henry Lane Eno detailing his commitment "to help [Dorr] meet his obligations." See also "Meeting Tribute to George B. Dorr," *Bar Harbor Times* (September 8, 1920). While Dorr does not leave a paper trail of his reaction to this testimonial, within two weeks he sends Rockefeller a letter "in recognition of that cooperation…from the period of commencement and the over-coming of initial difficulties to one of attainment." September 12, 1922. RAC. III.2.I.B.85.f.839.

[14] Dorr to Rockefeller, December 19, 1920. RAC. III.2.I.B.86.f.847.

[15] Dorr to Rockefeller, January 12, 1921. RAC. III.2.I.B.110.f.1103; the RAC contains a list of deeds (1921–1930) received by Rockefeller from Mr. Dorr (RAC. III.2.I.B.85.f.839). No fewer than 145 parcels were "mediated" by Dorr—without compensation—during this decade.

[16] Rockefeller to A. H. Lynam. RAC. III.2.I. B.86.f.847.

[17] Rockefeller to Charles O. Heydt, July 12, 1922. RAC. III.2.I.B.74.f.767.

[18] Cammerer to Dorr, September 15, 1920, National Archives and Records Administration. RG79. NPS. CCF. Acadia. B.3.f.121.

[19] See Dorr's publications on this theme: "A Glorious Tribute to France: The New Lafayette National Park on the Maine Coast," *La France* (September 1920), 590–593 and "Our Seacoast National Park," *Appalachia* 15 (1920): 174–182.

[20] *Dorr Papers*. B.1.f.14. Bar Harbor Historical Society.

[21] G. B. Dorr, "Study for Permanent Development of Lafayette National Park Land Area," January 8, 1922. Chapman Archive. Map Room. A. H. Lynam file. The same file contains a legal document that uniquely attributes to Dorr ownership of a motorboat called *Dorothy*.

[22] Jeffrey Killion and H. Eliot Fould, *Cultural Landscape Report for the Historic Motor Road System, Acadia National Park*. (Brookline, MA: National Park Service and Olmsted Center for Landscape Preservation, 2007), 23.

[23] Neil Maher, "Acadia National Park Motor Roads: Park Loop Road," 19–20.

[24] *Dorr Papers*. B.1.f.14; B.2.f.6.

[25] Richard W. Sellars, "Manipulating Nature's Paradise: National Park Management Under Stephen T. Mather, 1916–1929," *Montana: The Magazine of Western History* 43 (1993): 4. For more on this theme, see his *Preserving Nature in the National Parks: A History* (New Haven: Yale University Press, 1997).

[26] Ann Rockefeller Roberts, *Mr. Rockefeller's Roads: The Story Behind Acadia's Carriage Roads*. 2nd ed. (Camden, ME: DownEast Books, 2012), 101–103. For many years this title was out of print, but a second edition (2012) includes a timely interview with David Rockefeller Sr. (the only surviving son of John D. Rockefeller Jr.) and an illuminating new chapter by then–Wildwood Stables director Ed Winterberg on the restoration of the carriage roads in the early 1990s. In Pepper's autobiography, *Philadelphia Lawyer* (Philadelphia: J. B. Lippincott, 1944), he described his strenuous activity on Mount Desert, including a seventeen-mile one-day trek from Bar Harbor to Northeast Harbor over nine intervening mountains.

[27] William D. Rieley, *Cultural Landscape Report for the Carriage Road System:*

Acadia National Park, Mount Desert Island, Maine (Charlottesville: Riley & Associates, Landscape Architects, 1993), 189.

[28] "Papers Relating to Road Hearing Before Secretary Work." March, 1924. ANP. SRC.

[29] ANP. SRC. B.24.f.10.

[30] "The Club's Permanent Camps," *Appalachia* 16 (1924): 367–68; *Dorr Papers.* B.1.f.2. See also *Echoes of Echo: Memories of Echo Lake Camp.* Ed. Mary P. Mitchell (Boston: AMC, 1989).

[31] *Bar Harbor Times.* August 9, 1922.

[32] Gleason to Burbank, January 11, 1923. *Papers of Luther Burbank.* B.5. Library of Congress; the largely unknown Herbert Wendell Gleason collection is preserved at the Sawtelle Research Center.

[33] "Lafayette National Park." Advertisement. *Papers of Luther Burbank.* B.5

[34] *The Boston Transcript.* February 15, 1910. Quoted in Finis Dunaway, *Natural Visions: The Power of Images in American Environmental Reform* (Chicago: University of Chicago Press, 2005), 17.

[35] Eliot to Rockefeller, August 9, 1922. RAC. III.2.I.B.59.f.441 referring to HCTPR lot #52.

[36] Eliot to Greene, July 19, 1922, quoted by Henry James Jr., *Charles W. Eliot: President of Harvard University 1869–1909* (Boston: Houghton Mifflin Co., 1930), II., 302–303.

[37] Edward H. Cotton, *The Life of Charles W. Eliot* (Boston: Small, Maynard & Co., 1926), 302–304. See also the illuminating Friends of Acadia address by the late Harvard theologian Peter J. Gomes on "The Preservation Legacy of Charles William Eliot," Northeast Harbor, ME. August 21, 2007.

[38] Dorr to Rockefeller, August 9, 1922. RAC. III.2.I.B.59.f.441 referring to HCTPR lot #52.

[39] H. M. Albright, *Reminiscences of Horace M. Albright* (New York: Columbia University Oral History Office, 1960), 92.

[40] Eugene P. Trani, "Hubert Work and the Department of the Interior, 1923–28," *Pacific Northwest Quarterly* 61 (1970): 31–40.

[41] *Harvard College. Class of 1874. Fiftieth Anniversary Report.* 1924, 87. Harvard University Archives. *Records of Honorary Degree Recipients.* University of Maine, Raymond H. Folger Special Collections. MUO B. 130. See also K.C. Elkins, "Honorary Degrees at Harvard," *Harvard Library Bulletin* 12, #3 (1958): 326–347.

[42] *Bar Harbor Times.* September 12, 1923.

[42] Robert Sterling Yard, *The Book of the National Parks* (New York: Charles Scribner's Sons, 1919). On Yard's administrative career, see *The National Parks and Conservation Association Papers, 1898–2002.* MSS CONS 225. Denver Public Library. Denver, CO.

[44] John C. Miles, *Guardians of the Parks: A History of the National Parks and Conservation Association* (Washington: Taylor & Frances, 1995), 151. The preservationist credo of the NPCA was at odds with the earlier mission of the aforementioned National Conservation Association. Before its demise in 1923, the NCA fostered the resource management philosophy of its founder, Gifford Pinchot. See Char Miller, *Gifford Pinchot and the Making of Modern Environmentalism* (Washington, D.C.: Island Press, 2001), 226–227.

[45] R. S. Yard, *An Analysis of Lafayette National Park* (Washington, D.C.: National Parks and Conservation Association, 1924), 19–26. See also Paul S. Sutter, *Driven Wild* (Seattle: University of Washington Press, 2002), 113.

[46] R. S. Yard, *An Analysis,* 40.

[47] Dorr to Rockefeller, December 22, 1923. RAC. III.2.I.B.85.f.839; Dorr to Mather, November 14, 1924. NARA. RG79.CCF.1907–39. Acadia.

[48] G. B. Dorr, "David B. Ogden," *The New York Times,* October 31, 1923.

[49] Fosdick, *John D. Rockefeller, Jr.*, Ch. 15–16. See also John Ensor Harr and Peter J. Johnson, *The Rockefeller Century* (New York: Charles Scribner's Sons, 1988), 214–217.

Chapter Sixteen: ATTACK MAY COME AGAIN

[1] "Papers Relating to the Road Hearing before Secretary Work, March 26, 1924." ANP. SRC. Resource Management Records. New Series. 2012.I.B.5.f.1.

[2] W. D. Rieley and R. S. Brouse, *Historic Resource Study for the Carriage Road System Acadia National Park. Mount Desert Island, Maine* (Charlottesville: Rieley & Associates, 1989) 141; see Richard Quin and Neil Maher. *Acadia National Park. Motor Roads. Bar Harbor Vicinity. Hancock County, ME.* (Washington, DC: National Park Service. Historic American Buildings Survey/Historic American Engineering Record #ME-11, 1994–97) for a thorough assessment of the March hearing. Library of Congress.

[3] William James, "The True Harvard," *Memories and Studies.* (New York: Longmans, Green, & Co., 1912), Ch.14.

[4] Richard W. Hale Jr., *The Story of Bar Harbor* (New York: Ives Washburn, 1949), 191–192, 199–200.

[5] Rockefeller contributed to a fund to cover twenty percent of the administrative and travel expenses of the hearing. Correspondence dated February 12 and 24, and May 8, 1924. RAC. III.2.I.B.109.f.1085.

[6] Stebbins to Peters, March 15, 1924. *Roads in National Park Hearings. Hon. John A. Peters Papers.* Hale & Hamlin, LLC. Ellsworth, ME.

[7] Peters to the Hon. John E. Nelson, March 17 and 19, 1924. *Hon. John A. Peters Papers.*

[8] Peters to Hersey, March 14, 1924. *Roads in National Park Hearings. Hon. John A. Peters Papers.*

[9] Arthur M. Allen to Peters, March 13, 1924. Lafayette National Park file. Douglas B. Chapman Archive. Bar Harbor, ME.

[10] Eliot to Work, February 1, 1924. *Records of the President of Harvard. Charles W. Eliot.* Harvard University Archives. B.95.

[11] *The Harvard Crimson,* March 20–22 and December 15, 1924. See also the Harvard Alumni Association publication, *The Ninetieth Birthday of Charles William Eliot* (Cambridge: Harvard University Press, 1924) and a comprehensive collection of greetings and testimonials from students, faculty, academic institutions, and learned societies from around the world in *The Papers of Charles William Eliot: an Inventory.* 2008. B.1–7, 13. Harvard University Archives.

[12] Henry James, *Charles W. Eliot: President of Harvard University, 1869–1909.* (Boston: Houghton Mifflin Co., 1930), v. 2, 303.

[13] Dorr to Eliot, March 18, 1924. *The Papers of Charles William Eliot.* B.95.

[14] Rockefeller to Eliot, April 8, 1924, RAC. III.2.I.B.59.f.441.

[15] Virginia S. Mackay-Smith to H. G. Work, March 17, 1924; B. Farrand to H. G.

Work, March 10, 1924. National Archives and Records Administration. RG79. CCF. Acadia. Misc. Rpts.

[16] Pepper to Peters, March 17, 1924. *The Papers of Charles William Eliot.* B.95.

[17] Peters to Hubert Work, March 20, 1924. Unboxed Misc. Park Papers. Chapman Archive.

[18] Eliot to Work, March 22, 1924. *The Papers of Charles William Eliot.* B.95; this is the only first-hand description of Dorr's disability from one of his contemporaries.

[19] The September 2009 discovery of a Gleason event announcement in the Chapman Archives provided new evidence of Park Service support for Dorr's efforts.

[20] H. W. Gleason, "Distinguished Specialists Remove Obstructions in Lafayette Park Motor Road Case." *Boston Evening Transcript,* Aug. 8, 1924, 3.

[21] *Lafayette National Park. Hearing Transcript. March 26, 1924.* NARA. RG79. CCF.1907–39. Acadia. Misc. Reports. B. 4; see also RAC. III.2.I.B.109.f.1085. Of critical importance are the "Papers Relating to the Road Hearing before Secretary Work, March 26, 1924," 130 pages of historical documentation complied by Sawtelle Research Center staff at Acadia National Park. Resource Management Records. New Series. 2012.I.B.5.f.1.

[22] RAC. III.2.I.B.109.f.1085.

[23] H. L. Martin to Charles O. Heydt, April 2, 1924. RAC III.2.I.B.109.f.1085.

[24] Dorr to Rockefeller, April 29, 1924, RAC. III.2.I.B.74.f.763. The Chapman Archive of unboxed Lafayette National Park memorabilia contains documentation of Dorr's daily activities during late summer 1924 in the form of daily hour-by-hour journal reports kept by a park ranger in his company.

[25] Dorr to Cammerer, January 10, 1940. RAC. III.2.I.B.115.f.1154.

[26] Rockefeller to J. B. Murphy, May 8, 1924. RAC III.2.I.B.109.f.1085.

[27] In his *Memoirs* (New York: Random House, 2002) David Rockefeller Sr. does not mention his reaction to not being included in the 1924 trip, emphasizing at length his "first extended trip with his parents" two years later.

[28] Raymond B. Fosdick, *John D. Rockefeller, Jr.: A Port*rait (New York: Harper & Brothers, 1956), 306–312. For more specific documentation, see *Worthwhile Places: Correspondence of John D. Rockefeller, Jr. and Horace M. Albright.* Ed. Joseph W. Ernst (Bronx, NY: Fordham University Press, 1991), 22–32.

[29] Donald Swain, *Wilderness Defender: Horace M. Albright and Conservation* (Chicago: University of Chicago Press, 1970), 153–155.

[30] Dorr to Rockefeller, June 25, 1924. Chapman Archive. *JDR Jr. Papers.* B.148. D53. The group consisted of "Mr. Lynam…as Chairman, Mr. [Clarence E.] Dow, who is always in close touch with me, Mr. Simpson as chief engineer, and Mr. Hill, park engineer, immediately in charge of the work." See Richard Quinn and Neil Maher, *Acadia National Park. Rockefeller Carriage Roads.* HABS/HAER. ME-13: 34

[31] Richard Quinn and Neil Maher, *Acadia National Park. Motor Roads. Cadillac Mountain Road.* ME-11.

[32] G. B. Dorr, *The Story of Acadia National Park* (Bar Harbor: Acadia Publishing Co., 1997), 102.

[33] Work to Dorr, July 1924. NARA. RG79.CCF.1907–39. Acadia. Misc. Reports. B.4.

[34] Jeffrey Killion and H. Elliot Foulds, *Cultural Landscape Report for the Historic Motor Road System, Acadia National Park* (Boston: National Park Service and Olmsted Center for Landscape Preservation, 2007), 25.

Chapter Seventeen: BEGINNINGS AND ENDINGS

[1] Martha Harmon, "C. C. Little and the Founding of the Jackson Laboratory," *The History Journal of the Mount Desert Island Historical Society* III (2000), 5.

[2] Dorr to Eliot, November 13, 1924. *Records of the President: Charles W. Eliot Papers.* Harvard University Archives and the *C. C. Little Papers.* RG 1.1. The Jackson Laboratory Archives. Bar Harbor, ME.

[3] For background, see Charles K. Hyde, *Independent Automakers: Nash, Hudson and American Motors* (Detroit: Wayne State University Press, 2009), Ch. 5.

[4] John D. Rockefeller Jr. to R. Jackson, June 18, 1927. RAC. III.2.I.B.75.f.770; MDIBL Executive Committee Chairman Hermon C. Bumpus shortly thereafter published a plan that incorporated elements of Little's vision. See *Reports of Dr. Hermon C. Bumpus on Studies Made in 1929 on Educational Projects in Acadia National Park and Yellowstone National Park.* National Park Service Harpers Ferry Library Center. Historical Collection. RG19.B.K1810.

[5] Mount Desert Island Biological Laboratory Archives; see also E. K. Marshall Jr. "A History of the Mount Desert Island Biological Laboratory, 1898–1962", *A Laboratory by the Sea*, Ed. Franklin H. Epstein (Rhinebeck, NY: River Press, 1998), 59. The cumulative financial support from JDR Jr. for the MDIBL from 1929 to 1934 was $18,500 (buying power in 2014: $330,000.).

[6] Little to Jackson, undated. RAC. III.2.I.B.75.f.770.

[7] Jackson and Little to JDR Jr., November 5, 1926. RAC. III.2.I.B.75.f.770.

[8] Joel Holstein, *The First Fifty Years at The Jackson Laboratory*. Ed. William L. Dupuy. (Bar Harbor: Jackson Laboratory, 1979), Ch. 1.

[9] Martha Harmon, "C. C. Little," n. 36 and n.41.

[10] Anne Kozak quoting laboratory director Rick Woychik in "Jackson Lab Enjoys Growth," *Mount Desert Islander*. December 7, 2007; on Nobel, see October 15, 2009 issue.

[11] *Dorr Papers*. B.2.f. 4. Bar Harbor Historical Society.

[12] Ralph Brewster to G. B. Dorr, August 21, 1925. Case III. *Correspondence (1924–26)*. f.9/10. Robert Abbe Archives. Abbe Museum. Bar Harbor.

[13] William Lawrence, *Robert Abbe Memorial Essay*. ANP. SRC. B.32.f.18.

[14] R. Abbe, *The Beginnings of a Museum,* Robert Abbe Archives. Case II.f.2; see also R. H. Epp, "Establishing Dr. Abbe's Museum in Mr. Dorr's Park," *The History Journal of the Mount Desert Island Historical Society* V (2003): 22–36.

[15] Case II.f.2. Robert Abbe Archives.

[16] Dorr to Mather, November 14, 1924. National Archives and Records Administration. RG79. CCF. Acadia. 1907–39. The "Indians" in question were the Wabanaki. See Harald E. L. Prins and Bunny McBride, *Asticou's Island Domain: Wabanaki Peoples at Mount Desert Island 1500–2000.* (Boston: National Park Service Northeast Region Ethnography Program, 2007), I, especially 345–346. A more approachable study from the same authors is *Indians in Eden: Wabanakis and Rusticators on Maine's Mt. Desert Island* (Camden: Down East Books, 2009).

[17] Lawrence to Abbe, August 25 and September 26, 1926. Case III.f.2. Robert Abbe Archives. Also Abbe to JDR Jr., September 12, 1927. RAC III.2.I.B.74.f.760. Colby College geology students began a yearly event of visiting Lafayette National Park, according to Stephen Mather. *Report of the Director of the National Park Service to the Secretary of the Interior, Fiscal Year Ended June 30, 1926* (Washington, DC: GPO, 1926),

7; a 1926 LNP annual report from Superintendent Dorr was included, 149–150. Of the 100,000 park visitors—a new record—more than 15,000 arrived in automobiles.

[18] JDR Jr. to Abbe. September 15, 1927. RAC. III.2.I.B.74.f.760 and B.77.f.783.

[19] These personal remarks are drawn from the massive *William Otis Sawtelle Collection, 1692–1941.* ANP. SRC. A seventy-eight-page finding aid is available. Information regarding Sawtelle's teaching career at Haverford College was provided by the institution archivist, Diana F. Peterson. March 3, 2010 email.

[20] Farrand to Abbe, April 8, 1927. *Correspondence* (1924–26).f.9/10. Robert Abbe Archives; see also Farrand to Dorr, May 20, 1927. *Facilities.* C.1.f.1. Robert Abbe Archives. See also Bernice Kert, *Abby Aldrich Rockefeller: The Women in the Family.* 2nd ed. (New York: Random House, 2003), Ch. 17.

[21] Ann Rockefeller Roberts, Interviewed in Southwest Harbor, Maine. August 26, 2003.

[22] *The New York Times,* April 24, 1927. X15.

[23] *Bar Harbor Times,* March 7 and 14, 1928.

[24] *Minutes,* 1928. Bar Harbor Village Improvement Association. Bar Harbor Historical Society.

[25] Newton Drury to Fletcher Wood, April 29, 1944. Case III.f.9. Robert Abbe Archives. NPS Land Ownership Record. Tract 27. Deed No. 24. Robert Abbe Archives. I.3.

[26] *Robert Abbe Birthday Correspondence,* 2 Vols. April 12, 1921. G. B. Dorr. Robert Abbe Archives.

[27] *Daily Kennebac Journal,* July 8, 1925.

[28] This highly publicized ascent was documented in print and moving film that circulated widely. See Philip R. Shorey, "Maine Celebrities Climb to Katahdin's Peak," *In the Maine Woods* (Bangor: Bangor and Aroostook Railroad Co., 1926), 94–99; unfortunately, the film is no longer extant.

[29] G. B. Dorr, "Mt. Katahdin as a Forest Reservation." *Sieur de Monts Publications* XVIII (1916).

[30] The addition of other tracts of land led to the establishment in 1933 of the "forever wild" Baxter State Park. See Thomas A. Urquhart, "Land Conservation in Maine, 1900–2000," *Twentieth-Century New England Land Conservation: A Heritage of Civic Engagement.* Ed. C. H. W. Foster (Cambridge: Harvard University Press, 2009), 42–45.

[31] Shorey, "Maine Celebrates Climb," 97.

[32] In the early 1930s, Dorr was joined by Benjamin Hadley and other rangers in climbs to Katahdin's summit. See S. Herbert Evison, *Oral History Interview of Ardra Tarbell. October 21, 1971.* National Park Service Historical Collection. RG37.E1. Harpers Ferry, WV.

[33] *Bar Harbor Times,* August 12, 1925. On the second day of Brewster's visit, he joined Mr. Dorr to speak to the Appalachian Mountain Camp community at Echo Lake, visiting Charles W. Eliot in Northeast Harbor and Mrs. John S. Kennedy at Kenarden Lodge. The planned activities were not complete until the party attended a concert at the Building of the Arts, dinner at the Pot and Kettle, and a Navy Ball at the Swimming Club.

[34] NPS Harpers Ferry Center Library, Historical Collection. Conferences. Box A40. See the *Report of the Director of the National Park Service, 1926.*

[35] Dorr to JDR Jr., February 14, 1926. RAC. III.2.I.B.85.f.839.

[36] Cammerer to JDR Jr., August 17, 1926. RAC. III.2.I.B.84.f.835.

[37] Dorr to Arno Cammerer, April 24, 1925. NARA. RG79.CCF.1907–39/Acadia. B.1.f.1.

[38] Michael McGiffert, "*Mount Desert: A History,*" *The History Journal: Mount Desert Island Historical Society* II (1999): 57–59. See S. A. Eliot to W. O. Sawtelle, December 16, 1924 and editorial correspondence with Houghton Mifflin & Co. See also Dorr's November 11, 1924 response to S. A. Eliot's request for information. Northeast Harbor Library. Charles W. Eliot II archival documents.

[39] Henry James, *Charles William Eliot: President of Harvard University, 1969*–1909 (Boston: Houghton Mifflin Co., 1930), II, 321–326.

[40] RAC. III.2.I.B.59.f.441.

[41] Arthur Cushman McGiffert Jr., "*Pilot of a Liberal Faith*" *Samuel Atkins Eliot 1862–1950* (Boston: Beacon Press, 1976), 150.

[42] Henry James, *Charles W. Eliot.* II, 331.

[43] *The New York Times,* August 23, 24, 25, 1926.

[44] *The New York Times,* March 21, 1927.

[45] Eliot to Endicott, September 15, 1926. *Endicott Family Papers.* B.24.f.34. Massachusetts Historical Society. Boston. According to Charles W. Eliot II, "It would take thirty years to settle Grandfather's estate," for much of the difficulty involved opposition of some family members to the donation of land atop Asticou Hill to Acadia National Park. *Eliots and Asticou Foreside.* Northeast Harbor Library Archives. Typescript.

[46] I.1.A.1. Hancock County Trustees of Public Reservations Archives. Ellsworth, ME.

[47] The Trustees of Reservations, *1926 Annual Report.* 8–10.

[48] Paul Revere Frothingham, "A Great Character," *All These* (Freeport, NY: Books for Libraries Press, 1969 [1927]), 309.

[49] See the insightful and lively essay by the late Reverend Peter J. Gomes, "The Preservation Legacy of Charles William Eliot," delivered to Friends of Acadia, Northeast Harbor, Maine. August 21, 2007.

[50] Raymond Fosdick, *John D. Rockefeller, Jr.: A Portrait* (New York: Harper & Brothers, 1956), Ch. 15.

[51] Fosdick, *John D. Rockefeller, Jr.*, 417–422, passim.

[52] See Charles W. Eliot, *The Durable Satisfactions of Life* (New York: Thomas Y. Crowell & Co., 1910).

[53] Judith S. Goldstein, *Triumphs and Tragedies: Charles W. Eliot, George B. Dorr, and John D. Rockefeller Jr. and the Founding of Acadia National Park.* (Somesville, ME: Port In a Storm Bookstore, 1992), 28–30.

Chapter Eighteen: "THE OLD ORDER CHANGETH!"

[1] *The Hancock County Trustees of Public Reservations: A Historical Sketch and a Record of the Holdings of the Trustees.* (Bar Harbor: 1939), 11.

[2] *Hancock County Registry of Deeds.* Revised Index. January 1, 1927 to December 31, 1936. There are 215 deeds recorded under the grantor name of George B. Dorr; John D. Rockefeller Jr. is the grantee for 185 of these deeds.

[3] *City of Boston Police Record,* December 24, 1927. ANP. SRC. B.2.f.1.

[4] *Harvard College Class of 1874,* Fourteenth Report. 1928. Harvard University Archives.

[5] *Endicott Family Papers,* B.34.f.14. Massachusetts Historical Society. Boston, MA.

[6] *Bar Harbor Times,* April 11, 1928.

[7] Rev. ed. by Samuel A. Eliot. (Boston: Houghton Mifflin Co., 1926).

[8] Ann Rockefeller Roberts, *Mr. Rockefeller's Roads: The Story Behind Acadia's Carriage Roads.* 2nd ed. (Camden: Down East, 2012), 132.

[9] Charles W. Eliot II, *The Future of Mount Desert Island* (Bar Harbor: Bar Harbor Village Improvement Association, 1928). See Ethan Carr, "The 'Noblest Landscape Problem': Thomas C. Vint and Landscape/Historic Preservation," *Design with Culture: Claiming America's Landscape Heritage.* Eds. Charles A. Birnbaum and Mary V. Hughes (Charlottesville: University of Virginia Press, 2005). See also the Mather-approved "Memorandum of a Development Plan for Lafayette National Park." Acadia National Park. ANP. SRC. B.KW. f.24.

[10] Ethan Carr, *Wilderness by Design: Landscape Architecture and the National Park Service* (Lincoln: University of Nebraska Press, 1998), 7–8.

[11] Rockefeller to Cammerer, September 7, 1926. Quoted by Roberts. *Mr. Rockefeller's Roads,* 135.

[12] Roberts, *Mr. Rockefeller's Roads,* 130.

[13] *Superintendent Monthly Reports,* July 1929. National Archives and Records Administration. RG79. CCF. Acadia.

[14] Erwin J. Raisz, "The Scenery of Mt. Desert Island: its Origin and Development," *Annals of the New York Academy of Sciences* XXXI (September 18, 1929): 121–186, esp.130.

[15] Van Dyke to Dorr, August 16, 1928. *Dorr Family Correspondence,* Temple University Libraries Special Collections. Philadelphia, PA.

[16] Cammerer to Rockefeller, October 10, 1928. RAC. III.2.I.B.84.f.835.

[17] Cammerer to Rockefeller, December 8, 1928. RAC. III.2.I.B.84.f.835.

[18] See the 1929 article by W. O. Sawtelle, "Acadia National Park: Random Notes on the Significance of the Name," *http://digitalcommons.library.umaine.edu/mainehistory/83/*

[19] Cammerer to W. B. Acker, February 18, 1927. Douglas B. Chapman Archive. Map Room. A. H. Lynam file. Bar Harbor, ME. See also "Superintendent Dorr to Continue Work," *Bar Harbor Times,* December 12, 1928.

[20] Cammerer to Rockefeller, October 8 and 10, 1928. RAC. III.2.I. B.84.f.835.

[21] Ibid.

[22] The origins of the term "Acadia" derive from accounts from fishermen and traders brought across the Atlantic Ocean by explorers in service to Henry IV. G. B. Dorr, "A Glorious Tribute to France," *La France,* September 1920, 590. On Mather's view of the renaming, see *Report of the Director of the National Park Service* (Washington: Government Printing Office, 1929), 4. In our own day many believe that it is derived from the native *Mi'kmaq* term *akadie* or *cadie,* meaning a piece of land (generally with a positive connotation), which was rendered *l'Acadie* by the French who explored and settled in present-day Maine and Maritime Canada. In a May 2, 1917 letter to the U.S. Commissioner of Patents, Dorr explains that "the word Acadia has never had a place in English geographic usage…the French word was Acadie, not Acadia; that after the Treaty of Utrecht in 1713…the name even in the French form ceased to apply to any region, except historically." Chapman Archive. JDR Jr. Papers. B.143.D3.

[23] Tom Butler. *Wildlands Philanthropy: The Great American Tradition.* (San

Raphael, CA: Earth Aware, 2008), 19.

[24] Robert Shankland, *Steve Mather of the National Parks* (New York: A. Knopf, 1951), Ch. 20.

[25] January 15, 1929. RAC. III.2.I.B.83.f.827.

[26] *Bar Harbor Times,* September 10, 1930; *Worthwhile Places: Correspondence of John D. Rockefeller, Jr. and Horace M. Albright.* Ed. Joseph W. Ernst (Bronx, NY: Fordham University Press, 1991), 110–111. According to the CPI, the 2014 buying power of Mr. Rockefeller's investment would be nearly $56 million.

[27] G. B. Dorr, "Early Road Systems and What They Led To." 1939 typescript. ANP. SRC. B.3.f.6. Brandon Wentworth's *The Fabulous Radio* NBD (Southwest Harbor, ME: Beech Hill Publishing Co., 1984) remains the best account of what was considered "to be the most important and the most efficient radio station in the world." The details of the exchange of properties are best explained in *Schoodic: Draft General Management Plan Amendment and Environmental Impact Statement* (Bar Harbor: Acadia National Park, 2004).

[28] George B. Dorr, *The Story of Acadia National Park* (Bar Harbor: Acadia Publishing, 1997), 112–119.

[29] For recent developments, see *Schoodic,* v., 6–9.

[30] *Bar Harbor Times,* September 10, 1930; *Worthwhile Places,* 110–111.

[31] G. B. Dorr, "Early Road Systems."

[32] Jeffrey Killion and E. Eliot Foulds, *Cultural Landscape Report for the Historic Motor Road System. Acadia National Park* (Brookline, MA: National Park Service and Olmsted Center for Landscape Preservation, 2007), 32–33.

[33] Shirley J. Fiske, *The Tarn: Community Recollections and Reflections* (Boston: National Park Service, 2012), 42

[34] Susan L. Klaus, "'Such Inheritance as I Can Give You,' The Apprenticeship of Frederick Law Olmsted, Junior." *Journal of the New England Garden History Society* 3 (1993): 7.

[35] September 18, 24, October 2, 14, November 14, and December 23, 1929. RAC III.2.I.B.110.f.1097; B.119.f.1203.

[36] Rockefeller to Henry V. Hubbard. September 18, 1929, and Dorr's December 4, 1929 response to Hubbard. RAC. III.2.I.B.110.f.1097; B.85.f.839.

[37] "A Century of Trust," *Ellsworth American* Supplement, September 13, 2001.

[38] See Walter J. Hickel, Secretary of the Interior, Citation for Meritorious Service to Ardra Tarbell. National Park Service. Harpers Ferry Center Archives. Harpers Ferry, WV.

[39] See S. Herbert Evinson, *Oral History Interview of Ardra E. Tarbell. October 21, 1971. NPS Historical Collection.* RG37.E1. Harpers Ferry Center. This transcript is the sole surviving park office view of Dorr as employer and gentleman. I am indebted to Tarbell's niece, Frances LaCourse of Hollis, Maine, for the April 20, 2006 interview about her aunt's duties.

[40] S. B. Sutton, *Charles Sprague Sargent and the Arnold Arboretum* (Cambridge: Harvard University Press, 1970), 321.

[41] NARA. RG79. CCF. *Superintendent Monthly Reports.* May 1931. Acadia.

[42] S. Herbert Evison. *Oral History Interview of Ardra E. Tarbell. October 21, 1971.*

[43] Peterson quote referred to by NPS historian Richard H. Quin, "Cadillac Summit Road." Historic American Buildings Survey/Historic American Engineering Record

ME-58. 1994. 15, n. 42. Library of Congress.

[44] R. W. Sellars, "Science or Scenery? A Conflict of Values," *Wilderness* 52 (Summer 1989): 29–38.

[45] Ann W. Spirn, *The Language of Landscape* (New Haven: Yale University Press, 1998), 24.

[46] *Home Geographic Monthly* 2, #1 (1932): 43–48; in 2007, Frances LaCourse uncovered this long-lost G. B. Dorr publication among Ardra Tarbell's memorabilia.

[47] June 10 and 16, 1930 correspondence, *Worthwhile Places*, 101–108; see also Rockefeller to Albright, June 20, 1930. RAC. III.2.I.B.84.f.835.

[48] ANP. SRC. B.3.f.6.

[49] *Bar Harbor Times*, December 3 and 10, 1930.

[50] *Bar Harbor Times*, February 11, 1931.

[51] *Bar Harbor Times*, December 17, 1930.

[52] Ann Rockefeller Roberts, *Mr. Rockefeller's Roads*, 107.

[53] By the end of the 1932 visitor season, 237,596 people visited Acadia—a 46-percent increase over 1931.

[54] See Ethan Carr, *Mission 66: Modernism and the National Park Dilemma* (Amherst: University of Massachusetts Press/Library of American Landscape History), 2007.

[55] Rockefeller to Atterbury, May 27, 1932. RAC. III.2.I.B.73.f.755; Albright to Rockefeller, June 13, 1932. RAC.III.2.I.B.84.f.835.

[56] *Bar Harbor Times*, June 22 and 29, 1932.

[57] Wilbur to Rockefeller, June 27 and June 29, 1932. RAC. III.2.I.B.83.f.827.

[58] *Superintendent Monthly Reports*, NARA. RG79. CCF, July 1932, Acadia.

Chapter Nineteen: CADILLAC SUMMIT ROAD DEDICATION

[1] On these "reportorial tactics—and comebacks," see B. M. Havey, "Acadia—A Boyhood Dream Come True," *Maine Highways* (1932–33), 11, 29, 30.

[2] *Bangor Daily* News, January 1, 1932. *The New York Times* gave the event advance coverage as well, July 17, 1932. See also "Old Cadillac Story as Road is Dedicated," *Bar Harbor Times*, July 27, 1932.

[3] "Dedication Exercises, Cadillac Mountain Road," and "Suggested Draft for Assistant Secretary Dixon's Talk at Acadia National Park on July 23." Typescript. *Joseph M. Dixon Papers 1772–1944.* Mss 055. K. Ross Toole Archives, Mansfield Library, University of Montana, Missoula, MT.

[4] *Portland Sunday Telegram*, July 24, 1932; see also *Bar Harbor Times*, July 27, 1932.

[5] Shingles painfully debilitated JDR Jr. and left him weakened for the next several months. Rockefeller to Cammerer, September 24, 1932. RAC. III.2.I.B.84.f.835.

[6] See Chris Mather, "National Parks from a Mather's Perspective," *Ranger* (Spring 2015), 6–8. Dorr's position on the placement of plaques other than this one is clearly delineated in a letter to attorney Richard W. Hale less than a month after the summit celebration: "…that no notices or placards, no monuments, plaques or memorials shall be placed…out-of-doors whether on the summit or along the roadside leading to it to distract people's attention from the one purpose of the road: to exhibit the landscape."

[7] September 8, 1932. RAC III.2.I.B.110.f.1093.

[8] Endicott to Dorr, July 24, 1932. *Endicott Family Papers*. B.24.f.41. Massachusetts Historical Society. Boston.

[9] Robert B. Keiter, *To Conserve Unimpaired: The Evolution of the National Park Idea* (Washington, D.C. : Island Press, 2013), 97–98; see also George C. Coggins and Robert L.Glicksman, "Concessions Law and Policy in the National Park System," *Denver University Law Review* 74 (1997): 729–759.

[10] Robert Shankland's chapter on "Concessions and Concessioners" is definitive. *Steven Mather of the National Parks (*New York: Alfred A. Knopf, 1951), Ch. 10.

[11] Peters to JDR Jr., March 10, 1934. RAC III.2.I.B.62.f.619; JDR Jr.'s September 24, 1936 letter to David Rodick well summarizes the evolution of concessions atop Cadillac. RAC III.2.I.B.62.f.619. For summit background, see Peter Morrison, *The Cadillac Mountain Summit. Acadia National Park, Maine: Archaeological and Landscape Reconnaissance* (Bar Harbor, ME: National Park Service and the Abbe Museum, 2008).

[12] The Rockefeller Archive Center contains nearly a hundred pages of Acadia Corporation correspondence covering the years 1933–1941. III.2.I.B.62.f.619.

[13] Cammerer to Rockefeller, April 27, 1939. RAC. III.2.I.B.62.f.619.

[14] August 9, 1932. National Archives and Records Administration. RG79. CCF. Acadia. Miscellaneous Reports.

[15] RAC. III.2.I. B.42.f.380.

[16] JDR Jr. to Lynam, November 7, 1932, and May 4, 1933. RAC. III.2.I.B.85.f.840.

[17] H. Eliot Foulds and Lauren G. Meier, *Cultural Landscape Report for Blackwoods and Seawall Campgrounds. Acadia National Park* (Boston, MA: National Park Service and Olmsted Center for Landscape Preservation, 1996), 14.

[18] Donald C. Swain, "Harold Ickes, Horace Albright and the Hundred Days: A Study in Conservation Administration," *Pacific Historical Review* 34 (1965): 455–465.

[19] Swain, "Harold Ickes," 461.

[20] *Conservators of Hope: The Horace M. Albright Conservation Lectures* (Moscow, ID: University of Idaho Press, 1988), 24; see also H. M. Albright, "My Trips with Harold Ickes," *Washington History* 2, #1 (1990): 28–50.

[21] "Early in the Winter of 1933." ANP. SRC. B1. f.15; see also G. B. Dorr, *The Story of Acadia National Park* (Bar Harbor: Acadia Publishing, 1997), 120–121.

[22] Ethan Carr, *Mission 66: Modernism and the National Park Dilemma* (Amherst: University of Massachusetts Press/Library of American Landscape History, 2007), 41.

[23] See also Horace M. Albright, *The Birth of the National Park Service: The Founding Years, 1913–33* (Salt Lake City, UT: Howe Brothers, 1985), 291–303.

[24] Albright to JDR Jr., June 1, 1933. RAC III.2.I.B.84.f.835.

[25] Donald C. Swain, *Wilderness Defender: Horace M. Albright and Conservation* (Chicago: University of Chicago Press, 1970), 218–219.

[26] *Bar Harbor Times,* May 31, 1933.

[27] The definitive work is Neil M. Maher's *Nature's New Deal: The Civilian Conservation Corps and the Roots of the American Environmental Movement* (New Haven: Yale University Press, 2008); see also John C. Paige, *The Civilian Conservation Corps and the National Park Service, 1933-1942: An Administrative History* (Washington, D.C.: Department of the Interior, 1985) and J. Moreira, P. Dean, and K. Champney. *The Civilian Conservation Corps at Acadia National Park* (Orono: University of Maine Folklife Center, 2002).

[28] *Official Annual Report, 1937. First CCC District.* ANP. SRC. B.32.f.4; see also NARA. Northeast Region. Waltham, MA. RG.79.B.13.

[29] Margaret Coffin Brown, *Pathmakers: Cultural Landscape Report for the Historic Hiking Trail System of Mount Desert Island* (Boston, MA: National Park Service and Olmsted Center for Landscape Preservation, 2006), 126–137.

[30] See Jack Russell, "Bob Patterson's First Work on MDI" and his companion piece, "The CCC in Acadia," *Friends of Acadia Journal,* 14, #1 (2009): 14–15; 13, #2 (2008): 12–13.

[31] "Narrative Report for February, 1934. Eagle Lake Camp, NP-1." NARA. RG.79.B.2. Waltham, MA.

[32] Swain, "Harold Ickes," 465.

[33] Albright to JDR Jr., August 10, 1933. RAC. III.2.I.B.84.f.835.

[34] JDR Jr. to Albright, October 10, 1933 and Albright's response of October 28. RAC III.2.I.B.84.f.835.

[35] Dorr to T. W. Ward, November 1933. *Samuel Gray Ward and Anna Barker Ward Family Papers.* III, 263, 264. Harvard University.

[36] Mount Auburn Cemetery Historical Collection, #4474 and 1151, Cambridge, MA; ANP. SRC. B.1.f.2, f.11.

[37] *Class of 1874, Fifteenth Report.* 1934. 14–15. Harvard University Archives.

[38] Peter J. Gomes, "The Preservation Legacy of Charles William Eliot," Friends of Acadia Address. Northeast Harbor, Maine, August 21, 2007.

[39] *Annual Meeting of the Garden Club of America, July 11, 12, and 13, 1934.* Garden Club of Mt. Desert. Program and penciled notes. *Mabel Choate Papers.* Naumkeag. Trustees of Reservations. Stockbridge, MA. See Bernice Kert, *Abby Aldrich Rockefeller: the Woman in the Family,* 2nd ed. (New York: Random House, 2003), Ch. 17; Patrick Chasse, *The Abby Rockefeller Garden* (David & Peggy Rockefeller, 1990). See also *Bar Harbor Times.* July 18, 1934.

[40] Albright to JDR Jr., August 31, 1934. RAC. III.2.I.B.110.f.1099.

[41] "National Park Glories Appear on New Stamp," *The New York Times,* August 19, 1934.

[42] Phyllis Sylvia to Albright, May 5, 1935. RAC. III.2.I.B.85.f.840.

[43] He wrote to physician Alfred E. Cohn that Lynam "for many years has been my lawyer and confidential representative here in Maine and because I think highly of him as a friend, I am anxious to have everything done to prolong his life." September 15, 1933. RAC. III.2.I.B.74.f.764.

[44] December 5 and 16, 1933. RAC. III.2.I.B.74.f.764.

[4]5 A. H. Lynam obituary. *Bar Harbor Times,* December 19, 1934.

[46] HCTPR member Herbert L. Satterlee, husband of Louise Pierpont Morgan, expressed a prevailing conviction—that Lynam's talents were irreplaceable. March 21, 1935 letter to the "Sieur des Monts" (i.e., G. B. Dorr). ANP. SRC. B.38.f.10.

[47] Albright to JDR Jr., December 26, 1934. RAC. III.2.I.B.85.f.840.

[48] Ickes to Dorr, December 29, 1934. NARA. RG79. CCF. Acadia, Miscellaneous Reports.

[49] JDR Jr. to Dorr, December 28, 1934. RAC. III.2.I.B.85.f.840.

[50] Kert, *Abby Aldrich Rockefeller,* Ch. 16, 28, and 32.

[51] G. B. Dorr, "History of a Tract of Land." ANP. SRC. B.5. f.6; see also B.2. f.2. For background, R. C. Laughlin, "Glaucoma," *Bulletin of the Institute of the History of Medicine* II, #3 (May 1934): 141–163; H. S. Sugar, "An Essay on the History of Glaucoma," *Historia Ophthalmologia Internationalis 1* (1979): 55–65; H. S. Sugar, "Glaucoma–History Since 1850," *Historia Ophthalmologia Internationalis* 3 (1985): 347–381.

[52] March 14, 1935. RAC. III.2.I.B.86.f.846.

[53] Nancy Wynne Newhall, *A Contribution to the Heritage of Every American: the Conservation Activities of John D. Rockefeller Jr.* (New York: Alfred A. Knopf, 1957): Preface.

[54] Allen K. Workman, "Saving Schoodic: A Story of Development, Lost Settlement, and Preservation," *Maine History* 45, #2 (June 2010), 118. For a fuller account, see his *Schoodic Point: History on the Edge of Acadia National Park* (Mount Pleasant, SC: The History Press, 2014). Detailed documentation provided by James J. Lee III, *U.S. Naval Station—Apartment Building: Historic Structure Report. Acadia National Park, Bar Harbor, Maine* (Lowell, MA: NPS Historic Architecture Program, 2009), 13–31.

Chapter Twenty: THE MATHER ERA CLOSES

[1] G. B. Dorr, "Dorr Point." Acadia National Park. ANP. SRC. B.3.f.7.

[2] Jack Russell, "The CCC in Acadia," *Friends of Acadia Journal* 13, #2 (2008), 12.

[3] Maurice Sullivan, "Museum Monthly Reports. May to December 1936." ANP. SRC. B.2.f.11.

[4] "Oldfarm Inventory," 1945. ANP. SRC. B.3.f.100.5.

[5] Oldfarm. ANP. SRC. B.2.f.1.

[6] Dorr to R. W. Hale, March 13, 1939. Hale to Dorr, March 16, 1939. Douglas B. Chapman Archive. JDR Jr. Papers. B.13.f.18.

[7] June 11, 1936. ANP. SRC. B.2.f.11.

[8] Dorr to Schiefellin, July 12, 1936. ANP. SRC. B.1.f.6.

[9] Dorr to I. F. Storey, October 6, 1939. National Archives and Records Administration. RG79. CCF 1933–1949. Acadia. General. B. 797. Dorr's letter provides rich background to issues about the final version of *Acadia National Park* (Bangor: Burr Printing Co., 1942).

[10] Neil Rolde, *The Interrupted Forest: A History of Maine's Wildlands (*Gardiner: Tilsbury House, 2001), 308–311.

[11] Rolde, *The Interrupted Forest*, 309–311.

[12] See Samuel E. Morison, *Three Centuries of Harvard, 1636–1936* (Cambridge: Harvard University Press, 1936) and supportive resources in *Harvard University Tercentenary Celebration Documents* (Cambridge: Harvard University, 1936). See also Clark A. Elliott, "The Tercentenary of Harvard University in 1936. The Scientific Dimension," *Osiris* 14 (1999), 153–175; and "Cambridge Birthday," *Time Magazine*. September 28, 1936.

[13] Dorr to T. W. Ward Jr., December 23, 1936. ANP. SRC. B.2.f.10.

[14] See Diana W. Laing, "The Cushing-Endicott House: 163 Marlboro Street," *Proceedings of The Bostonian Society*, 1960, 15–52; knowledge of the interior of Oldfarm is based on a few photographs from a single photo shoot, incidental remarks from Dorr's memoirs, a 1944 estate listing, and a small assortment of Oldfarm furnishings housed at the Sawtelle Research Center.

[15] Walter Muir Whitehill, *William Crowninshield Endicott (*Salem: Peabody Museum, 1938), 5.

[16] See the diaries and engagement books of Mrs. Endicott for May 7, 1933. *Endicott Family Papers. Louise T. Endicott Papers*, 1863–1958. B.32.f.12. Massachusetts Historical Society. Boston.

[17] *Dorr Papers.* B.1.f.1. Bar Harbor Historical Society.

[18] Gilbert Murray, husband of the daughter of the Dorr family friends, Rosalind and George Howard (the Earl of Carlisle), was held in high regard for his scholarly and still definitive study, *The Rise of the Greek Epic* (Oxford: University Press, 1934).

[19] Rollo Walter Brown, *Harvard Yard in the Golden Years (*New York: A. A. Wyn, 1948), 74.

[20] Dayton Duncan and Ken Burns, *The National Parks: America's Best Idea* (New York: A. Knopf, 2009), 281–284.

[21] See T. C. Vint to Dorr, August 25, 1936, and other relevant documents on the status of projects at Great Meadows, Kebo Mountain, Blackwoods Campground, and the Otter Creek Causeway. Chapman Archive. JDR Jr. Papers. B.8.f.555. Bar Harbor, ME.

[22] "Park Official Sees New Era for Mt. Desert," *Bangor Daily Commercial,* January 17, 1937.

[23] "Congressmen Pay Visit to Mt. Desert Island," *Bar Harbor Times,* June 17, 1937.

[24] "Edith Wharton, 75, Dead in France," *The New York Times*, August 13, 1937.

[25] See *The Autobiography of a Curmudgeon* (New York: Reynal & Hitchcock, 1943).

[26] *The Secret Diary of Harold L. Ickes,* Vol. 2 (New York: Simon & Schuster, 1953), 202–203.

[27] Dorr to Cammerer, December 3, 1937. RAC. III.2.I.B.114.f.1152.

[28] June 27, 1938. *Worthwhile Places: Corrsepondence of John D. Rockefeller, Jr. and Horace M. Albright,* Ed. Joseph W. Ernst. (New York: Fordham University Press, 1991), 166–175.

[29] Ibid. Also contained in this letter is a summary of Albright's discussion with writer Mary Roberts Rinehart about her desire to assist Mr. Dorr with his property decisions, notable because it references a singular example of Dorr's strong use of negative language about another person; that is, Charles Pike, a "pig-headed fellow," whose influence over financier Potter Palmer's decisions was an obstacle to completion of the Park Loop Road.

[30] *Worthwhile Places*, 175–182.

[31] Rockefeller to Serenus Rodick, November 18, 1938, December 9, 1938. Chapman Archive. JDR Jr. Papers. B.9.f.588.

[32] December 1 and 13, 1938. RAC III.2.I.B.114.f.1152.

[33] January 5, 1939. ANP. SRC. B.1.f.10.

[34] ANP. SRC. B.1. f.11; Mount Auburn Cemetery. Historical Collections. # 4474, Letters of January 4 and 13, 1939. Cambridge.

[35] Dorr to David Rodick, April 12, 1939. *Sieur de Monts: Acadia National Park. Draft Document.* 1999. ANP. SRC.

[36] Dorr to Drury, April 15, 1941. ANP. SRC. B.4.f.1.

[37] See David Lowenthal, "Not Every Prospect Pleases: What is Our Criterion for Scenic Beauty?" *Landscape* 12, #2 (1962–63): 19–23.

[38] E. Carr, *Wilderness by Design: Landscape Architecture and the National Park Service* (Lincoln: University of Nebraska Press, 1998), 9.

[39] Stephen Mather, *Department of the Interior. Report of the Director of the National Park Service. 1919.* (Washington, DC: GPO, 1919).

[40] *Twentieth-Century New England Land Conservation.* Ed. C.H.W. Foster (Cambridge: Harvard University Press, 2009).

[41] G. B. Dorr, "Address at Opening of the Sieur de Monts National Monument,"

Sieur de Monts Publications II (1916).

[42] G. B. Dorr, "Man and Nature," *Sieur de Monts Publications* VII (1916).

[43] G. B. Dorr, "Man and Nature."

[44] Dorr to Drury, April 15, 1941. ANP. SRC. B.4.f.1.

[45] Dorr to JDR Jr., January 9, 1922. Douglas B. Chapman Archive. Map Room. A. H. Lynam file.

[46] G. B. Dorr, *Dorr Papers*. B.1.f.14.

[47] Judith S. Goldstein, *Majestic Mount Desert* (Mount Desert: Somes Pond Press, 1996), 45.

[48] G. B. Dorr, "Acadia National Park," *Dorr Papers*. B.2.f.4; B.1.f.14.

[49] Albright to JDR Jr., May 3, 1939. RAC. III.2.I.B.52.f.380.

[50] JDR Jr. to Dorr, September 9 and 15, 1939. RAC. III.2.I.B.85.f.840.

[51] Dorr to Cammerer, January 10, 1940. RAC. III.2.I.B.115.f.1154.

[52] Dorr to JDR Jr., December 9, 1939; JDR Jr. to Serenus Rodick, January 12, 1940. RAC. III.2.I.B.114.f.1150; see also Ann Rockefeller Roberts, *Mr. Rockefeller's Roads: The Story Behind Acadia's Carriage Roads*, 2nd ed. (Camden: Down East Books, 2012), 162–166.

[53] August 1940. Roscoe C. E. Browne Appreciation. Anne Funderburk Collection. Seal Harbor, ME.

[54] Bill Horner, M.D., "Deasy: A Maine Man," *Chebacco* XI (2010): 22.

[55] *The New York Times*, July 19, 1940, 24.

[56] There were family ties with the James family. Ward's mother (Anna Barker Ward) was related by marriage to Jennet Barker (1814–1843), the sister of Henry James Sr. (1811–1882), who fathered philosopher William James and his novelist brother, Henry.

[57] Margaret Snyder, "'The Other Side of the River' (Thomas Wren Ward, 1844–1940)," *The New England Quarterly* 14, #3 (1941): 423–436.

[58] *Brazil through the Eyes of William James*. Ed. Maria Helena P. T. Machado. (Cambridge: Harvard University Press, 2006),14.

[59] "Notes on Matters to Tell About." Typescript. *Dorr Papers*. B.1.f.13.

[60] *The Tracy Log Book: 1855*. Ed. Anne Mazlish. (Bar Harbor: Acadia Publishing Co., 1997).

[61] Dorr to Franklin D. Roosevelt, August 1, 1940. ANP. SRC. B.4.f.1.

[62] In an unattributed and unsigned two-page letter in the Chapman Archive (JDR Jr. Papers. B.13.f.22) the claim is made that on April 1, 1940 Dorr sold the nursery property to its manager, Clarence Dow. The arrangement meant that "the Bank has taken over all Mr. Dorr's property, and will take care of the taxes, insurance, and upkeep of said property…[while] Mr. Dorr will be allowed to live in Storm Beach cottage." Without corroboration, it appears that Dorr was free to offer F. D. R. the gift of his property even in the shadow of this loss of control.

[63] Franklin D. Roosevelt to Dorr, August 21, 1940. ANP. SRC. B.4.f.1.

[64] For Cammerer's resignation letter, see RAC. III.2.I.B.52.f.380.

[65] Undated two-page typescript. ANP. SRC. B.3.f.7.

[66] *New York Herald Tribune*, May 1, 1941. RAC. III.2.I.B.52.f.380.

Chapter Twenty-One: A FULL AND USEFUL LIFE

[1] Dorr to Edward Taylor, March 28, 1941. Acadia National Park. Sawtelle Research Center. B.4.f.1.

[2] Dorr to Horace M. Albright, January 17, 1941. ANP. SRC. B.4.f.1.

[3] Benjamin Hadley file memorandum, January 15, 1945. ANP. SRC. B.3.f.10.

[4] Dorr's attorney acknowledged as much in a letter to Rockefeller's office. "Ben Hadley…is actually running the Park for Mr. Dorr now." David Rodick to Jay Downer, February 5, 1941. RAC. III.2.I.B.62.f.620.

[5] JDR Jr. to Dorr, January 8, 1941. ANP. SRC. B.45.f.1.

[6] Albright to Dorr, January 21, 1941. ANP. SRC. B.4.f.1.

[7] Dorr to Taylor, March 28, 1941. ANP. SRC. B.4.f.1.

[8] A. E. Demaray to B. Hadley, July 2, 1941. ANP. SRC. B.4.f.1.

[9] Dorr to Taylor, March 28, 1941. ANP. SRC. B.4.f.1.

[10] *Bangor Daily Commercial,* May 1, 1941. Using the CPI Inflation Index, the Dorr estate's value in 2014 would have been $2,430,000.

[11] See excerpts from Congressional testimony, Luther S. Winsor. "Acadia National Park: A Study of Conservation Objectives to its Establishment and Boundary Adjustments." Typescript. 1955. 27–28. ANP. SRC. B.HB.f.16.

[12] *Bar Harbor Times.* May 6, 1941.

[13] Demaray to Dorr, July 11, 1941 Douglas A. Chapman Archive. JDR Jr. Papers. B.8.f.513. Bar Harbor, Me.

[14] Dorr to Demaray, July 26, 1941. ANP. SRC. B.3.f.11.

[15] Ibid.

[16] *The Yellow House Papers. The Laura E. Richards Collection.* Gardiner Library Association and Maine Historical Society, Portland, ME. RG 17, 18.

[17] Dorr to Demaray, July 28, 1941. ANP. SRC. B.3.f.12.

[18] Demaray to Dorr, September 27, 1941. Chapman Archive. JDR Jr. Papers. B.13.f.06.

[19] A. E. Demaray to B. L. Hadley, December 19, 1941. Chapman Archive. JDR Jr. Papers. B.13.f.06. See also Dorr to JDR Jr., December 23, 1941. RAC III.2.I.B.85.f.840.

[20] Drury to Dorr, February 21, 1942. ANP. SRC. B.3.f.10; see also *Portland Sunday Telegram,* January 11, 1942. C–9; and Department of the Interior January 11, 1942 press release. RAC. III.2.I.B.83.f.823.

[21] JDR Jr. to D. Morris, July 10 and 30, 1941. RAC. III.2.I.B.63.f.632.

[22] M. Sullivan to Dorr, October 16, 1941. ANP. SRC. B.3.f.1.

[23] Demaray to Dorr, September 27, 1941. ANP. SRC. B.3.f.11.

[24] Brad Emerson, "Athens in the Wilderness," *Portland Monthly Magazine* 29, #2 (April 2014): 37 ff. and Serenus Rodick to JDR Jr., April 18, 1942. RAC III.2.I.B.63.f.632.

[25] April 18 and May 29, 1942. RAC. III.2.I.B.63.f.632.

[26] Drury to JDR Jr., March 9, 1942. RAC. III.2.I.B.62.f.622.

[27] See Rosemary Nusbaum, *Tierra Dulce: Reminiscences from the Jesse Nusbaum Papers* (Santa Fe: Sunstone Press, 1980), 73–79.

[28] J. Nusbaum to Dorr, January 19, 1942. RAC III.2.I.B.83.f.823.

[29] Duane A. Smith, *Mesa Verde National Park: Shadows of the Centuries.* Rev. ed. (Boulder: University Press of Colorado, 2002), Ch. 7.

[30] Nusbaum to Dorr, January 19, 1942.

[31] May 7, 1942. Dorr Estate Correspondence. *Hon. John A. Peters Papers.* Hale & Hamlin, LLC. Ellsworth, ME.

[32] Peters to Hale, May 8, 1942, and Hale to Peters, May 11, 1942. Dorr Estate Correspondence.

[33] Harold Ickes and A. E. Demaray acknowledged receipt of copies. July 13, 1942. National Archives and Records Administration. RG79.CCF.1933-49. Acadia. B.791.

[34] *The Story of Acadia National Park* was published in 1948, combining Dorr's earlier title with the incomplete sequel. Not an autobiography, the publication has been in print more than sixty years.

[35] Benjamin Hadley, "Preliminary Report on Isle Au Haut." June 1943. ANP. SRC. BJV.f.22. Whether Dorr's companionship with two Bowditch grandsons, Charles and Henry, had any bearing on the gift could not be resolved through contact with relatives.

[36] Benjamin Hadley, June 1943. A social ethnographic report on *The Park Lands of Isle au Haut: A Community Oral History* (Boston, MA: National Park Service, 2013) by Douglas Deur provides for the first time a published account of the Bowditch family influence; unfortunately, it ignores the relevance to park development of the long-standing relationship between the family of the park superintendent and descendants of Nathaniel Bowditch. The justification for acquisition of offshore islands was a recurring theme for decades after Dorr's death; see the October 1968 report of chief naturalist Paul G. Favour Jr., "Justification for Offshore Islands," ANP. SRC. B.24.f.7.

[37] Dorr to JDR Jr., December 31, 1943. RAC. III.2.I.B.85.f.840.

[38] Oakes to JDR Jr., January 11, 1944. RAC. III.2.I.B.85.f.840.

[39] Hadley to Horace Albright, June 1944. Quoted in a June 20, 1944 letter from JDR Jr. to G. L. Stebbins. RAC. III.2.I.B.85.f.840.

[40] George L. Stebbins, "Random Notes on the Early History and Development as a Summer Resort of Mount Desert Island and Particularly Seal Harbor." RAC. III.2.I.B74.f.761.

[41] At the request of the trustees, JDR Jr. wrote Morris's obituary for "one of the finest men who ever lived on Mount Desert Island." RAC. III.2.I.B.93.f.700.

[42] Stebbins to JDR Jr., June 20, 1944. RAC. III.2.I.B.73.f.757.

[43] Stebbins to JDR Jr., July 15, 1944. RAC. III.2.I.B.85.f.840.

[44] *Bar Harbor Times*, June 19, 1944.

[45] Dorr to Drury, July 12, 1944. NARA. RG79. CCF. Acadia. Miscellaneous Reports.

[46] Stebbins to Rockefeller, July 15, 1944. RAC. III.2.I.B.85.f.840.

[47] Hadley to Demaray, August 6, 1944. NARA. RG79.CCF.1933-49. Acadia. B.791; on the cause of Dorr's death, see File #4414, Mount Auburn Cemetery Historical Collection. Cambridge.

[48] August 7, 1944. NARA. RG79.CCF.1933–49. Acadia. B.795.

[49] JDR Jr. to Horace Albright, *Worthwhile Places*, 222.

[50] Mount Auburn Cemetery Historical Collections, #4474.

[51] August 8–11, 1944. *Bar Harbor Times, Ellsworth American, Portland Sunday Telegraph.*

[52] "Our Debt to G. B. Dorr," *Boston Herald*, August 6, 1944.

[53] Hadley to H. Albright, August 14, 1944. ANP. SRC. B.218.f.10.

[54] Sargent Collier's *The Triumph of George B. Dorr (*Bar Harbor: S. Collier, 1964) first gave rise to this much-repeated fiction which resurfaced in Dayton Duncan and Ken Burns's celebrated film and book, *The National Parks: America's Best Idea* (New York: Alfred A. Knopf, 2009), 195.

[55] Superintendent's Monthly Report, August 1944. NARA. RG79.CCF.1933–49. Acadia. B.794.

[56] Hadley to Drury, August 17, 1951. ANP. SRC. B.2.f.1.

[57] Hadley to Albright, August 14, 1944. Letter. ANP. SRC. B. HJ.f.10; See also Hadley to R. W. Shankland, March 20, 1949. ANP. SRC. B.2.f.1.

[58] NARA. RG79.CCF.1933–49. Acadia. B.794.

[59] See Demaray to Drury, September 11, 1944, and Tolson to Drury, September 19, 1944 and December 15, 1944. NARA. RG79.CCF. Acadia. Misc. Reports; also Acadia. B.791.

[60] August 9, 1944. NARA. RG79.CCF. 1933–49. Acadia. B.791.

[61] T. J. Allen to Drury, September 19, 1944. NARA. RG79.CCF. Acadia. Misc. Reports.

[62] Drury to Farrand, September 2, 1944. NARA. RG79.CCF. Acadia. B.791.f.201–006.

[63] Hadley to Drury, September 20, 1944. Demaray to Hadley, September 11, 1944. NARA. RG79.CCF. 1933–46. Acadia. Misc. Reports.

[64] Dorr Mountain Case Study Decision, United States Board on Geographic Names. USBGN Archives. June 15, 1945.

[65] Charles R. Tyson and Tom Blagden Jr., *First Light: Acadia National Park and Mount Desert Island.* (Boulder, CO: Westcliffe Publishers, 2003), 6–10.

Chapter Twenty-Two: EPILOGUE

[1] Richard Waldron Hale Jr., *The Story of Bar Harbor: An Informal History Regarding One Hundred and Fifty Years in the Life of a Community* (New York: Ives Washburn, Inc., 1949). Ch. 8 is devoted to Mr. Dorr.

[2] Benjamin Hadley, "Oldfarm Inventory to U.S.A. Inventory of Personal Estate of George B. Dorr." Douglas B. Chapman Archive. Bar Harbor, ME. JDR Jr. Papers. B.12.f.05.

[3] Chapman Archive. JDR Jr. Papers. B.3.f.05.

[4] At the time of Dorr's death, he owned thirty-one small parcels of land in Bar Harbor alone, roughly one hundred acres appraised at just over $10,000. Harry L. Crabtree. Ellsworth attorney of record. December 8, 1944. Chapman Archive. JDR Jr. Papers. B.13.f.05.

[5] B. L. Hadley to Serenus B. Rodick, March 12, 1945. Chapman Archive. JDR Jr. Papers. B.13.f.05.

[6] "Healy and the Dorrs," *Athenaeum Items* No. 33 (February 1945). The 75.9 x 63.8 cm. portrait is owned by the Athenaeum. Email correspondence with David B. Dearinger, the Susan Morse Hilles Curator of Paintings, November 27, 2011.

[7] JDR Jr. to John A. Peters, July 20, 1945. RAC. III.2.I.B.98.f.968.

[8] Peters to JDR Jr., June 21 and July 31, 1945. RAC. III.2.I.B.98.f.968.

[9] David Rodick to JDR Jr., November 30, 1945; November 5, 1947. RAC. III.2.I.B.98.f.968.

[10] J. A. Murray to Serenus Rodick, October 4, 1944. Chapman Archive. JDR Jr. Papers. B.13.f.05.

[11] United States Board on Geographic Names Archive.

[12] In a related action, Peters contacted Mount Auburn Cemetery and arranged for installation of a simple memorial stone adjacent to the grave of Dorr's parents and

childhood nurse. Peters to G. R. Sands & Sons, November 20 and 23, 1945. *Hon. John A. Peters Papers.* Dorr Estate. Memorials. Hale & Hamlin, LLC. Ellsworth, ME

[13] Linda M. Cox, *The Charles River Esplanade, Our Boston Treasure.* 2000. *www.esplanadeassociation.org/about-the-park/park-history/*

[14] Peters to Serenus Rodick, February 4 and 6, 1946. Chapman Archive. JDR Jr. Papers. B.13.f.05.

[15] Hadley to Peters, February 11, 1946. *Hon. John A. Peters Papers.* Dorr Estate. Also [Hadley] to Serenus, March 13, 1946. Chapman Archive. JDR Jr. Papers. B.13.f.05. See Jack Russell, "Bob Patterson's First Work on MDI," *Friends of Acadia Journal* 14, #1 (Spring 2009).

[16] Peters to Mary Hale, January 22, 1946. *Hon. John A. Peters Papers.* Dorr Estate Correspondence.

[17] Hadley to Peters, February 7, 1946, refers to memorial placement "on a rocky crag on the Emery Path just above Sieur de Monts Spring." *Hon. John A. Peters Papers.* Dorr Correspondence. See also Peters to Serenus Rodick, February 25, 1946. Chapman Archive. JDR Jr. Papers. B.13.f.05.

[18] Hadley to Peters, March 28 and April 29, 1946. *Hon. John A. Peters Papers.* Dorr Estate. On access to the summit related to the Acadia Corporation, see David Rodick correspondence, June 22 and December 7, 1945. RAC. III.2.I.B.62.f.621–622.

[19] *Dedication of the George Bucknam Dorr Memorial. August 29, 1947.* (Ellsworth: Hancock County Trustees of Public Reservations, 1947); in addition to this published booklet, the HCTPR archives at the Woodlawn Museum in Ellsworth contain black-and-white images of the event, photographed by Sargent Collier.

[20] HCTPR. *Dedication of the George Bucknam Dorr Memorial.* Typescript. Sieur de Monts Spring. Acadia National Park. RAC. III.2.I.B.73.f.752.

[21] C. C. Little, "My 'adventure in faith.'" Jackson Laboratory Archives. Bar Harbor. B.73.f.13.

[22] L. F. Cook. "The 1947 Forest Fire Record: One Third of Acadia Burned." *National Parks Magazine* (January–March 1948): 20–22.

[23] "John D. Rockefeller Jr. and Acadia National Park," undated report attached to January 10, 1969 letter from Martha Rockefeller to David Rockefeller. RAC. III.2.I.B.83.f.821.

[24] Peters to Hale, November 26, 1947. *Hon. John A. Peters Papers.* Dorr Estate.

[25] November 20, 1947. RAC. III.2.I.B.73.f.756; costs associated with both memorials were solicited through public subscriptions.

[26] During the first six months of 1947, written dissatisfaction with the pace of Serenus Rodick's processing of the Dorr estate is documented in the Peters archive: Hale to Peters, February 27 and May 6, 1947. JDR Jr. feared that Serenus might be "on the edge of a break down." JDR Jr. to Peters, June 9, 1947. *Hon. John A. Peters Papers.* Dorr Estate.

[27] Probate records and copies of seven Bar Harbor Banking and Trust Company checks are found in the *Peters Papers,* issued November 24, 1947. In 2015 dollars, the estate value was $273,500.

[28] Sylvia to Peters, July 1, 1947. Also Peters to JDR Jr., September 18 and October 5, 1945 and reply from JDR Jr. RAC. III.2.I.B.85.f.840; B.98.f.968. On memory, see Hadley to T. J. Allen, December 4, 1946. National Archives and Records Administration. RG79. CCF. 1933–49. Acadia. B.791.

[29] Mary N. Hale to Hillory Tolson, NPS assistant director. December 24, 1946. NARA. RG79. CCF. 1933–49. Acadia. B.791.

[30] Edwin W. Small to T. J. Allen, December 17, 1946. NARA. RG79. CCF.1933–49. Acadia. B.791.

[31] Harvard University, Houghton Library to Mrs. Hale, April 8, 1945. *Hon. John A. Peters Papers.* Dorr Estate. Acknowledgments from other institutions receiving estate gifts are contained therein.

[32] *Bar Harbor Times*, July 12 and 26, 1945. See R. H. Epp, "Guide to the George Bucknam Dorr Papers," a 2004 typescript finding aid to the unprocessed papers at the Bar Harbor Historical Society Museum.

[33] Sawtelle Research Center documents were gathered over the decades from park staff that inherited—and presumably selectively discarded—files from their predecessors.

[34] Robert Pyle to R. Epp, March 10, 2003. Correspondence.

[35] Dorr to Edward T. Taylor, March 28, 1941. ANP. SRC. B.4.f.1; this expectation ("asking nothing in return but its right use") is repeated in this letter to Taylor, Chairman of the House Appropriations Committee.

[36] J. H. Denniston and Aloysius J. Higgens, Field Report on "Old Farm." Acadia National Park. September 16, 1946. Typescript. ANP. SRC.; see also "Treasures of Oldfarm" by College of the Atlantic student Kathryn Harmon. See the *Internet Archive* for an online version.

[37] Drury to Hadley, October 22, 1948. ANP. SRC. B.3.f.10.

[38] August 18, 2004. Earle G. Shettleworth Jr. interview. Maine Historic Preservation Commission. Augusta, ME.

[39] Sylvia to JDR Jr., July 17, 1954. RAC. III.2.I.B.85.f.840.

[40] JDR Jr. to Conrad Wirth, September 17, 1954. RAC. III.2.I.B.83.f.821.

[41] Wirth to JDR Jr., February 4, 1955. RAC. III.2.I.B.83.f.821.

[42] Howard R. Stagner to Conrad L. Wirth, "Interpretive Plan for Acadia National Park," February 2, 1955. RAC. III.2.I.B.83.f.821. See also Stagner's *Preservation of Natural and Wilderness Values in the National Parks* (Washington, D.C: GPO, 1957).

[43] Wirth to JDR Jr. February 4, 1955. RAC. III.2.I.B.83.f.821.

[44] JDR Jr. to Wirth, May 2, 1955. RAC. III.2.I.B.83.f.821.

[45] Stephen J. Hornsby, "The Gilded Age and the Making of Bar Harbor," *Geographical* Review 83, #4 (1993): 457–459.

[46] Stagner, Interpretive Plan for Acadia National Park," 3.

Index

A

B

C

D

E

F

G

H

I

J

K

L

R

S

T

U

V

W

Y

Z

About the Author

RONALD H. EPP, Ph.D. is a historian and professor of philosophy with a background in scholarly publishing and academic library leadership. His research over the last two decades into the Massachusetts families that influenced the development of conservation philanthropy has resulted in numerous talks and publications for Acadia National Park, Hancock County Trustees of Public Reservations, Mount Desert Island Historical Society, and many other organizations. He served as a consultant for the Ken Burns documentary *America's Best Idea: The National Parks* and has uncovered and inventoried hidden collections of documents relating to the history of Acadia National Park.

About Friends of Acadia

Founded in 1986, Friends of Acadia is an independent nonprofit organization working to preserve, protect, and promote stewardship of the outstanding natural beauty, ecological vitality, and distinctive cultural resources of Acadia National Park and surrounding communities for the inspiration and enjoyment of current and future generations. A leading example of citizen stewardship at national parks, Friends of Acadia is a place where personal connections to Acadia are translated into a remarkable collective impact.

To learn more, visit www.friendsofacadia.org.